The Long Sexual Revolution

The Long Sexual Revolution

ENGLISH WOMEN,
SEX,
AND CONTRACEPTION
1800–1975

Hera Cook

OXFORD
UNIVERSITY PRESS

OXFORD
UNIVERSITY PRESS

Great Clarendon Street, Oxford OX2 6DP

Oxford University Press is a department of the University of Oxford.
It furthers the University's objective of excellence in research, scholarship,
and education by publishing worldwide in

Oxford New York

Auckland Bangkok Buenos Aires Cape Town Chennai
Dar es Salaam Delhi Hong Kong Istanbul Karachi Kolkata
Kuala Lumpur Madrid Melbourne Mexico City Mumbai Nairobi
São Paulo Shanghai Taipei Tokyo Toronto

Oxford is a registered trade mark of Oxford University Press
in the UK and in certain other countries

Published in the United States
by Oxford University Press Inc, New York

British Library Cataloguing in Publication Data

Data available

Library of Congress Cataloging in Publication Data

Data available

ISBN 0-19-925239-4

1 3 5 7 9 10 8 6 4 2

Typeset by Kolam Information Services Pvt. Ltd, Pondicherry, India
Printed in Great Britain
on acid-free paper by
Biddles Ltd,
Guldford and King's Lynn

To

Julie and Leris

my mother and my aunt

Acknowledgements

One of the great pleasures of writing this book has been the many arguments and discussions I have had with colleagues who have read portions of it or listened to me at research seminars and conferences. I would like to express my gratitude to them for their contribution to the work. I am especially grateful to Pat Thane who supervised the doctorate with which this book began and to Marybeth Hamilton who has discussed the ideas and read drafts seemingly endlessly over the years. Both have provided me with constant support and intellectual stimulation. The staff of Birkbeck College, University of London, where I took my first degree were an inspiration to me at that time and have continued to support my research and offer me encouragement in many ways since then. I would like to thank Richard Evans, Joanna Bourke, David Feldman, and Dorothy Porter. The first year of the doctorate was spent at the London School of Hygiene and Tropical Medicine where Margaret Thorogood and Klim McPherson kindly gave access to their files of epidemiological research on the pill. Although little of that material has found its way into the finished book, it has informed the research. At this time I met Diana Kuh, who gave me confidence in the use of statistics, and graciously obtained permission for me to use the Research Council's National Survey of Health and Development data. I would also like to thank the staff and the architect of the University of Sussex, who provided much needed breaks away from London's harder edges.

This work would not have been possible without the Economic and Social Research Council, which awarded me the doctoral fellowship with which the book began. Thanks must go to the Leverhulme Foundation, which awarded me a Studentship held at the University of Sydney, Australia, thus introducing a comparative dimension to my work. Charlotte MacDonald, the head of History, Victoria University, Wellington, offered me space and support as a Visiting Researcher for six weeks. Responses to the numerous research papers I have given over the years have contributed much to the development of the book, and it has given me immense pleasure to debate my ideas with informed and ethically engaged audiences. In particular my thanks go to the seminar participants at the Centre for Population Studies, University of Cambridge, the History Department of the University of Bristol, and the Department of Demography at the Australian National University and to Sally Alexander and Jane Lewis who commented on papers I presented. The Women's History Seminar at the Institute of Historical Research, London, and the History Work in Progress seminar at the University of Sussex have been a source of support and friendship as well as intellectual stimulation.

I should also like to thank Anna Davin, Jenny Carpenter, Saul Dubow, Amy Erikson, Ian Gazeley, Lesley Hall, John Lowerson, Angus McLaren, Alison McKinnon, Peter McDonald, and Eve Setch. Chris Sparks was a constant support and provided much needed advice on my fellowship applications. I would like to thank Simon Szreter and the other anonymous academic reader for Oxford University Press for their helpful suggestions. Natalie Higgins kindly sent me her forthcoming Oxford doctoral thesis on marriage in north England. I am grateful to Rose Hacker, Stephen and Olive Peet, Sir Benedict Hoskyns, Angela Phillips, Lindsay Christopherson, Joanna Norcross, and Rosalind Stanwell Smith who allowed me to interview them and gave me valuable insights into themselves and their times. I would like to thank Ruth Parr, Kay Rogers, and Jackie Pritchard at Oxford University Press. Shereen Colvin, Ross Wollard, and Raymond Rogers at the University of London Library, Senate House, went beyond the call of duty. The Brook Advisory Service, the British Medical Association, and *Pulse* magazine kindly allowed me to use their archives. Gill, Zak, and others at 56 Charing Cross Road must be thanked for their efforts in supplying me with otherwise unobtainable primary sources. No one other than myself has typed a word of the book but for giving me help in countless far more important ways, I would like to thank: Kate Duke, Jane Hawkesley, Chris Katic, Oision Murphy-Lawless, Clare Neely, Ben Patrick, and my extended family Damon, Megan, Nigel, Rolf, Simon, and Walter who have been supportive and patient on occasions past counting.

H.C.

Contents

List of Figures   xi
List of Tables   xii
Abbreviations   xiv

Introduction   1

PART I   *Inventing Contraception*

1. Birth Rates and Women's Bodies: Reproductive Labour   11

2. 'Nature is a Blind Dirty Old Toad': The Withdrawal Method   40

3. 'Conferring a Premium on the Destruction of
   Female Morals': Fertility Control and Sexuality
   in the Early to Mid-Nineteenth Century   62

4. 'One Man is as Good as Another in that Respect':
   Women and Sexual Abstinence   90

5. Mastering the Sexual Self:
   Contraception and Sexuality 1890s–1950s   122

6. 'Physical "Open Secrets" ': Hygiene, Masturbation,
   Bowel Control, and Abstinence   143

PART II   *Sexuality and Sex Manuals*

7. English Sexuality in the Twentieth Century:
   Ignorance, Silence, and Gendered Sexual Cultures   165

8. 'The Wonderful Tides': Sexual Emotion and
   Sexual Ignorance in the 1920s   187

9. 'The Spontaneous Feeling of Shame':
   Masturbation and Freud 1930–1940   207

10. 'Thought Control': Conjugal Rights and
    Vaginal Orgasms 1940s–1960s   225

11. 'The Vagina too, Responds': Vaginal Orgasms, Clitoral
    Masturbation, Feminism, and Sex Research 1920–1975   245

PART III   *The English Sexual Revolution*

12. Sexual Pleasure, Contraception, and Fertility Decline   263

13. 'Truly it Felt Like Year One':
    The English Sexual Revolution   271

14. Population Control or 'Sex on the Rates'?
    Political Change 1955–1975   296

15. 'A Car or a Wife?' The Northern European
    Marriage System and the Sexual Revolution   318

Conclusion: Living through Changing Sexual Mores   338

Appendix A: Analysis of the Sex Manual Authors   341
Appendix B: List of Sex Manual Authors   347

Bibliography   355
Index   393

List of Figures

1.1. Gross reproduction rate 1751–1976   15
4.1. Illegitimate live births per 1,000 total live births   102
12.1. The cumulative percentage of the first use of
      the pill by the MRC 1946 cohort   269
15.1. Period by which first use of the pill pre-dates the
      year of marriage, as a percentage of the total pill
      use before marriage   333

List of Tables

4.1.   Illegitimate live births per 1,000 total live births   103
4.2.   The percentage of the population reporting they
        had ever used birth control, by marriage cohort,
        in various surveys   113
4.3.(*a*) Birth control use by class, marriage cohort, and
        (*a*) those who had at any time used appliance methods,
        (*b*) those who had only used non-appliance methods   113
4.3.(*b*) Birth control use by class, marriage cohort, and
        (*a*) those who had at any time used appliance methods,
        (*b*) those who had only used non-appliance methods
        (including the pill)   114
5.1.   Inter-war contraceptive effectiveness estimates:
        failure rates   140
7.1.   Age at which people became interested in the
        opposite sex by date of birth   174
15.1.   Female age at first intercourse   320
15.2.   Married women and single women who reported
        coitus before marriage   326
15.3.   Women who reported premarital coitus with
        their husbands before first marriage, by year
        of marriage   327
15.4.   Use of contraception before marriage by married
        women in different social class and age at interview
        cohorts who reported premarital sexual relations
        with their husbands   327
15.5.   Women in age at interview cohorts, by social class,
        who were first married by age 20   329
15.6.   Women in age at interview cohorts, by social class,
        who reported premarital sexual relations   330

15.7. Length of time before first marriage sexual relations
with husband started, for women first married in
different years   332

15.8. Ever married women who first used the pill before
the year of marriage, in the same year as marriage,
and following the year of marriage   334

15.9. Use of the pill between first marriage or 'going steady
with your husband' and first birth and following
birth intervals by women married in different years   335

15.10. Married and single women aged 15–64 in
paid employment   336

Abbreviations

BMA	British Medical Association
BMJ	*British Medical Journal*
CA	*Contemporary Authors*
FPA	Family Planning Association
GP(s)	general practitioners, family doctors
GRR	gross reproduction rate
IUD	intrauterine device
LA(s)	local authorities
MOH	Medical Officer of Health
MRC	Medical Research Council
NHS	National Health Service
NMGC	National Marriage Guidance Council
STD	Sexually transmitted disease
TFR	total fertility rate

Introduction

In 1961, when the pill was introduced to Britain, women pushed their, often reluctant, doctors to give them the drug. By the late 1960s, young women were talking about a revolution in women's sexual attitudes, but since then the suggestion that the pill just meant women couldn't say no has been widely repeated, alongside negative assessments of the 'sexual revolution'. As early as the 1880s, there had been suggestions that fear of pregnancy gave wives an excuse for denying to their husbands their conjugal right of sexual intercourse. By the early 1990s, over 80 per cent of British women of reproductive age since the early 1960s had taken the pill. What was the impact of contraception and, in particular, the oral contraceptive pill on women's sexuality? Historical analysis of change in heterosexual women's sexuality has often remained trapped in debates that began in the 1890s. Some feminists continue to argue, even in the late twentieth century, that contraceptive technologies can be seen not as emancipating women but as making women available to men and ensuring they alone bore the responsibility for preventing pregnancy. This argument has been extended to include the notion that contraception was part of making sexual pleasure rational and scientific, reducible to the internalizing of norms.[1]

My first encounter with the notion that these ideas had any contemporary purchase was at a research seminar in the mid-1990s. The speaker announced authoritatively that the pill had not given women greater sexual freedom, rather the drug had merely made them subject to male sexual demands. 'Not all women,' I responded. Many young women of my generation, including myself, enjoyed extensive sexual experimentation. Only a decade or so earlier such casual, low-risk sexual activity had

---

[1] e.g. A. Dugdale, 'Inserting Grafenberg's IUD into the Sex Reform Movement', in J. Wajcman and D. MacKenzie (eds.), *The Social Shaping of Technology* (1999), 320–1.

not been possible for young women. Many thousands of intelligent, self-possessed girls had 'fallen pregnant' and been hustled out of sight into institutionalized mother and baby homes until their babies were adopted or risked unsafe illegal abortions during the 1950s and 1960s. The difference between those women and my generation was evidently not that we were more intelligent, less neurotic, or more competent, but that we had access to female-controlled contraception backed up by safe, legal, affordable abortion. Feminism, though frequently presented as monolithic and the source of the argument that the pill meant women could not say no to sex, has contributed greatly to young women's growing capacity to insist upon their own desires.[2] This argument was, in any event, founded on a fundamental misapprehension; women had never possessed the right to say no—or yes—to sex on the basis of their own desire. Sexual intercourse outside marriage, if discovered, and particularly if pregnancy occurred, often earned girls and women the treatment of social outcasts or even institutionalization. In the case of married women, there was a powerful customary belief that a woman had no right to deny her husband regular sexual intercourse. This was backed up by the law, which held that in entering a contract of marriage a woman had given consent to intercourse with her husband and she could not retract this.[3]

However, the pill did produce a situation in which these pre-existing social conditions led to a new twist on male sexual exploitation of young

---

[2] The idea that the pill meant women couldn't say no to sex appears to have originated in the USA. The earliest source encountered was A. Dell'Olio, 'The Sexual Revolution Wasn't Our War', in *The First Ms. Reader* (1972), 124. More influential was S. Hite, *The Hite Report* (1976), 332.

[3] The legal doctrine concerning rape within marriage was based upon a statement in *History of the Pleas of the Crown* by Sir Matthew Hale (1609–76): 'The husband cannot be guilty of a rape committed by himself upon his lawful wife, for by their mutual matrimonial consent and contract the wife hath given herself up in this kind unto her husband which, she cannot retract.' The *actus reus* of rape is sexual intercourse without consent and therefore if the wife could not consent she could not be raped. The first recorded case of a man being prosecuted for the rape of his wife during marriage was *R. v. Clarke* in 1949. In *R. v. R.—* (Rape: marital exemption) [1991] 4 All ER 481, [1992] 1 AC 599, the House of Lords changed the law as to rape within marriage on the grounds that there had been very significant changes in the nature of marriage and the status of women. Parliament gave this legislative endorsement with section 142 of the Criminal Justice and Public Order Act 1994, amending section 1 of the Sexual Offences Act 1956. P. Dobson, *Criminal Law*, 5th edn. (1999), 81.

single women in the 1960s. Throughout the nineteenth and twentieth centuries, the family, the Church, and later schools had attempted to supervise and control unmarried women's sexual behaviour. In this social setting women might have had to struggle against persuasive male arguments and persistent groping but they had the entire weight of society, backed up by the ultimate sanction of pregnancy, supporting them if they did not wish to have intercourse. In the 1960s the arrival of the pill meant that for the first time women could have confidence that they would not get pregnant. There is a new sense of excitement and possibilities present in many accounts by heterosexual women who were young and single at this time. In choosing to reject the control of their sexual behaviour they saw themselves as rejecting control over their lives as a whole. However, abandoning the traditional moral position left many confused, with no substantial arguments against casual or dishonest male sexual exploitation. By the early 1970s, men assumed fashionable young women were on the pill and statistics show that well over half actually were. For this generation of young single women the widespread use of the pill did mean some men assumed that if women could not get pregnant they had no reason to say no.

Women were brought up to accept, and prioritize, other people's needs, not to express their own feelings or desires.[4] There was also a societal rejection of emotion as insufficient when opposed to rational argument. The fact that a woman did not feel desire was not an adequate argument—for or against anything. Women had no right to sexual autonomy. This term describes the extent to which women have control over their lives. Autonomy includes the extent to which women can play an active role in the family and society, whether women have a real say in making and carrying out decisions, how much freedom they have to develop bonds with other people, to move about and to interact with the outside world, the ability to obtain information and use it as the basis for making decisions about one's private concerns and those of one's intimates, control of economic resources: all of this constitutes women's

---

[4] For the need to stop being nice: E. Phillips, 'Introduction: Libertarianism, "Egotism", and Liberation', in Eileen Phillips (ed.), *The Left and the Erotic* (1983), 22–3. A. Coote and B. Campbell, *Sweet Freedom: The Struggle for Women's Liberation* (1982), 223–7.

autonomy.[5] The level of female autonomy shapes women's experience of their sexuality.

This book began as a project about sexuality and contraception in which maternity had no part. This is how sexuality has been constructed in Western cultures since the mid-twentieth century, but this was the first period in which it was possible for heterosexual women to separate physical sexual activity from the reality of frequent conceptions and births. Even those few who were infertile lived in a society dominated by this experience. The importance of this became obvious during the research and the physical impact of motherhood upon birth rates and hence upon female sexuality has become central to the book. However, although historians have produced valuable research focusing on the impact of eugenic thought and the state on concepts of motherhood during the early twentieth century[6] there is no evidence that the pressure this placed upon women had any impact upon birth rates. Birth control was almost entirely a matter of self-help and levels of use of contraception rose persistently from the 1890s when survey records began. When birth rates altered during the twentieth century, it was not according to the desires of eugenicists and population controllers. For this reason, these ideas and those who held them are touched upon only briefly.

The definitions of class used by the researchers and other writers whose work has been drawn upon in this study have varied even within the same period. It is not possible to reconcile these different approaches, and the range of sources used has meant there was no alternative but to accept the terminology used by those cited and the resulting imprecision. The research has focused on the experience of white Protestant or secular English women. There was regional variation within England and the experience of women elsewhere in the British Isles is likely to have varied considerably. Scotland, for example, has had different illegitimacy rates and a stronger commitment to education for several centuries. Large-

---

[5] S. Jejeebhoy, *Women's Education, Autonomy, and Reproductive Behaviour: Experience from Developing Countries* (1995), 7.

[6] The germinal article was A. Davin, 'Imperialism and Motherhood', *History Workshop* (1978). See also R. A. Soloway, *Birth Control and the Population Question in England, 1877–1930* (1982). R. A. Soloway, *Demography and Degeneration: Eugenics and the Declining Birth Rate in Twentieth-Century Britain* (1990).

scale black and Asian immigration only began in the 1950s; these women brought a different cultural heritage to bear on sexuality and even in that period the sources used herein may not be relevant to their experience. The differences between the USA and England have been commented on throughout the book. There are also considerable similarities between all the Anglo cultures, Australia, Canada, New Zealand, the USA, and the British Isles. These include the relative strength and independence of women, which can be seen in the prominence of feminism. Also relevant were the increasing availability of contraception and abortion, the strong social purity movements in the late nineteenth century, rising levels of female education, movements of women out of and into the paid work-force, and the expectation that marriage will entail setting up a separate household rather than the wife moving in with her new in-laws. Increasingly during the course of the research, and to a greater extent than is visible in the finished work, comparisons provided a means of asking what was the probable impact of these different factors on women's sexuality.

As the focus of this study is contraception and sexuality, the relevant physical sexual event is heterosexual penetrative penile-vaginal inter-course. For variety, this act is referred to as coitus, intercourse, penetrative intercourse, sexual intercourse, and sex. This usage is not intended to suggest that heterosexual coitus is *sex*. The research has drawn extensively on surveys of sex and fertility. There has been no survey research into sexuality that can be defended as methodologically perfect and as com-pletely free from distorting constraints imposed by funding. Nonetheless, the most important limitation upon these surveys was probably the unwillingness of many respondents to answer the questions put to them fully. This reticence must be placed in the context of societal injunctions against speaking of personal sexual experience, the lack of a common understanding of sexuality between men and women, and the inappropriateness of an increasingly 'scientific' survey methodology in such conditions. There are no alternative sources to round out the picture provided by demographic statistics and qualitative sources such as sex manuals, biographies, and novels. Those who undertook such surveys were intelligent, aware of their own times and culture, and did the best they could often in the face of considerable pressure. The results accur-ately reflect the trends revealed in other sources. Notwithstanding the evidence of concealment, in this study the testimony of individual women and men concerning their own desires and behaviour has been treated as accurate, except where there is direct evidence this is not the case. Eve Kosofsky Sedgwick has called the denial of the right to define one's own desire, which was central to approaches to the sexuality of individuals throughout the century, 'an act of intimate violence'.[7] Accepting that people often were able to describe what they felt, and respecting their testimony, creates new challenges. It leads to different and fruitful questions.

The gender/sex divide has been central to scholarship in women's history for the previous decade. This is the division of women's experience into sex, the fixed biological difference between men and women, and gender, which is socially constructed. The central concern of this study is the impact of women's changing experience of conception and reproduction, the foundation of the biological difference that is labelled sex. Use of the term gender to delineate that which is socially constructed and therefore subject to change is not accurate. Sex is also socially constructed. Bodies and their activities are not an unchanging template upon which society writes its message. Hence the gender/sex divide is not used in this study. However, sexed bodies are also unchanging in some senses. Sex, the biological difference, results in some physical responses which it is possible to employ to measure the impact of socially constructed events such as the quality of nutrition, housing, repeated pregnancies, disease in varying cultures and periods. Maternal deaths, births, breastfeeding are all such events.

In Part I of the book, *The Development of Contraception*, the physical burden that reproduction places upon women is analysed, and the effect of the period of unusually high fertility around 1800 upon women's motivation to control births is considered. The problems of developing and using contraception are examined in an effort to explain the low levels of use. The interaction between desires for fertility control, women's economic status, and their sexuality in the nineteenth century is the subject of Chapters 3 and 4. Few women encountered information about birth control and those who did seemed to have little to gain from the practice.

---

[7] E. K. Sedgwick, *Epistemology of the Closet* (1990), 26.

How high is the probability that middle-class men who wanted to control their fertility relied upon prostitution? A revised chronology of the changes in Victorian women's sexuality is produced by placing the limited evidence of sexual behaviour in the context of the birth rates and the early twentieth-century evidence. The birth control methods used in the first two-thirds of the twentieth century, including abstaining from sexual intercourse, are described in Chapters 5 and 6. The accompanying changes in attitudes to the body and sexual attitudes necessary to achieve this are considered in these chapters. Why and to what extent did the use of birth control require modification of individual's sexual response, and of gender roles in physical sexual activity?

These questions continue to be important in Part II, *Sexuality and Sex Manuals*. This begins in Chapter 7 by charting change in sexual behaviour during the first two thirds of the twentieth century, looking at the impact of ignorance of physical sexuality and reproduction, the estrangement of the genders, and a deep-seated reticence on English sexual mores. The next four chapters use sex manuals and related sources to create an intellectual history of heterosexual physical sexual practice in this period. What did women's new confidence and the growing use of contraception in the century contribute to the modernization of sexual practice? What did this consist of and to what extent did the contradictory and contested re-emergence of male domination within the genre in the 1940s and 1950s play a part in this modernization? The influence of first-wave feminism and of the need for sexual continence to control fertility receded into the past during these decades. The third and final part of the book, *The Sexual Revolution*, argues that from the 1930s to the 1950s birth rates rose due to rising rates of coitus. The availability of the pill then precipitated a transformation in sexual mores. The public debate and legislative changes generated by women's demand for the new female-controlled method and for abortion resulted in a huge increase in the availability and acceptability of all methods of birth control. It is argued that the resulting reduction of the real and substantial economic and social risk of pregnancy has transformed new generations' attitudes to sexuality.

Norbert Elias commented in 1939 that 'Life sometimes seems to us uncertain enough today, but this bears no comparison with the insecurity of the individual in medieval society. The greater control of sources of fear that is slowly established in the transition to our social structure is indeed one of the most elementary preconditions for the standard of conduct that we express by the concept of "civilization".[8] In the last third of the twentieth century, historians became wary of claiming that progress has occurred. The catastrophe that overtook Elias and his generation only a few months later has overshadowed interpretations of the whole century. Concepts such as civilization have been called into question. However, other positive changes affected the lives of millions of people during the century. The introduction of reliable contraception is one among many changes that increased the control of fear, and allowed a greater experience of pleasure and increased emotional aspirations. There have been substantial improvements, amounting to a transformation, in the lives of English women over the past two centuries. The generation of women who came of age in the 1950s and early 1960s lived through a period in which this process came to a head and female sexual mores were transformed. Their confusion and astonishment is evident in the sources, as well as in the stories they have told me. This book has been written for them.

---

[8] N. Elias, *The Civilizing Process: State Formation and Civilization* (Oxford, 1939; 1976), 253.

PART I

Inventing Contraception

Birth Rates and Women's Bodies: Reproductive Labour

Population growth results first and foremost from the physical labour that only the biological female can perform. This labour, which is performed by the woman's body, can be described as reproductive labour and it includes the processes of menstruation, pregnancy, birth, and breastfeeding. These have been defined as natural processes or events, things that just happen, rather than as work performed by the woman, but like all other forms of labour these activities require energy and drain physical resources. The decline in levels of fertility that has taken place throughout much of the world has been a decline in the level of this reproductive labour, but most scholars dismiss the notion that women had or have a particular motivation to reduce fertility. The pains and pleasures of the body are assumed to be perennial factors that are always present and therefore do not create change. However, changes in fertility rates show us that the burden of reproductive labour borne by the average woman has risen and fallen sharply over generations. In the seventeenth century English women had been having an average of four to five children, but fertility rates rose with increasing speed throughout the eighteenth century until they peaked in 1816. In the first decades of the nineteenth century the average married woman had nearly eight children.[1] Research suggests that after four to five births the risk of maternal complications, stillbirths, and maternal mortality

---

[1] E. A. Wrigley, J. E. Oeppen, R. S. Schofield, and R. S. Davies, *English Population History from Family Reconstitution, 1580–1837* (1997), table 7.1, 335.

increases for women in all societies.[2] Thus, although individual women's physical tolerance varies widely and some women are able to produce much larger families without ill effects, for most women there is a ceiling on the rate of births that can be achieved without causing damage to their body. Research in the developing world has shown that women do affect fertility. Most obviously, increasing women's level of education invariably leads to a lowering of fertility, whereas increasing that of men does not necessarily do so. The desire to control and, when needed, to reduce their burden of labour is present in all human beings. Reproduction places a burden upon women that does not exist for men.

These alterations in fertility rates also tell us more than any other evidence can about the sexual experience of the majority of women but historians of sexuality have ignored reproduction. This is in keeping with their wider attitude to the physical body. Those who write about sexuality have been concerned with desire and identity or the regulatory activities of the state, and the physical body and its sensations have largely been treated as a given.[3] There has been an unexamined assumption that while the social conditions of sexuality and/or discursive sexualities are open to change and thus to history, the body itself is an unchanging and inflexible substratum. Physical acts are accepted as natural and unchanging; only the meanings that are attached to them by culture alter. This book is about the reproductive act, heterosexual penile-vaginal intercourse and its material consequences, to which desire is peripheral and risk is central. The greatest of these consequences is pregnancy. Unlike sexually transmitted diseases, pregnancy can be an intensely desired outcome of women's sexual activity. This does not make it less of a risk. The connection between pregnancy and female sexual expression is not an essentialist, natural, or spiritual connection (although for some women it may also be all of these). It is a banal, dull connection. Pregnancy has had enormous consequences because babies entailed physical and economic costs. Often women could not afford to enjoy sex. The risk made it too expensive a pleasure. An emphasis on the commercialization of sexuality today diverts

---

[2] I. Loudon, *Death in Childbirth* (1992), 242. A. Rosenfield, 'Maternal mortality and morbidity', in B. P. Sachs, R. Beard, E. Papiernik, and C. Russell (eds.), *Reproductive Health Care for Women and Babies* (1995), 272–3.

[3] e.g. E. Kosofsky Sedgwick, *Epistemology of the Closet* (1990), 29.

attention from the real decoupling of physical sexual activity and economics. The result of the introduction of contraception is that physical
sexual events between men and women no longer carry an uncontrollable and incalculable risk of major economic consequences.

Men and women were not equally exposed to this risk. Men can be
likened to passive smokers: under some circumstances they do, and under
other circumstances they do not, have the choice to get up and leave a
smoke-filled atmosphere. Male risk varied: within stable societies where
the man and woman's behaviour was likely to be observed and there was a
norm that said men must accept responsibility, male risk of exposure to
the economic costs of pregnancy was higher. Where it was acceptable,
men could reject the risk: they might desert the woman when pregnancy
occurred, or men might pay the prostitute, usually another young
woman, a small fee in return for which she accepted full responsibility
for the economic risk of a pregnancy. In refusing to accept such a fee, an
unmarried woman in love was refusing to allow the man to limit his
responsibility for the consequences. In practice, she often had little power
and he could simply ignore or evade his share of the risk. This option was
only rarely open to her. Young women who 'fell' provided examples that
warned other young women that the consequences were substantial.
Sexual pleasure had the potential to create ongoing economic burdens,
so there was an incentive for parents to prevent their daughters behaving
in ways likely to arouse their own sexual desires or those of men in
response to them (often not the same behaviours). Married men acquired
some of this risk but women's exposure continued to be greater. It is likely
that the relative male freedom from the economic consequences of
sexuality played the major role in creating society's deep anxiety about
uncontrolled male sexual activity, including masturbation and homosexuality.

The general neglect of demographic evidence by historians of sexuality
has also occurred because the statistically driven discipline of historical
demography has tended to diminish the importance not just of bodies and
sexuality, but of women themselves. This omission was created in part by
the difficulty of constructing relevant variables using the limited forms of
data that can be analysed statistically. It has encouraged the mistrust of
statistical methods felt by some feminists and historians of women and

sexuality, despite the enormous advantages such methods offer. In *Trust in Numbers: The Pursuit of Objectivity in Science and Public Life* (1995), Theodore Porter explains that the development of a rigorous language of mathematics has provided a universalizing language, which makes communication possible amongst different groups. Objectivity, in this instance, is a strategy for dealing with distance and distrust. This language, he argues, has been criticized from the left because it must, in order to operate, slice away the complexity and richness of the individual. However, it can also be used to create openness and to undermine existing certainties. For example, equal pay or equal opportunities legislation depends on the use of statistics to reveal discrimination. In the context of this research, not just fertility rates, but the proportion of women marrying, the infant mortality rate, and a host of other measures, reveal changes over decades and centuries, creating a picture of women's lives that is available through no other source. Throughout this research fertility rates have been used to reveal the level of reproductive labour and the direction of change in women's lives.

FERTILITY RATES

Changes in fertility can be measured in a number of different ways. The actual number of babies born each year is called the crude birth rate, but whether one woman has ten babies or ten women have one baby each the rate will be the same. This does not give much information about women's actual experience. For this purpose we need rates that show the average number of babies born per woman. This is called a woman's (or couple's) completed family size. Such rates show alterations in the number of babies born per fertile or fecund woman, generally taken to be those between the ages of 16 and 44. The total period fertility rate (TFR) does this. This rate is that most commonly referred to when discussing the sharp decline in fertility from the 1870s. If the period is considered only from 1841, then this decline from the 1870s gains greatly in significance, and it has been the focus of extensive research. However, in the 1980s, the Cambridge Population Group used parish reconstitution data to produce fertility rates from before 1841. Calculating the TFR still requires more information than is available for the period before 1841 and only the

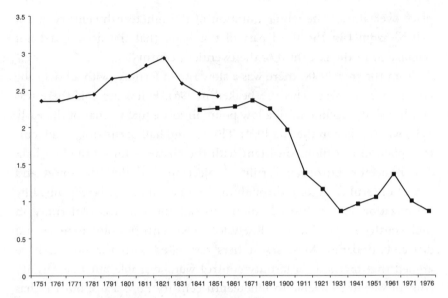

Fig. 1.1 Gross Reproduction Rate 1751–1976

Source: 1751–1851 E. A. Wrigley, et al., *English Population History From Family Reconstitution 1580–1837* (1997). Table 8.7, 532. 1841–1976, *Birth Statistics, Historical Series of Statistics from Registrations of Births in England and Wales, 1837–1983* OPCS Series FM1 no. 13 (1983). Table 1.4, 26.

gross reproduction rate (GRR), which shows the number of daughters born per woman, can be obtained for the entire period from 1751 to 1976. (See Fig. 1.1.) This reveals that after rising slowly from the 1600s fertility began to rise sharply from 1751. According to the GRR it then peaked in 1816, the second decade of the nineteenth century. The late eighteenth and early nineteenth centuries were a period of great change in women's employment patterns and there was a major shift in ideas about women's proper role, and in attitudes to marriage and sexuality. In the 1820s and 1830s there was a very sharp decline in the birth rate, but this decline then slowed down. There was an aggregate rise from the mid-1840s to the mid-1870s but the fertility of some occupational groups was declining as early as the 1850s. The relation of the nineteenth-century fertility decline to sexual mores is examined in Chapters 2–4. The aggregate fertility of the nation did tip sharply downwards again from the 1870s on, rushing towards the low point in the birth rate, which was reached in the early 1930s. Thus, the fertility decline must be considered as a process that took place over almost the whole duration of the nineteenth century and it will be argued in the third part of this book that the decline did not stabilize until the last third of the twentieth century.

From the mid-1930s, there was a slow rise in fertility, with a brief baby boom after the war. This rise peaked in 1964. Following this there was another sharp decline until a low point almost equal to that of the early 1930s was reached in the late 1970s. This second half of the story is difficult to explain in a fashion consistent with the changes during the first half. The Princeton European Fertility Project showed that the onset and spread of fertility decline throughout Europe could not be explained by urbanization and industrialization. Instead the patterns of fertility in nineteenth-century Europe closely followed centuries-old language and dialect boundaries. Most researchers associated with the project have argued that methods of fertility control were available but that fertility control was unthinkable to nineteenth-century Europeans; but this has been contested.[4] There has been increased interest in 'demand for children' and in ideological factors such as secularization.

Fertility had been controlled primarily through marriage. In England, for several centuries, there was a low level of illegitimacy, most births took place within long-term relationships recognized by the community (whether formal marriage or not), and contraception was either non-existent or relatively ineffective. This meant that a rise or fall in the proportion of women who were married and in the age at which they married produced a rise or fall in fertility rates. This is because a higher age at marriage meant women spent fewer years married and having sexual intercourse, so therefore fewer years at risk of pregnancy. In England there was a high average age at marriage and a high proportion of people who never married at all right up until the 1940s. In 1965, John Hajnal described this unique pattern of late and infrequent marriage as the

---

[4] For a summary see G. Alter, 'Fertility of Theories Decline: A Nonspecialist's Guide to the Current Debate', in J. R. Gillis, L. A. Tilly, and D. Levine (eds.), *The European Experience of Declining Fertility: A Quiet Revolution 1850–1970* (1992). See also J. Knodel and E. van de Walle, 'Lessons from the Past: Policy implications of Historical Fertility Studies', in A. J. Coale and S. Cotts Watkins (eds.), *The Decline of Fertility* (1986). For the origins of these ideas, see F. W. Notestein, 'Population: The Long View', in T. W. Schultz (ed.), *Food for the World* (1945). S. Szreter, 'The Idea of the Demographic Transition and the Study of Fertility Change: A Critical Intellectual History', *Population and Development Review*, 19/4 (1993).

north-west European marriage system because it has occurred only in that area. He showed that not only was the marriage age late, at around 26 to 27 or older for men, and for women at 23 to 24, but 10 to 15 per cent of the population never married at all.[5] In most societies nearly 100 per cent of women marry and they tend to do so at a younger age. The age at marriage in Britain did not rise or fall because plebeian couples intended to have a smaller or larger completed family size. But communities were aware that delaying marriage delayed the start of childbearing, and that marrying when a woman was very young often resulted in a large family. So individual caution backed up by community sanctions stopped most couples from marrying unless they had sufficient savings and income to support a new separate household containing a wife and children.

Premarital sexual intercourse was regulated by this system. Most unmarried women would not have sexual intercourse except with a partner who had agreed to marriage, and the man would not make this offer until he could afford to do so. Note that this is not the same as delaying intercourse until marriage was imminent, and there is no way of proving statistically which of these behavioural choices couples made. There was probably considerable leeway if the woman did not become pregnant. Under the old poor law, if a man tried to evade responsibility for a pregnancy, then the woman could appear before a magistrate and swear her coming child's paternity. If parish officials accepted the testimony of the woman and those who supported her they would then force the father to contribute to its support to avoid the charge on the parish.[6] E. A. Wrigley and R. S. Schofield found that average wages were so low many men and women could not afford the cost of household formation and it was this that caused the low rate of marriage.[7] They describe this as a homeostatic system with a rising and falling nuptial valve, that is, marriage, adjusting family size to available resources independent of the individual's conscious decisions. There was a lag of several decades between real wage movements and shifts in fertility, which they were unable

---

[5] J. Hajnal, 'European Marriage Patterns in Perspective', in D. V. Glass and D. E. Eversley (eds.), *Population in History* (1965).

[6] A. Clark, *The Struggle for the Breeches: Gender and the Making of the British Working Class* (1995), 188–9.

[7] E. A. Wrigley and R. S. Schofield, *The Population History of England, 1541–1871* (1981), ch. 10.

to explain. Nonetheless, in England there is a clear connection between food prices and employment patterns (the economy), which encouraged or discouraged household formation, through marriage (coitus), to realized fertility (births). There was a greater degree of sexual autonomy permitted to young single women within the context of English community control than was the case in other cultures, such as those of southern Europe. Both men and women chose their own partners, the age difference was usually small, and premarital sex was accepted as a stage of courting. Women were not rigidly chaperoned by their family members or by employers and they often had a degree of freedom to accept and reject their own partners.[8] It had been argued that this system of prudential marriage had broken down as a result of industrial and social change prior to 1870, and that by then fertility was managed by the use of contraception or not at all. However, Simon Szreter recently found that people continued to delay marriage throughout 'the protracted period during which the planned control of fertility within marriage became established as a behavioural norm'.[9] Szreter was referring to the period from the 1860s to the 1940s but, as will be shown in the final chapter of this book, the transition away from the north-west European marriage system in England was not fully completed until the mid-1970s, some twenty-five years later.[10]

Women's reproductive capacity and experience has been extensively analysed by demographers in order that the different components can be defined and then treated as statistical variables. The resulting theory both extends understanding of women's reproductive labour and limits interpretations of women's role in changing fertility rates. Porter explains that the creation of statistical knowledge involves the defining of information, such that it is appropriate to that purpose. Existing objects must often be redefined in order that they can be counted. Using occupational classifications as his example, he shows that:

---

[8] Hajnal, 'European Marriage Patterns'. D. Levine, *Reproducing Families: The Political Economy of English Population History* (1987). J. Schwarzkopf, *Women in the Chartist Movement* (London, 1991), ch. 1. A. MacFarlane, review of *The Family, Sex and Marriage in England 1500–1800*, by Lawrence Stone, *History and Theory*, 18 (1979), 114.

[9] S. Szreter, *Fertility, Class and Gender in Britain, 1860–1940* (1996), 391.

[10] See Ch. 15.

The dependence of categorisation on particular circumstances would seem to imply that the categories are highly contingent, and hence weak. Once put into place though they can be impressively resilient. Legions of statistical employees collect and process numbers on the presumption that the categories are valid. Newspapers and public officials wanting to discuss the numerical characteristics of a population have very limited ability to rework the numbers into different ones. They thus become black boxes, scarcely vulnerable to challenge except in a limited way by insiders. Having become official then, they become increasingly real.[11]

A 'black box' is an artificial, constructed entity which is presented and used as a unit by the producer of the knowledge and cannot be taken apart by the recipient. The black boxes of the scientist may be material objects but they can also be causal claims, categories, or laws.[12] The statistical categories that are used to analyse fertility function as a black box. The intellectual spadework on the assumptions that underlie statistical categories cannot be done and redone constantly. It exists as a foundation that enables the models to be refined, a process that continues over decades. As these models are tightened and improved, the categories narrowed and focused over the decades, the arguments or concepts on which the assumptions are based may be being developed in opposite directions, opened up as categories, widened, and shown to be untenable. The breaking down of reproductive experience into component parts was based upon assumptions that now need to be re-examined.

PROXIMATE AND REMOTE DETERMINANTS

A number of biological and behavioural factors have a direct influence on fertility. 'Direct influence' means that the factors involve the bodies of women and, to a lesser extent, the bodies of men. These factors include use of contraception. In 1956, Judith Blake and Kingsley Davis proposed a set of eleven such factors, which they called intermediate factors. Modernization, or 'cultural factors', such as industrialization and mass education, which were then thought actually to cause fertility decline, could

[11] T. Porter, *Trust in Numbers: The Pursuit of Objectivity in Science and Public life* (1995), 42.
[12] For black boxes, see B. Latour, *Science in Action* (1987), 2.

control fertility only through these intermediate factors. Their analysis identified factors such as the differing interests of men and women. They included sexuality, although they believed that levels of sexual activity were only minimally malleable, and that at great cost.[13] In 1978, this list was refined by John Bongaarts, who labelled the factors associated with modernization 'remote determinants', and Davis and Blake's intermediate factors 'proximate determinants'.[14] Gender relations were dismissed entirely from Bongaarts's list and sexuality was relegated to being a biological rather than a social function. It is not clear why he removes these factors but it may have been because they had proved hard to measure. Bongaarts believed that the proximate determinants were factors that could play only an intermediate role. This means that either they are seen as physical processes beyond the boundary of consciousness, or they are altered by the remote determinants, which are the factors that cause change. The proximate determinants are biological variables related to body parts or systems.[15] Society and conscious behaviour create the conditions under which these factors operate, such as access to coitus, or the adequacy of nourishment. The flow of causation is always from society and behaviour to body parts. Bongaarts and Robert Potter produced this list of proximate determinants:

1. marriage (and marital disruption);
2. the onset of permanent sterility;
3. post-partum infecundability;
4. natural fecundability or frequency of intercourse;
5. use and effectiveness of contraception;
6. spontaneous intrauterine mortality;
7. induced abortion.

Bongaarts and Potter suggested that marriage and the onset of permanent sterility, or menopause, determine the duration of the reproductive

---

[13] K. Davis and J. Blake, 'Social Structure and Fertility: An Analytic Framework', *Economic Development and Cultural Change*, 4 (1956).

[14] J. Bongaarts, 'A Framework for Analyzing the Proximate Determinants of Fertility', *Population and Development Review*, 4 (1978).

[15] J. Bongaarts and R. G. Potter, *Fertility, Biology, and Behaviour: An Analysis of the Proximate Determinants* (1983), 5.

period, and the other five factors determine the rate of childbearing and the duration of birth intervals.[16] The list is about body parts, not people or social structures. Marriage, for example, is only significant because this event marks the meeting of penises and vaginas. Often this meeting actually happened before marriage, but marriages could be discussed openly in academic discourse and, more importantly, they could be counted. Obtaining accurate rates of cohabitation still creates immense problems for researchers. The list is presented as non-gendered; however, the factors listed and the way they are defined relate almost solely to women's bodies. This reflects the social construction of reproduction as well as the fact that women's biological role in reproduction is much greater and more complex than that of men.

1. Marriage is included because the period of time for which women have the potential to bear children is the most important factor in population growth. The age at puberty was and remains relatively unimportant. Until the 1960s, courtship and marriage determined the start of most British women's sexual and reproductive career. The age at which men marry makes little difference to completed fertility, and the varying extent to which male sexual activity is confined within marriage in different societies, and in the same societies at different times, has not been considered relevant to fertility rates.[17]

2. The onset of permanent sterility refers to menopause in women. 'Couple sterility' occurs as a result of both male and female problems; however, infertility levels in both sexes are believed to be relatively constant and thus insignificant.[18]

3. Post-partum infecundability refers to the period after a birth in which a woman is not ovulating and, therefore, is unable to become pregnant. This is extended to a varying degree in different societies and in

[16] Ibid. 5.

[17] A. McLaren, *Reproductive Rituals: The Perception of Fertility in England from the Sixteenth Century to the Nineteenth Century* (1984), 65.

[18] A high prevalence of gonorrhoea and genital tuberculosis is a major cause of sterility in some contemporary African populations. There seems to have been no modern research on whether STDs would have had an influence on fertility in England in the 19th and early 20th centuries. Szreter comments on this but his reference is to research done for the Royal Commission on Population during the 1940s, at which point, as Pfeffer shows, infertility was little understood. Szreter, *Fertility*, 428 n. 173. N. Pfeffer, *The Stork and the Syringe: A Political History of Reproductive Medicine* (1993).

individual women by breastfeeding. This may or may not be consciously intended to delay conception, and it is not a reliable method of doing so for the individual woman.

4. Natural fecundability is defined as the probability of conceiving within a month among fecundable women; that is, excluding women who are pregnant, sterile, or not menstruating; and in the absence of measures intended to reduce fertility. The probability of conceiving as a result of any one episode of coitus is primarily controlled by biological factors. In the list this is coupled with coital frequency, which greatly affects the likelihood of conception. The inclusion of frequency in this category stemmed from the widely held belief that levels of sexual activity were biologically determined, and it is treated as an element of the woman's fecundability by Bongaarts and Potter. It is increasingly evident that coital frequency can also differ according to social and cultural beliefs and needs, and alterations in frequency are unlikely to be solely the responsibility of women.

5. Contraceptive effectiveness refers to the degree of reliability of the method in preventing pregnancy. In practice it arises from a combination of the available technology and the knowledge and resources of the individuals using the methods.

6. Spontaneous intrauterine mortality refers to miscarriages.

7. There is evidence for the use of induced abortion by women throughout recorded history. The incidence has been impossible to ascertain prior to the legalization of abortion.

This list specifies the physical biological processes involved in reproduction, and reveals how they interact over the course of women's lives. However, it is assumed that these bodily practices and processes do not cause change. In some instances the events do occur without the conscious volition of the individual: for example, menopause. But in the other instances it is believed that external forces or events motivate the individual to take action to produce the resulting event: induced abortion for example. Within this framework the cause for the abortion is never the pregnancy but instead the social forces that make the pregnancy undesired. If we take this premiss to its logical conclusion then no pregnancy is undesired solely because the woman does not want a pregnancy or a child. Presumably, according to this, in some ideal or natural circumstance the woman would want every pregnancy.[19] Unless some negative external factor intervenes a pregnancy would always proceed. There is no internal dialogue of desire and rejection here. The woman's body has no needs and makes no demands upon her consciousness, say, for respite.[20]

The exterior forces are labelled the remote determinants, and lists of these have included industrialization, urbanization, feminism, structural changes in family function, female wages, child labour rates, and mass education. Much interest has focused on the economic costs of children. The list of proximate determinants was concerned, legitimately enough, with (primarily) female body parts, not with women as mothers and wives, but the list of remote determinants also fails to include factors which relate to these activities/roles. This latter list is not concerned with the body nor, with limited exceptions, has it been concerned with women. The clearly gendered exceptions were feminism and women's wage rates. The consequence of the division of factors affecting fertility into these two lists is that thinking rational, male, economic actors and feminists or working women respond to the remote determinants, but women in their traditional roles of wives and mothers are passive. So women were only active, that is, capable of affecting fertility, when they were in or claiming traditional male roles. At no point were women in the roles of wife and mother considered as possible agents of change. On the face of it the strong tendency of researchers to ask women but not men questions about fertility appears to contradict this, but women were asked about their fertility rather as if they were record-keepers for the couple. Only by questioning both men and women is it possible to treat women as decision-makers in their own right.[21] There is now research undertaken

[19] This was the belief of 19th-century French socialists who rejected contraception. A. McLaren, *Sexuality and Social Order* (1983), 86.

[20] It is arguable that the demands of the male body were included. As explained, Bongaarts and Potter assumed that the body would require a constant rate of coitus and hence that coital frequency, or sexual desire, was a biological factor. The notion of a physical need for sexual relief has been seen as typical of male but not female sexuality. However, they were writing in the late 1970s, a moment at which female sexual desires were being newly acknowledged, and so such a conclusion cannot necessarily be drawn.

[21] e.g. G. Rowntree and R. M. Pierce, 'Birth Control in Britain: Part One', *Population Studies*, 15/1 (1961). E. Slater and M. Woodside, *Patterns of Marriage: A Study of the Marriage Relationships of the Urban Working Classes* (1951).

by demographers which examines the role wives and mothers play in fertility decline, but even in this the female body remains passive as they continue to use a variant of remote and proximate determinant analysis.[22]

The apparent logic of the division of the determinants into these categories of remote and proximate, that is, causal and non-causal, reflects the importance of these relatively simple polarized dichotomies to Western culture. The Cartesian opposition between mind and body sets up a dualism in which the mind and rational thought are opposed to, and separate from, the body and emotions. Feminist philosophers have highlighted the strength of the association of the mind and rationality with males and of the body and emotion with women. Reliance on this polarization has limited the understanding of fertility rates. We should be alert for possible absences when we see, as is the case with this model, that specifically female experience is consigned to the category of the non-rational, the body, something which occurs below consciousness. Simply introducing women as conscious choice-making subjects within the framework of remote and proximate determinants does not encompass female reproductive experience (though doing so has produced insights). The body is the primary site for potentially different attitudes to fertility for women and for men but women's physical experience is placed outside consciousness.

The construction of the woman as passive in demographic theory was reinforced by the work of Richard Easterlin in the 1970s. He produced a model which extended remote and proximate determinants analysis in order to elucidate the route between modernization and fertility. This model is not concerned with biological factors but with consciousness; the intention is to map the private individual decision-making process that leads to fewer babies. Thus it should account for the impact of embodied experience. Easterlin drew on the work of the 1950s Chicago school of household economists who had attempted to explain fertility decision-making.[23] They had argued that the demand for children depended on the household's balancing of its subjective tastes for goods and children against externally determined constraints of price and income in a way that

---

[22] For a summary of recent research, see S. Jejeebhoy, *Women's Education, Autonomy, and Reproductive Behaviour: Experience from Developing Countries* (1995).

[23] G. Becker, 'An Economic Analysis of Fertility', in National Bureau of Economic Research (ed.), *Demographic and Economic Change in Developed Countries* (1960).

maximized its satisfaction. The household unit or couple made decisions about fertility. Parents might develop a taste for children who embodied greater inputs of time and goods, leading to a growing emphasis on the quality rather than the number of children. The Chicago school model was adopted by Easterlin, who proposed that between the remote and proximate determinants a new stage be inserted, which included (1) supply of children, (2) demand for children, and (3) regulation costs of fertility control. This brought the level of analysis down from societal factors, for example, mass education, to the decision-making processes of the couple.

Easterlin's model was widely accepted, but there has been growing comment on the gender blindness of the approach since the late 1980s. Historical demographer Wally Seccombe commented that treating the reproductive couple as a unified subject allows no theoretical space for wives and husbands to have different interests.[24] The blindness this creates is revealed in Ron Lesthaeghe and Johan Surkyn's argument that the fertility decline since the Second World War resulted from a prioritizing of hedonism and individualism and a lessening of responsibility, sacrifice, altruism, and the respect for the sanctity of long-term commitments.[25] They use gender-neutral language except in comments such as that the 'generation that produces the baby boom is also the one that starts the incipient quest for perfectionism . . . for instance . . . in the form of greater educational investment in daughters'.[26] There is an unavoidable implication that educational investment in sons was necessary but that for daughters it was a luxury. However, it is clear that, before the Second World War, the survival of individuals, including men, women, and children, often depended on the stability of the family unit and its successful interactions with the surrounding society.[27] As a result,

[24] W. Seccombe, 'Men's "Marital Rights" and Women's "Wifely Duties"': Changing Conjungal Relations in the Fertility Decline', in Gillis et al., *The European Experience*, 66.

[25] R. Lesthaeghe and J. Surkyn, 'A Century of Demographic and Cultural Change in Western Europe: An Exploration of the Underlying Dimensions', *Population and Development Review*, 9/3 (1983), 429.

[26] R. Lesthaeghe and J. Surkyn, 'Cultural Dynamics and Economic Theories of Fertility Change', *Population and Development Review*, 14/1 (1988), 38.

[27] For a discussion of the costs to women of lone parenthood and their responses in the 19th century, see J. Humphries, 'Female Headed Households in Early Industrial Britain: The Vanguard of the Proletariat', *Labour History Review* (1998).

individual interest often coincided with the interest of the kin group. The period in which 'individualism' has been prioritized has seen the creation of the welfare state and rising levels of female employment. This resulted in an extremely sharp fall in the relative risk to the family unit if women expanded their role and their aspirations. It is on this basis that women have changed their behaviour. And, in fact, today women continue to undertake the major part of long-term care of the chronically ill and of children. There are many responsible and caring men; nonetheless, women's lives are characterized to a greater extent by responsibility, altruism, and a respect for the long-term commitment they have made in having children.[28] The underlying construction of passive and remote determinants militates against demographers perceiving these changes in risks. In the earlier society, the absence of the embodied female subject means the gendered nature of the sacrifices that were required to maintain the family unit is not visible. In the modern period the focus on the couple means that specific changes in women's role due to changes in society are ignored. Thus Lesthaeghe and Surkyn characterize the change as ideological and ignore the substantial decrease in women's domestic and reproductive labour. Seccombe's research showed how an awareness of differing gender interests might produce positive results He argued that in British working-class couples of the late nineteenth and early twentieth centuries women had the motivation to limit family size but the methods available were male methods. So birth rates did not fall until changes in the family economy led to husbands' interests converging with those of their wives, while at the same time feminism and doctors' advice was giving wives more confidence to resist their husband's sexual demands.[29]

Alison MacKinnon has criticized the lack of female agency in demography.[30] To illustrate this she used an article by Solvi Sogner, a female

[28] See e.g. A. Garnham and E. Knights, *Putting the Treasury First: The Truth about Child Support*, Poverty Publication 88 (1994).

[29] W. Seccombe, 'Starting to Stop: Working-Class Fertility Decline in Britain', *Past and Present*, 126 (1990).

[30] A. MacKinnon, 'Were Women Present at the Demographic Transition? Questions from a Feminist Historian to Historical Demographers', *Gender and History*, 7/2 (1995), 222.

demographer. Sogner's response to criticism from historians of women is worth quoting at length:

Did [historical demographers] . . . not measure fertility per woman-year, make in depth studies of breastfeeding practices, discuss post-partum amenorrhoea? Did they not . . . discuss virtually all problems separately for each sex, and thus highlight living conditions for women as well as for men? Surely the historical demographers were safe against any possible accusation of discriminating against women. They were appalled when such criticisms were levelled against them. This self-righteous attitude is justified only up to a point. It tends to overlook women as historical actors in their own right—albeit passive actors.[31]

Even once the issue of women as actors is drawn to Sogner's attention, even though she has given the matter considerable thought, women remain at most 'passive actors'. This is because the model on which she bases her analysis prevents her from seeing them in any other fashion. As the analysis of proximate determinants has shown, the category that is constructed as passive is not the woman, it is the reproductive body parts and processes of the woman. In the existing analytical framework the remote determinants are factors external to embodied women and men, and these create motivation for the 'couple' to reduce fertility. This leads us to treat motivation as if it is synonymous with the remote determinants. Thus, for example, the take-up of education can be treated as synonymous with the will to be educated. The individual with his or her mind and his or her will to be educated need not be discussed. The space that the mind and will occupy between the body parts on the one hand and the remote determinants on the other hand does not exist in the model. However, the woman's mind and will may be expressed in relation to her body parts. For example, a wealthy middle-class wife with no paid occupation may decide to prevent a further birth because she is physically exhausted by her previous pregnancies. If a means to prevent the birth is available or her husband agrees to restrict sexual intercourse, her decision will contribute to fertility decline, but no remote determinants, ideological or economic, need enter this mother's decision-making process. The only relationship is that between her body parts and

---

[31] S. Sogner, 'Historical Features of Women's Position in Society', in N. Frederici, K. Oppenheim Mason, and S. Sogner (eds.), *Women's Position and Demographic Change* (1993), 245.

her will, so in the model of remote and proximate determinants her decision-making process is hidden.

Thus in this analytical framework factors external to the woman are treated as if they were the same as factors external to the body parts. It is assumed that the rational, thinking actor is motivated to reduce fertility by the remote determinants. Causal effects flow from external factors *inward* to the body parts where the reproductive/sexual events take place. Decline or rise in the number of births occurs because factors external to the individual produce effects on the reproductive body parts. There is no theoretical space for the relationship of the individual to their body to be examined. A flow *outward* from the body parts causing the individual to act is not possible in this framework. Yet we are all familiar with the causal relationship between our own body and our mind. There are circumstances in which we know absolutely that the body forces the mind to take action. The most extreme and obvious of these is physical pain. In *The Body in Pain* (1985), Elaine Scarry examines the difficulty of describing the experience of pain. She comments that for 'the person whose pain it is, [the pain] is "effortlessly grasped" (that is even with the most heroic effort it cannot *not* be grasped)'.[32] The unavoidable thrust of physical pain into conscious awareness that Scarry describes is a response fundamental to human experience (though it may be delayed in extreme circumstances). This does not mean that a person necessarily acts to reduce pain when it occurs. Though they cannot choose not to *feel*, people can choose not to *act* in response to their physical sensations. For example, those with chronic illness may be habituated to pain to the extent that they regard it as the normal state of being. However, when people do not attempt to prevent their own pain this is interpreted by observers as revealing that something is preventing them from doing so. It would be extremely surprising in the case of such major physical experiences as pregnancy and birth if the flow of causation passed in one direction only, from the external causes to the body. Pain is only one category of sensation. Pleasures (from a desired child or sexual activity) provide other such categories. All aspects of sexuality and reproduction involve this interrelationship between the feeling body and the thinking mind. Female experi-

[32] E. Scarry, *The Body in Pain* (1995), 4.

ence is central to this book but the male interrelationship of the mind and body is also absent from this theoretical structure. The layer missing between the proximate and remote determinants is embodied experience. This absence may seem justified because it is assumed that the mind and body interrelationship, and the elements of embodied experience not affected by the remote determinants, are transhistorical and thus play no role in causing change. However, as has been explained, rises and falls in fertility cause immense change in women's physical experience, in their burden of reproductive labour.

Some researchers have expressed ambivalence about describing the activities involved in loving or caring for others as labour. For example, Pam Carter, who undertook research into breastfeeding, felt uneasy about describing situations in which women breastfeed their babies as 'working conditions'. She cites other researchers who feel that representations of, for example, mothering or caring for elderly parents as labour misrepresent fundamental relationships, which cannot be contained or limited.[33] It is vital that loving attention to others is not treated reductively. Reproduction is the most fundamental act of creation that human beings can perform and creative work is for most people intensely meaningful and rewarding. Women often took pride in the immense amount of hard work involved in bearing and raising several children. To call their physical contribution labour does not diminish the love and altruism that often accompanied their achievement. The intellectual need to separate labour and love is a comment on how work is perceived, how rare it is that people find work that is fulfilling and in which they have control over the conditions of their labour. The demographer John Caldwell has discussed the obscuring of relative work inputs:

Work traditionally has been a matter of *drudgery*... The distinction frequently made between 'productive work' and 'household work' tends to obscure the value of some forms of work. Indeed, the whole subject of peasant labor inputs is so obscured by conventional wisdoms, convenient to the powerful, that it is difficult to interpret research or to discount the prejudices of researchers... [T]here is a continuous downgrading of the value of women's work that misrepresents its significance. Those peasant households with insufficient

[33] P. Carter, *Feminism, Breasts and Breastfeeding* (1995), 78.

female inputs are in just as reduced a condition as those with insufficient male inputs.[34]

Conventional wisdom also excluded women's reproductive labour. Even analysts such as Caldwell, or feminists who have examined women's domestic labour, do not include the labour of the body in their definition of work. Reproduction, and by implication the physical labour this involves, is mentioned by a number of theorists including Karl Marx, but it is not included in any actual analysis of labour.[35] The result is that the labour involved, and the cost of this to the woman, escapes analysis.

Reproductive labour can be compared with coal mining, an occupation that has been of great economic and symbolic importance in Britain. Mrs Lawther, a miner's wife, told the annual Labour Party conference in 1927, 'It is four times as dangerous to bear a child as it is for you to go down a mine. You are seeking legislation to make your occupation safe; will you still go on allowing your wives to suffer under this ban [on birth control]?'.[36] She was speaking about maternal mortality. However, when comparing the risks a miner's life entailed with that of men in white-collar occupations, we would include the wearing down of the miner's body resulting from the hard labour, and the risk of serious injury and emphysema.[37] The latter were occupational safety or medical issues but the wearing down of the body was simply part of the job. In the same way, the normal physical labour of reproduction, and the consequent wearing down of women's bodies, was not a medical issue, except when exhaustion or injuries seriously hampered their continuing labour in the household. Even actual injuries to the mother caused by pregnancy or childbirth, that is, maternal morbidity, were considered impossible to measure. This means there are no adequate statistics except for maternal deaths.[38] Nonetheless, damage from childbirth and miscarriage caused many women chronic pain, constant tiredness, and difficulties with future

---

[34] J. C. Caldwell, *Theory of Fertility Decline* (1983), 160–1.

[35] C. C. Williams, *Examining the Nature of Domestic Labour* (1988), 13.

[36] 'The Twenty Seventh Annual Report of the Labour Party', cited in L. Hoggart, 'The Campaign for Birth Control in Britain in the 1920s', in A. Digby and J. Stewart (eds.), *Gender, Health and Welfare* (1996), 223.

[37] T. Griffiths, *The Lancashire Working Classes: c.1880–1930* (2001), 196.

[38] Loudon, *Death*, 365.

births.[39] Middle- and upper-class women were more often able to take long periods of rest in order to recover but for many, and for working-class women, enduring such difficulties was part of the usual course of their lives, part of their primary occupation. There are now very few men in the developed world willing to undertake jobs that involve the level of risk, or require the hard physical work, that coal mining did. Why would women, especially those who already had several children, have continued to undertake a high-risk, hard-labour occupation with low rewards?

In the absence of reliable and safe individual methods of birth control women had limited choices. Most women dearly wanted some children, and the considerable positive outcomes of reproductive labour can include much loved children, higher status, and support in old age. Either a woman married and struggled with as many pregnancies as fate sent her, or she did not marry and usually had no children. Therefore changes in family size cannot be directly related to the hypothesis that women desired to reduce their labour. However, women's breastfeeding choices can be treated as a separate issue from their desire to have children. This was the only element in a woman's reproductive labour that could be performed by other women. Therefore, women could have control over this aspect of their work even when birth control was not available to them.

BREASTFEEDING AS REPRODUCTIVE LABOUR

Women's response to breastfeeding suggests strongly that they were, and are, not passive in relation to the biological processes that take place in their bodies; they did act to reduce their reproductive labour. Breast milk does not come from nowhere. It is produced by the labour of the woman's body. The fact that this is a biological process, an automatic mechanism, does not mean the woman will be unaware that milk production and feeding makes demands on her body, nor, as the historical record reveals,

[39] See Ch. 5 for inter-war estimates of such damage in birth control clinic patients. M. Llewellyn Davies, *Maternity: Letters from Working Women Collected by the Women's Co-operative Guild* (1915).

does it mean that she is passive in relation to the process.[40] The consequences of breastfeeding for women who do not have adequate resources or control of their fertility have been documented. At the extreme the cumulative effect on women of a high number of births and prolonged lactation causes 'maternal depletion syndrome'. This involves a severe breakdown in maternal health including weight loss and premature ageing, with chronic infections and heavy daily workloads additional contributory factors.[41] However, even well-nourished women experience tiredness and disruption of their other activities when breastfeeding. Moreover, breastfeeding can result in painful conditions. Valerie Fildes explains that:

At all periods (including the present) the major problem for breastfeeding women has been sore or infected nipples, usually the result of small cracks becoming infected.... The types of problems which affected the nipples were: i) soreness (especially in first time mothers); ii) cracks, clefts and fissures; iii) ulcers and loss of the nipples; iv) nipples obstructed or deformed by scar tissue from suckling a previous child.... [S]evere problems such as loss of a nipple due to breastfeeding were not infrequent in the 17th century and there was probably a high incidence of infections of all degrees of severity until very recent times.[42]

These health problems are a part of the routine burden of labour, just as the numerous minor injuries, such as broken fingers, sustained by coal miners were a routine part of their occupation. Well-nourished women with adequate resources can often cope with these difficulties, and find pleasure in breastfeeding, enjoying feelings of intense closeness to the baby and sensual delight in the physical experience. Feminist researchers have pointed out how cultural disincentives against breastfeeding could and should be removed and this discussion is not intended as an argument

[40] Maher points out that 'the socio-biological and frequently the medical discussion of the relationship between mother and child gives us to understand that it depends on automatic mechanisms over which mother and child have little control...To these authors, the care given by the mother, especially in the early period, is almost involuntary, a passive affair.' V. Maher, 'Breastfeeding or Maternal Depletion', in V. Maher (ed.), *The Anrothropology of BreastFeeding: Natural Law or Social Construct* (1992), 156.

[41] Ibid. 160, citing D. B. Jelliffe and E. F. Jelliffe, *Human Milk in the Modern World: Psychological, Nutritional and Economic Significance* (1978).

[42] V. Fildes, *Breasts, Bottles and Babies: A History of Infant Feeding* (1986), 139–40.

against breastfeeding. But historical and modern research suggests that in the existing societal context the majority of women will take advantage of alternatives that enable them to cease working so hard.

Falls in the rate of breastfeeding have been recorded in many historical societies. For example, Fildes has shown that use of wet-nurses by wealthy English women increased through the seventeenth century, and by the early eighteenth century even those with a relatively modest income often hired other women to breastfeed their infants.[43] The use of wet-nurses declined in the late eighteenth century as feeding vessels such as the 'bubby pot' made hand-feeding babies possible. She comments that such large numbers of these pots exist in varied materials that it is evident that they must have been in use by the poor also.[44] French women's reliance on wet-nurses began earlier and was even greater.[45] Kirsten Hastrup explains that in Iceland during the seventeenth and eighteenth centuries, to the horror of contemporary observers, only the very poorest of mothers breastfed their children. Most babies were fed on cow's milk, butter, and fish, and because of this, although birth mothers were regularly having ten, twelve, or more babies, only two or three would survive to adulthood.[46] John Knodel undertook a study of the Bavarian village of Anhausen over two and a half centuries 1692–1939. He found that there had been a demographically significant shift away from breastfeeding in the mid-nineteenth century. By 1904–7 68.6 per cent of women in the area did not breastfeed their babies at all.[47] Fildes's examination of reports by the Medical Officers of Health in the 1900s shows that although the median percentage of English women breastfeeding in the first month of the baby's life was very high at 89.3 per cent, in wealthier areas more

[43] Ibid. 99–100.

[44] Ibid. 168, 346, 348. Wrigley has disputed Fildes's argument, using statistical sources to argue that stillbirth rates would account for the rise in fertility at this time, and thus breastfeeding rates may not have fallen. E. A. Wrigley, 'Explaining the Rise in Marital Fertility in England in the "Long" Eighteenth Century', *Economic History Review*, 51/3 (1998).

[45] D. Hunt, *Parents and Children in History* (1970), 100–22. P. Aries, *Centuries of Childhood: A Social History of Family Life* (1962), 374–5.

[46] K. Hastrup, 'A Question of Reason: Breastfeeding Patterns in Seventeenth and Eighteenth Century Iceland', in Maher (ed.), *Anthropology*, 93, 96, 98.

[47] J. Knodel, 'Two and a Half Centuries of Demographic History in a Bavarian Village', *Population Studies*, 24 (1967), 355.

women chose not to breastfeed.[48] In 1930, Lella Florence found that the majority of the Cambridge birth control clinic working-class patients breastfed their children as long as possible for reasons of convenience and economy. By 1980, when Britain had become a much wealthier society, only 26 per cent of women breastfed for as long as four months, the period recommended by the Department of Health and Social Security working party in 1974.[49] Leonore Manderson found that in colonial Malaya, breastfeeding declined from the later nineteenth century as a result both of earlier weaning and of women opting to bottle-feed from birth.[50] There are many other such examples throughout the world.

In spite of the wealth of examples, and numerous comments by contemporary observers, recent researchers have been very reluctant to draw the conclusion that many women find breastfeeding 'a troublesome task' that they do not wish to undertake.[51] They emphasize external factors that influenced the decision to refuse the infant the breast. This is another example of the unwillingness to see the responses produced by the body, or the interaction between the body and the consciousness, as causal. Manderson attributed the Malayan decline to an association between bottle-feeding and modernity, promoted especially by the infant feeding practices of expatriate and wealthy local women, and the growing availability of paid work outside the home, making continued breastfeeding difficult. More recently baby food manufacturers are seen to be manipulating women. It is important that the unscrupulous advertising of inadequate breast milk substitutes is prevented; nonetheless, this explanation cannot explain the continuities with the behaviour of women before the advent of mass advertising. In England breastfeeding declined among wealthy women before they moved into paid employment. The decline in breastfeeding in the cities of developing countries has

[48] V. Fildes, 'Infant Feeding Practices and Infant Mortality in England, 1900–1919', *Continuity and Change*, 13/2 (1998), 253–4, 259. R. I. Woods, P. A. Watterson, and J. H. Woodward, 'The Causes of the Rapid Infant Mortality decline in England and Wales, 1861–1921 part II', *Population Studies*, 43 (1989), 116 n. 42, 114.

[49] L. Secor Florence, *Birth Control on Trial* (1930), 95. Maher, 'Breastfeeding', 152.

[50] L. Manderson, 'Women and the State: Maternal and Child Welfare in Colonial Malaya, 1900–1940', in V. Fildes, Lara V. Marks, and H. Marland (eds.), *Women and Children First: International and Maternal Welfare, 1870–1945* (1992), 163.

[51] Carter, *Feminism*, 7, citing W. Cadogan, *Essay on Nursing* (1749).

also been correlated with the increasing number of hospital births. Again this cannot explain declines before this shift to institutions began.[52] For centuries writers have suggested that husbands prevailed upon their wives to cease feeding because they wanted to resume sexual relations, or they resented the attention given to the child.[53] The advent of birth control means this issue no longer appears directly relevant, and breastfeeding researchers now pass over it in silence. In the 1960s, William Masters and Virginia Johnson undertook research on sexual activity during pregnancy, post-partum, and while breastfeeding.[54] They found that both male and female attitudes to sexuality can reduce desire to breastfeed, and additionally husbands were often intolerant of periods of enforced continence. Data from other cultures suggests that in the absence of effective birth control continence is usually necessary while the infant is at the breast if another pregnancy is not to occur too rapidly.[55] Overall the impression is that, aside from paid employment or the husband's attitudes in some instances, these factors would not be powerful enough to prevent women from breastfeeding without an underlying factor reinforcing them.

In a review of contemporary research since the 1960s, *Women's Education, Autonomy, and Reproductive Behaviour: Experience from Developing Countries* (1995), demographer Shireen Jejeebhoy revealed an apparent contradiction in women's behaviour. She commented that the relationship between better-educated women and lower infant and child mortality is one of the most pervasive and consistently observed, to the point that it has been

[52] Ibid. 5, 90, making a similar point about milk substitutes, 222–3. Carter also found that the belief that feeding causes breasts to lose shape, and discomfort about breastfeeding in front of others, are also major problems for British women, 21–3. For an unselfconscious male response confirming this problem, see D. Coleman and J. Salt, *The British Population: Patterns, Trends, and Processes* (1992), 43. Maher, 'Breastfeeding', 155.

[53] Fildes, *Breasts*, 102–5. Hunt, *Parents*, 106–8. Couples now use birth control so researchers consider this irrelevant, although there are still questions about women's sexual desires and male partners' sexual pressure while mothers are feeding.

[54] This was based on observations of six women, and interviews with 111 women and 79 husbands of these women. This research was undertaken in the USA during the 1950s and 1960s, a low point for breastfeeding. W. H. Masters and V. E. Johnson, *Human Sexual Response* (1966), 139–68.

[55] J. C. and P. Caldwell, 'The Role of Marital Sexual Abstinence in Determining Fertility: A Study of the Yoruba in Nigeria', *Population Studies*, 31/2 (1977), 197.

described as 'boringly inverse'.[56] In spite of this evidence of women's effective concern for their children, and the fact that breastfeeding contributes considerably to the health of infants, women with even a small amount of education also breastfeed for shorter periods and do so less exclusively. This relationship holds in different societies regardless of varying per capita income, female literacy rates, or gender disparity in literacy. There is little evidence that education must rise to a given level, or threshold, before breastfeeding rates start to decline. Increased levels of women's education are also strongly associated with falls in levels of fertility but in this case there is a threshold. This is because even a small amount of education usually causes breastfeeding to decline, so fertility rises. Higher levels of education are required before other factors associated with education, such as use of contraception, increase, and fertility begins to fall.[57] Reduced fertility is interpreted as revealing a conscious desire to reduce 'family size'. As breastfeeding can reduce fertility, reduced breastfeeding appears inconsistent with this aim. However, both shorter breastfeeding episodes and lowered fertility reduce women's reproductive labour. Viewed from this perspective, there is no inconsistency in women's actions. It should be noted that stopping breastfeeding definitely reduces the individual woman's reproductive labour while for many women continued breastfeeding will not prevent fertility returning. If we hypothesize that women's primary need is to reduce their reproductive labour, and reduced fertility is only one means by which they can achieve this, then lower rates of breastfeeding are wholly consistent with other effects of education such as increased use of contraception. Women are likely to have greater control over their infant feeding choices than over the use of contraception. Women's response to breastfeeding suggests that where they had control they were not passive in relation to the biological processes that take place in their bodies. They did act to reduce their reproductive labour.

INFANT MORTALITY AND WOMEN'S MOTIVATION

Infant mortality provides some information about the health of mothers over long periods. *Exogenous* infant mortality includes deaths attributable to

[56] Jejeebhoy, *Women's Education*, 97.   [57] Ibid. 81–4.

causes separate from the mother's health such as infection, injury, or poor treatment. The *endogenous* infant mortality rate, on the other hand, includes deaths caused by the trauma of birth or lack of independent viability resulting from, for example, low birth weight or premature birth.[58] The general health and nutritional status of the mother are crucial in determining the endogenous infant mortality rate. In England this remained almost level for at least a century. The rate was twenty-eight deaths per 1,000 from 1838 to 1854, and from 1906 until the end of the 1930s it averaged twenty-four deaths per 1,000. Yet the mortality rate for children under 5 fell from the 1870s, and the exogenous infant mortality rate, that is deaths from external causes, fell over 60 per cent from 93.7 to 35.8 per 1,000.[59] The fact that there was almost no improvement in the endogenous rate suggests that the health of mothers did not improve over these decades.[60] A recent statistical study of fertility decline found that in the late nineteenth and early twentieth centuries infant mortality was strongly parity dependent. That is, the more babies a woman had the more likely the next baby was to die. This shows, yet again, that women's health worsened as they had more children, and so direct a link increases the likelihood that in a period of high fertility women's embodied experience would give rise to the desire to reduce births. The study did consider the issue of women's health and concluded that it was an important factor. Unfortunately, the authors continued to perceive women as passive: fertility decline occurred, they argue, because 'there was a

[58]   Wrigley, 'Explaining', 438.

[59]   Ibid. 448. See also R. I. Woods et al., 'The Causes of the Rapid Infant Mortality Decline in England and Wales, 1861–1921 Part II' *Population Studies* 43 (1989).

[60]   See summary and graph of infant, neonatal, post-neonatal, and maternal mortality. Loudon, *Death*, 1992. 488–91. However, the conduct of the birth by midwives or doctors also made a difference. Loudon gives an example of areas in England where, from 1910 to 1934, obstetrical practice raised maternal mortality to the extent that poverty actually resulted in lowered rates of death, as these mothers were too poor to afford doctors, 243–6. On the other hand, Fildes argues that efforts by local government to improve mothers' nutritional status from 1900 to 1920 had a direct and rapid effect on both neonatal and post-neonatal mortality, trends in which are very similar to endogenous mortality. So endogenous infant mortality could have been both rising as a result of poor obstetric practice, and falling as a result of improved maternal nutritional status from 1900 to the 1930s. Fildes, 'Infant feeding practices', 261. Peretz casts some doubt on this: E. Peretz, 'The Costs of Modern Motherhood to Low Income Families in Inter-War Britain', in Fildes et al., *Women.*

recognised premium laid by the men in the community on maintaining the health of wives and women in general'.[61]

This discussion could be taken to imply that because women suffer the physical costs of reproduction, they are inherently more inclined to want a smaller family size (something close to current Western norms, for example). It may suggest that they will accept the idea of fertility control more quickly than men, and thus, they will adopt birth control without question, or faster than men, when it becomes available. The experience of developing countries, as well as that of England, shows women's response is more complex. Nor do they necessarily have a choice. Where women do have influence there is a complex equation between the rewards and costs of childbearing. Children are regarded as a blessing, and they often bring women (and men) great joy and pleasure. The question that arises is not why women have four or five children but why they continue childbearing beyond that number. They may do so because, for example, bearing many sons is how they best ensure their own prestige or even survival in the event of widowhood.[62] Women also have varying degrees of strength and stamina so that for some women large families are very much less physically stressful than is the case for others. However, the level of British fertility around 1800 was briefly and unusually high. Gross reproduction rates rose from 2.35 in 1751 to 2.68 in 1801 and peaked in 1821 at 2.93. By 1851 the rate had gone down to 2.42.[63] In such a circumstance established societal structures do not exist to support high fertility rates. This fertility rise took place during a period of industrialization, change in female employment patterns, and social upheaval. Mothers often had little control over an unstable environment, and an unusually large family did not make them the subject of special social respect or praise. Thus there was no reward for their high burden of reproductive labour. In this context it seems reasonable to assume that sharp rises in family size will not be occurring by choice.

[61] E. Garret, S. Szreter, A. Reid, and K. Schurer, *Changing Family Size in England and Wales: Place, Class and Demography, 1891–1911* (2001), 434; parity, 200.

[62] For a discussion of these issues, see A. M. Taj and K. Oppenheim Mason, 'Differences between Women's and Men's Reproductive Goals in Developing Countries', *Population and Development Review*, 13 (1987).

[63] Wrigley et al., *English Population History*, table 8.7, 532.

The contribution that women's desire to diminish their reproductive labour has made to fertility decline is difficult to analyse and has therefore probably been underestimated as a causal factor. Unusually high fertility rates could well provide motivation for an innovative attempt at direct and individualized control of births. This argument that in the first half of the nineteenth century English women had a new motivation to limit pregnancies because the *average* number of births was becoming physically insupportable is very different from the notion that women had always felt a strong motivation to limit births directly. The diffusion of knowledge about birth control by radicals, such as Francis Place, who wished to improve the lot of working-class people began in the 1820s just after the gross fertility rates peaked. The next chapters challenge the argument that knowledge of birth control already existed, then consider the advances in knowledge and technology and the major shifts in sexual behaviour required to control fertility directly, instead of through marriage and other indirect means.

2

'Nature is a Blind Dirty Old Toad': The Withdrawal Method

During the 200 years from the 1770s to the 1970s there was a slow transformation of women's reproductive experience. These changes in fertility rates and in marriage can best be understood as the result of a long-drawn-out shift from communal, indirect control of fertility to effective, direct, female control of fertility. Indirect methods of fertility control include delaying marriage, male recourse to prostitution, breast-feeding, and sexual abstinence for reasons other than fertility control. Fertility change has largely remained the province of demographers, whose interest is in population change, so arguments about the causes of shifts in fertility rates have attracted little critical attention from historians of women. Until recently historical demographers gave only passing mentions to the connection between changing sexual mores and fertility rates. They claimed, correctly, that historians have shown that individual, direct control of fertility had always been possible. Historians have described a host of methods, with varying degrees of effectiveness, which could be used to prevent population growth. Infanticide and abstinence from sexual intercourse are very effective methods, withdrawal and traditional methods of abortion less so, while methods such as the use of herbal pessaries or the early skin condoms were probably highly ineffective. There were also a number of 'methods', including, for example, wearing amulets and getting up and walking around the room after intercourse, that had no effect on fertility at all.[1] The claim that

---

[1] N. E. Himes, *The Medical History of Contraception* (1936; 1970). A. M. Carr-Saunders, *The Population Problem* (1922). A. McLaren, *A History of Contraception from Antiquity to the Present Day*

fertility control has always been possible and therefore contraceptive methods are largely irrelevant ignores the nature of the change that has taken place in the past 200 years. The innovation is not the control of fertility within marriage, but the control of fertility without repression of sexuality or excessive physical costs (damage) to women.

Scholars interested in social relations argue that the societal context gives rise to techniques of birth control, not the other way around. Some demographers and historians argue that this is because birth control methods have always existed, but others believe that the methods are so obvious that they would have been constantly reinvented in each generation.[2] However, the desire for fertility control preceded effective means to achieve that end by thousands of years. One might as soon say the story of Icarus proves that flying was always possible. Preventing conception while having sexual intercourse is not easy or self-evident. Modern physiological knowledge of the body and rubber technology are necessary. In this chapter I argue that the English did not even begin to develop the knowledge and means of *effective* direct control of their fertility until the publication of information about contraception began in the 1820s. This changes the picture. If control of fertility were only possible through preventing sexual expression, then we would expect a direct and enduring link between sexual mores, and rises and falls in fertility. The development of contraceptive technology will thus be central to the changes in fertility rates and sexual mores in the last two centuries. And the issue of whether motivation to control fertility existed has to be considered in the context of existing contraceptive knowledge and usable methods. This chapter looks first at the evidence for the use of withdrawal before 1800 and then at the new advice given in the birth control tracts published in the 1820s and 1830s.

(1990). J. T. Noonan, *Contraception: A History of its Treatment by Catholic Theologians and Canonists* (1965). J. M. Riddle, *Contraception and Abortion from the Ancient World to the Renaissance* (1992).

[2] For a summary of these arguments, see J. and P. Schneider, *Festival of the Poor: Fertility Decline and the Ideology of Class in Sicily, 1860–1980* (1996), 150. R. Lesthaeghe, *The Decline of Belgian Fertility* (1977), 99, 136–7. A. MacKinnon, *Love and Freedom* (1997), 103. A. McLaren, *Sexuality and Social Order* (1983), 22. McLaren, *History*, 154–7. G. Santow, 'Coitus Interruptus and the Control of Natural Fertility', *Population Studies*, 49 (1995), 32–8.

WITHDRAWAL

The two most important direct methods of birth control before the
development of adequate rubber technology and understanding of
human reproductive biology were abortion and withdrawal. It is probable
that, in the 200 years from 1770 to 1970, withdrawal became the method
most frequently used to lower fertility. This method involves the removal
of the man's penis from the woman's vagina just before ejaculation takes
place. The historian of contraception Angus McLaren has said there was
little doubt that Europeans understood the use of withdrawal in the
eighteenth century. In a recent article, demographer Gina Santow
reinforces this, arguing that withdrawal is an effective method which
has been central to the management of fertility over centuries.[3] If withdrawal was such an obvious technique, so widely known and self-evident
that any man could work it out for himself, then why would intelligent
men in conditions of desperation not have used it? Francis Place (1771–
1854), who produced the first birth control handbills in 1820, provides an
example. His autobiography reveals that he was anxious to learn about
and undertake anything that might enable him to improve his position in
the world. The meticulous bookkeeping he described with great pride
reveals that he was also conscientious and methodical. Although Place
believed that the growing sexual prudery of the early nineteenth century
was desirable, he regretted the passing of more relaxed sexual mores, and
before his early marriage, he led a sexually active life. Had withdrawal been
common knowledge, Place would have known of the method, and he
would have had the self-control and sexual awareness to use it successfully. His wife, whom he greatly loved, had fifteen children between 1792
and 1817, of whom five died in infancy.[4] Yet even during and after the
couple had endured a terrible period of poverty early in their marriage he
did not try to control his fertility, about which he was fatalistic. In his
autobiography he described his attitude to fertility in the early years of his
marriage: 'I saw the certainty that I should have a large family, and that

---

[3] McLaren, *History*, 154–7. Santow, 'Coitus', 32–8.

[4] 'I loved her as well at the close of Thirty Six years after our marriage... When young
she was a most beautiful figure, my delight and consolation under all kinds of difficulties
and privations' F. Place, *The Autobiography of F. Place (1771–1854)*, ed. M. Thale (1972), 255.

nothing but wretchedness awaited us, if I did not contrive to get into business.'[5] Other examples of men who were responsible and loved their wives and children but did not restrict their fertility are not hard to find.[6]

It is thought that Place had no knowledge of contraception until 1818, which was one year after the last of his children was born in 1817. This may be a coincidence, as his wife was then 43 years old.[7] It would be ludicrous to suggest that Place was a passive, uncontrolled, or unthinking man. If he did not believe controlling his family size was possible, then for the vast majority of the English population contraception did not exist. Even if methods are mentioned in occasional records, or they appear so easy to use that they could just be reinvented, in practice they were not available in the early nineteenth century.

What of Place's wife Elizabeth, who may have had even greater motivation to control births: why did she not use abortion? Abortion has played (and continues to play) a vital role in women's control of their fertility. In sources throughout history, and from other cultures, abortion is mentioned with much greater frequency than contraception.[8] Spontaneous miscarriages must have provided a regular reminder that pregnancies could be interrupted before they reached full term, making abortion self-evident in a fashion that contraception, a preventive technique, was not. Place undertook research into abortion, observing women who lived with journeymen tailors and plumbers of his acquaintance, and who then had children after marriage either with these men or with other men. They acknowledged to him that they had abortions. The occupations given, and Place's comments, suggest that abortion was not respectable.[9] Place was not a conventional or a religious man and a possible reason is that the risk of damage to the woman was so high that prudent couples avoided abortion if possible. A similar argument may apply to the use of herbal pessaries or abortifacients by women. A recent analysis of

---

[5] Ibid. 137.

[6] e.g. J. Bowd, 'The Life of a Farm Worker', unpublished MS, (1889), 300. Cited in D. Vincent, 'Love and Death and the Nineteenth-Century Working-Class', *Social History*, 5/2 (1980), 228.

[7] Dudley Miles, F. Place 1771–1854: The Life of a Remarkable Radical (1988), 140–3.

[8] Noonan, *Contraception*. R. F. Spencer, 'Primitive Obstetrics', *Ciba Symposia*, 11 (1949), 1187–8.

[9] Draft letter to R. Carlile. Place Collection, British Library, Set 68.

traditional recipes using herbs and so forth from classical times to the nineteenth century confirms that some of the ingredients did possess abortifacient or contraceptive properties.[10] It is probable that women preferred to take abortifacients as soon as they had any doubt as to the arrival of their menstrual period.[11] Modern medical understanding has led researchers to claim that many women taking abortifacients would not have been pregnant and so the drugs would have been credited with ending pregnancies that never existed. But recent research based on hospital records from the 1830s has confirmed the impression given in other sources that women possessed a close knowledge of their menstrual cycles, and it is likely that many women were aware they had conceived by the date of the expected period.[12] Over 50 per cent of early miscarriages are still acknowledged to be due to unknown causes even today and the possibility that women were able to end a pregnancy using abortifacients cannot be rejected. However, anthropological research does not suggest a wealth of effective methods were present in pre-modern cultures, and, in any event, by the late nineteenth century the knowledge required to make effective and safe potions from plants was lost, if it had ever existed.[13]

What then is the historical evidence for people's use of withdrawal in early modern England? The history of sexuality and women is producing increasingly detailed accounts of gender and sexual cultures, making it obvious that approaches to contraception would have varied considerably in different cultural contexts and therefore only the scanty English sources are relevant. G. R. Quaife found a small number of reports by seventeenth-century peasant women who reported that their husbands used withdrawal. These women complained of lack of sexual satisfaction. One married woman said of her husband that 'what seed should be sown in the right ground he spent about the outward part of her body'. A young

[10] Riddle, *Contraception*.

[11] This has also been true in other cultures. See L. F. Newman (ed.), *Women's Medicine: A Cross-Cultural Study of Indigenous Fertility Regulation* (1985).

[12] M. Levine-Clark, 'Testing the Reproductive Hypothesis: Or What Made Working-Class Women Sick in Early Victorian London', *Women's History Review*, 11/2 (2001), 184–5, 190.

[13] No evidence is presented of use of effective, safe potions, and women's search for new methods reinforces this absence. See P. Knight, 'Women and abortion in Victorian and Edwardian England', *History Workshop* (1977). A. McLaren, 'Women's Work and Regulation of Family Size: The Question of Abortion in the Nineteenth Century', *History Workshop*, 4 (1977).

woman who, according to Quaife, had been 'seduced' in the rye 'obviously did not appreciate her lover's precaution'. She said that 'he had fouled her clothes' and she would have 'to make them clean'.[14] Examples such as these, which unambiguously refer to withdrawal, are few. There are other more questionable examples. One man was reported to have said in 1617 that he had 'to do with wenches when he list and would choose whether he beget them with child or not'.[15] In a deposition from an adultery trial a maid was reported to have said she saw 'Mr Germain's y[ard] come from the Duchess, reeking, slimy and limber, casting his sperm about the room'.[16] It is not certain these references actually do refer to withdrawal. Nonetheless, taken together the sources do make the case that a few people did discover withdrawal and use it successfully before the nineteenth century.

People did not openly discuss or write about stigmatized physical sexual practices and the relative absence of sources might be because contraception could not be openly discussed, rather than because it was not used. Yet this or any other birth control method was definitely not widely available when people wanted to prevent pregnancy. Adulterous lovers, for example, would surely have prevented pregnancy had it been possible or practical. Aristocrats appear to have been no more knowledgeable than the government servant Samuel Pepys (1633–1703). His diary reveals that he made a great effort to pick married women as his mistresses with the intention that any pregnancy would be placed at the husband's door. He panicked on one occasion when his mistress appeared to have conceived while her husband was absent from home.[17] Other diaries of men with extensive sexual experience do not reveal use of contraception. The farm servant John Cannon (1684–1743) got into considerable difficulty as a

[14] G. R. Quaife, *Wanton Wenches and Wayward Wives* (1979), 133, 171–2.

[15] Ibid. 172. See also A. McLaren, *Reproductive Rituals: The Perception of Fertility in England from the Sixteenth Century to the Nineteenth Century* (1984), 77 n. 26, 81. McLaren, *History*, 154–7.

[16] L. Stone, *Road to Divorce: England 1530–1987* (1990; 1995), n. 69, 251. Stone believed an uneducated servant girl must have been prompted to use such vivid and obscene language. If he was correct (as well as patronizing) then the evident exaggeration, 'about the room', which suggests withdrawal, may not have come from the eyewitness anyway.

[17] Stone, *Road to Divorce*, 242, 290, 312. L. Leneman, *Alienated Affections: The Scottish Experience of Divorce and Separation, 1684–1830* (1998), 125, 167, 177. Pepys in Stone, *Family*, 560, 552–61.

result of getting a servant pregnant.[18] James Boswell (1740–95) suffered from the delusion that the expensive condoms of the day would enable him to avoid further bouts of gonorrhoea. Yet he did not use withdrawal (or condoms) even when his wife, whom he desired, refused him his 'conjugal privilege' due to her fear of further pregnancies.[19]

There appear to be almost no written sources telling men how to use withdrawal as a method of birth control and even sources condemning the practice are rare. The brief biblical verses describing Onan spilling his seed on the ground lest he should give seed to his brother do not provide a how-to guide.[20] The clergy, who were the group best versed in biblical knowledge, were also most likely to be aware of the prohibitions against birth control. The generosity of the vicar of Weaverham in Cheshire was far from usual. He was denounced in 1590 as 'an instructor of young folks how to commit the sin of adultery or fornication and not beget or bring forth children'.[21] It is also easy to overestimate clerical knowledge. The historian of contraception and Catholic theology, John Noonan, found contraception was mentioned less often than abortion, although there was little attention paid to either in Catholic texts from the time of the Romans.[22] Upper-class men travelled in Europe and might have learnt of the method, but such men were likely to patronize prostitutes or practise adultery, making birth control unnecessary, and, in any event, they had little incentive to share information with plebeians.[23] In total, the evidence

---

[18] T. Hitchcock, 'Sociability and Misogyny in the Life of John Cannon, 1684–1743', in T. Hitchcock and M. Cohen (eds.), *English Masculinities, 1660–1800* (1999). T. Hitchcock, *English Sexualities: 1700–1800* (1997), 32–8.

[19] Condoms had been sold in London since the early 18th century but were expensive, unreliable, and unpleasant to use. J. Boswell, *Boswell's London Journal, 1762–1763*, ed. F. A. Pottle (1950), 227, 231, 255, 262. P. Fryer, *The Birth Controllers* (1965), 30–3. Himes, *Medical History*, 190, 197–201. Stone, *Family*, 554, 589–90.

[20] Genesis 38: 7–10. In the 1820s and 1830s, R. Carlile and C. Knowlton both use the term onanism to refer to masturbation, not withdrawal, though McLaren cites an example of it being used to refer to withdrawal. M. L. Bush (ed.), *What is Love? Richard Carlile's Philosophy of Sex* (1998), 98. C. Knowlton, 'Fruits of Philosophy . . .' (1832), repr. in S. Chandrasekhar (ed.), *'A Dirty, Filthy Book': The Writings of Charles Knowlton and Annie Besant on Reproductive Physiology and Birth Control and an Account of the Bradlaugh–Besant Trial* (1981), 100. McLaren, *History*, 154–6.

[21] Stone, *Family*, 422.

[22] Noonan, *Contraception*, 16–25, 164. He also comments on the infrequent mention of withdrawal in the penitentials, 161; 94, 155.

[23] Boswell does not appear to have learned from his travels. Stone, *Family*, 581, 596–7.

is sufficient to prove that withdrawal was used, but it also reveals that the knowledge was not commonplace. The method must have been invented and reinvented only occasionally by individuals and the information passed on orally, if at all.

Under what circumstances, and when, is it likely that people reinvented withdrawal? How did people 'invent' or improve their knowledge of other bodily skills based upon observation and practice? Anthropological evidence can provide insight into this question. In some non-Western societies such skills are raised to a high degree while in other societies they are rudimentary. Robert F. Spencer summarized data on obstetrical practice in non-Western societies with a low degree of material complexity. He provides some examples of efforts to manipulate the child in the womb externally in order to facilitate birth. These covered the range from 'what by our standards is a most brutal extreme', to timid and inexpert attempts, and societies where the midwives possess 'considerable practical skill'.[24] Thus this bodily skill was acquired and transmitted to others in some cultural settings, but not others, as was the case with withdrawal in European cultures of the eighteenth and nineteenth centuries. Contraception is preventive medicine, which means individuals will receive no positive gain, only an absence of undesired consequences, in return for their effort. Early users of withdrawal in England had to decide on the basis of their own observations whether their attempts were effective at preventing conception. The amount of effort the method involved at the time of use, including loss of sexual pleasure or stress, would go into the equation. In the early 1950s, anthropologist Charles Erasmus undertook research in Quito, a village in Ecuador, where health workers were attempting to introduce new practices. He found that there was 'no resistance to modern medical practices in so far as those practices may be judged . . . on an empirical basis'.[25] The local people had quickly accepted that the doctor was best qualified to treat venereal disease or

---

[24] Spencer, 'Primitive Obstetrics', 1182–4. Spencer defined primitive as referring to material technology and insisted he did not intend a value judgement. These anthropologists do take a positivist approach and are interested in the use of empirical evidence, but they reject the notion that this is solely the province of Western science.

[25] C. J. Erasmus, 'Changing Folk Beliefs and the Relativity of Empirical Knowledge', *Southwestern Journal of Anthropology*, 8 (1952), 419.

appendicitis, because they could see the results. They did not accept that teething children got intestinal infections and diarrhoea from sucking objects that had been on a dirty floor. Intestinal infection in teething children was so frequent that parents believed teething itself was the cause. Following the advice would also have involved much work supervising the infants.[26] In this instance preventive advice was resisted because it operated at a theoretical level which did not lend itself to confirmation by empirical observation. The people of Quito were fully capable of critical thinking but they were assessing the new medical advice in the light of their own observations. In the 1990s, medical ethnographers are still arguing that traditional systems of ethnomedicine are not consensual and complacent. Experimentation is used and they involve considerable critical thinking.[27] This suggests that if withdrawal was not used it was because the invention of the method was not self-evident, as scholars have tended to assume.

It is not usually possible to observe directly the sexual practice of other people, so, as a number of demographic historians have observed, discussion, questioning, casual gossip, and other forms of communication would have played an important role in spreading information about birth control.[28] It is believed that withdrawal was the major method used to lower French fertility rates, which fell well before those of the British.[29] French and English sexual cultures in the eighteenth and nineteenth centuries differed in the attitude to open discussion of sexuality. French pornography, novels, and medical texts reveal a sexual culture that encouraged more interest in technique and in which people discussed sexuality more openly and in greater physical detail.[30] In a culture where

[26] Ibid. 416, 423. See also W. S. Laughlin, 'Primitive Theory of Medicine', in I. Galdston (ed.), *Man's Image in Medicine and Anthropology* (1963), 121.

[27] Introd. in M. Nichter (ed.), *Anthropological Approaches to the Study of Ethnomedicine* (1992), p. xii.

[28] D. Gittins, *Fair Sex, Family Size and Structure, 1900–39* (1982), 88–92. Schneider and Schneider, *Festival*, 151, citing S. Cotts Watkins, *From Provinces into Nations: Demographic Integration in Western Europe, 1870–1960* (1991) and Santow, 'Coitus.' S. Szreter, *Fertility, Class and Gender in Britain, 1860–1940* (1996), 555–6.

[29] McLaren, *Sexuality*, 26, 126. Szreter, *Fertility*, 544.

[30] P. Cryle, *Geometry in the Boudoir: Configurations of French Erotic Narrative* (1994). B. Leckie, *Culture and Adultery: The Novel, the Newspaper, and the Law, 1857–1914* (1999), 20–8, 244–5. M. Mason, *The Making of Victorian Sexuality* (1995), 182. McLaren, *Sexuality*, 120–1, 166. R. D. Owen, *Moral Physiology* (1834; 1842), 23–4. P. Wagner, *Eros Revived: Erotica of the Enlightenment in England and America* (1988; 1990).

this is the case there will be more opportunity for men and women to share observations and increase the probable accuracy of their conclusions. The English unwillingness to discuss sexuality, aside from bawdy humour lacking in explicitness, would probably have retarded the invention and spread of knowledge about withdrawal.

Gina Santow has claimed that withdrawal was a highly effective method, which, if correct, would have increased the likelihood that men who experimented with withdrawal would continue to use the method. As proof she cites an Australian study undertaken in the 1980s that found only around 14 per cent of first-time users (the least efficient group) of withdrawal could be expected to conceive accidentally during the first year of use.[31] Is this research finding from the 1980s relevant to the use of withdrawal in the eighteenth and nineteenth centuries? Santow assumes that the method involves only the use of a transhistorical body, and a penis and vagina, the properties of which are obvious and unchanging. The varied social contexts and the possibility of varying physical sexual practices have been disregarded. This estimate of method effectiveness is near the top of the range of results found in the second half of the twentieth century. In 1975, Margaret Bone compared levels of method failure in a number of studies showing considerable variation in results from different study populations. At that time, she commented that coitus interruptus was 'an ancient technique and one of the least effective now in use'.[32] A study by G. I. Swyer et al. reviewed research undertaken prior to the mid-1960s and including studies in developing countries. They found the failure rate of withdrawal varied from 38 to 10 per cent. In 1971, an American study found an extended-use-effectiveness failure rate of 23 per cent.[33] The rates of

[31] Santow, 'Coitus'. Citing G. Santow and M. Bracher, 'Premature Discontinuation of Contraception in Australia', *Family Planning Perspectives*, 24 (1992), 60, and J. Trussell and K. Kost, 'Contraceptive Failure in the United States: A Critical Review of the Literature', *Studies in Family Planning*, 18 (1987), 246. In an earlier article, Santow discussed a wider range of estimates of method effectiveness for withdrawal. G. Santow, 'Coitus Interruptus in the Twentieth Century', *Population and Development Review*, 19/4 (1993).

[32] M. Bone, *Measures of Contraceptive Effectiveness and their Uses* (1975), 1.

[33] G. I. Swyer, W. D. M. Paton, N. W. Pirie, N. R. Morris, and R. G. Edwards, 'The Scientific Basis of Contraception', supplement 'Towards a Population Policy for the United Kingdom', *Population Studies* (1970), 37. N. B. Ryder and C. F. Westoff, *Reproduction in the United States, 1965* (1971), 335.

success at preventing pregnancy evidently vary greatly. Why would this be so?

Measuring the effectiveness of methods of preventing pregnancy has proved to be very complex. There are now three measures of contraceptive effectiveness. Theoretical effectiveness refers to use without human error, in laboratory conditions or an equivalent. Use effectiveness measures the prevention of pregnancy in actual use, allowing for carelessness on the user's part, as well as method failures. Extended use effectiveness measures effectiveness of a method over a given period of time, so that if users discontinue a method frequently, because it is expensive, or not 'well tolerated', which means unpleasant to use, this is taken into account.[34] Even with these refinements the method failure rates still do not relate directly to men and women's actual experience. This is because coital frequency alters the risk of failure. For example, if one group of women has sexual intercourse half as often as another group of women, the method failure rate will be the same for each act of intercourse, but the cumulative method failure rate in the first group will be half that of the second group. Although research has demonstrated that different populations do have different rates of coital frequency, studies of effectiveness have not included this variable.[35] A recent text commented that '[o]nly a few studies provide estimates of effectiveness because of the difficulties encountered in measuring it'.[36]

Clinicians in the mid-twentieth century were surprised when birth control researchers reported high effectiveness rates for withdrawal as their experience had suggested that withdrawal was a most unreliable method.[37] It was assumed that clinical experience was not an accurate guide but it is probable that method effectiveness had improved. The increased knowledge that couples bring to the use of contraception must be considered. For example, it was not widely understood that semen

[34] Bone, *Measures*.

[35] J. R. Udry, 'Coitus as Demographic Behaviour', in R. Gray, H. Leridon, and A. Spira (eds.), *Biomedical and Demographic Determinants of Reproduction* (1993), 86–7.

[36] J. Bongaarts and R. G. Potter, *Fertility, Biology, and Behaviour: An Analysis of the Proximate Determinants* (1983), 66.

[37] C. Tietze, 'The Use-Effectiveness of Contraceptive Methods', in C. V. Kiser (ed.), *Research in Family Planning* (1962), 368.

could live for relatively long periods after ejaculation. Twentieth-century birth control and sex manual authors went to some effort to explain this to their readers. T. H. van de Velde, the author of around eighty papers on gynaecological and obstetric matters, described the problem this lack of understanding created in 1931:

A man ... performs the sexual act [with his wife while wearing a condom]. All is well—but after ejaculation, he again inserts his member into the vagina for a few moments, after removing the condom, though without having a second emission. A very natural caress. But, if he has omitted to clean his member thoroughly from traces of semen, and to urinate vigorously, thus clearing the urethra as well, both he and the woman he loves and desires to protect, may have a terrible surprise. Another man or a woman—may touch the vulva with fingers on which semen has hardly dried[,] with a sponge containing drops of semen, or with linen which has been moistened with semen.[38]

This problem would be more extreme where couples were relying on withdrawal alone. The depth of confusion still existing even in the late 1920s can be gauged by the fact that van de Velde believed 'anatomical contraception', or partial withdrawal, lowered the chance of pregnancy. This consisted of coital positions in which the male ejaculated within the vagina, but conception was supposedly minimized by the positioning of the penis at an angle away from the cervical os (the opening of the canal to the uterus). Marie Stopes's *Contraception* (1923) contains similar material.[39] This cannot be considered a method of birth control at all, yet two intelligent people with scientific training, one of whom was a gynaecologist, repeated it in print. Seriously considering such accounts reveals that the assumption that the body has obvious properties enabling the control of fertility and that these will be revealed to any conscientious observer is false. Housing standards, including availability of running water, heating, and privacy, also make a considerable difference to the use of withdrawal. This would help explain why Swyer et al. found much higher method failure rates in non-Western countries, as housing and sanitation standards are likely to have been considerably lower than was the case in

[38] Th. H. van de Velde, *Fertility and Sterility in Marriage: Their Voluntary Promotion and Limitation* (1931), 288–9.

[39] Ibid. 304–14, 353; See also Th. H. van de Velde *Ideal Marriage: Its Physiology and Technique* (1928; reset 1943), 186. M. Stopes, *Contraception: Theory, History and Practice* (1923; 1925), 61–3.

Australia or America, sources of results showing high method effectiveness. The much greater effectiveness of withdrawal in the research cited by Santow probably relates to greater knowledge of conception combined with routine standards of hygiene. Couples in wealthy, hygiene-obsessed, modern Australia might well use a clean towel to wipe away the sperm every time they had intercourse. They would probably take a bath or shower at least once a day, and would know that they must never have intercourse a second time without washing in between. These results cannot be read back into Britain in the 1950s, let alone the 1800s and before.

Another factor could have misled eighteenth-century couples who were dependent on their own observations. In the study Gigi Santow cites, she and M. Bracher found that effectiveness increased strongly with age. The size of the improvement suggests that it was due more to young men's growing control of their sexual response than to women's falling fertility. In the first year of use 27 per cent of teenagers conceived, but only 14.5 per cent of women aged 20–4 years, and only just over 2 per cent of women aged 25 and older.[40] As the discussion below shows, the early birth control tracts reveal that, to the authors' chagrin, men did need practice to achieve good results.[41] When couples felt unable to discuss use of the method with others who were more experienced a high initial failure rate might have led them to discontinue the method. This would have been exacerbated by the fact that the most fertile couples for whom the method was most likely to fail will start trying to control their births first. This is because such couples will be the first to reach a point at which they want to prevent a further pregnancy. In such circumstances, empirical observation and critical thinking would lead the highly fertile couple to conclude the method was not effective. The capacity for invention attributed to early users must be considered in light of the uncertain return for their efforts.

To summarize, there have always been some individuals who used withdrawal. But 'inventing' the method was not straightforward, especially given the absence of discussion about physical sexual practice in

---

[40] Santow and Bracher, 'Premature Discontinuation', 772.
[41] For practice, also see Schneider and Schneider, *Festival*, 225–6, 260.

England and women's desire to have a share of sexual pleasure. Effectiveness in use was lowered by limited understanding of conception, and poor housing and hygiene. The majority of couples probably did not have access to this or any other effective, direct method of birth control in the eighteenth and early nineteenth centuries.

THE EMERGENCE OF BIRTH CONTROL

In the 1820s, the first publications intended specifically to inform men and women about birth control appeared. The men who wrote these first works were major figures in the history of British working-class radicalism. Francis Place was a force in the struggle for working-class political representation. He persuaded Richard Carlile (1790–1843), who spent years in jail in the cause of press freedom, to support birth control. Carlile then went on to write and publish 'What is Love?' in his journal the *Republican* in 1825, and followed this in 1826 with a book, *Every Woman's Book: or, What is Love?*, which was an extended version of the essay.[42] Robert Dale Owen (1801–99) was the son of Robert Owen, a self-made factory owner who started co-operation as an anti-capitalist social movement with the hope of setting in place a new social system.[43] Dale Owen wrote *Moral Physiology* as a genteel alternative to Carlile's brash avowal of female sexual freedom. Some difficulties faced by isolated individuals in inventing and reinventing withdrawal have been suggested above. In contrast there is a clear path leading from Place's intellectual and personal awareness of population growth, to his conception of birth control, and from there to his search for actual methods. His experience of a large family, which has already been described, was one shared by many people in this period. Fertility had risen throughout the eighteenth century, and from around 1750 the marriage habits of the common people and the upper and middle classes had begun to reverse. The age at marriage of the latter groups began to rise, while the average age at which plebeians married fell, and by

---

[42] 'What is Love?', *Republican*, 11 (6 May 1825), 545–69. *Every Woman's Book: or, What is Love?* (4th edn. 1826). Both are reprinted in Bush (ed.), *What is Love?* Place's key letter to Carlile of 17 Nov. 1822 is reprinted in full in M. Stopes, *Contraception*, 305–13.

[43] The contribution of these men to birth control is described in Fryer, *Birth Controllers*.

the1800s they were marrying at much younger ages than the propertied classes. As Garret et al. point out, the Revd Thomas Robert Malthus was undoubtedly influenced by this shift in marriage habits, as well as by the growth of population, when he wrote the *Essay on the Principle of Population*, first published in 1798.[44] In this he argued that population growth would outstrip food production, and could be controlled only by the *positive* checks of wars, famines, disease, and misery. The radical utopian philosopher William Godwin, who had been Mary Wollstonecraft's husband, pressed upon him the idea of a *preventive* check. Malthus accepted this, but only in the form of moral restraint, or delay of marriage. Vice was rejected by him, including promiscuous intercourse, adultery, and 'improper arts to conceal the consequences of irregular connections'.[45]

Malthus' ideas stimulated immense debate throughout British society, including amongst men, such as Place, interested in political economy and in the condition of working people. These conditions were the opposite of those faced by the isolated individual inventing withdrawal for personal use in previous centuries. In 1822, Place published *Illustrations and Proofs of the Principle of Population*, in which he rejected moral restraint and put the theoretical social and economic case for the preventive or physical checks, that is, contraception. Norman Himes commented that 'One might read the *Essay* through without so much as surmising that women had anything to do with reproduction or population.'[46] Even so, Place wrote that these references to 'physical checks' were taken only 'with the concurrence of friends who were themselves afraid to encounter the certain obloquy of such allusions'.[47] The information Place gave

---

[44] E. Garret, S. Szreter, A. Reid, and K. Schurer, *Changing Family Size in England and Wales: Place, Class and Demography, 1891–1911* (2001), 425, 429. See also J. Weeks, *Sex, Politics and Society: The Regulation of Sexuality since 1800* (1981; 1989), 29.

[45] T. R. Malthus. *An Essay on the Principle of Population* (1872; 1914), i. 14.

[46] N. E. Himes, introd. to F. Place, *Illustrations and Proofs of the Principle of Population*, ed. N. E. Himes (1930), 285.

[47] Quoted in Miles, *Place*, 145. F. Place to McLaren, 25 Nov. 1830, Place Collection, Set 62, 165. These friends included Place's middle-class associates, who were no better than he was at restricting their families. Himes commented, 'Small wonder [Place] should write to G. Ensor of "moral restraint, which has served so well in the instances of you & I—and [J.] Mill and [Edward] Wakefield—mustering among us no less I believe than 36 children ... rare fellows we to teach moral restraint."' Place, *Illustrations*, ed. Himes, 10.

probably originated in France. Place's biographer, Dudley Miles, argues that he did not know of any practical birth control methods until Robert Owen returned from visiting France in 1818 with several pieces of 'spunge' and knowledge of withdrawal.[48] Robert Owen later denied such an event had taken place but, even if this were true, the French Revolution and then the Napoleonic Wars increased the movement of people across the channel. It is likely that many others returned to England from France with knowledge of birth control in these decades. A musical instrument maker named Ben Aimé, whose name suggests another French connection, gave Place the draft of a handbill similar to the final version.[49] Mary Wollstonecraft, who been in France during the revolutionary period, even mentioned the concept, albeit disparagingly, in *A Vindication of the Rights of Women*, published in 1792.[50] Birth rates in France had only begun to fall in the late eighteenth century, and thus it would appear that once the French had begun to use birth control widely, there was fairly rapid transmission of this knowledge across the channel.

These birth control tracts were the first attempts at recognizably modern research and critical analysis of methods of contraception.[51] Research into contraception is not simply medical research. Much of this book is devoted to describing the extent to which birth control required modification of the sexual behaviour of healthy individuals, and of gender roles in physical sexual activity. Doctors rejected involvement in these areas of behaviour because they were not within the province of medical knowledge. Yet contraceptive research also required knowledge of the interior workings of the body that was being developed within medicine. This combination of behavioural change and medical knowledge was central to the development of methods of contraception

---

[48] Miles, *Place*, 140–3.

[49] Place Collection, Set 68. No more is known about Aimé than his occupation and address. Bush (ed.), *What is Love?* 31. Fryer found no evidence that Place or Bentham obtained information from prostitutes, another possible source. Fryer, *Birth Controllers*, 77.

[50] 'Surely nature never intended that women, by satisfying an appetite should frustrate the very purpose for which it was planned.' M. Wollstonecraft, *A Vindication of the Rights of Women* (1792), 152. Cited in McLaren, *History*, 169.

[51] Himes, *Medical History*, 234–5.

in England.[52] Birth control methods first required new ideas about proper sexual behaviour and only then could new technologies, or new knowledge, be put to use. The modification of behaviour did not happen by accident or without effort; instead it was the result of countless small, conscious acts on the part of individuals. These acts can be seen dimly, submerged within the smooth descriptions in the birth control texts. There are four different versions of Place's handbills on birth control, which were distributed widely in 1823. Withdrawal was only included in the first one: 'The other method to be resorted to . . . is for the husband to withdraw, previous to emission, so that none of the semen may enter the vagina of his wife.' Place then omits withdrawal from the following three versions.[53] Carlile proffers a reason why withdrawal might be rejected: 'Complete withdrawing before emission is certainly effectual in all cases; but not so easily observed by all persons.' There are echoes here of conversations describing failure, perhaps joking and self-deprecating, perhaps fearful of a dreaded pregnancy.

Contraceptive use effectiveness measurements do not include skill on the part of the user as a factor, yet that was obviously called for in the use of withdrawal. Carlile introduced the distracting concept of 'partial withdrawal': 'Another [method] is, not to inseminate the female by observing a partial or complete withdrawing at the moment of seminal emission'. Carlile did add that the 'latter is the more certain means', yet he still felt that '[p]artial withdrawal is effectual on some women'.[54] This must have offered a tempting alternative to men who were struggling to gain adequate control over their responses. Dale Owen is far more straightforward. He claims withdrawal is effective in all cases, the loss of

---

[52] This may not have been the case in other societies, where embodied sexual and reproductive knowledge was more easily accumulated and shared. The tradition of well-trained midwives enabling women to gather and pass on reliable information may help explain why the use of female methods of contraception, as well as abortion, was much higher in Germany and France than in England by the end of the 19th century. I. Loudon, *Death in Childbirth* (1992), 179. McLaren, *Sexuality*, 166. A. McLaren, 'Abortion in France: Women and the Regulation of Family Size', *French Historical Studies*, 10 (1978). J. Woycke, *Birth Control in Germany, 1871–1933* (1988).

[53] Place Collection, Set 61, pt. II, 42–3. The handbills are reprinted in Himes, *Medical History*, 214–7.

[54] Bush (ed.), *What is Love?*, 100–1.

enjoyment is trifling, and few men have so little control that they cannot practise it. In the appendix to the fifth edition he added some accounts given to him by successful users. But he was producing propaganda, glossing over the difficulties that led Place to recommend only the sponge, and Carlile to include partial withdrawal. By the 1850s, Dale Owen was forced into admitting that:

I can readily imagine men who in part from temperament, but much more from the continued habit of unrestrained self-indulgence, may have so little command over their passion as to find difficulty in practicing [withdrawal] and some it may be who will declare it impossible ... I am at least convinced the number is exceedingly small; not a fiftieth part of those who at first imagine such to be the case.[55]

These texts disclose real and substantial difficulties. And these authors were the enthusiasts, the men who were willing to put their reputations on the line to promote a highly stigmatized practice. This must have been the most optimistic and positive account of withdrawal that it was possible for honest and, with the exception of Carlile, pragmatic men to produce.

These early authors believed that women should control the method used. Owen, in particular, explained that in this way women could protect themselves from male selfishness and lack of consideration. Place preferred the use of a sponge inserted into the vagina, as this method 'seems most likely to succeed in this country as it depends upon the female'. Users appear to have reported back failures to him because in the first handbill he recommends 'a piece of sponge about an inch square', but by the last handbill this has grown; the sponge must be 'large enough, that is; about as large as a green walnut or a small apple, [then] it will prevent conception ... without diminishing the pleasures of married life'.[56] Carlile explains that users have had difficulties: 'The piece of sponge has been questioned as to its efficacy in some cases; in others, it has been found certain; and the inference is that variance in habit or construction of parts may vary its effects.'[57] Dale Owen does not recommend the sponge, as he

<hr />

[33] R. D. Owen, *Moral Physiology* (10th edn. 1858), 65.
[56] Place Collection, Set 61, pt. II, 42–3.
[57] Bush (ed.), *What is Love?* 100.

knows three men for whom it failed, nor the 'baudruche', or condom of the day, which was 'in every way inconvenient'.[58]

The first doctor to enter the field was an American, Charles Knowlton (1800–50), who published his book in 1832. An English edition appeared in 1834. This introduced a new method, douching or syringing with chemical spermicides.[59] Historian Michael Mason has recently argued that this practice rapidly became usual. He argues that 'to judge from the evidence of *My Secret Life* it was anyway *common* for women to wash out their vaginas after intercourse, in the hope of preventing conception' (italics added).[60] This erotic memoir covers the mid-Victorian period. The anonymous author, Walter, knew about sponges and condoms, methods that had been used by some prostitutes since the eighteenth century, but his descriptions of women usually refer only to washing their external genitalia, such as 'washing her quim', or 'she took my basin, and washed herself'.[61] Walter also makes frequent references to cleaning his own genitals and it was important to him that women's genitals be clean. He probably recorded this for that reason. There are numerous references to clean linen, and some to being careful so that linen may remain clean. Laundry had to be paid for and the women may have been anxious to prevent semen stains, or they may, like modern prostitutes, have used getting up to wash as a way of telling the client that his time was up.[62] However, in one episode, 'Kitty', a young girl, examines sperm in her fellow servant Bet's basin. Bet seems to have scooped the semen out of her vagina with her fingers (after intercourse with a lover) and there are other occasions when this seems to be what is described.[63] This is an interesting, albeit ineffective, new addition to the range of pre-modern contraceptive

[58] Owen, *Moral Physiology* (1834; 1842), 36, 39. Dale Owen had been born in Glasgow, but the experiences he described must have been largely American, as his father had soon immigrated with him to that country.

[59] Knowlton, 'Fruits', 136–9.

[60] Mason, *Sexuality*, 58, repeated 60, and in his second volume M. Mason, *The Making of Victorian Sexual Attitudes* (1994), 184.

[61] Walter, *My Secret Life* (1880; 1995), 'French Letters', iii. 19; 'She Washed' i, ch. 14, 197.

[62] e.g. S. Boyle, *Working Girls and their Men* (1994), 5. J. O'Connell Davidson, 'Prostitution and the Contours of Control', in J. Weeks and J. Holland (eds.), *Sexual Cultures, Communities, Values and Intimacy* (1996), 185.

[63] Walter, *My Secret Life*, iv. 92, 95–6.

The Withdrawal Method 59

procedures. But there is no suggestion in *My Secret Life* that women are using modern appliances such as syringes or douching, which would flush out the vagina with fluid. In one episode Walter is told about a man who is insisting on using withdrawal, which is new to Walter. This is unsurprising, as he takes no responsibility for fertility, merely recording women's anxieties about pregnancy from time to time.[64] *My Secret Life* confirms the supposition that some women and men were aware of and wanted to control their fertility but that the sales of the early texts were not sufficient to spread knowledge of new methods widely.

Janet Farrell Brodie argues for the high growth in nineteenth century America of birth control propaganda and sale of female appliances. American women had a higher rate of use of female methods than English women did in the twentieth century. There is no reason to believe that use of female methods in England would have fallen around 1900 when use of birth control was rising and surveys begin, so it must be taken that they were never popular. In the USA the mass production and wide distribution of common household goods began earlier, and was facilitated by higher average incomes for the white population than was the case in England. There was also a stronger tradition of self-doctoring as a result of the isolation and long distances in rural and frontier America. These factors would have increased acceptance of female methods.[65] Brodie may also be exaggerating the impact of the events she describes in the USA. She attributes the decline in the birth rate to this cause, rejecting the explanation that partial sexual abstinence was one of the chief means by which couples achieved low birth rates. According to the figures she cites the marital fertility rate of white native-born women was reduced by almost half (from 7.04 to 3.56 children per woman) during the nineteenth century. Twenty-five per cent of this decline occurred before 1840 yet only three of the birth control texts she cites, those by Owen, Knowlton, and Hersey, were published as early as the 1830s, and there were no lecturers on the topic in this decade. Therefore a substantial part of the decline had already taken place before birth control information, and possibly syringes also, became widely available. The early establishment

64 Ibid., withdrawal, iv. 323–4; anxiety about pregnancy, iv. 277, 317, iii. 16.
65 J. Farrell Brodie, *Contraception and Abortion in Nineteenth Century America* (1994).

of sexual restraint would explain the considerable evidence for low coital frequencies or partial sexual abstinence in US sexual culture. The relatively earlier and higher use of female methods is then consistent with the widespread observation of the greater assertiveness of American women and the more substantial evidence of female sexual pleasure in that culture but it is not relevant to England.[66]

The first English doctor to write a substantial work on birth control was Dr George Drysdale (1825–1904) who published *Physical, Sexual and Natural Religion* in 1854. He was still trying to promote the sponge, but he explains the benefits of female control differently: 'Any preventive means, to be satisfactory, must be used by the *woman*, as it spoils the passion and impulsiveness of the venereal act, if the man have to think of them' (italics in original).[67] This shift away from promoting women's own sexual needs is consistent with the growing denial of female sexuality by mid-century, although Drysdale promotes women's need for paid employment and their interests in other areas.

Annie Besant (1847-1933) was a feminist secularist, union organizer, journalist, and orator, who later became a theosophist. In 1877, she and Charles Bradlaugh (1833–1891), a republican freethinker, who became an MP in 1881, republished a new edition of Knowlton's *Fruits of Philosophy*. A complaint from an unidentified source led to them being tried and convicted of publishing an obscene libel. They were sentenced to six months in prison but the Court of Appeal overturned the sentence on a technicality. The trial was accompanied by huge press publicity and led to an immense increase in awareness of birth control in England.[68] It has been estimated that at least a million, and perhaps as many as two million, tracts were sold in Britain between 1876 and 1891, as the decline in fertility rates

[66] O. Banks, *Faces of Feminism* (1981; 1986). R. Evans, *The Feminists: Women's Emancipation Movements in Europe, America and Australasia 1840–1920* (1977). See also Ch. 4. On sexual pleasure, no English equivalent has been found of the 19th-century diaries presented by Brodie, *Contraception*, ch. 1, or M. L. Todd's diaries in P. Gay, *Education of the Senses: The Bourgeois Experience, Victoria to Freud* (1984).

[67] G. Drysdale, *Physical, Sexual and Natural Religion: By a Student of Medicine* (1855), 350. For Drysdale's life, see M. Benn, *Predicaments of Love* (1992).

[68] This edition of Knowlton's pamphlet, which is unchanged except for annotations by Dr George Drysdale, and a brief account of the trial, and the lives of those involved, is reprinted in Chandrasekhar (ed.), '*A Dirty, Filthy Book*' 87–147.

began to pick up speed.[69] In 1884 Annie Besant published *The Law of Population*, which she claimed was updating Knowlton's pamphlet. There was very little new information about methods but in Besant's hands the radical ideas about female sexuality that Place had tried to prevent Carlile making public, that Dale Owen had softened and made kind, that Drysdale had altered to include women's paid employment and respect for the prostitute, disappeared. What remained was the claim that birth control would not result in unchastity but instead make early marriage possible, and in so doing end young men's degrading dependence on prostitution and enforced, childless celibacy for women. Population control, a safer topic, became far more prominent, and Besant cited research on poverty and medicine at length.[70] This separation of birth control and sexuality became increasingly marked in late nineteenth century pamphlets and continued to shape the public discourse on birth control well into the 1960s.[71]

In the English context, the point at which public discussion of contraception emerged has been regarded as more or less irrelevant to fertility decline because the start of the fall has been taken from the 1870s when aggregate fertility rates began to fall sharply in England. However, researchers into fertility decline are now becoming aware of the importance of events in the first half of the nineteenth century when the furious growth in population of the late eighteenth and early nineteenth centuries slowed dramatically.[72] This brings their interests into line not just with the origins of printed birth control publicity, but also with the trajectory of women's sexuality and of gender relations in the nineteenth and first half of the twentieth centuries. The way in which this trajectory shaped, and was shaped by, fertility control is the subject of the next two chapters.

[69] Himes, *Medical History*, 251. For the diffusion of contraceptive information in this period, see also J. A. and O. Banks, 'The Bradlaugh–Besant Trial and the English Newspapers', *Population Studies*, 8 (1954). Angus McLaren, *Birth Control in Nineteenth Century England* (1978), 221–5. J. Peel, 'The Manufacture and Retailing of Contraceptives in England', *Population Studies*, 17 (1963), 113.

[70] A. Besant, 'The Law of Population' (1884), repr. in Chandrasekhar (ed.), '*A Dirty, Filthy Book*'.

[71] e.g. H. A. Allbutt, *The Wife's Handbook* (1886).

[72] Garret et al., *Changing Family Size*, ch. 7. S. Szreter and E. Garret, 'Reproduction, Compositional Demography and Economic Growth: Family Planning in England Long before the Fertility Decline', *Population and Development Review*, 26/1 (2000).

3

'Conferring a Premium on the Destruction of Female Morals': Fertility Control and Sexuality in the Early to Mid-Nineteenth Century

The response to birth control methods in nineteenth-century England can only be understood in the context of the shifts taking place in women's sexual behaviour. There were major alterations, not just in the perception of female sexuality during the nineteenth century but in women's actual experience. In the early nineteenth century it was assumed that women had passionate sexual feelings. By the early twentieth century there is evidence that many, if not most, women repudiated physical sexual desire. A large proportion of women took little pleasure in genital sexual activity, and those who did so usually felt unable to admit to this openly. In the interval the economic position of women relative to men of their own class worsened in all classes. Consideration of the level of female sexual and economic autonomy in nineteenth-century English culture helps provide an answer to the question of why women came to repudiate sexual pleasure. This chapter and the following one lay the foundations for an understanding of the changes that occurred in twentieth-century sexuality. The nineteenth-century sources I have used are well known to historians but, when examined in the context of fertility rates and the more copious twentieth-century sources, a new understanding of the changes in heterosexual sexuality that took place can be suggested.

FEMALE SEXUAL BEHAVIOUR

In the absence of widely available birth control, a fall in fertility rates means that the majority of women (and men) are having sexual intercourse less frequently. Thus substantial changes in sexual behaviour are revealed by changes in fertility rates. The fertility rate (GRR) in England rose slowly from the seventeenth century, then took off sharply from the 1780s. Births probably reached a peak in 1816, after which the rate declined very suddenly in the 1820s and then continued to fall slowly until the end of the 1840s. There was then a slow rise, which peaked in the 1870s, after which fertility fell sharply, reaching a nadir in the early 1930s.[1] There is a complex relationship between this uneven but essentially downward movement in fertility rates and the changes in sexual behaviour and sexual mores taking place in the nineteenth century. Identifying and tracking these changes is not an easy task, as they differed by class and by region, and knowledge of the sexual mores of plebeians and even of the middling classes is largely statistical or mediated through official sources. Nonetheless since the 1970s there has been a wealth of exciting new research into marriage, prostitution, and sexual violence by historians of women and the family. When this is placed beside the existing histories of sexuality, a clearer picture of the changes in sexual activity from 1800 to 1900 begins to emerge. It is evident that in the late eighteenth and early nineteenth centuries sexual mores varied considerably within and between communities. A very substantial proportion of the female population had casual sexual relationships, settling down when they became pregnant or if it suited them, for as long as they or their partner wished to continue the arrangement.[2] This

---

[1] See Fig. 1.1.

[2] F. Place, *The Autobiography of Francis Place (1771–1854)*, ed. M. Thale (1972), e.g. 87, 96. P. Colquhoun, *A Treatise on the Police of the Metropolis* (1796), ch. 7. M. Ryan, *Prostitution in London* (1839), 168–9. On cohabitation, see J. R. Gillis, *For Better, for Worse: English marriages, 1600 to the Present* (1985). Anna Clark, *Women's Silence, Men's Violence: Sexual Assault in England 1770–1845* (1987), 27. On the rise in illegitimacy and premarital pregnancy, which peaked around 1800, see R. Adair, *Courtship, Illegitimacy and Marriage in Early Modern England* (1996). E. A. Wrigley, 'Marriage, fertility and Population Growth in Eighteenth Century England', in R. B. Outhwaite (ed.), *Marriage and Society: Studies in the Social History of Marriage* (1981). For an earlier debate on the causes of this rise see E. Shorter, *The Making of the Modern Family* (1975). L. A. Tilly, J. W. Scott, and M. Cohen, 'Women's Work and European Fertility Patterns', *Journal of Interdisciplinary History*, 6/3 (1976).

sexual behaviour became increasingly unacceptable to the emerging working classes, especially women, during the course of the nineteenth century. The reasons for their shifting attitudes can be found by putting the changes taking place in the labour market together with those in women's reproductive lives.

In the early eighteenth century plebeian culture had been characterized by heterosocial work patterns and negotiated gender relations. Usually a woman worked within the household under the authority of her husband or another male, but women and men worked side by side and, within her own area of activity, a woman's skills and her contribution to household production endowed her with a degree of power. Community pressure forced men as well as women to take financial responsibility for children, the products of their mutual sexual activity. Irregular or free unions were frequent and stable as a result. By the nineteenth century, the virtual demise of live-in-service employment for men, the rise of homosocial work environments, increasing urbanization, and mobility had reduced the surveillance of both sexes that made community pressure effective as well as the means by which it could be applied.[3] The New Poor Law of 1834 introduced a bastardy clause, which prevented parish officials from forcing fathers to support their children. They had done so to prevent unmarried mothers and babies becoming a charge on the parish and instead of this the mothers were required to go into the workhouse to obtain relief. There were regional differences. For example, research by Barry Reay suggests that in some rural areas families could successfully apply pressure on men even in the mid-nineteenth century, but for most unmarried urban women their vulnerability in the event of pregnancy had greatly increased by the 1830s and 1840s.[4]

---

[3] A. Clark, *The Struggle for the Breeches: Gender and the Making of the British Working Class* (1995), 188–95. M. Jackson, ' "Something More than Blood": Conflicting Accounts of Pregnancy Loss in Eighteenth Century England', in R. Cecil (ed.), *The Anthropology of Pregnancy Loss: Comparative Studies in Miscarriage, Stillbirth and Neonatal Death* (1996), 200–1. T. Hitchcock, 'Sociability and Misogyny in the Life of John Cannon, 1684–1743', in T. Hitchcock and M. Cohen (eds.), *English Masculinities, 1660–1800* (1999), 32. K. D. M. Snell, *Annals of the Labouring Poor: Social Change and Agrarian England, 1660–1900* (1985), chs. 1 and 2.

[4] B. Reay. 'Sexuality in Nineteenth-Century England: The Social Context of Illegitimacy in Rural Kent', *Rural History*, 1/2 (1990).

Working-class women's economic position also worsened from the last third of the eighteenth century as the new patterns of employment altered class and gender boundaries. There was a long-term shift away from household production to wage labour, which disadvantaged women compared to men. Employment opportunities for women contracted in agriculture, and though there was growth in industrial employment following the Napoleonic Wars this too declined from the mid-nineteenth century. Overall the nineteenth-century picture is one of growing female dependence on men and their wages with pockets of improvement associated with factory work.[5] Historian Barbara Taylor explains that 'premarital pregnancy or free unions... became symptoms of domestic insecurity and personal degradation... [and] the comparative stability of legal marriage became more desirable. [Such women's] poverty and vulnerability made them too close to prostitutes.'[6] Thus in the second quarter of the nineteenth century the boundaries between respectable women and others hardened. Lone mothers, in particular, were amongst the poorest groups in society. Mothers had difficulty providing even the basic necessities without the financial contribution of a man.[7] When women cannot support themselves and their children by their own labour then marriage or cohabitation becomes their trade.[8] In such a society men can demand female subordination, and a successful wife will ensure she does not threaten her security by unwanted boldness, flirtatiousness, or displays of sexual knowledge. Thus there is a strong link between women's economic autonomy and their sexual behaviour.

Some authors present affection or love as a characteristic that defines a sexual relationship as non-mercenary, but women who were financially dependent on men could not separate their needs in so simple a fashion. In the late 1840s Henry Mayhew interviewed a 20-year-old needlewoman,

[5] S. Horrell and J. Humphries, 'Women's Labour Force Participation and the Transition to the Male-Breadwinner Family, 1790–1865', in P. Sharpe (ed.), *Women's Work: The English Experience 1650–1914* (1998), 172, 195–6. L. A. Tilly and J. W. Scott, *Women, Work and Family* (1989).

[6] B. Taylor, *Eve and the New Jerusalem* (1983), 204–5.

[7] J. Humphries, 'Female Headed Households in Early Industrial Britain: The Vanguard of the Proletariat', *Labour History Review*, 63 (1998).

[8] For arguments that marriage is women's trade, see W. R. Greg, 'Queen Bees or Working Bees?', *Saturday Review* (8 Oct. 1859). W. R. Greg, 'Why are Women Redundant?' *National Review* (14 Apr. 1862). C. Hamilton, *Marriage is a Trade* (1909).

who reportedly told him, 'I struggled very hard to keep myself chaste, but I found that I couldn't get food for myself and my mother, so I took to live with a young man.' Her economic need was overwhelming. He was a tin man who made fourteen shillings a week whereas she could barely obtain three on average. But she also says, 'I was very fond of him and had known him for two years before he seduced me.'[9] Her emotional and her economic needs were intertwined. When Mayhew met this woman, she told him she was pregnant and had not seen her tin man for six months. And having failed at marriage, she could see no future for herself but to go on the streets. In this context, working-class women had considerable incentive to adopt a more cautious approach to sexual contact. Anna Clark argues that as 'the middle class gained moral and political power, the working class as a whole had to choose between libertine and respectable strains of plebeian sexual culture. Ultimately,' she concluded, ' "respectable" sexual attitudes became hegemonic.'[10] There are routes by which the middle class could conceivably have imposed such attitudes, including the growing police forces, the influence of domestic service, and evangelical religion. But it is difficult to see why, for example, many female radical secularists should have accepted such attitudes, as they did, had the middle classes provided the force behind the move to greater sexual respectability. Nor would this explain the growing gender conservatism of the radical male working class from the 1840s. Gareth Stedman Jones has pointed out that the working classes successfully resisted attempts to convert them to active Christianity even in the late nineteenth century and there was only one policeman for every 980 persons in 1861, hardly sufficient to enforce sexual probity.[11] Domestic service is more likely to have had an impact, although only 22 per cent of all unmarried women were categorized by the census as being in domestic employment in 1851, and middle-class dissatisfaction makes it clear that female servants frequently did not accept middle-class

---

[9] *The Unknown Mayhew: Selections from the Morning Chronicle 1849–50*, E. P. Thompson and E. J. Yeo (eds.) (1971), 147–9.

[10] Clark, *Struggle*, 62. Taylor argues that pressure for change came from both above and below. Taylor, *Eve*, 204–5.

[11] G. Stedman Jones, *Languages of Class: Studies in English Working Class History, 1832–1982* (1983), 195–7. D. Taylor, *Crime, Policing and Punishment in England, 1750–1914* (1998), 88–9.

mores.[12] However, there is no need to postulate such forces pushing women away from sexual risk-taking and toward greater sexual caution. In the absence of birth control and economic autonomy, the benefits to women of a libertine or even libertarian sexual culture are extremely questionable.

By the early twentieth century women were profoundly ill at ease with sexuality, suggesting that nineteenth century working-class women had responded to the increased risk of betrayal by men with a growing mistrust.[13] Mayhew reported that the seamstress told him she lied to her mother, telling her that the tin man had married her, and it was his sister she blamed for his betrayal, not the man himself. She would probably have been less credulous when faced with a potential seducer of any daughter of hers and, knowing her own fate, more suspicious and demanding of information than her own mother had been. This would have been an intelligent response to the growing risk which unmarried pregnancy created for women in the absence of societal restraints on men, and it is consistent with the broad shift toward a more prudish and respectable female working-class culture in nineteenth-century England.

Middle-class women's emotional and economic needs were equally inseparable. Women in the emerging middle classes became increasingly financially dependent on husbands, parents, and male kin in the first half of the nineteenth century. Separation of the home from the place of work, and an education that was not intended to prepare them for paid employment, meant that middle-class women had great difficulty in earning a living if their husband or family were unable to support them. Over a third (35 per cent) of all women aged between 25 and 34 years were single or widowed in 1851 and a disproportionate number of these were middle class. Some had income from family trusts and an unknown proportion ran small businesses, but the considerable attention paid to the plight of governesses reveals that middle-class women were highly aware of their own economic vulnerability even in

[12] 1% of all married women and 7.1% of all widows were categorized as in domestic service. M. Anderson, 'The Social Position of Spinsters in Mid-Victorian Britain', *Journal of Family History* (Winter 1984), table 3, 384.

[13] See Ch. 4.

the 1840s.[14] Several historians have observed that romantic love was immensely important to middle- and upper-middle-class Victorians.[15] Nonetheless, the vast majority of middle-class Victorians chose a person to love from among those in their own economic class and, even more importantly, they increasingly delayed marriage or did not marry at all due to financial concerns. Thomas Malthus' (1766–1834) delay of his own marriage until his mid-thirties was already becoming typical of behaviour among the emerging middle classes when he was writing in the late eighteenth century. By the 1830s any sensible middle-class man (or working-class man with aspirations) deferred marriage until he could afford to maintain himself and a wife and children at the standard he was accustomed to. The poet Alfred Lord Tennyson (1809–92) ended his informal engagement with Emily Sellwood (1813–96) around 1840. They met again only by chance, and when they eventually married in 1850, he was 41 years old and she was 37. In the interval she remained at home caring for her father.[16] By 1851, the average age at marriage of professional men was 30 and this rose further to 33.5 in 1901–6. These men were also more likely not to marry at all.[17] Men and women may have been intensely in love but their financial position determined their romantic career.

It is probable that in the late eighteenth century the proportion of women from among the middling classes who were sexually active outside marriage had risen, as did that of plebeian women. This is the impression

[14] Lady Eastlake (née E. Rigby), 'Review *Vanity Fair, Jane Eyre*, and *The Governesses' Benevolent Institution—Report for 1847*', *Quarterly Review*, 84 (1848), 176, 179. M. J. Peterson, 'The Victorian Governess: Status Incongruence in Family and Society', in M. Vicinus (ed.), *Suffer and be Still: Women in the Victorian Age* (1972), 4. M. Vicinus, *Independent Women: Work and Community for Single Women, 1850–1920* (1985), 23, 26. L. Davidoff and C. Hall, *Family Fortunes: Men and Women of the English Middle Class 1780–1850* (1987), 312–13. *Marriage and Divorce Statistics: Historical Series of Statistics on Marriages and Divorces in England and Wales, 1837–1983*, FM2 no.16 (1990).

[15] M. J. Peterson, *Family, Love, and Work in the Lives of Victorian Gentlewomen* (1989). F. B. Smith, 'Sexuality in Britain, 1800–1900: Some Suggested Revisions', in M. Vicinus (ed.), *A Widening Sphere: Changing Roles of Victorian Women* (1977), 187. J. Tosh, *A Man's Place: Masculinity and the Middle Class Home in Victorian England* (1999).

[16] A. Thwaite, *Emily Tennyson: The Poet's Wife* (1996), 141–2.

[17] S. Szreter and E. Garret, 'Reproduction, Compositional Demography and Economic Growth: Family Planning in England Long before the Fertility Decline', *Population and Development Review*, 26/1 (2000), 66. S. Szreter, *Fertility, Class and Gender in Britain, 1860–1940* (1996), 306. For an example of the impact of nuptiality on a 19th-century family, see B. Caine, *Destined to be Wives: The Sisters of Beatrice Webb* (1985), 114.

given by the histories of women such as Sarah Stoddard (b. 1774), later William Hazlitt's wife, who had sexual experience before their marriage.[18] Evangelical moralists, both male and female, made many complaints about moral laxity in the midding class. Historian Linda Colley has shown that women's public and patriotic activities increased and they were gaining in confidence in the decades before 1825. She argues that the deluge of prescriptive literature warning women that their place lay in the private sphere was prompted by a determination to reverse this growing female incursion into public life.[19] Sexual activity, however independent, is not in itself political but it is another aspect of women's autonomy. Much of the late eighteenth-century prescriptive comment on female sexuality probably sprang from a desire to control women's growing sexual activity.

It is probable that men exercised the power women's vulnerability created; visitors observed that middle-class English husbands insisted on obedience from their wives to a much greater extent than their American and French equivalents.[20] One aspect of male dominance was an insistence on sexual restraint in the widest sense. Increasingly women had constantly to prove their respectability by exhibiting an appropriate femininity, which included inhibiting their movements, voice, dress, and conversational topics.[21] Modesty and deference to familial and other

---

[18] A. C. Grayling, *The Quarrel of the Age: The Life and Times of William Hazlitt* (2001), 120, 287. Davidoff and Hall, *Family Fortunes*, 397–8. The most prominent example is Mary Wollstonecraft, whose experience of romantic betrayal while pregnant and financial desperation once she had a child also provides an exemplary case of the risks which sexual activity posed for women. The best biography is still C. Tomalin, *The Life and Death of Mary Wollstonecraft* (1974).

[19] L. Colley, *Britons: Forging the Nation 1707–1837* (1992), 248–50.

[20] M. Clarke, *Thackeray's Women* (1995), 29–30. M. Mason, *The Making of Victorian Sexuality* (1995), 116–7. C. Norton, 'Letter to the Queen on Lord Chancellor Cranworth's Marriage and Divorce Bill, by Pearce Stevenson, Esq', (1839) repr in J. O. Hoge and J. Marcus (eds.), *Selected Writings of Caroline Norton: Facsimile Reproductions* (1978), 105. F. Tristan, *Flora Tristan's London Journal, 1840* (1980), 195–7.

[21] For many middle-class daughters, this included restricting their physical liberty. Davidoff and Hall, *Family Fortunes*, 403–5. See also E. D. Rappaport, *Shopping for Pleasure: Women in the Making of London's West End* (2000), 105, 137–8. C. N. Rolfe, 'Sexual Delinquency', in H. Llewellyn Smith (ed.), *The New Survey of London Life and Labour* (1935), 295–6. E. Wilson, *The Sphinx in the City* (1991), 30–1. Nead argues the restraints on lower-middle-class women have been exaggerated, but her evidence reveals considerable limitations on the behaviour of those who did move about the city alone. L. Nead, *Victorian Babylon: People, Streets and Images in Nineteenth-Century London* (2000), 66–9.

authority was central. Sarah Taylor (1793–1867), from a well-to-do middle-class Unitarian East Anglian family, was said to be bold and often incautious in testing her attractions. Her specific failings are unknown but were certainly very minor; even so her husband-to-be, John Austin (1790–1859), referred in his marriage proposal to 'those slight stains on your reputation'.[22] The difficulties that later faced actresses of middle-class origin late in the century trying to conform to the requirements of respectability reveal the restraint expected of women.[23] In 1887, a theatre critic announced that the 'freedom of life, of speech, of gesture, which is the rule behind the curtain, renders it almost impossible for a woman to preserve that simplicity of manner which is after all her greatest charm'. These were among 'the things that make it impossible for a lady to remain a lady' if she becomes an actress.[24] Thus the constraints created by the demands of middle-class femininity stretched well beyond actual physical sexual behaviour.

WOMEN'S RESPONSE TO BIRTH CONTROL

The authors of the major nineteenth-century birth control publications all believed that contraception would particularly improve the lot of women by enabling greater female sexual autonomy. This included recognition of women's sexual desires and their entitlement to sexual satisfaction. During the 1820s and 1830s, Francis Place and Richard Carlile made concerted attempts to introduce these ideas and techniques to the secular and politically radical sections of the working class, among whom were many women. It was another fifty years before wide-scale publicity was once more given to birth control techniques, and these radical women provide a unique example of the initial response of English women to birth control ideas and techniques. Many expressed strong opposition to birth control, and their response can help us to understand

---

[22] L. and J. Hamburger, *Contemplating Adultery* (1992), 16, 26, 28–9, 34, 35, 38.

[23] Davidoff and Hall, *Family Fortunes*, 438.

[24] T. C. Davis, *Actresses as Working Women: Their Social Identity in Victorian Culture* (1991), 94, cited from 'Does the Theatre Make for Good?', interview with C. Scott, 'critical doyenne' of the *Daily Telegraph*, in *Great Thoughts*, an evangelical Christian magazine, in 1987.

the delay in the adoption of birth control and the changes in nineteenth-century working-class women's attitudes to sexuality. Historians have previously described the rejection of Francis Place's birth control handbills by Mary Fildes, who had been on the committee of the Manchester Female Reform Society, and was 'memorable for her courage' in the Peterloo Massacre in 1819.[25] In 1823, someone, presumed to be Place, sent her a packet of birth control handbills along with a letter asking her to distribute them. She opened the packet in the presence of her father-in-law, and suspicion was aroused, presumably in him, that she had agreed to do this. She made a complaint to the Attorney General, which brought no result, and then wrote to radical periodicals. Thomas Wooler of the *Black Dwarf* published her letter, the text of the leaflet, and a condemnation of it. Richard Carlile, who produced the *Republican*, ignored the letter until 1825, when he named her in his essay 'What is Love', and then in *Every Woman's Book*, as a convert to contraception, implying she had been secretly promoting the methods. Her husband denied that she had been thus converted.[26] The effort that Fildes made to ensure that people knew that she was not a supporter of birth control reveals the seriousness of the threat to her reputation. The involvement of her husband and her father-in-law reveals that this also concerned the men in her family. Why should association with birth control so threaten Fildes?

Birth control had the potential to increase female sexual autonomy greatly. Rejection of female sexual autonomy was grounded in day-to-day social and economic relations of power and endured well into the twentieth century. Women's reputations depended upon their sexual behaviour to a much greater extent than did those of men. Historians have argued that gossip about sexual reputations regulated female behaviour, while financial probity and keeping their word were central to male reputation. However the impression given is largely that the importance of female sexual behaviour to women's reputation was ideological and customary. Anna Clark does suggest that a 'clash in material as well as moral interests,

[25] M. L. Bush, *What is Love? Richard Carlile's Philosophy of Sex* (1998), 41, 72.

[26] M. Fildes to R. Carlile, 7 Sept. 1823, Place Collection, British Library, Set 68. T. J. Wooler, *Black Dwarf*, 11 (1823) 404–11. *Republican*, 14 (1826), 31. 11 (1825), 561–3. Bush, *What is Love?*, women's opposition to birth control, 121–2, 126. There was also protest from men, 121–3, 130.

divided ordinary women and women who engaged in sexual commerce from each other. If a man associated with prostitutes or kept a mistress he diverted money from the household exchequer and could expose his wife to venereal disease.'[27] This description of sexual expression as having costs is important, because many historians treat sexual activity as if these do not exist. Yet Clark's statement gives sexual agency to men and omits the greatest cost arising from sexual activity, which was children. It had been theorized that children's wages and labour made them an economic asset and so couples chose to have large families. Karl Ittman has challenged this in a study of Bradford in the second half of the nineteenth century. He argues that neither the availability of waged work for children, nor the wages paid to those children who did work, substantiates the theory that they made an economic contribution of such importance to families with an employed father that couples would choose to have larger families on this basis.[28] This is argued in relation to money wages only. If the cost of women's reproductive and domestic labour for their offspring is put into the equation the contribution made by children's wages and household labour was even less important. It is important not to confuse labour that is necessary only because children exist with the creation of a surplus necessary to make them an economic asset. Jane Humphries has shown that lone mothers, women whose children ought to have been an asset according to the theory, were poor and getting poorer throughout the nineteenth century.[29] In sum, when a woman became pregnant she was creating an ongoing financial expense not a financial asset. Thus in a culture without contraception the basis of a woman's good reputation, her sexual behaviour, was not unrelated to the basis of a man's reputation, that is, financial probity and straight dealing. To maintain their reputa-

[27] A. Clark, 'Whores and Gossips: Sexual Reputation in London 1770–1825', in A. Angerman et al. (eds.), *Current Issues in Women's History* (1989), 231, 241. Place links male financial and female sexual immorality as the failings in his master's family. Place, *Francis Place*, 71–2, 78–82.

[28] K. Ittmann, 'Family Limitation and Family Economy in Bradford, West Yorkshire 1851–1881', *Journal of Social History*, 25/3 (1992), 555, 569 n. 72. He and others have also shown that many parents voluntarily kept their children from work and paid for schooling well before the 1870s. See also K. Ittmann, *Work, Gender and Family in Victorian England* (1995), 200. D. Vincent, *The Rise of Mass Literacy: Reading and Writing in Modern Europe* (2000), 25, 34–5.

[29] Humphries, 'Female Headed Households', 47.

tions both sexes had to avoid incurring debts they could not repay, and a man's willingness to take responsibility for children he had fathered was also an aspect of financial probity.

Throughout the nineteenth century those opposed to birth control accused women who desired sexual intercourse without the possibility of reproduction of being prostitutes, harlots, or courtesans. For example, T. J. Wooler, the editor of the *Black Dwarf*, wrote that promoters of birth control were 'conferring a premium on the destruction of female morals; and encourag[ing] the most extended scale of prostitution'.[30] Prostitute is a more formal synonym for the word whore, which was a powerful insult to women in the early nineteenth century, sufficient to justify a court case. The words 'whore' and 'whoring' remain insults used to imply allegedly sexual female behaviour outside a monogamous relationship even today. Those who opposed birth control were using prostitute in this sense, not according to the narrow definition only fully accepted in the second half of the twentieth century; that is, women who exchange a clearly defined sexual act for more or less immediate payment in cash.[31] In the nineteenth century, a woman who obtained sexual pleasure outside a long-term monogamous relationship could be identified as a prostitute even if she made no financial gain from her sexual activity.[32] The fear of pregnancy was thought to prevent women from responding to their own desires for sexual pleasure, hence the argument that birth control, by removing the fear of pregnancy, would turn women into prostitutes. Fildes's father-in-law probably interpreted her apparent interest in birth control as evidence of illicit sexual desires. Such desires might lead a woman to reject spousal or parental influence.

Freethinkers and republicans were particularly vulnerable to accusations of sexual immorality and lack of familial virtues. This, as well as women's economic vulnerability and their corresponding need to please their husbands or partners, increased the likelihood that a woman like

[30] T. J. Wooler, *Black Dwarf*, 11 (1823), 410. Also see *Lancet* (10 Apr. 1869), 499–500. Taylor, *Eve*, 186. E. P. Thompson, *The Making of the English Working-Class* (1980), 803. P. Fryer, *The Birth Controllers* (1965), 184–5. Clark, 'Whores'.

[31] For use of the term in the inter-war period, see Rolfe, 'Sexual Delinquency', 296.

[32] According to the *OED*, in the early use of the term prostitute, meanings included women who were offered or exposed to lust, or behaved licentiously, and men who were basely venal, and devoted to infamous gain.

Fildes would feel obliged to defend herself against the accusations of support for birth control. In *Every Woman's Book* Carlile dismissed the sexual conventions that maintained respectability; birth control removed the necessity for such restrictions, he argued. Unmarried women should have sex but not children, and women should take the initiative in sexual matters if they were attracted to a man. Women and men, Carlile decided, differ only in reproduction, and sexual desire is as strong in women as in men. Indeed, 'passion for this intercourse is a principle that turns all our wisdom and calculations into folly'.[33] He provided an example of female sexual desire:

Of one woman, the wife of a poor labourer, I have heard a singular anecdote of resolution. She would resist his importunities for months after each birth, and even arm herself with a knife to resist him if he became violent; but all would not do; she could never defend herself throughout a year; she was generally the first, after a few months to propose a honourable capitulation.[34]

Carlile presented female sexual behaviour associated with prostitution as desirable, indeed he defined prostitutes as women who follow the dictates of a natural appetite, the very thing he was suggesting birth control would free all women to do.[35] There was considerable female support for Carlile but his personal conduct confirmed the worst interpretations that could be placed on his ideas.[36] His wife Jane was a radical heroine, having run Carlile's press and bookshop and then joined him in prison in the cause of press freedom.[37] In August 1833 Carlile was finally released from jail, and in September he let his supporters know that he was leaving his wife Jane and their three children, to enter a 'moral marriage' with a young woman from Bolton named Eliza Sharples. He embarked on a series of frantic lecture tours, often with Eliza, whose presence infuriated many audience members. Carlile was condemned for justifying the abandonment of mothers and children, and Eliza was described as 'your moral mistress', who was 'no better than a prosti-

[33] R. Carlile, *What is Love?* (1825), repr. in Bush, *What is Love?*, 67.

[34] Ibid. 67–8.

[35] Ibid. 79.

[36] Female support, ibid. 131–4. See also I. McCalman, 'Females, Feminism and Free Love in an Early Nineteenth Century Radical Movement', *Labour History*, 38 (1980), 7, 12, 13.

[37] J. Schwarzkopf, *Women in the Chartist Movement* (1991), 127–8.

tute'.[38] As M. L. Bush comments, his example must have helped convince women that birth control would undermine their security.

The reason usually given for working-class resistance to birth control is the influence of Thomas Malthus. He had claimed that overpopulation and not social injustice was at the root of all poverty. Both charity and proletarian efforts to raise wages by strikes and combinations were counterproductive; instead the poor must learn to check their breeding by delaying marriage or abstinence. Socialists argued that asking the working class to control their fertility was tantamount to accepting that it was their incontinence, and not an unjust society, which was responsible for poverty.[39] The importance of objections to Malthusianism is probably exaggerated; even the politically active Carlile initially rejected birth control as much because it was unnatural, similarly to Christians who believed the practice to be ungodly. The fears underlying this rejection should not be trivialized or seen only in terms of the social regulation of sexuality. Sexual intercourse and reproduction shape people's lives. Major negative consequences included unwanted pregnancy, venereal disease, maternal injury or death from abortion or in childbirth, and the birth of disabled infants (and perhaps the vicissitudes of love). Beliefs about what was natural and unnatural offered a means by which men and women attempted to gain an illusion of control over the course of distressing events.[40]

For those who did venture to use the new methods the gains were uncertain. The radical artisan William James Linton (1812–97) was converted to the use of birth control when he read Robert Dale Owen's *Moral Physiology*. He entered into an affectionate relationship with Emily Wade

---

[38] Bush, *What is Love?* 131; see also 120, 127. There was widespread rejection of Carlile's ideas about love and birth control in the radical press. J. H. Weiner, *Radicalism and Freethought in Nineteenth-Century Britain: The Life of Richard Carlile* (1983), 198.

[39] J. A. Banks, *Prosperity and Parenthood: A Study of Family Planning amongst the Victorian Middle-Classes* (1954), ch. 3. Clark, *Struggle*, 188–95.

[40] Bush, *What is Love?*, 22–5, Fryer, *Birth Controllers*, 88–9. Fears about the consequences of unnatural sex occur elsewhere, e.g. 'if it happen that they come together when the woman's menses are flowing, will notwithstanding proceed to the act of copulation, which is both unclean and unnatural; and the issue of such copulation will prove monstrous, as a just punishment of lying together when nature forbids.' *Aristotle's Master-Piece Compleated. In Two Parts...* (1782), 40.

(his deceased wife's sister, marriage to whom was illegal), and the couple decided to have four children. Emily was increasingly ill and finally died of consumption in 1856, but in spite of her poor health 'accidents kept happening'. Some confusing letters in 1839 suggest the couple may have had their first child in May 1839 though the birth was not registered until 1841. If these letters are disregarded the birth intervals of the couple's seven children vary between eighteen months and two years. Regardless of when their first child was born, the intervals do not lengthen after the birth of the fourth child. Thus Linton and Wade's use of birth control made no apparent difference to their fertility.[41] This couple had little of the rigidity and caution needed to use the available methods successfully. By contrast Sarah (née Taylor) and John Austin, who also used birth control, had only one child. Both were highly disciplined, and John's lack of sexual affection and tenderness probably reduced the chance that they would get carried away by physical passion, further increasing the effectiveness of their use of birth control.[42]

MIDDLE-CLASS MEN AND THE CONTROL OF FERTILITY

The Austins were extremely early middle-class adopters of birth control. In the 1860s, John Russell, Lord Amberley (1842–1876), lost the contest for the seat of South Devon when it became known that he had spoken up in favour of birth control at a meeting. The resulting reports and family papers reveal that birth control was being discussed among intellectual and forward-thinking sections of the upper middle classes, and that the example of low birth rates among the French and white Americans had been noted.[43] Historian Joseph Banks suggested that the mid-century fall

[41] William Wade Linton 21 Dec. 1841, Emily (Gypsy) 1844, Lancelot 1846, Edmund 31 May 1848, Margaret 1851, Ellen Sept. 1852, Eliza 1854. Emily died in Dec. 1856. F. B. Smith, *Radical Artisan: William James Linton 1812–97* (1973), 21, 42–3, 82, 114.

[42] Hamburger and Hamburger, *Contemplating Adultery*, 180. See also P. Hirsch, *Barbara Leigh Smith Bodichon* (2001), 65, 106–9, 112–13. Walter, *My Secret Life* (1880; 1995), iii. 19, iv. 92, 95–6, 323–4.

[43] B. Russell and P. Russell (eds.), *The Amberley papers: The Letters and Diaries of Lord and Lady Amberley*, vol. ii (1937; 1966), 170, 254, 268.

in birth rates within marriage in some middle-class occupations reflected the early adoption of birth control by middle-class men.[44] This was building upon an argument first put in 1924 by the Superintendent of Statistics at the General Registrar's Office, Dr T. H. C. Stevenson. He argued that the middle classes had initially begun to lower their family size using knowledge of birth control gained from printed neo-Malthusian propaganda and that the information had then percolated *downwards* from the 1870s when the birth rates of many working-class occupational groups began to fall.[45] Yet historian Norman Himes estimated the probable sales of Robert Dale Owen's and Charles Knowlton's books in England at only a thousand copies each a year from secularist publishers along with an increasing number of pamphlets, repeated editions, and short versions of George Drysdale's lengthy book.[46] Birth control could not be mentioned directly in newspapers and magazines. The absence of evidence, aside from statistical inference, that downward diffusion of birth control information from the middle classes had taken place is reinforced by the contradiction between this notion and the enduring association from the 1830s between birth control information, political radicalism, and secularism. It is more probable that birth control information percolated *outwards* from radical groups and from purveyors of erotic literature and condoms.

There has been an ongoing emphasis by demographic historians on men as the prime movers of fertility decline and, in the absence of birth control methods, their sexual activity must be highly relevant to this contention. The rising average age at marriage of professional men resulted in a life cycle different from that now seen as the norm. Most were single throughout much of their twenties, many remained so until considerably later in life, and a growing proportion never married. Given the absence of birth control methods, if men's desire to control fertility had been as high as or higher than that of women, and men's sexual activity had been restricted to marriage, then men should have been

[44] Banks, *Prosperity* J. A. Banks, *Victorian Values: Secularism and the Size of Families* (1981).

[45] Szreter, *Fertility*, 264. For a history of this idea, see S. Szreter, 'The Idea of the Demographic Transition and the Study of Fertility Change: A Critical Intellectual History', *Population and Development Review*, 19/4 (1993).

[46] N. Himes, *The Medical History of Contraception* (1936; 1970), 222, 224, 231.

equally committed to male sexual restraint. If men were equally committed to sexual restraint, it is difficult to explain why a sexual culture
developed in which women were seen as greatly lacking in sexual desire
when compared to men, as it did during the nineteenth century. If men
were not equally committed to sexual restraint then they must have
replaced marital sex with other sexual activity during their late teens,
twenties, and, often, thirties.

Unmarried, middle-class men, even the prudish or naïve, were part of a
more sexually open culture than were unmarried middle-class women.
By the second quarter of the century, the evidence that women of this
class were almost invariably virgins at marriage is overwhelming. Men
could, and some did, exploit female servants but this risked disrupting the
home.[47] Prohibitions against masturbation had already been promoted by
medics for over a century, and were in any event embedded in Christianity, but these were probably of serious concern only to a minority at mid-
century.[48] Prostitution provided an alternative, although there might be
additional problems such as the cost and availability of attractive, clean
women.[49] Lord Byron (1788–1824) coupled Malthus' name with prostitutes in *Don Juan* (1821):

> The mob stood, and as usual several score
>   Of those pedestrian Paphians who abound
> In decent London when the daylight 's o'er;
>   Commodious but immoral, they are found
> Useful, like Malthus, in promoting marriage[50]

Byron was suggesting ironically that a 'Paphian' or prostitute would
dissuade men from marriage just as would the methods of fertility control
Malthus proposed—continence and late marriage. Many contemporary
authors assumed that single men patronized prostitutes; however, the

[47] J. R. Gillis, 'Servants, Sexual Relations and the Risks of Illegitimacy in London, 1801–
1900', *Feminist Studies*, 5 (1979).

[48] A. Hunt, 'The Great Masturbation Panic and the Discourses of Moral Regulation in
Nineteenth and Early Twentieth Century Britain', *Journal of the History of Sexuality* (1998).

[49] These problems are mentioned regularly by Walter in *My Secret Life*.

[50] *Don Juan*, 11th canto. Paphians were attendants of Venus (Paphos in Cyprus was the site
of an ancient temple to Aphrodite). Quoted in K. Nield (introd.), *Prostitution in the Victorian Age:
Debates on the Issue from Nineteenth-Century Critical Journals* (1973).

lack of research on the male clients who made the trade possible contrasts with repetitious attempts at enumerating the prostitutes. Numbers of prostitutes were, and remain, impossible to ascertain from contemporary estimates. In part this is due to the fundamental instability of the term prostitute in the first two-thirds of the nineteenth century, as this resulted in observers including radically different populations of women in the category they were counting. All sexually active unmarried women, including those who were cohabiting, were frequently included in discussions of prostitution by reformers earlier in the century. Fully half the number of 'prostitutes' on the list made up by reforming magistrate Patrick Colquhoun in 1797 were in this category. In 1839, Michael Ryan wrote that 'Some writers maintain, that every one in three of the daughters of persons in the lower rank in life, become prostitutes, before they are twenty years of age. It is also asserted that there is one prostitute to every seven virtuous woman.'[51] The gradual development of police forces and increasing respect for the new science of statistics during the middle decades of the century led to increasing reliance on police statistics. However, even in the 1860s legislators were unable or unwilling to define 'a common prostitute' as covered by the Contagious Diseases Acts and felt it reasonable that police suspicion should fall on any unattached woman seen in the company of men within the subjected districts.[52] Thus, police figures were not more accurate; rather the police categorized women as prostitutes according to different criteria. Historians have differentiated sharply between sexually active unmarried women and prostitutes, so the available research into prostitution is of little help in illuminating the shift in working-class women's sexual behaviour that was taking place.[53] The

[51] Varied estimates were made by Colquhoun, *Treatise*, 340. Ryan, *Prostitution*, 168–9. William Bevan, *Prostitution in the Borough of Liverpool: A Lecture, etc.* (1843), 6–7. Bracebridge Hemyng, 'Prostitution', in Henry Mayhew (ed.), *London Labour and the London Poor* (1862), 255. William Tait, *Magdalenism: An Inquiry into the Extent, Causes and Consequences of Prostitution in Edinburgh* (1840), 6–9, 84. Ralph Wardlaw, *Lectures on Female Prostitution: Its Nature, Extent, Effects, Guilt, Causes and Remedy, etc.* (1842), 14–16.

[52] *Report of the House of Commons Select Committee on the Contagious Diseases Act*, PP 1868–9 (306), VII. L. Mahood, *The Magdalenes: Prostitution in the Nineteenth Century* (1990), 71. For the impact of police identification methods on women, see J. Jordan, *Josephine Butler* (2001), 167–8. C. Tomalin, *The Invisible Woman* (1990), 118.

[53] e.g. F. Finnegan, *Poverty and Prostitution: A Study of Prostitutes in Victorian York* (1979). J. R. Walkowitz, *Prostitution and Victorian Society: Women, Class and the State* (1980), 2.

worsening economic position of women suggests that the numbers of women undertaking sexual acts solely for financial return, as opposed to those engaging in 'immoral' sexual activity for pleasure, are likely to have increased by mid-century. Historian Judith Walkowitz has argued that the majority of Victorian prostitutes catered to a working-class clientele. However, working-class people formed a much greater proportion of the population, which means that absolute numbers of working-class women were far greater than the numbers of middle-class men, so the latter could have patronized prostitutes extensively without this overturning her conclusion.[54]

Syphilis mortality rates in England provide some indication of middle-class men's behaviour, obviously including both married and single men. Male intercourse with prostitutes was almost the sole method of transmission of the disease among the middle classes, as middle-class women almost invariably remained virgins until marriage and adultery was almost certainly rare. Syphilis has a very low rate of mortality, that is, most people who are infected do not die as a result, so syphilis mortality indicates a much higher prevalence of the disease in society. Dr T. H. C. Stevenson, the Superintendent of Statistics of the Registrar General, reported to the Royal Commission on Venereal Disease in 1914 that the syphilis statistics were known to be inaccurate.[55] This was due to diagnostic difficulties and to the reluctance of doctors in private practice to put syphilis on death certificates. He concluded, however, that the problem could be overcome sufficiently by including deaths from parasyphilitic diseases not widely known to be manifestations of syphilis, and therefore more accurately certified. The highest death rates from syphilis were found to have occurred among men of the unskilled labouring class and men of the middle and professional classes. Once exposed to the disease the unskilled had a higher chance of infection and death due to their already poor health, making middle-class men's probable level of exposure to infection even higher than the relative rate of mortality would suggest. The recorded rate of syphilitic mortality, including all classes, rose until 1868 and was followed by a plateau lasting until around

---

[54]   Walkowitz, *Prostitution*, 17–18.
[55]   *Report of the Royal Commission on Venereal Disease*, PP 1916 (8190), p. xvi.

1886, then by ten years of rapid decline. This decline is consistent with the growth of awareness and anxiety about syphilis in this period. The class-specific mortality rates do not apply to the mid-nineteenth century, but the aggregate rate and social attitudes at that time suggest that middle-class men would have been more likely to patronize prostitutes than was the case by the end of the century. Hence there seems no reason to believe the relative rates would have been substantially different in the earlier period.

During the period from 1850 to 1868 in which the recorded rate of syphilitic mortality, including all classes, rose enormously, non-commercial sexual activity is more likely to have been falling, if anything, and thus this increase may reflect a rise in men's contacts with prostitutes. This could be related to urbanization, as syphilis was 'essentially a town disease' just as prostitution was largely an urban phenomenon.[56] In the middle quarters of the nineteenth century there was massive growth in population accompanied by a substantial shift from small rural localities to the towns and cities. This means that the proportion of men in the population who had easy access to prostitutes increased because the proportion of men who were town dwellers increased. The mortality statistics are not broken down by region, but the high population growth areas in the north were built on coal and textiles, industries in which the workers had notably low rates of syphilis and there was only a small established middle class. Nonconformist religious adherence was also relatively high in the north and west, and direct evidence of less tolerance for prostitution can be found in the strong support for the anti-Contagious Diseases Acts campaign in the area.[57] This suggests that the increase in prostitution was probably greatest in the south, central, and, to a lesser extent, eastern England, the regions in which the majority of professionals and holders of existing wealth lived. These are the areas where the Established Church had its greatest strength and this corresponds with

[56] Ibid., appendix 1, para. 51, 18. The incidence of syphilis-related mortality was lowest among agricultural labourers.

[57] K. D. M. Snell and P. S. Ell, *Rival Jerusalems: The Geography of Victorian Religion* (2000), 26, 59, table A.1, 423. Szreter and Garret, 'Reproduction', 61. On the anti-Contagious Diseases Acts campaign; J. Walkowitz, 'Male Vice and Female Virtue', in A. Snitow, C. Stansell, and S. Thompson (eds.), *Powers of Desire: The Politics of Sexuality* (1983). Jordan, *Butler.*

the voting patterns of the Tory Party. These institutions and also the legislature, the medical profession, and the police generally saw prostitution as a regrettable necessity, evidenced in the resistance to the campaign against the Contagious Diseases Acts.

Middle-class Victorian sexual ideology was more strongly related to religion than to medical discourses, as historian John Maynard has pointed out.[58] Dissent and evangelical Christianity offered believers a 'new moral economy' in which sexual restraint accompanied sobriety and self-control. A disproportionate amount of evidence regarding individual sexual experience comes from such men rather than the more sexually relaxed Anglicans or non-churchgoers. Their numbers were growing fast in the 1830s and 1840s and the Nonconformist churches received 47 per cent, a little under half, of all church attendances recorded in the 1851 religious census.[59] This figure does not directly relate to a proportion of the population, and it included working-class believers. It is worth noting that contemporaries were shocked that perhaps only half of those able to attend services did so. There are also examples of Dissenters who did not maintain socially acceptable sexual mores. Ben Smith, a wealthy Unitarian, had an illegitimate family with Anne Longden, and then had a second concealed family with another woman after her death in 1833.[60] Nonetheless it seems probable that by mid-century most, Nonconformists and evangelical Anglicans remained largely chaste until marriage, a choice which brought its own problems. They were however only a minority of the population.

During the middle decades of the century, there was a growing difference between the sexual knowledge and experience of young single men and women. Unmarried middle-class girls appear to have been increasingly unlikely to be permitted the privacy needed for anything other than the most limited mutual physical intimacies with young men. It would have been unthinkable for middle-class Unitarian Sarah Taylor, who was already 'slightly soiled' by flirtation, to experiment sexually with

[58] J. Maynard, *Victorian Discourses on Sexuality and Religion* (1993), 36.

[59] J. Obelkevich, 'Religion', in F. M. Thompson (ed.), *The Cambridge Social History of Britain 1750–1950* (1990), 332–3, 337–8.

[60] Hirsch, *Bodichon*, 8–14, 96–7.

John Austin (and perhaps save herself from an unhappy marriage) during the course of their lengthy engagement.[61] Notwithstanding other such examples, historian Peter Gay has argued that 'for many middle-class couples, betrothal was an informal permission for extensive mutual sexual exploration, short only of sexual intercourse'. Susan Chitty, in her biography of Charles Kingsley, makes it evident that he and Frances Grenfell, whose experience Gay cites to support his argument, would not have had opportunity for anything more than brief touches of the body and kissing, albeit with considerable passion.[62]

On the basis of the available sources, it seems reasonable to suggest that throughout the first three-quarters of the century a growing proportion of middle-class men received their sexual initiation through contact with women they paid for sex. The coarsening impact of prostitution upon unmarried men is a trope of the nineteenth-century birth control literature, as well as that on prostitution and on the shortage of husbands for middle-class women.[63] But such repetition may not make it less likely to have reflected actual experience. Julia O'Connell Davidson has undertaken research into prostitutes and their clients today. The points she makes are equally relevant to commercial sexual exchanges in the earlier period. She described the woman with whom the client has sex as 'a person who is not a person'. She explains that:

[The prostitute's client pays] to step outside the complex web of rules, meanings, obligations and conventions, which govern non-commercial sexuality... It is not necessary to be socially or sexually skilled... In stepping outside this web of rules, the client is effectively securing access to a sort of twilight sexual realm wherein a man can have sex with a real, live flesh and blood person and yet evade

---

[61] Hamburger and Hamburger, *Contemplating Adultery*, 16, 26, 28–9.

[62] P. Gay, *The Tender Passion: The Bourgeois Experience, Victoria to Freud* (1986), 306. S. Chitty, *The Beast and the Monk* (1974), 59, 66, 82. For acceptable physicality in a loving upper-class engagement, see Russell and Russell (eds.), *Amberley Papers*, 291, 321.

[63] e.g. A. Besant, 'The Law of Population...' (1884), repr. in S. Chandrasekhar (ed.), '*A Dirty, Filthy Book*' (1981), 181–2, 183. Carlile, *What is Love?*, 74. G. Drysdale, *Physical, Sexual and Natural Religion* (1855), 343, 377–8. On Drysdale's sympathy when a doctor, see M. Benn, *Predicaments of Love* (1992), ch. 12. C. Knowlton, 'Fruits of Philosophy' (1832), repr. in Chandrasekhar (ed.), '*A Dirty, Filthy Book*', 102. R. D. Owen, *Moral Physiology* (1834), 25.

all the social obligations which go along with sexual relations between real, live people.[64]

When a man purchases a woman's consent to sex he does not learn how to arouse her desire to have intercourse or how to accept refusal. Such an unequal sexual relationship reinforces the man's perception of the woman as an object, which exists only in relation to him, in order to service his needs, demands, and expectations. Victorian middle-class men usually arrived at the marriage bed either entirely inexperienced or tutored solely by dehumanizing experiences with prostitutes or the exploitation of young working-class women.

This experience can be compared to the early eighteenth-century experience of John Cannon (1684–1743), who had a sexual relationship for several years with Mary Withers, a fellow servant of lower status in his uncle's household. Initially this consisted 'of kissing & toying when together in private', and they gradually progressed to 'a more close familiarity'.[65] Cannon's descriptions are reminiscent of 'petting' as it existed in the 1950s. Through taking pleasure in each other's body without risking intercourse, and over many hours on different occasions, Cannon and Withers learned how to sexually arouse and satisfy one another. In spite of his higher status she was free to withdraw from the relationship, as they were not married, and thus he had an incentive to learn how to arouse and please her both physically and emotionally (as did she him). The woman's vulnerability increased if, or when, a couple agreed to have intercourse, and, as has been described above, this system broke down in the nineteenth century.[66] Nonetheless this learning process was part of a culture in which it was assumed that both young men and women would seek out and enjoy sexual pleasure. Such possibilities were increasingly denied to young middle-class men and women during the nineteenth

---

[64] J. O'Connell Davidson, 'Prostitution and the Contours of Control' In J. Weeks and J. Holland (eds.), *Sexual Cultures, Communities, Values and Intimacy* (1996), 188–9. See also P. Rose, *Parallel Lives* (1983; 1994), 282.

[65] T. Hitchcock, *English Sexualities: 1700–1800* (1997), 34. Hitchcock, 'John Cannon', 31, 34.

[66] Eventually Mary Withers became pregnant but John Cannon refused to marry her. Crucially he was able to evade community pressure as he had left the area and obtained a job in the excise. Tim Hitchcock comments that this homosocial occupation largely divorced from local communities was an unusual early forerunner of 19th-century changes in male employment. Hitchcock, 'John Cannon'.

century. Middle-class late marriage evolved into a different sexual system from that created by late marriage among plebeians in the seventeenth and eighteenth centuries. The plebeian deferral of marriage and sexual attitudes had been based upon economic considerations and so too were middle-class sexual attitudes. But late marriage as practised by middle-class mid-Victorians involved the creation of highly gendered separate sexual cultures. Prostitution is symptomatic of a culture in which young men, even those who remained celibate, routinely had greater access to sexual knowledge than did unmarried women and most had some degree of sexual experience. Active, autonomous female sexuality was potentially stigmatized as 'innate depravity' while male sexual expression involved only 'the ordinary tribute to natural desires, [and] the common laxity of a man of the world'.[67]

What then did these men do when they married? Retreating from possible exaggeration of the Victorian husband's sexual activity in the 1960s, historians have since tended to argue that middle-class husbands had little contact with prostitution. In Catherine Hall and Leonore Davidoff's influential account of the provincial middle classes from 1780 to 1850 middle-class engagement with prostitution goes unmentioned, even in the guise of kept women (as do sexually exploited servants). John Tosh does argue that men indulged as bachelors, but he insists that once married they were faithful to their wives.[68] Yet there is no shortage of contemporary comments about married men and prostitutes or of evidence regarding individuals.[69] Thus the question is actually one of prevalence; did married middle-class men usually or often patronize prostitutes or was this unusual and exceptional behaviour? Recent research into working-class women and prostitution has used official sources such as police reports or rescue home records. These sources are biased toward women who worked on the street and thus are unlikely to include

---

[67] W. R. Greg, 'Prostitution', *Westminster Review*, 53 (1850), repr. in Nield (ed.), *Prostitution*, 474. See also Maynard, *Victorian Discourses*, 52, 73.

[68] Davidoff and Hall, *Family Fortunes*, 21, 222–3, 323–4, 403. Tosh, *A Man's Place*, 57.

[69] e.g. letter to Fanny Smyttan, 27 Feb. 1867. Cited in Jordan, *Butler*, 81. J. Talbot, *The Miseries of Prostitution* (1844), 42. W. E. H. Lecky, *European Morals from Augustus to Charlemagne* (1869), 282, 284. Among the many men whose biographies reveal they visited prostitutes are C. Dickens, W. Hazlitt, Holman Hunt, C. Kingsley (only once), D. G. Rossetti, R. L. Stevenson, A. Trollope.

women who profited from wealthier men. Bracebrydge Hemyng, Henry Mayhew's collaborator, noted in 1862 that 'police do not concern themselves with the higher class of prostitutes; indeed it would be impossible, and impertinent as well, were they to make the attempt'.[70] Many biographies contain references to married and unmarried men's experience of non-marital sexual activity that was recorded due to financial expense. A wide range of sexual relationships with women is revealed to have existed. There is a comparative absence of casual commercial sexual encounters reported in biographies, which raises the suspicion that such brief events went unrecorded.[71] However, many of the men for whom there is evidence belonged to atypical groups such as writers or artists, and it is unclear to what extent their behaviour can be generalized to more conventional men. Nonetheless, why would men who found obtaining sexual relief from prostitutes acceptable during the long years they spent as bachelors choose abstinence if fertility control or their wife's physical condition made sexual restraint necessary later in their marriages? There was considerable pressure to conceal sexual matters from middle-class women and the fervently religious, but there were few other societal sanctions to deter middle-class men. Concern about syphilis was growing but there was much confusion, and as late as the 1860s it was

[70] Hemyng, 'Prostitution', 215.

[71] The varied relationships include, for example, the essayist Samuel Butler (1835–1902), who visited a Madame Dumas on Wednesday afternoons from 1873 to 1893 in return for the sum of a pound a week. After fifteen years Butler gave her his name and address, after which she wrote him letters and came occasionally to tea. When she died of consumption in 1892 he arranged her funeral. He also visited prostitutes in Europe. P. Raby, *Samuel Butler: A Biography* (1991), 141–2, 182. Charles Blandsford Mansfield married a woman who he claimed was constantly unfaithful to him and eventually eloped to Australia. He then started keeping mistresses, including a working-class woman whom he described as the 'magdalen' and a Mrs Meredith. Chitty, *Beast*, 121. A number of men had second families, e.g. W. M. Clarke, *The Secret Life of Wilkie Collins* (1988); I. Gibson, *The Erotomaniac* (2001), 130, 148; Hirsch, *Bodichon*, 8–14, 97–8; D. Petre, *The Secret Orchard of Roger Ackerley* (1975); or long-term mistresses, see Thomas Buckle in R. Pearsall, *The Worm in the Bud: The World of Victorian Sexuality* (1969; 1993), 97–8, Tomalin, *Invisible Woman*. Brief encounters include Grayling, *Hazlitt*, 87–8; Tomalin, *Invisible Woman*, 87–91. There is also evidence of middle-class prostitutes, who are likely to have had middle-class clients, from rescue homes and other institutions. F. Barret-Ducrocq, *Love in the Time of Victoria* (1992), 192; Hemyng, 'Prostitution', 243. Mid-century rescue homes sent middle-class girls to different institutions or else segregated them from working-class girls. P. Bartley, *Prostitution: Prevention and Reform in England, 1860–1914* (2000), 37.

argued that '[s]yphilis, under favouring circumstances, may be generated spontaneously', that is without sexual contact.[72] Thus broad cultural support for male sexual continence was absent.

An examination of a couple who undoubtedly did not use birth control or recourse to prostitution on the husband's part, although it is likely they did take measures to control their fertility, suggests some implications of partial abstinence, the alternative method, for marital relationships. The writer and parson Charles Kingsley (1819–75) was an apostle of marital sexuality. He and his wife Frances Grenfell (1814–91) were loving and mutually physically passionate. Their first child was born ten months after their wedding in 1844. The following year, 1845, Fanny became pregnant again and suffered her first miscarriage. She also became unwell early in the second pregnancy, and was to do so during all her future pregnancies. The next child arrived in early 1847; there was then a gap of nearly five years before the birth of Mary in 1852. That birth left her weakened and the following year she had a further bad miscarriage. Her last child, Grenville, was not born until 1858, five years later. Fanny's varied and lengthy birth intervals suggest the couple had a low frequency of coitus or even abstained for long periods. From 1831 to 1861 falls in family size were accompanied by a 'marked clustering of children into the early years of marriage' along with a fall in the age of the woman when her last child was born. This suggests that as women or men reached a point where they ceased to want a further child they increasingly lowered their rate of coitus.[73] This is the pattern of the Kingsleys' family, in which the later children were spaced further apart even before childbearing ceased entirely. In May 1849, Charles wrote to Fanny that while 'I long to be back in your arms [all you my] cruel cold darling beauty [wish for is]

---

[72] *Report of the Committee Appointed to Enquire into the Pathology and Treatment of the Venereal Disease with the View to Diminish its Injurious Effects on the Men of the Army and Navy*, PP 1868, vol. XXXVII, p. vi.

[73] M. Anderson, 'The Emergence of the Modern Life Cycle in Britain', *Social History*, 10 (1985), 73, fig. 3, 74. M. Anderson, 'Highly Restricted Fertility: Very Small Families in the British Fertility Decline', *Population Studies*, 52 (1998), 178. E. Garret, 'The Trials of Labour: Motherhood Versus Employment in a Nineteenth-Century Textile Centre', *Continuity and Change*, 5 (1990), 123. I. Loudon, *Death in Childbirth* (1992), 242. H. Cook, ' "Unseemly and Unwomanly Behaviour": Comparing Women's Control of their Fertility in Australia and in England from 1890 to 1970', *Journal of Population Research (Australia)*, 17/2 (2000), 135–6.

to sleep by my side'.[74] Fanny had intensely desired children but by then she had two and the experience of sexual pleasure entailed a high risk of further painful experiences. It is little wonder her sexual desire should have waned even though her love for Charles did not. It is only thanks to the Kingsleys' frankness that Fanny's resistance to sexual activity cannot be mistaken for prudery or an initial lack of sexual interest.

Joseph Banks argued in 1954 that the initial decline in nineteenth-century family size was due to a future time planning perspective among middle-class men who recognized the new costly need to educate their sons.[75] Charles Kingsley certainly found the effort of supplementing his inadequate living as a parson exhausting, but the impact of another child upon this struggle was a relatively remote concern for him whereas the impact of a further pregnancy on Fanny was almost immediate. And it is Fanny for whom there is evidence, albeit limited, of resistance to sexual demands. Women's success at limiting their fertility is likely to have depended on their capacity to assert their own needs as well as co-operation from their husbands. Fanny came from a family that was of higher status and wealthier than that of Charles, and she had a forceful personality. Emma Darwin (1808–1896), another loving and loved wife, was a less assertive woman whose husband did not suffer from financial constraints. According to biographer Randal Keynes she was unable to slow the pace of childbearing in spite of her desire to do so.[76]

Completed family size varied greatly in the nineteenth century but, if presented as an average, the completed family size of couples with a husband in class I who married between 1851 and 1860 was just over six children.[77] This means that a high proportion of women had a family size well over the level of four or five births beyond which the risk of complications, stillbirths, and maternal mortality increases. It is important to remember that the high birth rates experienced by women from the late eighteenth century were historically unusual and so this high burden of reproductive labour was a new experience for women, which could create the motivation for fertility control. High fertility increased the likelihood

[74] Chitty, *Beast*, 137, also 98, 163, 189.

[75] J. A. Banks, *Victorian Values: Secularism and the Size of Families* (1981), 57–8.

[76] R. Keynes, *Annie's Box: Charles Darwin, his Daughter and Human Evolution* (2001; 2002), 10.

[77] Anderson, 'Modern Life Cycle', 80.

that male sexual demands would be unwanted. The nineteenth-century evidence on this point can be contested but there is twentieth-century research into women who lacked access to contraception. This shows that many, though not all, women who desired sexual activity when they had two or three children were likely to have lost interest once they had had six or seven pregnancies.[78] Thus in the absence of birth control, fertility has a major influence on the shaping of women's sexual experience.

This examination of the relationship between birth control and sexuality starts to reveal the complex interrelationships between male and female sexuality and economics that produced nineteenth-century sexuality and led to the deferral of widespread experimentation with birth control for three-quarters of a century. In spite of the obvious advantages that birth control appeared to offer women there were a number of powerful reasons why they might have resisted the practice in the nineteenth century. These included the threat to their own sexual reputations, the freedom from familial responsibility the practice potentially offered to men, the fear of unnatural practices, and the constraints the methods placed upon physical sexual passion. In a period of diminishing economic autonomy, vulnerability to male desertion, and high fertility, sexual restraint offered most women greater rewards. The small fall in the birth rate in some middle-class occupations was probably due to a variety of causes, including recourse to prostitution, as men took advantage of women's lack of economic alternatives. The next chapter describes the transformation of female attitudes to sexuality, the emergence of societal support for abstinence, and the probable impact of these factors upon the practice of birth control in England.

---

[78] M. Kerr, *The People of Ship Street* (1958), cited in J. Klein, *Samples of English Culture*, vol. i (1965), 72. The point was made more obliquely in N. Dennis, C. Slaughter, and F. D. Henriques, *Coal is our Life* (1956; 1969), 228. P. Shapiro, 'The Unplanned Children', *New Society* (1962).

4

'One Man is as Good as Another in that Respect': Women and Sexual Abstinence

In this chapter the signs of women's increasing confidence and assertiveness in the late nineteenth century and the growing female consciousness of the impact of sexuality upon women are briefly charted. The evidence for a shift toward female rejection of sexual pleasure during the nineteenth century is considered and it is argued that this took place. Women's belated, even churlish, acceptance of birth control in the twentieth century is then described. This produces an account of changing sexuality in the nineteenth century which is incompatible with the account by Michel Foucault that has dominated the history of Victorian sexuality over the last three decades. Foucault rejected the 'repressive hypothesis', that is the claim that sex had been increasingly repressed since the seventeenth century, and put a counter-argument that the Victorian period incited sexuality, producing a multiplicity of sexual discourses and the privileging of sexuality as the core of identity. Little attention has been paid to the limits Foucault placed upon his subject matter:

It is quite possible that there was an expurgation—and a very vigorous one—of the authorised vocabulary... Without question, new rules of propriety screened out some words: there was a policing of statements. A control over annunciations as well: where and when it was not possible to talk about things became much more strictly defined; in which circumstances, among which speakers and within which social relationships... This almost certainly constituted a whole restrictive economy... At the level of discourses and their domains, however... practically the opposite phenomenon occurred ... an institutional incitement to speak about [sex] and to do so more and more.[1]

So Foucault was not making an argument about everyday speech. This was increasingly subject to a 'restrictive economy' in which talk of sex was repressed. His rejection of the 'repressive hypotheses' referred to a phenomenon that was occurring primarily, perhaps only, at the level of discourses produced by institutions and disciplines. English women were far less willing to speak of sex than English men; indeed they were heavily stigmatized for doing so, they also had a lesser degree of involvement with institutions and disciplines until the late nineteenth century, and thus they contributed little to such discourses. A focus on women's engagement with discourses on sexuality, and on what is known of women's experience of physical sexual activity, foregrounds the restrictive economy.

Foucault saw the subject's construction of self as resulting from the internalizing of the disciplinary gaze and the acceptance of the demands of society as her or his own needs. The lived experience of the body was, thus, the historical outcome of power/knowledge formations: the product of discourses. The residual category of a natural, untrammelled transhistorical body and its pleasures was posited by him as the site of resistance to power. But the sexual body of which Foucault speaks is a male body. It is evident that in the period studied coitus was assumed to be the aim of sexual desire and means to sexual pleasure by the vast majority of people. Conception and pregnancy take place within the female body. The risk/consequence of pregnancy exists prior to discursive power/knowledge formations, institutions, or the state. The female body cannot be only a source of resistance, it must also be a source of restrictions and regulation in the lives of women. Conception and pregnancy impose physical constraints upon the woman, as does use of contraception. She can resist these by rejecting the pregnancy or the child but there is no natural, untrammelled female sexual body to act as the site of resistance to power. Female sexual pleasure could not act as resistance to internalized discipline, rather, one way or another, discipline was necessary in order that pleasure could be experienced. To put this into

[1] M. Faucault, *The History of Sexuality* (*LaVolonte de Savoir*) (1978:1984), 17–8. n. 1

Foucauldian terms, in relation to sexuality, the female body was not an active, unrestrained body that had to be rendered docile by the internalizing of controls which had previously been imposed externally. To remain active women had first to resist their own bodies. This theoretical basis for the emergence of resistance to sexuality from within female discourse suggests a radically different account of sexuality in this period, one in which sexual repression does not come only from external forces imposing a social order, but also wells up from within and below.

THE DOUBLE STANDARD

Mid-century middle-class England saw the apogee of the double standard of sexual morality; male sexual access to women was a necessity but any slip from sexual purity on a woman's part cut her off from respectable society. Josephine Butler (1826–1906), who later became the leader of the campaign against the regulation of prostitution, lived in Oxford in the 1850s. She described hearing strong rumours that a don had seduced a 'very young girl', who then bore his child. But, she explained, when she expressed the hope that the don would be brought to a 'sense of his crime' to a man whom she believed to carry moral authority in the university, he advised her that a 'pure woman ... should be absolutely ignorant of a certain class of evils in the world'. For women 'silence was thought to be the greatest duty of all on such subjects', she wrote.[2] Around the same time Barbara Leigh Smith (1827–1891, later Bodichon) was writing a pamphlet summarizing the laws of England as they concerned women. She was advised to omit any mention of prostitution as 'no more than is absolutely necessary should be said upon subjects, which are considered as forbidden to women'.[3] These statements were quite clear. The subject of male sexuality was *forbidden* to women. It was women's *duty* as women to be silent. The dominant sexual culture in mid-Victorian Britain was shaped

[2] J. Butler, *Recollections of George Butler* (1892), 96.

[3] The advice came from Matthew Davenport Hill, who was a Liberal MP and reformer of the criminal law. He found the project amusing. Barbara was herself illegitimate and the double standard had shaped her life. P. Hirsch, *Barbara Leigh Smith Bodichon* (2001), 89–90.

by the acceptance of purchased sexual relief for men and respectable women were forbidden to discuss it. This is the foundation of Victorian sexual hypocrisy, and it is intimately tied into the emergence of feminism because that silence was imposed upon women for the benefit of men. This mid-century double standard was a radically different position from the stance taken by moral reformers in the early nineteenth century, and still adhered to by Dissenters and evangelical Anglicans as they had demanded that men also be moral.

In his recent history of Victorian sexuality, Michael Mason argues that too much has been made of sexual hypocrisy. He tells us that '[a]s a matter of plain fact, sexual hypocrisy in the lives of notable Victorians is rare . . . it is interesting that when sexual secrets have been disclosed they have often been revelations of non-performance, as . . . it may be in the extra-marital life of Dickens.'[4] The sexual secret was the existence of Charles Dickens's (1812–70) extramarital life, not his sexual performance. The hypocrisy lay in the immurement of Ellen Ternan (1839–1914), Dickens's mistress, in a suburban villa to serve his sexual and emotional needs, while he continued to benefit economically from his professions of belief in Victorian family values. Dicken's sexual performance once he got to the villa is of almost no significance whatsoever in relation to hypocrisy. Such a life could be imposed upon a woman like Ternan because her family's financial resources were so slender that she had little choice but to seize the opportunity Dickens offered and no means of supporting herself if she tired of her isolation.[5] As Butler wrote, it angered her that such men were able to 'go about smiling at dinner parties' while the women they privately consorted with were '*branded* openly'.[6]

It was in this social context that concern about sexuality began to be voiced publicly by middle-class and upper-middle-class women. The topic

[4] M. Mason, *The Making of Victorian Sexuality* (1995), 43. It is unclear how Mason defines sexual hypocrisy. The OED 2nd edn. definition of hypocrisy can be summarized as the 'assuming of a false appearance of virtue or goodness, with dissimulation of real character or inclinations'. Examples that meet this definition abound. The Victorians certainly used the word in a sexual context: 'Behold one of our [brothel] patrons . . . apparently participating in the delights of a chaste wife . . . He "does the agreeable" to admiration. The arch hypocrite!' J. Talbot, *The Miseries of Prostitution* (1844), 37.

[5] For Nell Ternan's relationship with Dickens, see C. Tomalin, *The Invisible Woman* (1990).

[6] Letter to Fanny Smyttan, 27 Feb. 1867, cited in J. Jordan, *Josephine Butler* (2001), 81.

of male conjugal rights formed the starting point for a new public discussion by women of female sexuality. Leigh Smith was discouraged from speaking of prostitution, but in the finished pamphlet on English law, she wrote that 'A woman's body belongs to her husband; she is in his custody, and he can enforce his right by a writ of *habeus corpus*.'[7] Historian James Hammerton has used evidence from cases heard under the new Divorce Act in 1857 and the Matrimonial Causes Act of 1875, which permitted the granting of separation orders in the magistrates' courts. In court, husbands and wives revealed that both parties accepted normative social attitudes and beliefs, such as a wife's duty of submission to her husband and an acceptance of male conjugal rights. The household was both a set of relationships and a physical terrain in which wives had a rightful place. A husband's acceptance of these boundaries gave his wife a degree of customary authority and control. But the cases reveal the vulnerability of wives where husbands were unwilling to abandon expectations of literal and unquestioning obedience and service.[8] Hammerton argues that the publicity divorce cases gave to women's resistance to male domination, including insistence on their conjugal rights, contributed to the development of feminism.

Nationally the issue that had most salience among women was probably venereal disease. The Contagious Diseases Acts provided for the compulsory medical examination for venereal disease of prostitutes working in specified military districts, and were passed in 1864, 1866, and 1869.[9] Initially these Acts provoked little public attention. However the campaign for the repeal of the Acts continued for seventeen years, and during this period the medical understanding of syphilis and gonorrhoea grew substantially. Both the support for the Acts and the campaign against them can be thought of as publicity that raised people's awareness of the dangers of venereal diseases and of the high rates of infection. Treatments for venereal diseases remained highly unpleasant, and were of uncertain efficacy until the early twentieth century when the drug Salvarsan was introduced. Syphilis had a low mortality rate but as late as 1924 the disease killed 60,335, a year when only 50,389 died of cancer and

[7] Hirsch, *Bodichon*, 90.
[8] A. J. Hammerton, *Cruelty and Companionship* (1992), 6–7, 112–13, 132.
[9] See J. Walkowitz, *Prostitution and Victorian Society: Women, Class and the State* (1980).

41,103 of tuberculosis.[10] The open insistence by male supporters of the Contegions Diseases Acts on men's need for sexual relief in spite of the risks to wives and children alienated many women. Elaine Showalter has pointed out that men saw women working as prostitutes as the source of contamination, while women believed the source of the disease to be men.[11] The churches and the social purity movement exploited fears about venereal disease to reinforce the existing negative Christian association between sexuality and sin. Thus the emerging discourse on sexuality was powerfully negative and gender specific. Much effort had also been put into raising standards of personal hygiene over the course of the nineteenth century, increasing perceptions of the genitals as dirty and potentially disgusting.[12] In this context of sin, dirt, and disease, a growing distrust and perception of physical sexual activity as repugnant was unsurprising.

In the last quarter of the nineteenth century, working-class women's literacy was rising fast and the education of middle-class women was starting to be taken seriously.[13] Female education has been consistently associated with increased female autonomy. In 1995, demographer Shireen Jejeebhoy reviewed contemporary research on female education and reproduction since the 1960s. She found that educating women has been found to have a substantial downward impact on their fertility in a wide range of developing countries. Her complex analysis has much to offer beyond this point. Education works indirectly, enhancing women's knowledge, decision-making power, and confidence in interacting with the outside world. Their emotional closeness to their husband and children, and their economic and social self-reliance, are also increased.

[10] E. T. Burke, 'The Toll of Secret Disease', *Nineteenth Century* (1927), cited in R. Davenport-Hines, *Sex, Death and Punishment* (1991), 246.

[11] E. Showalter, *Sexual Anarchy: Gender and Culture at the Fin de Siecle* (1991), 193–8. See also L. Bland, *Banishing the Beast: English Feminism and Sexual Morality, 1885–1914* (1995), ch. 1.

[12] There is little existing historiography. S. Sheard, 'Profit is a Dirty Word: The Development of Public Baths and Wash-Houses in Britain, 1847–1915', *Social History of Medicine*, 13/1 (2000). A. Wear, 'The History of Personal Hygiene', in R. Porter and W. F. Bynum (eds.), *Companion Encyclopedia of the History of Medicine* (1993). Cleanliness is mentioned regularly in 19th-century sources, see e.g. G. Gissing, *New Grub Street* (1891; 1968), 278–9. F. Place, *The Autobiography of Francis Place (1771–1854)*, ed. M. Thale (1972), 108, 225. H. Wilson, *Harriette Wilson's Memoirs*, ed. L. Blanch (1825; 1957), 112–13, 131.

[13] D. Vincent, *The Rise of Mass Literacy: Reading and Writing in Modern Europe* (2000), 60–1.

The impact of education differed according to the degree of gender stratification, that is, equality or lack of it, in a given society. In very unequal circumstances, relatively high levels of education may be necessary to make a difference to levels of fertility. In settings that are more egalitarian, less education is required.[14] There was considerable regional variation in gender and sexual cultures in England. Thus the increase in education is likely to have enabled women to act upon their desire for fertility control and protection from venereal diseases more effectively but the impact would have varied in different communities.[15]

During the last quarter of the century, employment opportunities for lower-middle-class women began to widen and middle- and upper-class women were being elected to positions at the municipal level and on boards. There was increasing agitation in support of legislative changes, such as the Married Woman's Property Acts, that would ensure women were less vulnerable to unreasonable husbands.[16] In 1867, the London-based National Society for Women's Suffrage was organized. Similar groups sprang up in Manchester, Edinburgh, Bristol, and Birmingham, creating a loose federation of suffrage societies. By the end of the century, the struggle for women's suffrage was becoming a mass movement with support from women in all regions and classes.[17] The emergence of the movement and rising literacy suggest that women were growing in confidence and assertiveness.

[14] S. Jejeebhoy, *Women's Education, Autonomy, and Reproductive Behaviour: Experience from Developing Countries* (1995), 37, 178.

[15] Regional cultures, e.g. Ellen Ross, *Love and Toil: Motherhood in Outcast London, 1870–1918* (1993), 59–65. B. Reay, 'Sexuality in Nineteenth-Century England: The Social Context of Illegitimacy in Rural Kent', *Rural History*, 1/2 (1990). D. Gittins, 'Marital Status, Work and Kinship, 1850–1930', in J. Lewis (ed.), *Labour and Love: women's Experience of Home and Family 1850–1940* (1986).

[16] See M. L. Shanley, *Feminism, Marriage and the Law in Victorian England, 1850–1895* (1989).

[17] L. Leneman, 'A Truly National Movement: the view from Outside London', in M. Joannou and J. Purvis (eds.), *The Women's Suffrage Movement: New Feminist Perspectives* (2000). Jill Liddington and Jill Norris, *One Hand Tied Behind Us: The Rise of the Women's Suffrage Movement* (1978: 1994). An indication of the magnitude of movement by the early 20th century is given by the large-scale marches and the ability to sustain nationwide campaigns such as the arson attacks, see A. Rosen, *Rise up Women! The Militant Campaign of the Women's Social and Political Union 1903–1914* (1974). C. Jorgensen-Earp. '*The Transfiguring Sword': The Just War of the Women's Social and Political Union* (1997).

WOMEN AND SEXUALITY

There is limited evidence about women's physical sexual experience in the nineteenth century but what is available is consistent with the trajectory suggested by fertility rates. It is probable that a substantial alteration in women's experience of genital sexuality, and in their attitudes, was taking place in the second half of the nineteenth century. Early to mid-century accounts suggest that many women had passionate physical sexual desires and felt able to express these. Middle-class Effie Gray's (b. 1817) marriage in 1848 to the art critic John Ruskin (1819–1900) was, notoriously, annulled after six years because of his refusal to consummate it. It appears that Effie fully undressed on the first night of her marriage, that Ruskin held her in his arms, and that she allowed him to look at her body, probably including her genitals, in the light. Her letter to her parents entreating their help suggests that she questioned him at length about his reasons. Such readiness to speak of sexuality and her anger about his disgust at 'her person' suggests a confidence about her own sexuality, which is reinforced by the erotic success of her second marriage.[18] Erotic confidence comes through clearly in the letters, and/or descriptions, of Sarah Austin (1793–1867), Sarah Walker (b. approx. 1800), Fanny Kingsley (1814–91), and other women in the first half of the nineteenth century.[19] Even with no experience of physical sexuality other than that with her prudish and self-absorbed husband John Austin, Sarah Austin was aware of her body's potential for pleasure and deeply desired further sexual experience.

Effie's initial acceptance of Ruskin's behaviour suggests she was speaking the truth when she wrote that, before marriage, 'I had never been told the duties of married persons to each other and knew little or nothing about their relations in the closest union on earth.'[20] Fanny Kingsley had been similarly ignorant of what sexual intercourse entailed before her marriage but this did not prevent her from enjoying physical sexual desire.[21] By the last quarter of the century such ignorance of physical

---

[18] M. Lutyens, *The Ruskins and the Grays* (1972), 108–9, 184–5, 234, 284.

[19] L. and J. Hamburger, *Contemplating Adultery* (1992), 117–18; see also 119, 127. S. Chitty, *The Beast and the Monk* (1974). H. M. Sikes (ed.), *The Letters of William Hazlitt* (1978). See also J. Tosh, *A Man's Place: Masculinity and the Middle Class Home in Victorian England* (1999), 58–9.

[20] M. Lutyens, *Millais and the Ruskins* (1967), 155.   [21] Chitty, *Beast*, 74.

sexuality and reproductive processes was said to be frequently devastating for young women, and a rising chorus of blame was directed toward mothers of all classes who, it was claimed, had failed to teach their daughters about sexuality.[22] It seems probable that mothers' responsibility for educating daughters about physical sexual acts was a new requirement. Previously girls of all classes had probably obtained this information gradually in the course of observation, premarital sexual exploration as described in the previous chapter, and conversations with other women such as married cousins and elder sisters.[23] By the late nineteenth century, these avenues of information were increasingly strictly proscribed for young women in all classes and increasing numbers of young men.

The possibility for adolescent observation of adult sexual affection and reproductive processes diminished during this period as adults restricted their own behaviour. Historian M. J. Peterson has described the mid-century marriage of Lydia North (1815–95) and James Paget. This upper-middle-class couple appear to have had a mutually pleasurable physical relationship, but James wrote to Lydia that the 'extreme and ardour of affection when openly exhibited is as displeasing to me as, when privately shown, it is delightful'.[24] This retreat from easy acceptance of open physical affection as well as of physical sexuality appears to have taken place in many early and mid-Victorian households, and minimal physical demonstrativeness appears to have become increasingly usual in middle-class families.[25] When parents reject the open expression of sexual affection then children

---

[22] Mothers, e.g. M. Llewellyn Davies, *Maternity: Letters from Working Women Collected by the Women's Co-operative Guild* (1915; 1978), 44, 48, 50, 58, 64. Bland, *Banishing*, 139–43. P. Keating, *The Haunted Study: A Social History of the English Novel, 1875–1914* (1989), 188–9. Gittins, *Fair Sex*, 79–90. Ross, *Love*, 107. M. Stephens, *Women and Marriage: A Handbook* (1910; 1918), 40–1. L. Tait, *Diseases of Women and Abdominal Surgery*, vol. i (1889), 51–5.

[23] For sexual learning, see Chs. 7, 8.

[24] M. J. Peterson, 'No Angels in the House: The Victorian Myth and the Paget Women', *American Historical Review*, 89 (1984), 701.

[25] For comment on the emotional tone of the late 19th century, see P. T. Cominos, 'Late-Victorian Respectability and the Social System', *International Review of Social History*, 8/1–2 (1963). B. Caine, *Destined to be Wives: The Sisters of Beatrice Webb* (1985). 93, 127–8. R. Keynes, *Annie's Box: Charles Darwin, his Daughter and Human Evolution* (2001; 2002), 83, 216–17. G. Raverat. *Period Piece: A Cambridge Childhood* (1952), 110, 113. Davenport-Hines, *Sex*, 70–2, 124. His perceptive comments on male homosexuality and the denial of emotion in that context after 1885 are also relevant, e.g. Brian Masters, *The Life of E. F. Benson* (1991; 1993), 209, 245–6.

lose the opportunity to learn how this is expressed. There is a notion that women who live in a society that condemns female sexual passion are nonetheless able to express their sexuality fully in private, but this is difficult to accept when careful attention is paid to generational change.[26] Rather, it appears that the impact of changes in behaviour and attitudes related to sexual expression on succeeding generations grew over these decades.

Ruskin's behaviour calls for comment. Mary Lutyens argued convincingly that the reason for the non-consummation and breakdown of the marriage was due to Ruskin's horror of babies and his dishonesty in concealing his determination to avoid them from Effie before the marriage.[27] This horror would easily produce the disgust he evinced toward female genitals (not merely pubic hair) in a period when coitus could not proceed without risk of conception. He also felt intense anxiety about his masturbation. Ruskin was the only child of upwardly mobile, rigid, and disciplined parents. He belonged to one of the occupational categories, authors, editors, journalists, that Joseph Banks identified as pioneers of the small family in the 1850s, as did Thomas Carlyle and John Stuart Mill, also known to have had low levels of physical sexual interest.[28] But Banks's range of categories suggests that varied strategies were being employed to lower family size. For example, officers of the navy and marines and army officers were certainly not embracing new sexual inhibitions.[29] Venereal diseases in the army and navy reached record heights in the third quarter of the century. There was no norm of male sexuality in nineteenth-century England just as there was no norm of family size; rather, several male sexual cultures existed, shaped by factors such as religion, income, region, degree of urbanization, and homosocial environment as well as personal temperament and ambition.[30]

---

[26] See Ch. 7.

[27] Lutyens, *Ruskins*, 108–9.

[28] Also see D. Hudson, *Munby Man of Two Worlds: The Life and Diaries of Arthur J. Munby, 1828– 1910* (1972); for Thomas Carlyle, John Stuart Mill, see P. Rose, *Parallel lives* (1983; 1994), 64, 125–6.

[29] The other occupations were painters, sculptors, artists; civil, mining engineers; accountants, physicians, and solicitors; ministers of other than the Established Church. J. A. Banks, *Victorian Values: Secularism and the Size of Families* (1981), 40.

[30] M. Anderson, 'The Emergence of the Modern Life Cycle in Britain', *Social History*, 10 (1985), 80.

Newly married women's increasing lack of sexual knowledge and experience when compared to that of their husbands arises as a problem in the last third of the century. Daniel Minertzhagen (1842–1910) had extensive sexual experience while Georgina Potter (1850–1914) had none when the couple married in 1873. Their son wrote that 'Mother in her puritan chastity could not respond to father's exuberance.'[31] Daniel lacked the sensitivity and interest necessary for the creation of a mutual sexual relationship. As the marriage continued he spent as much time as possible away from home and did nothing to support Georgina during her frequent pregnancies. Edwin Lutyens (1869–1944) came to his marriage in 1897 'pure' although he was without the strong religious convictions that had previously been associated with such attitudes. Unlike John Austin (1790–1859) nearly a century earlier, he was also socially adept and skilled at pleasing others, yet Emily, his wife, later told her daughter that her honeymoon was 'a nightmare of physical pain and mental disappointment'. It appears Edwin lacked previous sexual experience, and had intercourse rapidly without any sensitivity to Emily's feelings, making the experience 'increasingly disagreeable to her', and one she came to find 'disgusting'.[32] Emily was probably hampered in any effort to alter his behaviour because both she and Edwin would have found it unacceptable for her to make sexual demands. In the absence of premarital sexual petting she would, in any event, have had little opportunity to learn how her needs might be met physically or emotionally. It is evident that other women did learn to enjoy coitus after marriage, but for many 'a sense of sin or degradation ... accompan[ied] the sexual act' and where this was so the woman's participation might be limited. Rosie Williams, who was physically repelled by a prospective second husband was told by her elder sister that 'One man is as good as another in that respect'.[33]

During the nineteenth century upper-middle-class sexual culture shifted substantially. In the early decades women and men were often aware of the possibility of physical passion and subdued their sexual desires with difficulty. By the middle decades of the century, there was a thriving culture of sexual commerce available, which many middle-class men took advantage of, but respectable women were expected to control their

---

[31] Caine, *Destined*, 95–6, *passim*.   [32] M. Lutyens, *Edwin Lutyens* (1980), 56, 76.
[33] Caine, *Destined*, 103.

sexual feelings.[34] By the later decades of the nineteenth century, there appears to have been considerable female and some male ignorance of physical sexual activity along with diminishing mutual sexual pleasure. Middle- and upper-working-class 'new women' were struggling with new ideas about sexuality from the 1890s, but few appear to have had much actual sexual experience.[35] Those women who did tentatively express positive support for female sexual expression in public insisted this was only possible in the context of continence and self-control.[36] The costs of defying sexual conventions were often high for those bohemians and radical socialists who attempted to live differently.[37]

Among the working classes illegitimacy and premarital conception rates reveal that premarital sexual intercourse between couples who had agreed to marry continued to be usual well into the nineteenth century.[38] From the 1840s, illegitimacy fell steadily, hitting a low point in 1901 when the ratio of illegitimate births to all live births reached 38.9 (Fig. 4.1). The twentieth-century trends make it evident that this reflects changing levels of sexual activity outside marriage. The ratio rose from 1900 in spite of improving contraception, and actually doubled between 1955 and 1980, during which period contraception became widely available to single women for the first time.[39] There are two sharp peaks, of 62.6 in 1918

[34] See Ch. 3.

[35] T. Thompson (ed.), *Dear Girl: The Diaries and Letters of Two Working Women 1897–1917* (1987), 80, 138–9, 154, 195.

[36] F. Mort, *Dangerous Sexualities: Medico-Moral Politics in England since 1830* (1987), 111–16. Bland, *Banishing*, ch. 7.

[37] e.g. Eleanor Marx's suicide on 31 Mar. 1898 followed repeated betrayals by her lover Edward Aveling. R. Brandon, *The New Women and the Old Men* (1990), 139–59. Ida Nettleship (1877–1907), who in 1901 married the painter Augustus John (1878–1961), invited his (first) mistress Dorelia McNeill (b. 1881) to share their home. Ida rapidly had four sons and was unable to continue with her own painting. In spite of her fondness for Dorelia she became deeply depressed. Dorelia's qualities enabled her to prosper. She had no personal ambitions other than to be an artist's muse, she did not demand fidelity from her lovers or herself, and she had little concern about personal comforts; e.g. giving birth to her first child alone in an isolated caravan did not disturb her. M. Holroyd, *Augustus John* (1974), 191–200, 244, 251.

[38] Garret et al., *Changing Family Size*, 281.

[39] The connection between illegitimacy and sexual mores was rejected by E. Shorter, J. Knodel, and E. van de Walle, 'The Decline of Non-Marital Fertility in Europe', *Population Studies*, 25 (1971), 376. For a more recent discussion, see R. Adair, *Courtship, Illegitimacy and Marriage in Early Modern England* (1996).

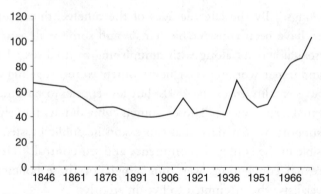

Fig. 4.1 Illegitimate live births per 1,000 total live births

Note: The arrows indicate the years when legislation expanding contraceptive provision took effect.

Source: Birth Statistics: Historical Series of Statistics from Registrations of Births in England and Wales, 1837–1983 OPCS Series FM1 no. 13. T. 1.1, 19.

and 93.3 in 1945, which clearly occur as a result of the First and Second World Wars. Male access to condoms increased during the wars but this seems to have had little impact.[40] During the war men were less likely to be present when women discovered their pregnancies and failure to marry is revealed by the relationship between the rise in the number of illegitimate births during the Second World War and the fall in pre-nuptial pregnancies.[41] If we put the two world wars to one side, then from 1875 until the 1950s the ratio stays below 50 (Table 4.1). From the inter-war period, some illegitimate pregnancies would have been prevented by use of contraception. However, the high numbers of pre-nuptial pregnancies reveal that the unmarried had difficulty obtaining such information and therefore the trends continue to reflect sexual mores. This period of sexual restraint is both consistent with and reinforces the other evidence about sexual behaviour.

There is little direct evidence of working-class women's physical sexual experiences but it is probable that many engaged in genital sexual petting

[40] C. Chinn, *They Worked All their Lives: Women of the Urban Poor in England, 1880–1939* (1988), 143. J. Peel, 'The Manufacture and Retailing of Contraceptives in England', *Population Studies*, 17 (1963), n. 60, 162.

[41] *Birth Statistics: Historical Series of Statistics from Registrations of Births in England and Wales, 1837–1983*, OPCS Series FM1 no. 13 (1983), tables 1.1, 5.5.

Table 4.1. *Illegitimate live births per 1,000 total live births*

Period	Ratio
1846–50	67.1
1851–5	65.9
1856–60	64.9
1861–5	63.6
1866–70	58.4
1871–5	52.1
1876–80	47.5
1881–5	48.0
1886–1890	46.3
1891–5	42.4
1896–1900	41.0
1901–5	39.5
1906–10	40.2
1911–15	43.1
1916–20	53.9
1921–5	42.7
1926–30	44.6
1931–5	43.5
1936–40	42.0
1941–5	68.7
1946–50	54.9
1951–5	47.5
1956–60	50.1
1961–5	69.0
1966–70	82.9
1971–5	86.8
1976–80	104.6

Source: Birth Statistics: Historical Series of Statistics from Registrations of Births in England and Wales, 1837–1983, OPCS Series FM1 no. 13 (1983).

with more than one partner before settling down. William Hazlitt's (1778–1830) bitter tirade against Sarah Walker (b. *c*.1800), the daughter of an artisan and a lodging house keeper, provides a unique account of a young woman experimenting with physical sexual pleasure. Walker enjoyed sexual activity, choosing from among the limited pool of male lodgers in her mother's house those to whom she was attracted. Hazlitt writes of her 'sitting in my lap, twining herself around me, [letting me enjoy her through her petticoats] looking as if she would faint with tenderness and modesty, admitting all sorts of indecent liberties'. She sat in his lap 'rubbing against' him, 'hard at it' for an hour at a time. Marriage with Hazlitt did not interest her; 'Why could we not go on as we were', she told him, 'and never mind about the word, *forever*?' He associates female physical desire with whoring, as is usual in nineteenth-century sources, but Sarah refused to be bought. Though he bribed her mother by paying the huge sum of £100 in advance for his lodgings, she returned his books and would not marry him.[42]

A minimum of around two-thirds of working-class women were engaged in small businesses or other paid employment.[43] There was less emphasis on self-control and discipline among the upper working classes and lower middle classes and many of these women had greater economic autonomy than did upper-middle-class women. Their sexual mores appear to have been relatively fluid. Where backgrounds are given for the small number of women who made successful careers associated with non-marital sexual activity, including prostitution, artist's models, mistresses, and actresses, they frequently came from the upper working classes.[44] Research by Ginger Frost into breach of promise cases between 1870 and 1900 reveals that most of the plaintiffs were respectable small businesswomen and either upper working class or lower middle class. Sexual intercourse was reported to have taken place in 25 per cent of the cases, including some women who had been cohabiting for long periods. Some men were willing to make false promises of marriage as 'all men do', but it is perhaps more important that if circumstances changed even men

[42] The square brackets are missing words added by the editor of the letters. Sikes (ed.), *Letters*, 63–72, 81–2, 263–4, 300–1.

[43] M. Anderson, 'The Social Position of Spinsters in Mid-Victorian Britain', *Journal of Family History* (Winter 1984), table 2, 380, source 1851 census.

[44] e.g. F. Barret-Ducrocq, *Love in the Time of Victoria* (1992), 51–5, 72–3. H. E. Blyth, *Skittles: The Last Victorian Courtesan: The Life and Times of Catherine Walters* (1970). T. C. Davis, *Actresses as Working Women: Their Social Identity in Victorian Culture* (1991), 72–3. B. Hemyng, 'Prostitution', in H. Mayhew (ed.), *London Labour and the London Poor* (1862), 216–17, 243, 255; 147. Hudson, *Munby*, 40–1. Wilson, *Memoirs*. This continued to be true into the 20th century; e.g. Dorelia McNeill's father was a mercantile clerk. Holroyd, *John*.

who had sincerely intended to marry felt able to change their minds.[45] The cases reveal that these women often desired sexual activity but they were anxious and aware of their vulnerability once intercourse had taken place. In these cases, the consequences of the breakdown of community control over young men described in the previous chapter can be observed. The falling illegitimacy rates are evidence of women's increasing sexual caution and diminishing opportunity for relaxed premarital sexual activity with a variety of partners, which would in turn have contributed to diminishing physical sexual pleasure.

Nonetheless, working-class women still had more opportunity to experience physical sexual activity before they began having children than did middle-class women. But given their poor nutritional status and living conditions it is probable that once they had children the impact of high fertility on working-class women's sexuality was even greater.[46] Two mid-twentieth-century studies of English women living in poverty with limited access to contraception found that their pleasure in sexual intercourse rapidly diminished with successive pregnancies.[47] In some regions working-class couples had already begun to lower their fertility by ceasing childbearing earlier in women's lives. This is achieved by couples having sexual intercourse less often later in marriage (or other long-term relationship).[48] This behaviour may not be parity specific, that is, dependent on the number of children already born (desired family size), as demographers have argued, but rather dependent on a woman's health and levels of fatigue, her willingness to continue sexual relations, and the degree of control she could exercise over her partner. From the 1870s, the slowing down of a half-century of rapid urbanization led to the establishment of more settled urban working-class communities enabling women (and parents) to establish networks of support and surveillance.[49] Respectability was

---

[45] G. Frost, *Promises Broken: Courtship, Class, and Gender in Victorian England* (1995), 11, 104–5, 114.

[46] For childbearing, see Llewellyn Davies, *Maternity*.

[47] M. Kerr, *The People of Ship Street* (1958), quoted in J. Klein, *Samples of English Culture*, vol. i (1965), 72. P. Shapiro, 'The Unplanned Children', *New Society* (1962).

[48] B. Reay, 'Before the Transition: Fertility in English Villages, 1800–1880', *Continuity and Change*, 9 (1994), 103, 108, 110.

[49] G. Stedman Jones, *Languages of Class: Studies in English Working Class History, 1832–1982* (1983), 27. M. Tebbutt, *Women's Talk? A Social History of Gossip in Working-Class Neighbourhoods, 1880–1960* (1995), 77–9. J. R. Walkowitz, 'Male Vice and Female Virtue', in A. Snitow, C. Stansell, and S. Thompson (eds.), *Powers of Desire: The Politics of Sexuality* (1983), 46.

increasingly central to working-class women's identity. Openly expressed enthusiasm for sexual pleasure, especially if it resulted in several affairs or was expressed by single women, became deviant and stigmatized behaviour. As with all such behaviour this does not mean that it did not take place but that the incidence was diminished because it was shameful and had to be hidden. Sexually active young women, such as Sarah Walker, still existed but the majority of women around them rejected such behaviour.

Nineteenth-century scholars now support a revisionist view of female sexuality, rejecting the construction of Victorian women as excessively prudish or anxious regarding sexuality. However, the evidence suggests that the error lay in placing the peak of these attitudes in the early or mid-nineteenth century and the presentation of them as monolithic and uncontested. By the late nineteenth and early twentieth centuries there is a wealth of evidence regarding a wide range of women, which reveals that the trajectory from the mid- to late nineteenth century was in the direction of increasing anxiety and diminishing sexual pleasure. This includes evidence relating to birth control use and sexuality, as well as autobiographies, and the testimony collected by oral historians.[50] Caveats include the probability that those women who did enjoy sexual intercourse were not willing to admit to such pleasure when interviewed by comparative strangers, but nonetheless, the responses obtained have been remarkably consistent, with only occasional hints of pleasure. The other potential source of bias toward a more negative view of female sexuality is quite simply the limited volume of sources available for the earlier period, including the over-representation of Nonconformists, who had stricter sexual mores than was then usual. However, the trends suggested by these sources are supported by the birth rates.

[50] Chinn, *They Worked*, 142–3. K. Fisher, ' "She was Quite Satisfied with the Arrangements I Made": Gender and Birth Control in Britain 1920–1950', *Past and Present* 169 (2001), 177. N. Higgins, 'Marriage in Mid 20th century North England' (D.Phil. thesis, 2003), 175–88. E. Roberts, *A Woman's Place: An Oral History of Working-Class Women, 1890–1940* (1984). Ross, *Love*, 162. W. Seccombe, 'Starting to Stop: Working-Class Fertility Decline in Britain', *Past and Present*, 126 (1990), 175–7. P. Townsend, *The Family Life of Old People: An Inquiry in East London* (1957), 75. M. Woodside, 'Orgasm Capacity Among 200 English Working-Class Wives', in A. Ellis and A. P. Pillay (eds.), *Sex, Society and the Individual* (1953), 105. More obliquely, P. Thompson, *The Edwardians: The Remaking of British Society* (1975; 1977), 75–80. Mixed experiences, see S. Rowbotham and J. McCrindle, *Dutiful Daughters: Women Talk about their Lives* (1977), 36–41.

If sexual pleasure is placed on a continuum, then in all classes there was a shift toward a higher proportion of women who did not enjoy physical sexual activity, while a smaller proportion than had previously done so did enjoy physical sexual activity. The percentage of women whose sexual behaviour and feelings were radically different from previous generations was substantial. No estimate can be made of the proportion of women who accepted their duty or whose husbands simply ignored their lack of sexual desire. However, a high and rising proportion of women remained unmarried.[51] Among couples who married from 1890 to 1899 more than a quarter (26.5 per cent) of all professional couples had only one or no children. Of manual couples in this cohort, 15 per cent had one or none.[52] It was not until the very late nineteenth century that any sizeable proportion even amongst the middle classes began using birth control methods. Therefore, so drastic a reduction in family size can only have been achieved by partial abstinence from sexual intercourse. Simon Szreter has explained that until recently it was thought that almost complete abstinence was required to prevent conception. However, he writes, it is now understood that 'even if attempted abstinence meant no more than that couples were restricting themselves to intercourse once every week, a definite spacing effect of about eight months would accrue'.[53] That means that a woman would on average take nearly a year to get pregnant. This is much longer than the average three to four months it takes to her to get pregnant if she is having the fifteen to twenty acts of intercourse that give her the maximum chance of getting pregnant in each menstrual cycle. It was not then known when ovulation occurred so it was not possible to plan intercourse to coincide with ovulation, and the figures are based on the result achieved when intercourse is spread over the month at random.

---

[51] Anderson, 'Social Position', table 1, 379, source 1851 census. *Marriage and Divorce Statistics: Historical Series of Statistics on Marriages and Divorces in England and Wales, 1837–1983*, FM2 no.16 (1990), table 1.1(b).

[52] M. Anderson, 'Highly Restricted Fertility: Very Small Families in the British Fertility Decline', *Population Studies*, 52 (1998), table 2, 181.

[53] S. Szreter, *Fertility, Class and Gender in Britain, 1860–1940* (1996), 395, citing J. Bongaarts, 'The Proximate Determinants of Natural Marital Fertility', in R. A. Bulatao and R. D. Lee (eds.), *Determinants of Fertility in Developing Countries* (1983), 116, table 4.

The importance of abstinence becomes clearer when the whole period of decline from the 1860s to the 1930s is analysed, as reported levels of birth control use cannot account for the fertility decline to the levels of the late 1920s and 1930s. In 1983, Douglas Sloan pointed out that to 'explain such a decline by contraception alone, social demographers must assume that nearly every Western couple was ... practising near perfect contraception throughout the second half of the female reproductive life span ... Yet, some 40 to 60 per cent of British and American couples who were then reproducing have denied any birth-control practice.'[54] Sloan criticized the reliance of demographers upon an untested common-sense belief that survey respondents were concealing use of birth control in order to explain this discrepancy. There is evidence of concealment of other sexual behaviours in a later survey, *Family Formation 1976* (1979) by Karen Dunnell. For this survey a random sample of 6,500 women between the ages of 16 and 49 was interviewed. This provided an opportunity to compare actual rates of two stigmatized behaviours, abortion and premaritally conceived births, with the rates reported by the survey respondents. Dunnell reports that:

Validation of pregnancy rates showed that pre-marital births and all abortions since the 1968 Act came into practice [i.e. since it was possible to compare the figures], were under reported by about 50%. Pre-maritally conceived live births occurring in the first seven months of first marriage appeared to be mis-reported rather than not reported at all, since by three years marriage duration the proportions of women having had a child compared very closely with registration data.[55]

These activities may still have been more highly stigmatized than the use of birth control had been more than half a century earlier; nonetheless this proven level of concealment reinforces the belief that birth control use was under-reported in the earlier surveys. Yet, even allowing this, the low effectiveness of the inter-war period methods (see Ch. 5) makes it unlikely couples could have reduced the birth rate to 1.72 in 1933, a rate only achieved again in 1976 when nearly 80 per cent of couples were using

[54] D. G. Sloan, 'The Extent of Contraceptive Use and the Social Paradigm of Modern Demography', *Sociology*, 17/3 (1983), 380, 383–4.

[55] K. Dunnell, *Family Formation 1976* (1979), 13.

effective modern methods.[56] Sloan also argued that the post-Second World War birth control surveys asked questions that would have excluded attempted abstinence and intended low coital frequencies.

The possibility of abstinence or sexual continence as a factor in fertility decline has been mentioned by historical demographers since the 1950s.[57] In the American context, Paul Davis and Warren Sanderson, in part using the well-known Clelia Mosher survey as evidence, have argued that the effectiveness of methods available for preventing pregnancy in the late nineteenth century was greatly enhanced because couples decreased their frequency of intercourse.[58] Using non-quantitative sources Seccombe argued in 1990 that in England abstinence from sexual intercourse among the working class was not uncommon and would have provided a method of bringing down the birth rate from the 1870s.[59] Simon Szreter undertook a re-analysis of the 1911 'fertility census' data by varied occupational groups, the small number of surveys produced in first decades of the twentieth century, the published collections of letters to Marie Stopes, the historiography of Victorian self-control, and middle-class feminism. He concluded that Sloan is correct, and that between the 1870s and the First World War 'attempted abstinence within marriage was the single most widespread and frequently used method of birth control'.[60] Szreter argues that men and women accepted the deferment of marriage, which

[56] M. Bone, 'Trends in Contraceptive Practice among Married Couples', *Health Trends*, 12 (1980), table 1, 87. Estimate 79% in Dunnell, *Family Formation*. Derived from table 8.3, 43. Fifty-three per cent of currently married women were using sterilization, IUDs, and the pill, all extremely effective methods, 22% were using the sheath, and only 8% were still using withdrawal.

[57] e.g. D. Kingsley and J. Blake, 'Social Structure and Fertility: An Analytic Framework', *Economic Development and Cultural Change*, 4 (1956), 219–20.

[58] P. A. David and W. C. Sanderson, 'Rudimentary Contraceptive Methods and the American Transition to Marital Fertility Control, 1855–1915', in S. L. Engerman and R. E. Gallman (eds.), *Long Term Factors in America's Economic Growth* (1986), 346–7. Dr Mosher's late 19th-century survey of American women's sexual experience is often cited as evidence that sexual repression has been exaggerated but it took her twenty-eight years to obtain replies from only forty-five women, almost all of whom were married to professional men and experienced limited sexual pleasure. C. Mosher, *The Mosher Survey: Sexual Attitudes of 45 Victorian Women* (1980). Also see C. N. Degler, 'What Ought to be and What Was: Women's Sexuality in the Nineteenth Century', *American Historical Review*, 79 (1974).

[59] Seccombe, 'Starting', 154, 159–61.

[60] Szreter, *Fertility*, 399.

he sees as a form of abstinence, until it was considered financially sensible, and then, having married late, opted for partial, or even complete, abstinence from coitus to control their fertility. The research undertaken for this book into sex manuals, sex research, community studies, and later surveys reinforces this conclusion. The sex manual authors are listed in Appendix B and a brief analysis of the genre given in Appendix A. The contents are discussed in Part II of this book. Here it is sufficient to say that in the early sex and birth control manuals abstaining from sexual activity is assumed to be a widely recommended approach to controlling births, and one that the authors believed their readers might well be using.[61]

American historians Linda Gordon and Ellen Dubois have argued that female sexual pleasure is a sign of resistance to sexual repression.[62] If this was so then it is remarkable that in England the decades of women's growing rejection of physical, especially genital, sexuality also saw the emergence of feminism as a mass movement of women. In fact, the nineteenth-century English legacy *is* one of resistance to sexual repression, but that resistance lay in the rejection, not the acceptance, of sexual pleasure. Married women had to endure the rigours of high fertility rates and exposure to venereal diseases while it was unacceptable for them to express sexual desires or to reject their husband's unwanted sexual

[61] e.g. G. Beale, *Wise Wedlock* (1922; 1926), 121–2. M. Fielding, *Parenthood: Design or Accident? A Manual of Birth Control* (1928), 27–30, 24. A. H. Gray, *Men, Women and God* (1923; 1947), 112,143, 148. N. Haire, *Birth-Control Methods (Contraception, Abortion, Sterilisation)* (1936; 1937), 52–5. A. Havil, *The Technique of Sex: Towards a Better Understanding of Sexual Relationship* (1939; 1959), 58. I. E. Hutton, *The Hygiene of Marriage* (1923), 102–3. M. Stopes, *Wise Parenthood*, 3rd edn. 1919 (1918; 1919), 6, 13. M. Stopes, *Contraception: Theory, History and Practice* (1923; 1925), 90. In the 1930s, some writers are confidently dismissing such suggestions: E. F. Griffith, *Modern Marriage and Birth Control* (1935), 75. In 1934, Scott referred to 'the passing of anaesthesia, deliberately cultivated as a contraceptive measure' after menopause. G. R. Scott, *The New Art of Love* (1934; 1955), 89. G. R. Scott, *Modern Birth Control Methods* (1933; 1947), 18, 61. P. Embey, *Women's Change of Life* (1955), 58. Some Anglican religious writers still argued as if a choice existed between contraception and abstinence in the post-Second World War period. C. Cuthbert and H. C. Warner, *Moral Problems* (1952), 54.

[62] L. Gordon and E. DuBois, 'Seeking Ecstasy on the Battlefield: Danger and Pleasure in Nineteenth Century Feminist Sexual Thought', in Feminist Review (ed.), *Sexuality: A Reader* (1987), 87–8. It is the authors' argument I am responding to rather than their evidence, which is from North America.

demands. Their acceptance of an ideology of wifely submission, and the increased economic powerlessness and diminishing autonomy of women during the mid-century decades, gave most wives few means of resistance to their husband's sexual demands other than minimizing their participation in sexual activity, which carried high risks and offered them little reward.

Robert Roberts commented about working-class Salford in the first decades of the twentieth century that:

During serious sex talk in workshop and factory what one heard most was exasperated complaint about wives so prudish, 'virtuous' or uninterested in bed that copulation lost much of its fascination . . . [One wife] swathed in clothes, permitted her husband only the act *per se* and, on her mother's advice, allowed no 'dirty' manual contact whatever. 'It's about as exciting', he said, 'as posting a letter!'[63]

Women such as these were not being passive; they were resisting male conjugal rights in the only way available to them. This interpretation appears to contradict blatantly the repeated assertion made by working-class women from the late 1890s to the 1960s that they did accept conjugal rights. But the point is that this is *all* the majority of women appear to have accepted by the late nineteenth century. Carl Chinn found that among working-class matriarchs in Manchester 'sex for enjoyment was looked on as a function peculiar to men; it was not in the sphere of matters in which wives were involved and so even very independent wives would have found it strange to withhold their consent, even though they found little pleasure in the act themselves.'[64] Mutual pleasure and tenderness was absent from these women's construction of marital sexuality. They had disengaged from mutual sexual activity; what they accepted was a duty. This did not leave women wholly without agency. One woman wrote that after her sixth pregnancy 'I went on

---

[63]   R. Roberts, *The Classic Slum: Salford Life in the First Quarter of the Century* (1971; 1973), 55–6.

[64]   Chinn, *They Worked*, 142, 148. See also E. Chesser, *Sexual Behaviour: Normal and Abnormal* (1949), 182. E. Chesser, *The Sexual, Marital and Family Relationships of the English Woman* (1956), 440. G. Gorer, *Exploring English Character* (1955), 133. Llewellyn Davies, *Maternity*, 67. S. Meacham, *A life Apart: The English Working Class 1890–1914* (1977), 66. E. Rathbone, *The Disinherited Family* (1924), ed. S. Fleming (1986), 197–9. Roberts, *Classic Slum*, 56. E. Slater and M. Woodside, *Patterns of Marriage* (1951), 167–9.

strike.'[65] A variety of strategies for avoiding intercourse consistent with sexual passivity are also described. These included staying up late at night working, sharing beds with children, complaining of pains, or, as Seccombe has pointed out, enlisting the doctor's support.[66] The frequency of intercourse will fall to some extent when women do not enjoy sex because, at the very least, they will not initiate sexual activity. An unknown, but possibly high, proportion of men gain less pleasure from sex with women who do not enjoy the experience, so their own motivation to engage in intercourse is diminished and they will initiate sex less often in such circumstances. Such domestic acts of resistance to male dominance were not 'political' but the female unhappiness and alienation they reveal contributed to, underpinned, and was in turn reinforced by the growing female political consciousness.

WOMEN'S ATTITUDES TO BIRTH CONTROL FROM THE LATE NINETEENTH TO THE MID-TWENTIETH CENTURY

Examination of levels of birth control use in detail during the first two-thirds of the twentieth century reinforces the claim that women provided the major impetus behind the decline in fertility. The earliest survey evidence showed that the reported use of birth control did not begin to rise sharply until 1910. Only 15 per cent of women married before 1910 reported that they had ever used birth control in the course of their married lives. But around 80 per cent of those married in the 1940s did so (Table 4.2). In all classes the reported use of birth control began with withdrawal, and then gradually shifted to condoms, caps, and spermicides (Table 4.3(a), Table 4.3(b)). The proportion of men using withdrawal declined over the period, but an increasing proportion of the population

---

[65] Llewellyn Davies, *Maternity*, 50.

[66] The following suggests that other wives did refuse directly: 'several wives said with pride "I've never refused him."' Woodside, 'Orgasm Capacity', 105. Gorer, *English Character*, 132–3. Rowbotham and McCrindle, *Dutiful Daughters*, 42. Seccombe, 'Starting', 179.

Table 4.2. *The percentage of the population reporting they had ever used birth control, by marriage cohort, in various surveys*

Surveys	Year of first marriage							
	Before 1910	1911–20	1921–5	1931–5	1941–5	1951–5	1961–5	1971–5
L-F 1946–7	15	40	58	63				
PIC 1967–8				71	82	89	91	
OPCS 1976						85	92	95

Source: C. M. Langford, *Birth Control Practice in Great Britain: A Review of the Evidence from Cross-sectional Surveys (1991), table. 3.2, 51*, citing E. Lewis-Faning, *Report on an Enquiry into Family Limitation and its Influence on Human Fertility during the Past Fifty Years*, Papers of the Royal Commission on Population, vol. i (1949). C. M. Langford, *Birth Control Practice and Marital Fertility in Great Britain: A Report on a Survey Carried out in 1967–68* (1976). K. Dunnell, *Family Formation, 1976* (1979).

Table 4.3.(*a*). *Birth control use by class, marriage cohort, and (a) those who had at any time used appliance methods, (b) those who had only used non-appliance methods*

	Social class					
	I		II		III	
Date of marriage	Appliance	Non-appliance	Appliance	Non-appliance	Appliance	Non-appliance
Before 1910	9	17	1	17	2	2
1910–19	15	45	11	28	5	28
1920–4	26	30	17	43	15	39
1925–9	37	21	21	39	15	48
1930–4	40	24	28	34	25	38
1935–9	53	20	34	34	25	29

Note: Non-appliance methods can be taken to refer to withdrawal only.

Source: E. Lewis-Faning, *Report on an Enquiry into Family Limitation and its Influence on Human Fertility during the Past Fifty Years*, Papers of the Royal Commission on Population, vol. i (1949), table 37, 52.

Table 4.3.(*b*). *Birth control use by class, marriage cohort, and (a) those who had at any time used appliance methods, (b) those who had only used non-appliance methods (including the pill)*

	Non-manual		Manual	
	Appliance	Non-appliance	Appliance	Non-appliance
1941–50	76	22	58	38
1951–60	88	12	75	23
1961–5	including pill 90	9	including pill 77	23

Source: Derived from C. M. Langford, *Birth Control Practice and Marital Fertility in Great Britain: A Report on a Survey Carried out in 1967–68*, (1976), table 6.1A, 106.

used birth control and so the actual number of couples depending on withdrawal continued to rise until the 1950s.[67]

For most women the use of withdrawal sharply diminished their sexual pleasure. For example, in the 1940s Moya Woodside concluded that among her urban working-class interviewees: 'the practice of *coitus interruptus* is responsible for much of women's lack of satisfaction, associated as it is with tension, anxiety, and physiologically less chance of reaching climax.'[68] In spite of this, few English women were willing to try the diaphragm. As late as the cohort of women married 1930–9 less than 9 per cent used the diaphragm.[69] The later surveys of contraceptive use suggest that douching and syringing, the other female methods, were hardly used

[67] E. Lewis-Faning, *Report on an Enquiry into Family Limitation and its Influence on Human Fertility during the Past Fifty Years*, Papers of the Royal Commission on Population, vol. i (1949), table 37, 52. A sample of 3,281 married, female, non-maternity patients in general hospital wards were interviewed for this report. Lewis-Faning divided the methods used into non-appliance and appliance categories. He suggested that non-appliance methods could be taken to refer to withdrawal only as the reported use of abstinence and the 'safe period' was minimal. Appliance methods included condoms, caps, and spermicides. C. M. Langford, *Birth Control Practice and Marital Fertility in Great Britain: A Report on a Survey Carried out in 1967–68* (1976), table 6.1A, 106.

[68] Woodside, 'Orgasm Capacity', 107. Also see Haire, *Birth-control Methods*, 66–7. Slater and Woodside, *Patterns*, 201. L. S. Florence, *Birth Control on Trial* (1930), 103. Walter, *My Secret Life* (1880; 1995), iii. 323.

[69] G. Rowntree and R. M. Pierce, 'Birth Control in Britain: Part Two', *Population Studies*, 15/2 (1961), 132–3. L. S. Florence, *Progress Report on Birth Control* (1956), 115.

in England. Around 20 per cent of couples in English marriage cohorts in the decades from 1930 to 1960 had used spermicides. This rose to nearly a third in the marriage cohort 1951–60 but only 1.5 per cent of these women used douches. This means that the spermicides were mainly used during intercourse.[70] Kate Fisher undertook an oral history of birth control use in Oxford and south Wales from 1925 to 1950. She found that husbands reported they inserted the spermicidal pessaries into their wife's vagina, and also that they, not their wives, purchased pessaries, so use of spermicides was a male-controlled method. Many of the female respondents also made it clear that their part in sexual intercourse was passive.[71] Thus the majority of women were unwilling to try any female-controlled methods despite the fact that withdrawal lessened female sexual pleasure. In fact, as a group women resisted the practice of birth control more strongly than did men well into the mid-twentieth century. It is unlikely that the late nineteenth-century feminists who rejected birth control had sufficient influence in this area to have created such feelings.[72] This suggests that the feminist rejection of birth control drew upon deep-rooted and widely shared attitudes to sexuality amongst English women.

In the mid-twentieth-century decades, birth control researchers Griselda Rowntree and Rachel Pierce interviewed both men and women. They found that male approval of birth control rose faster than that of women during the 1930s, and in the cohort who married 1940–9, male approval was significantly higher than that of women, who did not catch up until the 1950–60 marriage cohort.[73] In E. Lewis-Faning's survey only women were interviewed. Of the women married before 1910 whose husbands used withdrawal, over half gave 'lack of knowledge' as their reason for not using condoms or caps, and nearly

[70] F. Lafitte, *Family Planning in the Sixties: The Report of the Family Planning Association Working Party* (1963), ch. 2, 10.

[71] K. Fisher, 'An Oral History of Birth Control Practice *c.*1925–50: A Study of Oxford and Wales' (D.Phil. thesis, University of Oxford, 1997), 154, 258, 286. IUD use was also low. Dunnell, *Family Formation*, table 8.11, 47.

[72] O. Banks, *Faces of Feminism* (1981; 1986), 74–7. M. Benn, *Predicaments of Love* (1992), 142–3. B. Russell and P. Russell (eds.), *The Amberley Papers*, vol. ii (1937; 1966), 268.

[73] Rowntree and Pierce, 'Birth Control', T. 4. 11, 15. See also Gorer, *English Character*, 114–15.

30 per cent gave 'dislike of experimenting'. But the proportion of women who gave this reason *rose* to half of those who used withdrawal in the 1940–6 marriage cohort. Lack of knowledge slipped down to 16 per cent. This suggests that many women in the earlier cohorts would not have wanted to try other methods even if they had been available.[74] With increasing numbers of children, the dislike of trying appliance methods or 'experimenting' was overcome. Half the women with no children gave 'dislike of experimenting' but only 28 per cent of those with from five to seven children did so. This relationship between family size and method choice suggests strongly that most women who changed methods were doing so to control their fertility not to improve their sexual experience.[75]

The extent of women's rejection of more effective methods of birth control, including female-controlled methods, is surprising given that there is striking evidence of fear of unwanted pregnancies amongst women of all classes from the late nineteenth century on.[76] The use of abortion reveals an even higher level of desperation amongst women. In the late nineteenth century working-class women were innovative and willing to experiment with abortion methods they, or at least those initially involved, knew to be life threatening. Taking Diachylon, a lead-based compound, to produce an abortion was a new method that was not part of a folk tradition in which the risks may have been obscured, nor an instance of hapless victims purchasing patent medicines. In the 1890s, women in Sheffield observed, during an outbreak of lead poisoning after contamination of the city water supply, that those women who were pregnant aborted after being poisoned with the lead—some also died. Use of the substance spread through northern cities until what had been a

[74] Lewis-Faning, *Report*, T. 126, 183.

[75] Ibid. 182. Over the entire period between 7% and 14% also gave 'cannot be bothered' as a reason and there was a very high percentage of answers in the 'other' category, 9.5–30.7%. Florence, *Birth Control*, 19.

[76] Florence, *Progress Report*, 132. See also Slater and Woodside, *Patterns*, 187, 197. Klein, *Samples*, 72. I. Loudon, *Death in Childbirth* (1992), 210. There is less evidence of women's feelings in earlier periods. It is unlikely such fears were new although it has been argued that they reveal a decline in fatalism. Earlier fears, see L. A. Pollock, 'Embarking on a Rough Passage: the Experience of Pregnancy in Early-Modern Society', in V. Fildes (ed.), *Women as Mothers in Pre-industrial England* (1990), 47–9. Ross, *Love*, 91–2. 200. Thwaite, *Emily Tennyson*, 200.

common household item was finally, after several deaths, placed on the poison list in 1917.[77]

The best explanation for women's negative attitude is that use of birth control, initially withdrawal, was frequently a compromise between male desire for sexual relief and the female preference for sexual abstinence and fertility control at this time. Szreter has argued that withdrawal should be placed on a continuum with abstinence rather than being in the category of sexual practice. He writes that 'couples in British society who engaged in a regime of coitus interruptus were involved in essentially the same "game" of sexual restraint as those who were practising the various forms of conscious abstinence'.[78] Did 'couples' engage in this regime? If the gendered nature of the sexual experience is considered, then the answer must be no. Withdrawal is not a form of abstinence for women, as it is penetration of the vagina, not orgasm, which socially and legally constitutes sexual intercourse for the female sex. The use of the gender-neutral term 'couple' also implies that husband and wife have the same interest in sexual activity. This is contrary to every aspect of English sexual culture in the nineteenth and early twentieth centuries. The individual male using withdrawal must have desired to have sexual intercourse, but women were required to have intercourse whether they desired to or not—so their compliance cannot be proof of desire. Where woman do not want intercourse, withdrawal is not on a continuum with abstinence. Their immediate aim would be to avoid intercourse with control of fertility a secondary purpose. Withdrawal would be a failure of women's effort not to engage in sexual intercourse, rather than a partial success in the effort to practise birth control. However, it is consistent with other evidence to suggest that for men, and for women who desired sexual intercourse, withdrawal was on a continuum with abstinence as use of the method required them to control and to diminish their sexual pleasure. Hence, the Sicilian women interviewed by Jane and Peter Schneider saw use of withdrawal as a 'sacrifice' whereas by the end of the nineteenth century most English women did not.[79]

[77] A. McLaren, *Birth Control in Nineteenth Century England*, (1978), 242. See also Florence, *Birth Control*, 87. Chinn, *They Worked*, 148–9.

[78] Szreter, *Fertility*, 421.

[79] J. and P. Schneider, *Festival of the Poor* (1996), 262–3, 224–5.

A belief that positive change had taken place in working-class male attitudes to the family emerged in the 1950s and 1960s. Anecdotal evidence suggests similar change took place in middle class families but no equivalent research exists. In 1961, Ferdynand Zweig reported that there was a social change away from the 'stern, bullying, dominating and self-assertive father or of the absent father who took no interest in the children, leaving them to the mother. [This] is fast disappearing, and the new image of a benevolent, friendly and brotherly father is emerging.' He found the marital relationship was 'on the whole, more satisfactory now than it used to be a generation ago'. Zweig provided a reason for the decline in the authority of fathers; 'The husband is not the paymaster who can call the tune to the same extent.'[80] In their study of the urban working class, undertaken in the 1940s, Slater and Woodside also found that their respondents believed there had been a marked improvement over the past thirty years.[81] Zweig found connections between changes in the family world and the external or public sphere of paid employment:

Is the [marital] relationship moving towards greater equality of the sexes? A manager with whom I discussed this subject put his views in the most pungent way, linking this with the social change in the factory: 'The age of authority and abuse has passed. Men were bullied at work and they bullied back their wives and children. Now you cannot order your men about you have rather to coax and humour them.'[82]

This factory manager was assuming the point that so often has to be made explicitly; hierarchies of class and relations of authority in the home and in the outside world are not separate. By the 1950s there had been an immense social and legal improvement in the conditions of working people, of women, and, increasingly, of children. The authority of parents

---

[80] F. Zweig, *The Worker in an Affluent Society: Family Life and Industry* (1961), 23, 30, 31. Women told him that the most important single factor in the creation of more satisfactory relationships was the fall in heavy drinking. In 1935, Mrs Neville Rolfe also found that the fall in drunkenness had contributed to the decline in prostitution between 1900 and 1935. C. Neville Rolfe, 'Sexual delinquency', in H. Llewellyn Smith (ed.), *The New Survey of London Life and Labour* (1935), 339. See also Rathbone, *The Disinherited Family*, 195–6. R. Hoggart, *A Local Habitation (Life and Times, i: 1918–1940)* (1989), 19–20.

[81] Slater and Woodside, *Patterns*, 42. See also P. Wilmott and M. Young, *The Symmetrical Family* (1973). Fisher, 'She was quite satisfied', 191.

[82] Zweig, *Worker*, 30.

over their children, which had been central to the control of female sexuality, was also slowly disintegrating.[83]

Oral historian Elizabeth Roberts added a caveat; she argued that her research into women and families suggested many couples were moving into closer agreement over their aims by the 1940s, not that men necessarily felt they should abandon their authority over their wives.[84] This is relevant to birth control. In 1969, Gorer still found a 'widespread, if not very articulate, belief among the working classes that it is the husband's prerogative to determine whether any form of birth control should be used and that it is unseemly, almost unwomanly for the wife to take the initiative.'[85] The use of the word 'unwomanly' reveals the male rejection of women taking the sexual initiative. In this sexual context shared aims are relevant, not shared control.[86] Roberts's insight enables the early perceptions of improvement in male attitudes to be reconciled with women's demands for greater equality since the 1970s. Her conclusion is also consistent with Seccombe's argument that women had the motivation for fertility decline but men retained control of methods, hence it was not until men's desires converged with those of women in the early twentieth century that a decisive downswing in working-class birth rates occurred. He suggested that around 1920, 'after decades of "simmering tension, if not open conflict between spouses" it was now possible to conceive of a companionate marriage and female desire'.[87] Oral historian Kate Fisher has rejected Seccombe's picture of the working-class marriage as a site of disputes over fertility control.[88] However the average date of

[83] Thompson, *Edwardians*, 57.

[84] E. Roberts, *Women and Families: An Oral History, 1940–1970* (1995), 96.

[85] G. Gorer, *Sex and Marriage in England Today: A Study of the Views and Experience of the under-45s* (1971), 133. See also See also Wilmott and Young, *Symmetrical Family*, 20–1. M. Woolf, *Family Intentions* (1971), 76.

[86] For examples of such behaviour, see D. Sanders, *The Woman Book of Love and Sex* (1985), 79–80, 98.

[87] Seccombe, 'Starting', 187.

[88] Fisher claims that 'Stories of women suffering at the hands of indifferent men were prominent in clinic literature,' and that 'reliability on these stories has disproportionately influenced historians' analysis of gender roles in changing birth control practices'. Stories of indifferent men are usually carefully balanced by examples of caring husbands in published clinic literature. There is more than sufficient evidence available of 'indifferent', not to say violent, men to support those that are included. See P. Ayres and J. Lambertz, 'Marriage

birth in Fisher's oral history sample was 1912 and the average year of marriage was 1934.[89] Therefore, no conclusions can be drawn from her sample about marital relations or birth control use before the mid-1920s at the earliest. This average date of marriage is very close to the low point in the total marital fertility rate of 1933. By that time women had won the battle. Men had accepted the need to control their sexuality. Women of this generation reported that 'my husband was not lustful' and 'my husband was not highly sexed'.[90] Fisher's findings actually reinforce Seccombe's claim that the men have been persuaded. If the first quarter of the twentieth century was not a period of marital disputes and emotional alienation between men and women, these dates mean that Fisher's evidence cannot prove this. If, on the other hand, women's rejection of female sexual pleasure and their sexual passivity are factored in as resistance to male sexual demands then the argument presented here accounts for the sexual evidence, the survey findings on contraception and Fisher's evidence of male support for contraception.

By the late nineteenth century many working-class men were interested in the gains of respectability and it appears contradictory that their wives should have had to pressure them to control their fertility, as controlling family size was key to achieving and maintaining such gains. There were many loving fathers (in all classes); nonetheless male resistance probably existed because most men prioritized sexual access to their wives, not because they wanted many children.[91] Having children was part

Relations: Money and Domestic Violence in Working Class Liverpool, 1919–1939', in J. Lewis (ed.), *Labour and Love: Women's Experience of Home and Family 1850–1940* (1986). Chinn, *They Worked*, 155–66. A. N. and D. N. Chew, *Ada Neild Chew: The Life and Writings of a Working Woman*, ed. A. Davin (1982), 171, 181. Hammerton, *Cruelty*. Also upper-class male violence, 107. Rathbone, *The Disinherited Family*, 195–6, 184. Scott discusses the evidence presented in 1910 to the Royal Commission on Divorce by the Women's Co-operative Guild (and the strong male opposition to involvement in a campaign for divorce law reform). G. Scott, *Feminism and the Politics of Working Women: The Women's Co-operative Guild, 1880s to the Second World War* (1998), 83–4, ch. 5. N. Tomes, ' "A Torrent of Abuse": Crimes of Violence between Working-Class Men and Women in London, 1840–1875', *Journal of Social History*, 11 (1978). For a relevant theoretical analysis of the relationship between male violence and normal masculinity, see A. E. Jukes, *Men who Batter Women* (1999). For 19th-century feminists' campaigns against domestic violence, see Shanley, *Feminism*.

[89] Fisher, 'She was quite satisfied', 186, 189. See also Fisher, 'Oral History'.

[90] Chinn, *They Worked*, 148.   [91] e.g. Thompson (ed.), *Dear Girl*, 173.

of achieving adult masculinity and many men took considerable pleasure in their first and second children, but their interest often dropped off after that.[92] Studies of working-class people in the 1950s and 1960s found that adults mainly visited their mothers and that it was their 'Mum they supported, materially and emotionally'.[93] A compromise with women's desire for fertility control was produced in the 1920s as knowledge of contraception grew and increasing numbers of men realized that if they used contraception their wives would permit them to have intercourse. Thus men were, as Fisher claims, pivotal to changes in contraceptive behaviour, but that does not make them willing and early promoters of fertility decline in unity with their wives.

As we have seen in the two preceding chapters, fertility decline began in the first third of the nineteenth century when the only methods known to the majority of the population were abstinence and abortion. The existing ignorance about withdrawal was not dispelled until the late 1870s and only gradually did men accept the resulting discipline and loss of sexual pleasure. Thus, it was after a *century* of simmering tension that men and women could start to come to an agreement about controlling fertility. But by then abstinence had become women's preferred method and the adoption of contraception took place within that context. The next chapter examines men and women's changing attitudes to their bodies in order to understand the culture of abstinence more fully.

[92] Ross, *Love*, 97, 149–52.
[93] S. Brooke, 'Gender and Working Class Identity in Britain during the 1950s' *Journal of Social History* (2001), 786, citing M. Kerr, *The People of Ship Street* (1958), 166, P. Wilmott and M. Young, *Family and Kinship in East London* (1957), 78. Townsend, *Old People*, 83. There is considerably less evidence regarding middle- and upper-class men. For a generous interpretation of 19th century behaviour, see Tosh, *A Man's Place*, 97.

Mastering the Sexual Self: Contraception and Sexuality 1890s–1950s

In 1928, H. G. Wells wrote in the introduction to a contraceptive advice manual: 'When the adult citizen has gone through these pages he or she will know exactly the physical factors of the modern sexual problem. He or she will have all the mastery of his or her sexual self that knowledge can give.'[1] Wells had extensive opportunity to gain mastery of the existing methods and his penchant for sexually passionate affairs with young, unmarried middle-class women meant his contraceptive failures were recorded in an age when few such accounts survive. Amber Pember Reeves, the daughter of friends, did not become pregnant until she desired to do so, but Rebecca West seems to have become pregnant almost the first time she and Wells had intercourse.[2] Thus, Wells's mastery of the existing methods could not be relied upon to prevent pregnancy. When the sexually inexperienced poet Rupert Brooke had intercourse with Katherine Cox in 1912, he obeyed the instructions he had been given, Unfortunately this meant the couple waited until Cox's most fertile period, mid-month, and she probably syringed her vagina with quinine and water, a most inefficient method.[3] Cox became pregnant very quickly and then either miscarried or had an abortion. Contraceptive failure was

---

[1] M. Fielding, *Parenthood: Design or Accident? A Manual of Birth Control* (1928), 10. For a more extended discussion of birth control methods, including the economic costs in this period, see H. Cook, 'The Long Sexual Revolution: British Women, Sex and Contraception in the Twentieth Century' (Ph.D. thesis, 1999), ch. 3.

[2] R. Brandon, *The New Women and the Old Men* (1990), 184–5, 193.

[3] P. Delany, *The Neo-pagans: Friendship and Love in the Rupert Brooke Circle* (1987), 117, 170, 172, 180, 197.

devastating for these women. Having an illegitimate child kept West from active involvement in society while she was developing as a journalist and writer, while Cox was deeply distressed by her experience. Mastery of methods counted for little when the methods were grossly inefficient. In the early decades of the century success at preventing pregnancy depended on luck, a couple's fertility, and a willingness to sacrifice some degree of sexual pleasure. The first half of the twentieth century was a period of transition between ignorance and the inadequacy of nineteenth-century methods, and modern methods based upon widespread sexual knowledge. Contraception was necessary before women and men could allow themselves to relax the intense sexual control which has been described in the previous chapters. But the following examination of the methods reveals how difficult and frustrating they were to use. It becomes evident that controlling fertility required major alterations in sexual practice.

Historians have argued that the birth control methods available did not change from 1900 to 1960, but there was, nonetheless, an immense improvement in the effectiveness with which birth control prevented pregnancy and the extent to which methods permitted sexual pleasure.[4] In Britain in 1900, and even in 1920, contraceptives were 'generally crude, unreliable, expensive and difficult to obtain'.[5] There was wide advertising of appliances in the trade literature but most people were embarrassed and uncertain of what they needed and where to go to obtain it. Difficulties continued once the appliances had been purchased. There was no regulation of contraceptive aids, and quality control tests were carried out by many wholesalers and retailers for the purpose of grading second-quality articles in order to sell them at a cheaper price, rather than to reject any. The Birth Control Investigation Committee, set up in 1927, became the Scientific Advisory Committee of the FPA in 1939. This body released a schedule of approved chemical contraceptives in 1934, which was eventually extended to include sheaths and caps, and became the 'Approved List of Contraceptives'. There continued to be no British government quality control until the introduction of a British standard for condoms

[4] J. Peel, 'The Manufacture and Retailing of Contraceptives in England', *Population Studies*, 17 (1963), 116.

[5] F. Campbell, 'Birth Control and the Christian Churches', *Population Studies*, 14 (1960), 143.

in 1964.[6] The gradual imposition of such regulations is an important aspect of the huge improvement in contraception that took place over the course of the twentieth century.

However, the growth of widely available and accurate knowledge was probably the most crucial innovation of all in the history of birth control in Britain. At the beginning of the 1920s the few experts on birth control had limited knowledge as to which birth control methods were effective and why.[7] Contraception remained a matter of self-help in the face of advice that was often confusing at best. The situation improved rapidly from then on, as is shown in birth control manuals written between 1918 and 1960. These texts fall into a gap between the history of birth control and the history of sexuality that reflects the separation of birth control from sexuality, which took place in the mid-twentieth century, as a result of the effort to make birth control socially acceptable.[8] The birth rate of sections of the middle classes began to fall first and fastest, but twentieth-century research into the use of contraception has largely focused on working-class use of contraception. Together with the limited middle-class survey material, these birth control manuals offer a unique picture of middle-class use of contraception, as well as further illuminating the constraints on working-class users.

This chapter is based on the work of a number of manual writers, some of whom were drawing primarily on their own ideas and original research, and others who distilled workable summaries of the available knowledge. It is difficult to overestimate the innovativeness and importance of Marie Stopes's (1880–1958) first two books, *Married Love* (1918) and *Wise Parenthood* (1918), in kick-starting and shaping the discourse on heterosexual marital

[6] Peel, 'Manufacture', 123. Condoms were brought under the control of the American Food and Drug Administration in 1938, but this legislation did not apply to exports. C. Tietze, 'The Use-Effectiveness of Contraceptive Methods', in Clyde V. Kiser (ed.), *Research in Family Planning* (1962), 367, citing his own research: C. Tietze, *The Condom as a Contraceptive* (1960). On USA exports, H. Wright, review of *The Condom as a Contraceptive*, by C. Tietze, *Family Planning*, 913 (1960).

[7] E. Charles, *The Practice of Birth Control: An Analysis of the Experience of Nine Hundred Women* (1932), 155. E. F. Griffith, *Modern Marriage* (1935; 1947), p. ix.

[8] There is a copious secondary literature on sex manuals but Stopes's first slim manual on contraception, *Wise Parenthood* (1918), is the only text solely on birth control cited in this literature, and although Griffith's *Modern Marriage and Birth Control* (1935) is cited, it is as a marriage manual.

sexuality and contraception respectively in the 1920s.[9] Theodore van de Velde (1873–1937) had been a gynaecologist in the Netherlands, which means that in his texts he was not reflecting the physical experience of the English. This is an important caveat regarding his evidence; he was, however, enormously influential, and books written after 1928 follow his lead on many issues. A combination of personal experience and knowledge of the research that had been done prior to the First World War formed the ideas of both Stopes and van de Velde. Their beliefs produce a subtly different view of the body from that held by the next generation of writers, more porous, less mechanical, and less governed by rigid regularities of response; a more emotional body.

New writers had rejected this view of the body by the early 1930s. In their work the contracepting body was defined by mechanical barriers and the physical removal of sperm and was less sexualized and less emotional because of this. By the time Norman Haire's (1892–1952) *Birth Control Methods* (1936) was published, he had twenty-one years of medical practice, including fifteen years of practical birth control work with working-class women in clinics, and middle-class men and women in his Harley Street practice.[10] Dr Edward Fyfe Griffith (1895–1988), originally a general practitioner, became increasingly involved in sex education and providing birth control. One of the most frequently recommended of the early birth control manuals was *Parenthood: Design or Accident? A Manual of Birth Control* (1928) by Michael Fielding, the pseudonym of Maurice Newfield (1893–1949), doctor and editor of the *Eugenics Review*.[11] Some advice from George Ryley Scott (1886–1954), a professional writer, is included because, unlike the other authors mentioned, he was not concerned with ethical issues. In 1960, Dr Eleanor Mears (1917–92), then medical secretary of the British Family Planning Association (FPA), edited a British edition of a book on birth control by Alan Guttmacher (1898–1974), a gynaecologist,

---

[9] *Married Love* (1918) contains no information on methods of contraception though Stopes does defend the practice.

[10] See N. Haire, 'Contraceptive Technique', *Practitioner* (1923). N. Haire, *Birth-Control Methods (Contraception, Abortion, Sterilisation)* (1936; 1937). His involvement in sex reform is described in J. Weeks, *Sex, Politics and Society: The Regulation of Sexuality since 1800* (1981; 1989), 184–6.

[11] Obituary, *Eugenics Review* (1949), 103–16. Fielding, *Parenthood*. This book was recommended by several other writers, and in sex manuals, including those by N. Haire, H. Wright, and L. D. Weatherhead. By 1940, 150,000 copies had sold.

obstetrician, and president of the Planned Parenthood Federation of America.[12] This text represents the state of the art immediately prior to the release of the pill in 1961.

All these writers drew on users' responses, and their evidence has been supplemented by several better-known studies. *Birth Control on Trial* (1930) and *Progress on Birth Control* (1956) were written by Lella Secor Florence (1887–1966), an American from a working-class background.[13] Her sensitive and thorough discussions of working-class women's experience of birth control are based on interviews with patients attending the Cambridge birth control clinic and with patients who had failed to return to the Birmingham FPA clinic, respectively.[14] *The Practice of Birth Control* (1932), by Enid Charles (1894–1972), was based on evidence collected from the Birmingham birth control clinic and 432 completed postal questionnaires from middle-class women. Charles, a social biologist and a socialist, was born in Cape-Town and educated at Newnham College, Cambridge.[15] *Patterns of Marriage* (1951) was a study of 100 'neurotic' and 100 control couples, undertaken to investigate the extent of assortative marriage, that is of like people marrying like or otherwise, an issue which concerned eugenicists. It is unique in that both husbands and wives were interviewed separately, so sexuality and contraceptive use were placed in the context of the marriage. The project was undertaken by Eliot Slater (1904–83), a psychiatrist, and Moya Woodside, a social worker and researcher.[16]

BIRTH CONTROL METHODS

During the inter-war years, authors continued to recommend the sponge so beloved of the early nineteenth-century authors. Norman Haire explained that they were hard to clean and should be sterilized by boiling

[12] A. F. Guttmacher and E. Mears, *Babies by Choice or by Chance* (1960).

[13] See L. Secor Florence, *Lella Secor: A Diary in Letters, 1915–1922*, ed. M. B. Florence (1978).

[14] L. Secor Florence, *Birth Control on Trial* (1930). L. Secor Florence, *Progress Report on Birth Control* (1956).

[15] See *Who Was Who 1971–1980*.

[16] E. Slater and M. Woodside, *Patterns of Marriage: A Study of the Marriage Relationships of the Urban Working Classes* (1951).

in a saucepan of water. To increase the efficacy they could be soaked in a
1 per cent solution of lactic acid jelly and a soapy water douche should be
taken the next morning.[17] These precautions, if taken, would have made
the sponge a difficult method for women in working-class housing. In
1930, the 'vast majority' of Florence's working-class Cambridge patients
had no bathroom or suitable sanitary facilities.[18] The desire for privacy also
created problems with the use of all vaginal devices, as well as with
douching and reusable condoms. One woman, talking about the diaphragm, explained: 'Many's the morning I've come down in my slippers
before daylight so as to try and get it done [washed] before the children
were up. But one of them always heard me and then they were all at my
heels.'[19] Another woman 'spoke of the embarrassment of fixing it up in
the bedroom with her husband present'.[20] This embarrassment was usually not due to attempts to conceal use of contraception from husbands
but arose because women preferred to avoid display of anything connected with sexuality. The question of pleasure is addressed repeatedly in
the discussion of methods. Florence commented that 'we have never
found any patient who liked the method well enough to persist in its
use ... [One patient who was] instructed to soak the sponge in vinegar
found it cold and unpleasant to use, and her husband found the vinegar
much too stimulating, so that the climax in his case was very much
hastened.'[21] By the end of the inter-war period sponges were no longer
mentioned in England.

Methods such as 'sitting upright the moment after ejaculation has
taken place and coughing violently or taking some other exercise to
contract the pelvis' were not completely rejected until the mid-1930s.[22]
'Holding back' is the term for a deliberate attempt by a woman to prevent
herself from having an orgasm, in the belief that this would prevent

[17] Haire, *Birth-Control Methods*, 93. Stopes recommended the sponge but rejected regular
douching. Stopes, *Wise Parenthood* (1918), 17–18. Stopes, *Contraception: Theory, History and Practice*
(1923; 1925), 117–18, 133.
[18] Florence, *Birth Control*, 113.
[19] Ibid. 65.
[20] Florence, *Progress Report*, 129.
[21] Florence, *Birth Control*, 118–19. See also Charles, *Practice*, 46, 56.
[22] e.g. Th. H. van de Velde, *Fertility and Sterility in Marriage* (1931), 298–302; anatomical
contraception, 304–14, 353. Stopes, *Contraception*, 138–9, 61–3.

conception. Women who used this 'method' were found into the 1940s and 1950s.[23] Karezza consisted of penile insertion, with ejaculation inhibited by the mental concentration of both partners on the spiritual aspects of love. Van de Velde thought it 'obvious that most persons, and especially most men, would not consent to try it'.[24] There was one case of karezza in Charles's sample and two cases in which 'the form of intimacy adopted was not normal copulation nor coitus interruptus'.[25] This could have referred to placing the penis between the woman's thighs or to mutual masturbation.

It is often, perhaps even usually, assumed that oral and anal sex provided a route to sexual satisfaction without risk of pregnancy. However, recent surveys of sexual behaviour reinforce other evidence to suggest strongly that these sexual practices were unacceptable to most people in the first half of the twentieth century. This was not a new inhibition. Richard Davenport Hines found that in the seventeenth century oral acts were seen as wanton and the bidet was rejected from a moral, not hygienic, perspective. Such elaborate provision for cleaning the genitals was probably thought to be preparation for oral acts, confirming that oral–genital contact was considered debased.[26] Bidets were still rare and associated with sexual sin in the inter-war period. Richard Hoggart (b. 1918) commented that, amongst the working class, there was 'a great shyness about some aspects of sex—about discussing it "sensibly", about being seen naked, or even about undressing for the act of sex, or about sophistications in sexual behaviour'.[27] This was also true for many in

---

[23] Florence, *Progress Report*, 143. Haire, *Birth-Control Methods*, 67–8. J. Klein, *Samples of English Culture*, vol. i (1965), 71. Slater and Woodside, *Patterns*, 197–8. Stopes, *Contraception*, 56–8. Van de Velde, *Fertility*, 298–9. Earlier evidence of this belief is discussed in A. McLaren, *Reproductive Rituals: The Perception of Fertility in England from the Sixteenth Century to the Nineteenth Century* (1984), 20–1, 27.

[24] van de Velde, *Fertility*, 294–5. For the origins of karezza, see P. Fryer, *The Birth Controllers* (1965), 149–54.

[25] Charles, *Practice*, 29.

[26] R. Davenport-Hines, *Sex, Death and Punishment* (1991), 79, 82.

[27] R. Hoggart, *The Uses of Literacy* (1957), 83. See also P. Carter, *Feminism, Breasts and BreastFeeding* (1995), 106–31. Carter rejects the Newsons' use of 'prudish' to describe working-class people's attitude to sexuality. It is more useful to question why the term appears pejorative, 9. K. Dayus, *Where there's Life* (1985), 177. Klein, *Samples*, 65. J. and E. Newson, *Four Years Old in an Urban Community* (1968), 384.

the middle classes. Margaret Cole referred favourably to 'sophistications in sexual behaviour', and to 'love-play', which phrases referred to sexual activity other than coitus, such as oral sex or touching the genitals with the hands.[28] But Cole and Hoggart were part of a progressive intelligentsia and their acceptance of such activities was not typical of the majority.

Dr Eustace Chesser claimed to have asked some 800 of his patients about their sexual practices, probably around 1930. He recalled:

I was surprised and shocked at the proportionately large number of husbands and wives [more than 15 per cent] who admitted that they indulged, either occasionally or regularly, in anal intercourse. At first I wondered why they preferred this unnatural, and disgusting, method of union; and I asked some of them why they considered it more desirable than the normal sex act. In almost every case the reply was the same. *They did not prefer it, but indulged in it because it could not result in pregnancy.* (italics in original)[29]

This is a high rate of practice of anal sex but it is impossible to confirm this account, as other researchers were not willing to ask such questions. Chesser was a sympathetic questioner, who demonstrated a commitment to understanding sexual behaviour throughout his life, and there is no evidence of a bias that would lead him to misrepresent or to exaggerate this finding. Later evidence regarding anal sex suggests that it is likely that

[28] M. Cole, *The Life of G. D. H. Cole* (1971), 91–3. In the inter-war decades the phrase 'Love play' could be used to refer to 'everything that leads up to that stage of sexual communion which is usually called coitus'. This is an example of the sex manuals providing a new terminology. E. Chesser, *Love without Fear (A Plain Guide to sex Technique for Every Married Adult)* (1941), 39. See also A Buschke and F. Jacobsohn, *Sex Habits: A Vital Factor in Well-Being*, trans. E. and C. Paul (1932), 148. E. Charles, *The Sexual Impulse* (1935), 157–9. K. M. Walker (ed.), *Preparation for Marriage: A Handbook Prepared by a Special Committee on Behalf of the British Social Hygiene Council* (1932), 80–2. T. H. van de Velde, *Ideal Marriage* (1928; reset 1943), 126.

[29] This may have been in Manchester or Cinderford where Chesser worked as a GP after qualifying in 1926 and before moving to London in the early 1930s. My thanks to Lesley Hall for this information. E. Chesser, *Sexual Behaviour: Normal and Abnormal* (1949), 183. See also E. Chesser, *Live and Let Live* (1958), 31. The persistent negative attitude to anal sex can be seen in the comment of a sex manual author in 1966: 'Anal intercourse (*coitus in ano*) is also occasionally tried by some lovers eager for new sensations. but ... this can so easily degrade into a perversion ... it seems to me to lie outside the scope of a work such as this. Furthermore, this form of conduct is legally condemned as a criminal act.' V. Howarth, *Secret Techniques of Erotic Delight* (1966), 247. Woycke argues anal sex was increasingly used as birth control in Germany from the 1890s. If so, this is another example of the very different German attitude to the body. J. Woycke, *Birth Control in Germany, 1871–1933* (1988), 10.

many of these women did not obtain pleasure from the experience, and this is probably further testimony to women's fear of pregnancy and their acceptance of conjugal rights. The *Woman* magazine survey found that, in the 1980s, 'more than a third of wives regularly agree to things that they don't enjoy and which make them feel uneasy. In one in ten cases this is anal sex and, in nearly one in two, oral sex.'[30] The *Sexual Attitudes and Lifestyles* (1994) survey collected information on sexual practices from the 1950s, which was already well past the height of sexual prudery, to the 1980s. Even so, only 12 per cent of men and 11.6 per cent of women born 1935–50 admitted having ever had anal sex.[31]

In the 1994 survey, heterosexual non-penetrative sexual activities and oral sex were found to increase with higher social class and over time. Unfortunately, neither this study nor the 1985 *Woman* magazine survey distinguishes between cunnilingus and fellatio in the analysis. Overall, women were less interested in oral sex than men. Of all women aged 20 from 1950 to 1965, only 50 per cent reported experience of oral sex ever in their lifetime, while 62 per cent of men did.[32] An examination of letters to *Forum* magazine in the 1970s reinforces the impression gained from all the sources that women tended to be less interested in varied sexual acts or varied positions during coitus than were many men.[33] This lack of desire to experiment is consistent with women's more negative attitude to birth control.

Rates of breastfeeding declined with the birth rate and so it is unlikely that prolonged lactation was widely used as a method of birth control, although Florence found most women believed this would prevent them becoming pregnant.[34] Women and men did try to employ the safe period but, as Haire commented, there was 'practically no day, or group of days,

[30] D. Sanders, *The Woman Book of Love and Sex* (1985), 81.

[31] K. Wellings, J. Field, A. M. Johnson, J. Wadsworth, and S. Bradshaw, *Sexual Attitudes and Lifestyles* (1994), table 6.8, 164, table 6.12, 175.

[32] Ibid. 169; table 6.8, 164, table 6.12, 175.

[33] L. Coveney, L. Kay, and P. Mahony, 'Theory into Practice: Sexual Liberation or Social Control (*Forum* Magazine 1968–81)', in L. Coveney, S. Jeffreys, M. Jackson, L. Kay, and P. Mahony (eds.), *The Sexuality Papers: Male Sexuality and the Social Control of Women* (1984).

[34] Florence, *Birth Control*, 95. Also see M. Llewellyn Davies (ed.), *Maternity: Letters from Working Women Collected by the Women's Co-operative Guild* (1915; 1978), 146. Rejection of prolonged lactation, Stopes, *Contraception*, 41–2, 64–6. Van de Velde, *Fertility*, 293.

which has not, at some time or other, been described by some authority, and usually with some show of evidence, as absolutely or relatively infertile'.[35] All the post-First World War writers whose work has been examined rejected the safe period, but it is probable that many couples who were reducing their coital frequency chose to have intercourse on days they believed to be infertile.[36]

FEMALE CONTRACEPTIVE DEVICES

The methods discussed so far were free or very cheap. The most expensive methods were intra-cervical pessaries and intrauterine devices. The former consisted of a plate that sat in the vagina against the cervix with a stem which extended up the cervical canal, and in some devices there was a spring shaped like the letter V that expanded in the uterus. Stopes rejected such methods in 1918, but by the 1921 edition of *Wise Parenthood*, she recommended their use in women who had completed childbearing and had damage that prevented the use of a cap.[37] The devices were potentially harmful, as they provided a path for the introduction of infection into the uterus, although Haire described the 'Wishbone pessary' as also causing physical damage because of the pressure the V-shaped spring applied to the walls of the uterus.[38] Himes commented in 1936 that '[a]lmost all practitioners have now discarded intrauterine stems, "wish-bones," "butterflies" ... The Graefenberg ring is still suspect.'[39] The latter was an early precursor of the modern intrauterine device, the IUD, and Haire spent some decades using it before eventually rejecting it too as likely to produce infection. Even in 1936, he commented that this was an 'expensive method requiring many visits and a healthy genital tract' and that for the vast majority of women and doctors the vaginal diaphragm

[35] Haire, *Birth-Control Methods*, 59. Also Stopes, *Contraception*, 84–90.

[36] Fielding, *Parenthood*, 24. G. R. Scott, *Modern Birth Control Methods*, (1933; 1947), 50–8. M. Stopes, *Wise Parenthood* (1918; 3rd edn. 1919), 30. Van de Velde, *Fertility*, p. xiii.

[37] Stopes, *Wise Parenthood* (1918), 26; Stopes, *Wise Parenthood* (1918; 6th edn. 1921), pp. ix, 36–7;

[38] Haire, *Birth-Control Methods*, 131.

[39] N. E. Himes, *The Medical History of Conception* (1936; 1970), 305 n. 81. Charles, *Practice*, 29. One user in her sample.

was preferable.[40] Van de Velde and Fielding were against the use of the devices.[41] It is evident from practitioners' rejection of the devices that injuries and infections did occur and these devices would have provided some justification for those who claimed that contraception was injurious. There was only one user, even in Charles's middle-class sample, though like all female-controlled devices they were more widely used outside England.[42]

Devices that were placed in the woman's vagina to cover the cervix came in a large number of forms and materials. Robert Roberts claims that working-class girls in Edwardian Salford used vaginal 'pessaries of lard and flour'.[43] These would have been difficult to insert and ineffective at preventing pregnancy. Cervical caps are thimble shaped and fit over the cervix, which protrudes into the vagina, as a thimble fits over a finger. In the early 1900s there were rigid caps made of cellulose and metal, one version of which had sharp projections around the inside edge, designed to stick into the cervix, which has few nerves, so as to anchor the cap into position. These teeth produced small wounds and consequent infection.[44] They appear to have been little used in Britain.

Rubber caps were held in place on the cervix by suction. They stay in place more securely than diaphragms and cannot press on the bladder. The diaphragm is shaped like a shallow bowl made of rubber, larger in circumference, but less deep than a cervical cap. The diaphragm is placed with one edge over the cervix and the other edge resting against the pubic bone. A metal watch spring is encased in the rubber of the rim and this exerts pressure on the walls of the vagina, holding it in place. Doctors were uncertain as to how long women should be advised to leave caps in place, with some recommending that caps could be worn throughout the period between menstrual periods, or even continuously. It took until the

---

[40] Haire, *Birth-Control Methods*, 157.

[41] van de Velde, *Fertility*, 356; M. Fielding, *Parenthood* (1928; 3rd edn. 1934), 107.

[42] e.g. Florence, *Birth Control*, 37. J. F. Brodie, *Contraception and Abortion in Nineteenth Century America* (1994). J. C. Caldwell, C. M. Young, H. Ware, D. R. Lavis, and A. -T. Davis, 'Australia: knowledge, attitudes and practice of family planning in Melbourne, 1971', *Studies in Family Planning*, 4/3 (1973), 55–6. S. Seidlecky and D. Wyndham, *Populate and Perish: Australian Women's Fight for Birth Control* (1990), 39. Woycke, *Germany*, 41–3.

[43] R. Roberts, *The Classic Slum: Salford Life in the First Quarter of the Century* (1971; 1973), 51–2.

[44] Haire, *Birth-Control Methods*, 101–4. Van de Velde, *Fertility*, 340–3.

1930s for consensus to emerge that it was better for a woman to insert her cap every night, as leaving it in for long periods resulted in discharges and smells, and could cause inflammation.[45] The ignorance of doctors, as well as that of women, reveals how unusual and unnatural it seemed to many English people to place objects into a woman's vagina, outside the context of sex or birth, before the introduction of tampons and contraception. Cervical caps were slightly harder for women to insert and remove than diaphragms because the woman had to reach deeper into her vagina. Stopes had suggested in 1918 that self-fitting of rubber cervical caps should be possible.[46] But Haire wrote that 'women found it hard to fit', and self-fitting may not have been manageable by the majority of users. He believed that the doctor's skill in teaching a woman how to use the cap was the most important element in success with the method, but most doctors were not keen to become involved.[47] As a result problems with the supply of caps were considerable.

The use of these methods required a change in the conduct of sexual intercourse. Putting in the cap made intercourse premeditated and this reduced desire: 'Either a couple must decide before hand that it would be needed, in which case as one said, intercourse became a duty, or the wife must get out of bed to put in her cap, and often after that had lost her desire for intercourse.'[48] These complaints give a sense of the immediacy and instability of desire, and the brevity of the sexual act. Florence was able to elicit comments about a mutual experience in which the woman's desire was also important, as her own desire undoubtedly was to her.[49] However, many men and women felt the woman was taking the sexual initiative if she inserted the cap beforehand. Fielding wrote scathingly that some women saw inserting the cap into the vagina as a 'wanton act', 'an invitation to sexual intercourse', and that many men also found the cap

[45]   Haire, *Birth-Control Methods*, 121–2. Stopes, *Wise Parenthood* (1919), 16. Stopes, *Contraception*, 145–6. M. Sanger and H. Stone, *The Practice of Contraception: An International Symposium and Survey. From the Proceedings of the Seventh International Birth Control Congress, Zurich, Switzerland, September 1930* (1931), 12. Van de Velde, *Fertility*, 332, 338.

[46]   Stopes, *Wise Parenthood* (1919), 15. Stopes, *Contraception*, 141.

[47]   Haire, *Birth-Control Methods*, 105–7. Also in Charles, *Practice*, 110. Sanger and Stone, *Practice of Contraception*, 13.

[48]   Florence, *Progress Report* 130. Also see e.g. M. Macaulay, *Marriage for the Married* (1964), 206.

[49]   See Florence, *Letters, 1915–1922*.

unsuitable because they believed sex to be 'a manly pleasure, one in which women must indeed, by a deplorable necessity, have some part, but which no pure woman should ever enjoy'.[50] This was probably a widespread difficulty. Even in the 1960s Geoffrey Gorer found that working class men and women believed men should take the initiative in use of contraception.[51]

Other problems have obvious implications for women's sexual enjoyment, highlighting the result of high fertility rates. Giving birth frequently altered the shape of a woman's cervix and a cervical cap could not be fitted, although a diaphragm still could be used in some cases. In the event that the vagina had been badly torn or stretched in childbirth, resulting in a malposition of the uterus, a prolapse, laxity of the vagina, or a torn perineum, then the diaphragm, also, would not remain in position.[52] Of the sample of 1,250 women analysed in *Working Class Wives* (1939), 191, or 15 per cent, reported having gynaecological ailments, and of these seventy-seven, or 6 per cent, had received no treatment.[53] The actual number with problems was probably higher as these women were not actually examined and they had very low expectations as to good health. Patients who went to clinics were found to have more children on average than women in the population as a whole, so clinic findings are also not fully representative. Nonetheless, Florence found that a majority of the Cambridge birth control clinic's patients had suffered from injury in childbirth. For example, amongst the 247 patients who agreed to being examined, seventy-eight, or nearly a third, were found to have a lacerated cervix. Other injuries included fifty-six women with a torn perineum, twenty-three with a retroverted uterus, and eight with a severe prolapse.[54] Such women had little or no access to medical help prior to the introduction of the National Health Service in 1948 nor would this always have been to their advantage. Obstetric practice often demonstrated little respect for

[50] Fielding, *Parenthood* (1934), 105–6. See also Chesser, *Sexual Behaviour*, 182. Florence, *Birth Control*, 68. Slater and Woodside, *Patterns*, 176.

[51] G. Gorer, *Sex and Marriage in England Today: A Study of the Views and Experience of the under-45s* (1971), 142; see also 133.

[52] Haire, *Birth-Control Methods*, 125–6. I. Loudon, *Death in Childbirth* (1992), 365.

[53] M. Spring Rice, *Working-Class Wives: Their Health and Conditions* (1939; 1981), 61–2.

[54] Florence, *Birth Control*, 114, 155. Also see Fielding, *Parenthood* (1928), 56. M. Stopes, *The First Five Thousand: The First Report of the First Birth Control Clinic in the British Empire* (1923), 31.

women or their bodies.[55] Severe constipation meant the diaphragm might not remain in position. Florence thought nine-tenths of workers were constipated year in, year out.[56] In 1935, it was estimated that of the £2.5 million spent nationally each year on patent medicines, a large proportion went on purgatives.[57] For women who had adequate privacy and sanitation, caps could be more satisfactory than any other method, as Charles found in her middle-class sample.[58] Haire, van de Velde, and Fielding concluded that the diaphragm was the best method, if used in conjunction with a spermicide. In spite of this, caps and diaphragms were never used by more than a small percentage even among middle-class English women.[59]

SPERMICIDES

During the inter-war period it was discovered that while spermicides on their own were not very effective, combining them with appliance methods created a far higher level of effectiveness.[60] Spermicides were delivered in the form of pessaries and foam tablets inserted into the vagina, douches, and jellies or creams applied to the condom or cap. With manufactured products, the lack of regulation meant standards were variable.[61] Books included recipes for pessaries and jellies that could be made up at home.[62] Individual response varied considerably, with some

[55] For a discussion of obstetrics see J. Murphy-Lawless, *Reading Birth and Death: A History of Obstetric Thinking* (1998).

[56] Florence, *Birth Control*, 64. A few women found the diaphragm caused them pain. 73, 82. Fielding and Haire mention constipation. Haire, *Birth-Control Methods*, 11. Fielding, *Parenthood* (1934), 88.

[57] C. W. Hutt and H. H. Thomson (eds.), *Principles and Practice of Preventive Medicine*, vol. ii (1935), 1439.

[58] Charles, *Practice*, 52–4.

[59] G. Rowntree and R. M. Pierce, 'Birth Control in Britain: Part Two', *Population Studies*, 15/2 (1961), 132–3. Florence, *Progress Report*, 115.

[60] Charles, *Practice*, 19–20.

[61] Haire, *Birth-Control Methods*, 74–7.

[62] e.g. Fielding, *Parenthood* (1928), 57, 62–3. Stopes suggested several: Stopes, *Wise Parenthood* (1919). Stopes, *Contraception*. Van de Velde, *Fertility*, 346. Himes discusses those suggested by earlier writers, such as A. Besant or Dr H. A. Albutt, in detail, e.g. Himes, *Medical History*, 248, 252.

women and men able to tolerate quite strong chemicals, and others complaining of smarting, burning, or discharges as a result of use.[63] Soluble pessaries, made by Rendalls and consisting of quinine suspended in cocoa butter, were amongst the oldest. The popularity of the brand endured even though quinine produced local irritation in some women, and researchers C. I. Voge and J. R. Baker both found that its spermicidal power was low.[64] There were also aesthetic and practical objections to the 'soiling of underclothing and sheets, [and] the penetrating odour of cheap chocolate . . . Also cocoa butter is wholly unsuited for use in combination with any rubber . . . [diaphragms]; it injures the rubber and rapidly rots it away.'[65] Jellies were also found to be messy and unpleasant. In use, tablets and pessaries often failed to dissolve, or there could be difficulties in placing them high enough in the vagina. The cost per item of pessaries could create a disincentive to have intercourse. Even some of Charles's middle-class respondents commented on the expense.[66]

Vaginal syringing and douching were never popular methods in England. The reason given by the authors for dislike of the method was that use of douches or syringing alone, or as back-up in the case of condom failure, required the woman to get out of bed immediately the man had ejaculated. Fielding suggested dependence on syringing made a woman 'more reluctant to be wooed', that is, less interested in sex.[67] Haire's 1936 description is worth quoting at length:

If the weather is cold and the room where the douche has to be taken inadequately heated, the woman's disinclination [to get up immediately] is likely to be increased . . . douching is a nuisance even for the prosperous French woman with

---

[63]   Haire, *Birth-Control Methods*, 73. Also van de Velde, *Fertility*, 343.

[64]   J. R. Baker, *The Chemical Control of Conception* (1935). C. I. Voge, *The Chemistry and Physics of Contraceptives* (1933). See also Charles, *Practice*, 54–5. Himes, *Medical History*, 248–9. Peel, 'Manufacture', 117–18. Slater and Woodside, *Patterns*, 202. Van de Velde, *Fertility*, 344.

[65]   van de Velde, *Fertility*, 345. See also Charles, *Practice*, 54–5. Fielding, *Parenthood* (1928), 63. Haire, *Birth-Control Methods*, 76, 78.

[66]   Charles, *Practice*, 55. For working-class couples, see Florence, *Birth Control*, 67.

[67]   Fielding, *Parenthood* (1928), 47. In 1886 Albutt suggested that use of a bedpan with the syringe after intercourse removed the need for the woman to rise from bed. It took him half a page merely to describe how to set this up, and a less erotic procedure can scarcely be imagined. H. A. Allbutt, *The Wife's Handbook* (1886), 47–8. See also Charles, *Practice*, 56, 110. Himes, *Medical History*, 228. Stopes, *Wise Parenthood* (1919), 26.

her well-warmed bathroom, her bidet and her fountain douche. In Anglo-Saxon communities, where bathrooms are notoriously . . . the coldest and most cheerless rooms in our houses, where the presence of a bidet is regarded as almost a symbol of sin . . . immediate post-coital douching is more often a pious wish than an accomplished fact.[68]

It is obvious that Haire was not talking about working-class women. This was the experience of the privileged middle-class women who came to his Harley Street practice.

CONDOMS

Advances in the technology of condom manufacture came regularly but these were not sufficient to overcome the substantial problems in use until the early 1960s. The vulcanization of rubber, which had been developed in the 1840s, was probably not used for condoms until the 1870s. The crepe rubber used for these 'cement' condoms deteriorated within three months and gave off a strong odour. In America the substitution of liquid latex in the early 1930s led to thinner, odourless condoms that resisted ageing for three to five years, but European production continued to be mainly of the older type.[69] In 1931, van de Velde commented: 'Cheap condoms are a fatal form of economy . . . it is wisest to buy only products of firms with a large turnover, to buy in small quantities at a time . . . And never use the same article twice'.[70] Haire thought that 'highly intelligent people . . . would experience a higher percentage of success'.[71] All of the recommended precautions increased the cost of the method, revealing the role played by an adequate income in the 'intelligent' use of condoms. Once purchased, the non-lubricated condoms had to be carefully rolled on, after

[68]   Haire, *Birth-Control Methods*, 83.

[69]   Himes, *Medical History*, 201–6. Peel said the first latex condoms were made available in Britain from a US manufacturer in 1929. Peel, 'Manufacture', 122. G. R. Taylor, *Sex in History* (1953), described the 'early 1930s' invention of the latex process as a 'landmark in social history', 287.

[70]   van de Velde, *Fertility*, 323.

[71]   Haire, *Birth-Control Methods*, 99. Also see R. Pierpont (ed.), *Report of the Fifth International Neo-Malthusian and Birth Control Conference. Kingsway Hall, London, July 11th–14th, 1922* (1922), 294. Scott, *Modern Birth Control*, 47.

lubricating the penis, then the outside of the condom also needed lubrication, to avoid irritation to the genitals of both partners.[72] Enid Charles explained that the sheath was more comfortable when fitted wet: 'the penis [then] glides over the surface of the rubber without stretching it...this reduces the intra-urethral pressure, which perhaps accounts partly for the very pronounced disinclination of many males to use the sheath.'[73] The replies to her questionnaire did not disclose familiarity with this approach, so uncomfortable pressure on the urethra when putting on the condom may have been common.

Several authors suggested that some men could not sustain their erection or that premature ejaculation occurred while a man was pausing to put the condom on. Griffith wrote that 'many men dislike it and will not use it continuously...The woman frequently finds it more difficult to achieve an orgasm.'[74] The elasticity of the rubber was limited, which meant that it often gave way at one or more points, creating breaks so small that they would not be noticed.[75] Both Haire and van de Velde gave instructions for testing the condom after use, by filling it with water and observing whether any drips become visible.[76] In the event that a drip appeared they told readers that the woman must leap from the bed and douche immediately. Dr C. Killick Mallard, the MOH for Leicester, commented in 1922 that it 'is said that men object to [the condom]; but one must recognise that birth control involves self-control and self-denial...It is no use recommending a male method to the wife when the husband perhaps will not be bothered.'[77] The female researchers

[72] van de Velde *Fertility* 322–3.

[73] Charles, *Practice*, 38.

[74] Griffith, *Modern Marriage* (1935), 81. Even in the 1950s, when condoms were much improved, Florence found examples of this: 'Husband had tried to use the sheath, but couldn't manage it, as he could not maintain erection.' Florence, *Progress Report*, 149. Also see G. C. Beale, *Wise Wedlock* (1922; 1926), 137. Griffith felt this was still correct in the substantially rewritten *Modern Marriage* (1947), 94. Guttmacher and Mears, *Babies*, 29. N. Haire, *The Comparative Value of Current Contraceptive Methods, Reprinted from the Proceedings of the First International Congress for Sexual Research (Berlin October 10th to 16th, 1926)* (1928), 8. Haire, *Birth-Control Methods*, 95–8. Scott, *Modern Birth Control*, 47–8.

[75] Haire, *Birth-Control Methods*, 95. Griffith, *Modern Marriage*, (1947), 93

[76] Haire, *Birth-Control Methods*, 95. Van de Velde, *Fertility*, 324.

[77] Pierpont (ed.), *Report*, 288. Also see Haire, *Birth-Control Methods*, 97. Slater and Woodside, *Patterns*, 203. Nurses in Stopes's birth control clinics also commented on male rejection of

Charles and Florence were considerably more positive about condoms than the male writers, who particularly disapproved of the thicker reusable condoms as interfering with sensation to an unacceptable extent.[78] In 1930 the Cambridge clinic had made efforts to ensure a good-quality, affordable supply of reusable sheaths and Florence was relatively positive about their working-class patients' experience with this method. However, in 1950s Birmingham, she found that 'among manual workers the sheath is turned to more as a last resort'.[79] Charles's 1930s middle-class respondents had a very mixed response to condoms, but they were the most frequently used method. She concluded that the reusable sheath was a relatively acceptable and reliable method, which was not too troublesome for the average woman and did not interfere with the pleasure of intercourse to too great an extent.[80] In the late 1950s the modern condom, relatively thin, cheap, and easy to use, and, most importantly, pre-lubricated, arrived. Once introduced they captured over half the market within three years.[81]

CONTRACEPTIVE EFFECTIVENESS

This section examines some estimates of contraceptive effectiveness for the methods that were in use during the inter-war period. Statistical methods of assessing effectiveness were only beginning to develop and these estimates are flawed. The periods of use were not controlled, the samples from which the results were obtained were not properly selected, and so on. The reason to look again at this work is that it includes condoms in the form in which they were being used in the inter-war period and methods, such as sponges, that had been abandoned by the

condoms. D. A. Cohen, 'Private Lives in Public Spaces: Marie Stopes, The Mother's Clinics and the Practice of Contraception', *History Workshop*, 35 (1993), 110–11. Individual rejection, e.g. P. Bailey, *An English Madam: The Life and Work of Cynthia Payne* (1982), 58.

[78] Beale, *Wise Wedlock*, 137. Fielding, *Parenthood*, (1928), 66. Griffith, *Modern Marriage*, (1947), 93. Van de Velde, *Fertility*, 323–4.

[79] Florence, *Birth Control*, 43. Florence, *Progress Report*, 131. Slater and Woodside, *Patterns*, 203.

[80] Charles, *Practice*, 49–51, 166.

[81] *Which Report on Contraception* (1963). Peel, 'Manufacture', 122. For assumption of the reliability of earlier condoms, see Tietze, 'Use-Effectiveness', 416.

post-Second World War period, when more systematic attempts at assessing effectiveness were made. Norman Haire gave estimates of the contraceptive effectiveness of different methods in 1928 and in 1936.[82] The following discussion is arranged in the order of Haire's ranking of the methods from least to most effective. Enid Charles also gave estimates from her postal sample of users. Her detailed discussion of the conditions and periods of use contributed to the development of techniques for measuring statistical effectiveness. Eighty-three per cent of her sample was classified as middle class, the group understood to have the lowest birth rate. She suggested these women might also be unusually interested in birth control, given that they had taken the trouble to answer the questionnaire.[83] The

Table 5.1. *Inter-war contraceptive effectiveness estimates: failure rates*

Method	Haire—1928	Haire—1937	Charles—1932
Intra-cervical pessaries	unsafe		
Safe period/ holding back	100		
Cervical caps, incl. metal and celluloid	86		rubber only—27
Spermicides alone	70	75.0	quinine—useless
Syringing			73
Sponges	70		100
Withdrawal		69.5	34
Condoms		51.4	82
Grafenberg rings		30.0	
Combination methods	cap + S: 5	cap + S: 9 condom + S: 5	

Notes: Charles gives success rates. These have been reversed to make comparison easier. S = spermicide.

Sources: Derived from N. Haire, *The Comparative Value of Current Contraceptive Methods, Reprinted from the Proceedings of the First International Congress for Sexual Research (Berlin October 10th to 16th, 1926)* (1928); N. Haire, *Birth-Control Methods (Contraception, Abortion, Sterilisation)* (1936; 1937). E. Charles, *The Practice of Birth Control: An Analysis of the Experience of Nine Hundred Women* (1932). Page reference numbers are given in the footnotes to the text.

[82] Haire, *Comparative Value*, 2. Haire, *Birth-Control Methods*.
[83] Charles, *Practice*, 21, 23, 25.

much lower failure rates she recorded may, speculatively, be taken to represent the best results possible with these methods in this period.

Neither Haire nor Charles had sufficient experience of intra-cervical pessaries to give an estimate of effectiveness. Haire found holding back and the safe period would fail in 100 per cent of the cases.[84] In 1928, for cervical caps used alone, he found a high failure rate, over 86 per cent, but this included metal and celluloid caps, as well as rubber ones.[85] Charles found a much lower failure rate for cervical caps of only 28 per cent. For Dutch caps, she found only a 21 per cent failure rate.[86] This included only rubber caps, and some of her cases used chemicals, so they were actually combined methods. Her results may demonstrate the gains that could be made. If chemical methods were used alone failure was estimated by Haire to occur in about 70 per cent of cases, in 1928. By 1936, this estimate had risen to 75 per cent of cases.[87] Charles found that syringing alone failed in 73 per cent of cases.[88] Haire found that the reward for all the effort of cleaning sponges was that '[f]ailure may be expected sooner or later in about 70 per cent of cases'.[89] Charles's respondents reported no success at prevention of pregnancy for periods of over one year, when using this method.[90] Withdrawal failed in 69.5 per cent of Haire's cases, 34 per cent of Charles's;[91] condoms in 51.4 per cent of Haire's cases, 18 per cent of Charles's.[92] Haire found the Grafenberg ring, an intrauterine device, failed either because pregnancy occurred, or the ring was expelled from the uterus, in around 30 per cent of his cases.[93] He concluded that the 'combined method of occlusive rubber vaginal diaphragm, plus contraceptive jelly, plus douche, is in my opinion the best method of contraception for the majority of women . . . [It has a] 5 % failure rate *if used*.'[94] Charles found that a combination of the sheath and a soluble pessary or syringing was most effective, suggesting a 5 per cent failure rate.[95] The fact that the male researcher preferred caps, and the female researcher condoms, emphasizes just how unappetizing the methods were. It can

[84] Haire, *Comparative Value*, 2.   [85] Ibid.   [86] Charles, *Practice*, 34.

[87] Haire, *Comparative Value*, 2. Haire, *Birth-Control Methods*, 91.

[88] Charles, *Practice*, 35, 44.   [89] Haire, *Birth-Control Methods*, 93.

[90] Charles, *Practice*, 166.   [91] Haire, *Birth-Control Methods*, 65. Charles, *Practice*, 34.

[92] Haire, *Birth-Control Methods*, 99.   [93] Ibid. 156.   [94] Ibid. 124, 126.

[95] Charles, *Practice*, 47–8.

be concluded that before the First World War those couples who took the advice offered would obtain some degree of protection from pregnancy in return for considerable effort and some loss of sexual pleasure. Sponges, douches, and syringing offered little protection, and the condoms of the period were unreliable. Rubber caps and diaphragms were little used. By the 1930s, those women and men who had co-operative partners, self-discipline, an adequate income, and private washing facilities could, by using a spermicidal pessary, *and* a douche *and* either a condom, rubber cap, or diaphragm, obtain a high level of protection from pregnancy.

However, despite the loss of pleasure, especially for women, withdrawal continued to be more widely used than any other method. Use of abortion was widespread although no reliable estimates of prevalence can be obtained. Unlike contraception, abortion is not a sexual practice and it does not alter physical sexual activity, but the practice is likely to have increased women's fears regarding a further pregnancy. It is possible that abortion became easier for women after several births; nonetheless working-class women were aware they risked producing chronic ill health or worse. Florence recorded that one woman said she had 'often taken drugs to bring about a miscarriage . . . [and] was blind and deaf for three days as a result of taking too much quinine'.[96] Although middle-class women's experience with doctors was probably safer, financial exploitation, sexual abuse, poor hygiene, and inadequate medical care were reported in the post-Second World War period.[97] The possibility of abortion probably acted as a disincentive to sexual intercourse. The contracepted act of heterosexual coitus remained substantially different from that experienced by the 1960s. The diminished sexual pleasure resulting from successful use of the available methods must be considered a major factor in the sexual culture of a period in which the birth rate (TFR) had fallen substantially.

[96] Florence, *Birth Control*, 87. B. Brookes, *Abortion in England* (1988).
[97] P. Ferris, *The Nameless* (1967).

'Physical "Open Secrets"':
Hygiene, Masturbation,
Bowel Control, and Abstinence

Levels of birth control use were starting to rise sharply by the 1930s, yet contraceptive failure rates remained high in spite of many women's intense fear of pregnancy and many couples' shared desire for a small family. The reasons that lay behind people's difficulties were complex and not easy to overcome. In order to use contraception effectively in the inter-war period, people had to think about what they were doing, they had to be aware of and consider their sexual acts, not just perform them. In 1931, van de Velde commented:

Doctors succeed as a rule in the application of contraception in their individual lives because *they understand the main factors* . . . a few—very few—out of the hundreds of thousands of sperms, shed at the vaginal orifice, may be enough to cause pregnancy . . . [the doctor] *has the habit of vigilance* . . . this is . . . why he practices contraception with more success than the layman . . . The 'secret' of success here is—extreme care, precision and vigilance in executing whatever method has been chosen, and due allowance for *apparently* trivial matters. (italics in original)[1]

Outside the context of sex, the constant self-discipline, attention to minor details, and regulation of personal conduct required to achieve control of fertility had been central to middle-class Victorian thinking, and these attitudes became considerably more widespread throughout the population during the inter-war period. From the 1870s to the end of the 1930s,

[1] Th. H. van de Velde, *Fertility and Sterility in Marriage: Their Voluntary Promotion and Limitation* (1931), 286–9.

this attitude was more crucial to the decline in fertility than birth control information or appliances as such. H. G. Wells wrote that birth control meant that 'one thing at least will become impossible—the bestial and almost involuntary fumblings of an ignorant animal urgency'.[2] But there was resistance to this discipline from some progressive men. The publisher Victor Gollancz felt that 'contraceptives mean wilfulness, planning, preparation: they shackle freedom.' Abstinence was the only method available to his wife Ruth until the opening of the Marie Stopes Clinic in 1927. She then tried a spermicide, but that method failed in 1928 and she again insisted on abstention.[3] The physical sexual control needed to use contraception included, indeed required, a new emotional control.[4] Rising rates of birth control use show that the desire, whether that of men or of women, to control fertility usually won out over spontaneity.

HYGIENE, MASTURBATION, AND TOILET TRAINING

This new discipline combined with attitudes to the genitals to reshape many aspects of adult sexuality. Three areas offer some insight into such attitudes: hygiene, masturbation, and bowel control. No historical works cover genital hygiene, and even general improvements in personal hygiene are little written about. The genitals are a source of bodily secretions and excreta, and all societies have beliefs that ensure the separation of these from food in order to prevent disease. Avoidance of

---

[2] H. G. Wells, preface in M. Fielding, *Parenthood: Design or Accident? A Manual of Birth Control* (1928), 10.

[3] R. D. Edwards, *Victor Gollancz: A Biography* (1987), 155–6, 200. See also R. Brandon, *The New Women and the Old Men* (1990), 167–8. Eric Gill believed female control of contraception was 'essentially matriarchy'. B. Evans, *Freedom to Choose: The Life and Work of Dr Helena Wright, Pioneer of Contraception* (1982), 155–6. Holroyd suggests that Ida (née Nettleship, 1877–1907) and Augustus John (1878–1961), who married in 1901, were insufficiently disciplined to use contraception, but it is possible that Augustus held similar beliefs to Gollancz and Gill. Ida was unable to obtain an abortion in 1906 and she died of puerperal fever following the birth of her unwanted fifth child. M. Holroyd, *Augustus John* (1974), 191–2.

[4] Emotional control, see E. F. Griffith, *Emotional Development* (1944), 8. He repeats this sentiment in *Modern Marriage* (1935; 1947), 31.

touching the genitals was probably a sensible and functional aspect of pre-modern control of disease. Improvements in personal hygiene during the nineteenth and early twentieth centuries necessitated huge amounts of labour in the absence of running water in the home. Intense guilt and shame about being 'dirty' and rising disgust at others who were perceived to be unclean helped motivate this effort. These attitudes did operate as symbolic boundaries and as a means to impose definitions of class, but improved hygiene had substantial material consequences.[5] Measures such as the discouraging of spitting and the washing of hands and bodies have been accepted as a major causal factor in improvements in morbidity and mortality, amidst a general dismissal by historians of the extravagant claims made for the achievements of modern medicine.[6]

Sexual activity is the only human activity in which close association with the bodily secretions of the self or another person is deemed desirable. It is hardly surprising that people, especially girls kept ignorant of sexuality, confused the pleasurable mess of sex with the dirt of excreta. A woman recalled that, as a girl around 1915, she had been 'horrified at such intimacy with part of the body associated with "dirt" '.[7] Vera Brittain said, 'I thought I ought to know [about sexual matters], though the information is always intensely distasteful to me...I suppose it is the spiritual—& intellectual—development part of me that feels repugnance at being brought too closely into contact with physical "open secrets".'[8] The history of visible dirt, the kind that is removed with soap and water, is also relevant. Historically, concern for cleanliness had begun with the outer clothes, where it was visible, where it counted and gave some return for the effort, then moved to linen, and only in the eighteenth and nineteenth centuries did a concern with cleaning the skin emerge.[9] In

[5] At the symbolic level, Douglas offers insights into the internalization of new standards and Rose, a relevant Foucauldian discussion of self-governmentality. M. Douglas, *Purity and Danger: An Analysis of the Concepts of Pollution and Taboo* (1966; 1994). N. Rose, *Governing the Soul: The Shaping of the Private Self* (1990).

[6] A. Wear, 'The History of Personal Hygiene', in R. Porter and W. F. Bynum (eds.), *Companion Encyclopaedia of the History of Medicine* (1993), 1304–5.

[7] L. England, 'Little Kinsey', in L. Stanley (ed.), *Sex Surveyed 1949–1994: From Mass Observation's 'Little Kinsey' to the National Survey and the Hite Reports* (1995), 78.

[8] V. Brittain, *Chronicle of Youth: Vera Brittain's War Diary 1913–17* (1981), 30–1.

[9] Wear, 'Personal Hygiene'.

the 1940s, this process was still ongoing. A young woman working in a factory during the Second World War repeated the adage: 'My mother always used to say, suppose you were run over, in the street, and they took you to hospital, you wouldn't want to feel ashamed, would you?'[10] Cleanliness was still for show, as much to impress others as for the benefit of the self.

Genital hygiene is discussed in the sources on contraceptive methods. Van de Velde told his readers, especially the women, that they were insufficiently aware of genital hygiene. As a gynaecologist and obstetrician he would have had little exposure to male genitals.[11] Haire, who did, commented graphically that:

Every doctor who has to examine the genital organs of either sex must be struck frequently with . . . the dirty condition of the sexual organs . . . in a considerable proportion of cases. This is due, not to any innate perversity, but rather to ignorance and convention. Women who spend hours every day over their toilet, who take a complete bath once or more every day, who are manicured and pedicured . . . often display to their gynaecologist sexual organs bathed with foul discharges. Men who pride themselves that under the most trying conditions, they insist on their 'morning tub,' often think it quite superfluous to retract the foreskin and clean the glans, and are quite satisfied to go about with a sloppy, wet, evil smelling penis the head of which is smeared with a disgusting combination of stale smegma and stale urine.[12]

The extreme language used in this quotation, 'foul', 'evil smelling', 'disgusting', reflects the moral loading carried by the concept of cleanliness in this period. However, the probability is that approaches to genital hygiene were not those usually considered 'natural' or comfortable today. Van de Velde gave detailed advice beginning with explaining that men and women should clean their genitals both morning and evening, using filtered or boiled water and a fresh piece of surgical lint each time. The description emphasized that this cleansing was '[I]n addition to the usual

---

[10] C. Fremlin, *War Factory*, ed. D. Sheridan (1987), 39–40. See also R. Hoggart, *A Local Habitation (Life and Times,* i: *1918–1940)* (1989), 26. For a middle-class example, see *The Hygiene of Life and Safer Motherhood* [c.1929], 422. This guide was republished in a slightly different version as W. Arbuthnot Lane (ed.), *The Modern Woman's Home Doctor* (1939), 312.

[11] T. H. van de Velde, *Ideal Marriage* (1928; reset 1943), 27–9, 49–51.

[12] N. Haire, *Birth-Control Methods (Contraception, Abortion, Sterilisation)* (1936; 1937), 89–90.

baths and ablutions'.[13] This somewhat obsessive approach was reinforced by commercial advertising of douches and other cleaning products. One medical textbook gave an example of a 'young woman in her twenties [who] presented with a severe vaginal and vulval condition as the result of douching four times daily with Lysol, in an excess of zeal for cleanliness'.[14] This woman was aware of her genitals and of the need to clean them but her perception of her genitals as dirty was apparently so strong that she was unable to assess an appropriate level of care.

Measures taken to prevent children masturbating and to ensure regular bowel movements shaped their response to their genitals as adults. Prohibitions against masturbation endured well beyond the Second World War. As late as 1990, the authors of the *Sexual Attitudes and Lifestyles* survey reported with regret that 'questions on masturbation were excluded from the survey, because discussion of this practice had met with both distaste and embarrassment from respondents involved in the qualitative work on question design'.[15] Even middle-class, progressive parents were deeply upset by 'masturbation' in the 1930s. A mother who decided that her nine-month-old daughter was masturbating asked for advice at the hospital: 'Matron alarmed me by saying it was a form of self-abuse and she [the nine-month-old girl] would eventually go out of her mind unless the habit was broken. She advised smacking very hard.'[16] The mother instead wrote to Susan Issacs, a Freudian educationalist, who probably replied to her by citing Freud's theory that masturbation was universal in infancy. In his study of English nannies, Jonathan Gathorne-Hardy found

[13] van de Velde, *Ideal Marriage*, 271–3. Genital hygiene was also mentioned in E. Chesser, *Love without Fear (A Plain Guide to Sex Technique for Every Married Adult)* (1941), 60. W. de Kok, 'Woman and Sex', in Lord Horder, J. Malleson, and G. Cox (eds.), *The Modern Woman's Medical Guide* (1949; 1955), 137.

[14] E. Hunt, *Diseases Affecting the Vulva* (1943), 144. Vaginal douching for cleanliness was actively discouraged by a few inter-war writers, e.g. M. Stopes, *Wise Parenthood* (1918), 28.

[15] e.g. K. Wellings, J. Field, A. M. Johnson, J. Wadsworth, and S. Bradhaw, *Sexual Attitudes and Lifestyles* (1994), 146. E. Slater and M. Woodside, *Patterns of Marriage* (1951), 175.

[16] S. Issacs, *Social Development in Young Children* (1933), 150–1. Three cases of parents who did use, or were advised to use, splints imprisoning their child's limbs at night to prevent masturbation are described in the book. Issacs, whose book contained extensive observations of children supporting the Freudian view that infantile sexuality was universal, received considerable public attention. See W. A. C. Stewart, *Progressives and Radicals in English Education, 1750–1970* (1972), 256–61.

that responses by nannies to suspected or actual masturbation had become physically less harsh and the religious overtones were less prominent in the inter-war period, but fears about masturbation hardly seemed to lessen at all. For example:

[Simon T. (b. 1925)] can remember being slapped every time his hand so much as strayed in the direction of his genitals and once, when he and his sister were aged four and six, they were caught examining each other and soundly thrashed...[Alexander Weymouth] can remember he and his brother Christopher Thynne fiddling with each other's penises in the bath, perhaps the 'cleanest' place to do it. Nanny Marks said sharply, 'You're not being dirty are you?'[17]

Washing the genitals would not be sufficient to make them 'clean' for children brought up in this fashion and anything more thorough than a quick going over, even of their own genitals, would have attracted negative comment. Unsurprisingly, this behaviour was similar to that of many working-class mothers in this period, as the nannies were almost inevitably working class.[18] In 1965, a retired female doctor described the pre-First World War behaviour of an 'indomitable Lancashire lass' who had become the family's nanny following their mother's death. '[B]elieving, as she told me years later, that "self abuse was the evil rotting the world", [the nanny] insisted on supervision in the lavatory, and put us to bed with our hands tied, sometimes too tightly. I remember my piano teacher commenting on my scarred wrists.'[19] Gathorne-Hardy implies that that the lack of resources available to supervise working-class children would have resulted in a more relaxed environment for them to grow up in. But oral histories of working-class women reveal that their attitudes to sexuality were no less prudish, and it is probable the immensely more cramped housing made surveillance inevitable much of the time.[20] Robert Roberts explained that in pre-First World War working-class Salford, 'the water closet [was] the only place where a member of the household could be assured of a few minutes' privacy—a boon in an

[17] J. Gathorne-Hardy, *The Rise and Fall of the British Nanny* (1972), 270, 272.
[18] Ibid., ch.1.
[19] M. D. Marwick, 'Reminiscence in Retirement', *Family Planning* (Oct. 1965), 79.
[20] E. Roberts, *A Woman's Place: An Oral History of Working-Class Women, 1890–1940* (1984). C. Chinn, *They Worked All their Lives* (1988), 141–53.

overcrowded kitchen. With some boys, however, even this privilege was not allowed: there were parents with a phobia about masturbation who insisted that young sons should use the privy only with the door wide open.'[21]

The evidence on adult masturbation is very limited. Chesser reported in 1949 that he had asked 600 female general patients and 300 men whom he examined as an army medical officer if they had masturbated. Fewer than 30 per cent of the women admitted to having done so, whereas 100 per cent of the men claimed they had.[22] Chesser had considerable experience of asking patients about stigmatized activities and is more likely to have obtained accurate answers than other investigators, but there is no way of confirming his results. Nearly forty years later a questionnaire survey undertaken by *Woman* magazine asked, 'Do you ever masturbate?' Only two-thirds of unmarried women and 56 per cent of wives said yes. Even in the 1980s, nearly two-fifths of the unmarried women reported that they felt guilty doing so.[23] There is a trickle of accounts by men about discovering masturbation but only one account by a British woman found in the course of this research. Molly Parkin (b. 1932) became notorious for her wild sexual behaviour. Yet, her account encapsulates the contradictions that might be expected from the other evidence on women's approach to their genitals. She felt sexual pleasure was animal, 'like a dog', and touching herself would have been rude and forbidden, so she rubbed her vulva against the arm of a chair.[24] In a study of child rearing in Nottingham, undertaken in the 1960s, John and Elizabeth Newson found that 'the class trend in the mother's behaviour in response to masturbation is very marked indeed. Nearly all class V mothers try to stop the

[21] R. Roberts, *The Classic Slum: Salford Life in the First Quarter of the Century* (1971; 1973), 164.

[22] E. Chesser, *Sexual Behaviour: Normal and Abnormal* (1949), 126–7. The Himeses, from the USA, believed English investigators were unduly cautious about questioning patients, and Chesser's results suggest they were correct. N. E. and V. C. Himes, 'Birth control for the British Working Classes: A Study of the First Thousand Cases to Visit an English Birth Control Clinic', *Hospital Social Service*, 19 (1929), 588.

[23] D. Sanders, *The Woman Book of Love and Sex* (1985), 21. It is not clear from the text whether this is two-fifths of those who masturbate or two-fifths of all the unmarried women.

[24] M. Parkin, *Moll: The Making of Molly Parkin* (1993), 58. Men, e.g. Hall Carpenter Archives, *Walking after Midnight: Gay Men's Life Histories* (1989), 58. W. F. R. Macartney and C. MacKenzie, *Walls have Mouths: A Record of Ten Years Penal Servitude* (1936), ch. 23.

[1-year-old] child touching or playing with his genitals at this age; only a quarter of professional men's wives do so.'[25] They attribute this in part to greater working-class 'modesty', or prudery, and in part to advice from baby books, which, in a reversal of the inter-war period, were united in advising that 'genital play' was natural by 1960. However, by the time the children were 4 years old, 90 per cent of all mothers stopped such behaviour. Many of the 10 per cent who ignored it were doing so only because they believed this was 'bringing it out into the open' and would encourage the child to lose interest and stop.[26] There was a tremendous ambivalence implicit in the attempt to neutralize sex interest.

Toilet training was another area in which parents' attitudes to the genitals as well as to the shaping of the child's feelings are revealed. The educationalist Susan Issacs believed that 'the practice of very early and very rigid training in bowel and bladder routine' was *growing* in the inter-war period.[27] In a questionnaire-based survey undertaken in 1951, sociologist Geoffrey Gorer found that there was 'a large consensus of opinion ... that cleanliness training should be started before the baby is a year old (more than two-thirds of mothers say before it is six months old) ... and that children need more discipline than they get nowadays'.[28] Both Gorer and Gathorne-Hardy pointed out that toilet training below the age of six months is a waste of time, and the latter explained that this is because the sphincters that enable control of the bowels have not physically developed. Both the nannies and, in Gorer's sample, the parents of more than one child rarely appeared to have learned from experience and they continued trying to 'pot' later children before this age.[29] Older children were expected to be 'regular'. The nanny of Simon T. allowed him 'two "tries" separated by half an hour', and if he failed to produce he

[25] J. Newson and E. Newson, *Patterns of Infant Care in an Urban Community* (1963; 1965), 201. Class I and II 25%, class V 93%.

[26] J. Newson and E. Newson, *Four Years Old in an Urban Community* (1968), 385–6. See also Bibby, *Sex*, 116.

[27] Issacs, *Social Development*, 16.

[28] G. Gorer, *Exploring English Character* (1955), 163. This book was based on 5,000 of the questionnaires returned in 1951 in response to a request in *People*, a popular newspaper of the period.

[29] Gathorne-Hardy, *Nanny*, 262–6. Gorer, *English Character*, 164.

was then given a thorough smacking and Gregory's powder.[30] The limited diet, which led to chronic constipation in many adults, must have done the same for children, exacerbating the anxieties this regimen created.

WOMEN AND GENITALS

Women often felt considerable degrees of discomfort at touching their sexual organs. Margaret Mead has pointed out that, compared to boys, the 'female child's genitals are less exposed, [less] subject to maternal manipulation and self manipulation'.[31] There was no socially sanctioned reason for women to touch their genitals in the early 1920s. Even when washing her genitals, the female child would almost invariably have been taught to use a flannel, not to 'touch herself'.[32] This is in contrast to the male child who had to be given permission by those in authority to hold his penis in order that he could urinate. Female children would have little or no experience that would provide them with any pleasurable, or even neutral, sensations to refute the construction of their genitals as dirty, ugly, and fear inducing. Mothers very frequently did not tell their daughters about menstruation. There are numerous mentions of distress when girls discovered they were bleeding and thought they were seriously ill. One women recalled, 'When I was fourteen, I had the shock of my life—I couldn't think—I just screamed.'[33] Women in all classes report that they were given no explanation for the event. Beliefs that women should avoid washing during menstruation, that it must be concealed,

[30] Gathorne-Hardy, *Nanny*, 264.

[31] M. Mead quoted in P. D. and E. D. Kronhausen, *Sexual Response in Women* (1965), 95, also 103. See e. Chesser, *Sexual Behaviour*, 125. For a useful discussion, see J. H. Gagnon and W. Simon, *Sexual Conduct: The Social Sources of Human Sexuality* (1974), 55, 61–2.

[32] This was still the case for some girls in the 1960s, e.g. M. Warner, 'Our Lady of the Boarding School', in M. Laing, (ed.), *Woman on Woman* (1971), 36–7.

[33] D. Gittins, *Fair Sex, Family Size and Structure, 1900–39* (1982), 84. See also S. Alexander, 'The Mysteries and Secrets of Women's Bodies: Sexual Knowledge in the First Half of the Twentieth Century', in M. Nava and A. O'Shea (eds.), *Modern Times: Reflections on a Century of English Modernity* (1996). Chinn, *They Worked*, 141–2. K. Dayus, *Where there's Life* (1985), 95. C. Dyhouse, 'Mothers and Daughters in the Middle-Class Home c.1870–1914', in J. Lewis (ed.), *Labour and Love: Women's Experience of Home and Family, 1850–1940* (1986), 36. England, 'Little Kinsey', 81. J. Klein, *Samples of English Culture*, vol. i (1965), 65.

and problems with maintaining adequate sanitary protection added to negative feelings about the genitals—and femininity.[34] In the first decades of the century, ordinary protection consisted of washable towels made from turkish towelling. They were 'unpleasant to store and to wash either at home or in a laundry'.[35] The poor probably lacked even this provision: 'when the Suffrage Campaign brought women of education into Holloway Gaol, they found that no provision of any kind was made for women prisoners in this respect. If this means anything beyond abominable administration, it means that women of the class commonly committed to the gaol were not expected at that date to require such refinements.'[36]

By the 1930s, disposable sanitary pads were usual for those who could afford them, and the tampon, a commercial innovation, had begun to erode women's resistance to touching their genitals.[37] Some GPs and the Royal College of Obstetricians and Gynaecologists resisted women's use of tampons. This reveals the extent of discomfiture about the sexual body and the extent to which the medical profession endorsed and, where they had influence, reinforced apparently irrational female attitudes to their genitals. In a 1943 textbook, *Diseases Affecting the Vulva*, E. Hunt asserted that:

The insertion of a contaminated carton, without any attempt at cleansing the external surfaces of the genitalia, may be the source of actual danger to the woman who pushes the tampon upwards into the vagina, damaging the epithelium *en route* and introducing organisms which are retained in the vagina. The prolonged retention of the tampon by the woman who is careless in her habits leads to a suppurative condition, such as occurs with any foreign body. The psychical effect of the daily insertion of tampons in the vagina must also be considered, and the possibility that this practice may lead to masturbation.[38]

In interpreting this quotation in the absence of extensive historical research into sanitary hygiene products we must accept the possibility that the tampons of the 1940s promoted infection upon introduction. It remains

---

[34] G. R. Scott, *The New Art of Love* (1934; 1955), 27–8. Van de Velde, *Ideal Marriage*, 91. Women's Group on Public Welfare, *Our Towns: A Close up* (1943; 1985), 98.

[35] Women's Group on Public Welfare, *Our Towns*, 98.

[36] Ibid. 97–8. Some girls in factories were found to be using toilet paper and a few Second World War evacuees were using no protection whatsoever.

[37] Slater and Woodside, *Patterns*, 208. M. Macaulay, *The Art of Marriage* (1952; 1957), 58–9.

[38] Hunt, *Diseases*, 144.

difficult to believe they could have damaged the epithelium, or lining of the vagina. The reference to masturbation makes it evident there was a strong social component to the doctor's discomfort, which would have existed prior to the discovery of any physiological basis for unease. The suggestion that a woman who left her tampon in for prolonged periods was being careless ignores the confusion surrounding the issue. Around 1930, medical debates on the placing of contraceptive devices in the vagina reveal that some doctors were then happy to advise patients to leave devices in for long periods.[39] Van de Velde's suggestion that a fresh piece of surgical lint is essential each time the external genitals are cleaned comes from an opposing perspective, but both discussions suggest a lack of customary knowledge of the vagina. Even in the late 1950s, a gynaecology textbook advised that tampons were suitable only for 'married women', and were 'liable to set up vaginitis through inadequate drainage'.[40] No distinction was made between what would be seen now as separate social and medical rationales. Accepting the advice of the majority of the medical profession, even in the late 1950s, would often not have helped women to understand and interpret their own physical experience more positively. People's attitudes towards their genitals, whether this deviated from standards current today in terms of, for women, a lesser or a greater willingness to place objects in the vagina, or, for both sexes, a lesser or a greater concern with hygiene, should not be interpreted as irrational. There is no natural body, no natural range of sensations, pre-existing and free from the social context.

Working-class people were very much slower to begin using contraception, especially appliance methods, than were middle-class couples.[41] Looking back over the first half of the century, E. Lewis-Faning did not find pregnancy rates varied amongst method users by social class, which suggests that where working-class people were able and willing to use artificial methods they did so as effectively as middle-class couples.[42] But

---

[39] M. Sanger and H. Stone, *The Practice of Contraception: An International Symposium and Survey. From the Proceedings of the Seventh International Birth Control Congress, Zurich, Switzerland, September 1930* (1931), 12. See Haire, *Birth-Control Methods*, 123.

[40] F. W. Roques, J. Beattie, and J. Wrigley, *Diseases of Women* (1959), 107.

[41] See Ch. 4.

[42] E. Lewis-Faning, *Report on an Enquiry into Family Limitation and its Influence on Human Fertility during the Past Fifty Years*, Papers of the Royal Commission on Population, Vol. 1 (1949), 134.

for those who lived in poverty, maintaining the standards of hygiene sufficient to use contraception without promoting infection required efforts far greater than those that the same standards demanded of middle-class users of contraception. In the late Victorian period, lower-middle-class people still might not have running water in the home, and even in the inter-war period it was exceptional for working-class women to have unlimited water ready at hand, A private toilet also remained unusual in many areas.[43] It is probable that where there were inadequate facilities women frequently felt their genitals were dirty because they were; their feelings were not unreasonable and a reluctance to touch their genitals was not irrational. The use of birth control devices, including condoms or caps, may have required them to alter deep-seated and, within their context, functional ideas about their bodies. These women were unlikely to have had the attention to spare for the effort of preventing a future pregnancy by use of the recommended combined methods, nor is it likely that these would have seemed a sensible use of limited resources. Many of the women described in *Working-Class Wives* (1939) were ignoring existing painful diseases, and given that obtaining treatment for these was not possible, they certainly would not have had resources to spare for hypothetical gains in the future.[44] The label 'working-class' covers a range of incomes and housing conditions, and during the inter-war period much new housing was produced. There was an annual average of 150,000 new houses built in the 1920s, rising to over 300,000 annually during the 1930s.[45] Increasingly, working-class people did have internal running water, a privy that did not have to be shared with other tenants, and some degree of privacy in the home. But during the Second World War, 15 per cent of Britain's housing stock was destroyed and this loss was only slowly repaired. As late as the 1960s, Hannah Gavron

[43] H. Llewellyn Smith (ed.), *The New Survey of London Life and Labour* (1935), vi. 314. For the labour involved in laundry, see Chinn, *They Worked*. Middle-class toilet facilities, e.g. E. F. Griffith, *The Pioneer Spirit* (1981), 31. Roberts includes a picture of a toilet seat, with the cut-up squares of newspaper used by the respectable poor. Roberts, *A Woman's Place*, 132—4. G. Rattray-Taylor, *Sex in History* (1953), 190. Women's Group on Public Welfare, *Our Towns*, 87—8.

[44] M. Spring Rice, *Working-Class Wives: Their Health and Conditions* (1939; 1981), 28.

[45] M. J. Daunton, 'Housing', in F. M. Thompson (ed.), *The Cambridge Social History of Britain 1750—1950* (1990).

found that bad housing 'dominated the lives' of over 60 per cent of her sample of working-class London mothers.[46]

ABSTINENCE

Many women and men's apparent inability to use contraception properly in the first half of the twentieth century was due in part to feelings of distaste about their bodies. The feelings that discouraged women and men from being sexually adventurous or expressing tenderness through genital sexual activity were crucial in underpinning the acceptance of partial sexual abstinence. In 1886, Dr Henry A. Albutt published *The Wife's Handbook*, which covered the care of the wife and new baby and included information about contraceptive methods. He also explained that 'many young people injure their health considerably by indulging in intercourse too freely during the first months of marriage', and that 'Moderation should be observed.'[47] The early sex and birth control manual authors assumed abstaining from sexual activity was a widely recommended approach to controlling births which their readers needed to be dissuaded from using.[48] The manual authors are more flexible, even ambivalent, about the appropriate frequency of intercourse. In *Married Love* (1918) Stopes mentioned that this was one of the topics about which questions were most frequently asked. In *Enduring Passion* (1928) she devoted a chapter to the topic. In this she commented that 'some couples find after periods of mutual strength and enrichment, they can live without the physical act of union, deriving from each other all their natures require from the subtler mental, physical and spiritual

---

[46] H. Gavron, *The Captive Wife* (1966; 1968), 62. For conditions before the Second World War, see M. Llewellyn Davies, *Maternity* (1915; 1978). M. Pember Reeves, *Round about a Pound a Week* (1913; 1979).

[47] H. A. Allbutt, *The Wife's Handbook* (1886), 57–8.

[48] e.g. 'The alternative [to use of birth control]... is not merely the cessation of sexual intimacy, but also abstinence from all the endearing intimacies which are natural and spontaneous in married life. They must not only sleep apart but in many ways live apart. And this not only means pain of the heart... but also often leads to serious nervous trouble because of the strain which it involves... I believe conception control to be the better way.' A. H. Gray, *Men, Women and God* (1923; 1947) 112.

radiations'.[49] She also gave examples of high frequencies of intercourse. The evidence suggests this was a sexual culture in which there was a very much higher proportion of people at the low frequency end of a continuum, not that a full range of sexual behaviour was not taking place. Nor did a low frequency of intercourse necessarily mean a lack of enjoyment of sexual activity. However, in looking at the evidence from the late nineteenth century up to the Second World War, it is easy to forget or underestimate the obvious fact that those who were by today's standards inhibited in their sexual behaviour were also strongly inhibited in discussing sex. So reports of sexual behaviour largely come from those who were by the standards of their age uninhibited and atypical.

One of the indications that sexual restraint played an important role in bringing down the birth rate is the association of large families with sexual indulgence by working-class people. When people are using effective contraception there is no connection between the extent of sexual activity and reproduction. Where pregnancy is still seen as a sign of sexual indulgence then it is probable that birth control is not the sole and perhaps not even the primary means by which attempts to limit births are made. One woman described arguing with her father in 1914; 'My father was too easy going. I said, "No sooner do we get one baby grown up than another one comes." "Oh you brazen little madam," he said.'[50] The word brazen indicates the sexual content of what she had said. Embarrassment at being seen in public while pregnant was also common in the inter-war period.[51] Mass-Observation commented in 1945 that 'large families today are considered old-fashioned at best, at worst somehow indecent'. Comments made by respondents to the survey included a mother of four, who said, 'We have been called lustful and irresponsible producers.' A telephone engineer aged 30 described the 'Vague social feeling almost of immorality in having a lot of children'. A mother of three said, 'I was so ashamed when the third was expected, I wouldn't go out if I could help it.'[52] Terms such as

[49] M. Stopes, *Enduring Passion* (1928; 1931), 134–5.
[50] Roberts, *A Woman's Place*, 41.
[51] Gittins, *Fair Sex* 1982. 90. M. Stopes, *Married Love* (1918; 1937), 115.
[52] Mass-Observation, *Britain and her Birth Rate* (1945), 75.

'lustful' or 'immorality' reveal the continuing sexual connotation of reproduction.

There is evidence of sensitivity and concern on the part of some husbands. Where men were aware of their wives' feelings and a woman disliked sexual activity, it is reasonable to assume that there was often a lower frequency of intercourse. In 1964, a 32-year-old man, who described his wife as 'an alert and intelligent woman', described how both he and she had been brought up 'in an atmosphere of anti-sex education and thought'. He explained that his own and his wife's inhibitions led him to frequent prostitutes. Her 'initial efforts were a very brave attempt on her part to do what she thought was expected. Within a year of our marriage the old walls of inhibition and disgust had sprung up again; and because I don't like the indignity of rejection . . . we rapidly drifted apart, at least physically.'[53] Clearly a man's sensitivity to his wife could be limited and might not direct him into paths likely to improve their mutual sexual experience. One in four men told the Mass-Observation sex survey that they had visited prostitutes, although they did not state how often.[54]

In 1949, this Mass-Observation sex survey found that two out of five respondents insisted that it was possible to be happy without any form of sex life. Those who felt this tended to be older and there was a higher proportion of women.[55] Biographical evidence of partial or complete abstinence reinforces the impression that women were more likely to be accepting of this than men. For example, Herbert Morrison's wife was said to have refused to copulate with him for twenty years and his 'roaming hands' were blamed on her.[56] Nonetheless, writers of all kinds assumed that in the absence of sexual opportunity many people did not miss sexual fulfilment. One doctor argued that '[a]bstinence does no harm in the absence of sexual stimulus, as, for example, when a husband and wife occupy separate bedrooms; but if they lie in contact with one another there is sexual stimulus. Perhaps the stimulus may be unconscious and

---

[53] 'The Need for Prostitution', *Twentieth Century*, 172 (1964), 127.
[54] England, 'Little Kinsey', 143.
[55] Ibid. 155; example of abstinence, 156.
[56] B. Donoughue and G. W. Jones, *Herbert Morrison: Portrait of a Politician* (1973), 174, 309.

unrecognised, but it does occur and it is not recognised.'[57] Separate sleeping arrangements appear to have been an acceptable solution to many people, not just middle-class couples. There are mentions of working-class women who chose to sleep in another room with their children or in separate beds in the same room as their husband.[58] This level of avoidance could, and probably frequently did, go beyond the desire to control births into an active rejection of genital sexual activity by both sexes.

In *The Peckham Experiment* (1943), a report on a health clinic set up in the 1930s in Peckham, a working-class suburb of London, the authors noted that in 'the course of our work we found what we believe to be a high percentage of... non-consummation and of rarity of connection, as well as of the deliberate avoidance of childbearing by birth control methods... In these people what is usually presumed to be the pressing urgency of the sexual appetite remains unstirred to a surprising extent.'[59] Mentions of non-consummated marriages are particularly striking. *Sexual Disorders in the Male* (1939) was written by the Viennese E. B. Strauss and Kenneth Walker, whose career as a genito-urinary surgeon had begun before the First World War. They give a number of case studies that include abstinence over a long period. One married couple decided not to have children due to insanity in the immediate family. After their doctor recommended they not use birth control they remained abstinent for twenty-three years, at which point the wife wanted sexual experience and a child. They were described as having a 'moderately successful marriage'. In general, the authors said, 'feebly sexed patients are not uncommon'.[60] The absence of sexual activity did not mean

[57] Contribution by Dr W. H. B. Stoddart in R. Pierpont (ed.), *Report of the Fifth International Neo-Malthusian and Birth Control Conference. Kingsway Hall, London, July 11th–14th, 1922* (1922), 283. Beale, *Wise Wedlock*. Beale refers to the 'much debated question of separate or common bedrooms', 100.

[58] e.g. R. D. Laing, *The Facts of Life* (1976), 14. Chinn found this to be routine: C. Chinn, *They Worked*, 152. A middle-class example, J. Calder, *The Nine Lives of Naomi Mitchison* (1997), 10.

[59] I. H. Pearse and, L. H. Crocker, *The Peckham experiment: A Study in the Living Structure of Society* (1943), 258.

[60] K. M. Walker and E. B. Strauss, *Sexual Disorders in the Male* (1939; 4th edn. 1954), 76, 84. See also M. Cole, *The Life of G. D. H. Cole* (1971), 91. Stopes, *Enduring Passion* (4th edn. 1931); 'Undersexed Husbands', 54–6.

couples were unloving. Agnes Hughes, a close friend of Kier Hardie, and her husband Hedley Dennis remained abstinent throughout their married life but were close and very supportive of one another.[61] The historian Lesley Hall commented on the 'surprising number of correspondents [who] wrote to Stopes about unconsummated marriages, some of which had existed in this state for an extremely long period'.[62] Dr Joan Malleson, a well-respected female consultant on sexual problems, published her first article on non-consummated marriages in the *British Medical Journal* in 1942, and two further articles in the *Practitioner* in 1952 and 1954.[63] These were based upon hundreds of cases.

A detailed study was published in 1962 of non-consummated marriages treated by doctors over the three years that they participated in a Family Planning Association series of seminars. Only the wives were treated. They were given a medical examination and were then seen for a limited number of sessions. The author explained that such cases were not rare in the participating doctors' practices. It was estimated that each doctor saw an average of twenty-five to thirty 'virgin wives' a year, with the lowest estimate eight to ten women, and the highest fifty to sixty. Altogether, these ten doctors probably saw about 700 cases of non-consummated marriages, most of which patients were probably middle class, during the two and a half years of the study.[64] Of the 100 cases discussed in the seminar, 35 per cent, just over a third, had been married for the relatively short period of under one year, 37 per cent, again over a third, for one to four years, and 25 per cent for five to ten years. Three per cent had been married for over ten years.[65] There were few doctors willing or

[61] C. Benn, *Keir Hardie* (1992), 426.

[62] L. A. Hall, *Hidden Anxieties: Male Sexuality, 1900–1950* (1991), 102–3.

[63] J. Malleson, 'Vaginismus: Management and Psychogenesis', *BMJ* 2 (1942). 'Infertility due to Coital Difficulties: A Simple Treatment', *Practitioner*, 169 (1952). 'Sex Problems in Marriage with Particular Reference to Coital Discomfort and the Unconsummated Marriage', *Practitioner*, 172 (1954).

[64] L. J. Friedman, *Virgin Wives: A Study of Unconsummated Marriages* (1962), 11. A list of the medical experience of the ten, all female, participating doctors is given, 4–5.

[65] Ibid., derived from table 4, 126. The 100 cases discussed in the seminar were 'not a random sample' of those seen. The doctors tended to report those cases which they found difficult, 11–12. See also Alison Giles, 'Learning to Deal with Sexual Difficulties', *Family Planning*, 10/2 (1961). Many of the patients would have been referred from FPA clinics, which had a mainly middle-class clientele. A. Leathard, *The Fight for Family Planning* (1980), 76.

able to help their patients with sexual problems in this period. The large number of couples with these extreme sexual difficulties that found their way to the seminar participants is indicative of a much larger number who must have been unable to obtain professional advice.

Unsurprisingly, given that this was the late 1950s, these couples were not abstaining for contraceptive purposes but because they had profound difficulties with the expression of sexuality. The doctors found that:

Some women who have not consummated their marriages are in a sense asleep; they restrict conscious awareness of sexual feeling. They use the defence of 'not knowing' about their sexual organs to ward off anxiety ... Such women tend to think of their vaginas as too small for the penis and fear injury from intercourse.[66]

This explanation that the women were restricting conscious awareness of sexual feelings that nonetheless did exist reflects the broad acceptance within Western culture of the Freudian refusal to admit that a lack of sexual feelings is possible. This was the basis of the doctors' assumption that they knew more about these women than the women knew themselves. This validated their denial of the women's own testimony, which often spoke of an absence of sexual feelings. Many of the patients experienced vaginismus, where the vaginal muscles clamp tightly. The treatment offered consisted of talking with the woman and then inserting glass dilators into her vagina to enable her to overcome her fears about penetration of the vagina. Several of the doctors 'were anxious that using dilators might be seen as encouraging the patients to masturbate', a fear which now appears as 'irrational' as the patients' fear of intercourse.[67]

The aim of the treatment was to reconcile women to sexual intercourse and the seminar concluded that a patient's '[m]arked disgust for her genitals [has] been taken as bad prognostic signs but fear and anxiety have not'.[68] Some men also suffered from perceptions that sex was 'messy and disgusting'. Kenneth Walker explained that:

---

[66] Friedman, *Virgin Wives*, 39.
[67] Ibid. 105–6.   [68] Ibid. 111.

Many men marry not only in ignorance of the art of love-making but with entirely wrong attitudes to sexuality. Take, for example, a man who has grown up with the idea that sex is of a comic nature. From the start all manifestations of sexuality have been regarded by him as excellent material for ribald stories and obscene drawings . . . Is it surprising that when he marries his attitude remains the same? . . . the more he is in love with and admires his wife, the less likely he is to be able to associate her with such obscene behaviour as love-making. As a result he may even find himself impotent with his wife and capable only of love-making with prostitutes.[69]

Male participation in sexual badinage is not sufficient to indicate that they were any more comfortable and less anxious about genital sexual activity than their more obviously prudish wives. The problems these men and women faced were not usual by the 1950s. But their attitudes were assumed to be common in the manuals of the 1920s and before. The existence of so large a number of women with serious difficulties in the late 1950s reinforces the impression given by other sources that the proportion of couples in which one or both partners did not enjoy sexual expression, and thus did not find abstinence a sacrifice, was considerable in earlier decades.[70]

However, marital abstinence is not merely a method of birth control any more than is infanticide. Abstinence within marriage was a course of desperation that could be sustained only by imposition of a repressive sexual and emotional culture, initially by individuals of their own accord, and then, as they internalized those dictates, upon succeeding generations. The fertility decline that took place in Britain was of a wholly different nature from those that have taken place in the developing world since the arrival of effective methods of contraception in the 1960s.[71] The point that was reached in the 1930s was not a stable, low-growth population equilibrium, instead it was a highly unstable low-fertility regime

[69] K. M. Walker, *Love, Marriage and the Family* (1957), 133.

[70] In the late 1960s, Gorer found 'a couple' of instances. G. Gorer, *Sex and Marriage in England Today: A Study of the Views and Experience of the under-45s* (1971), 31.

[71] For an overview of fertility decline, see D. Kirk, 'Demographic Transition Theory' *Population Studies*, 50 (1996). R. Lesthaeghe and J. Surkyn, 'A Century of Demographic and Cultural Change in Western Europe: An Exploration of the Underlying Dimensions', *Population and Development Review*, 9/3 (1983).

maintained by sexual control. As contraception and living conditions improved during the inter-war period, the internalized sexual repression which had maintained this regime was gradually eroded, and fertility began to rise again.

PART II

Sexuality and Sex Manuals

English Sexuality in the Twentieth Century: Ignorance, Silence, and Gendered Sexual Cultures

I have found that people talk to me very frankly about sex, and I have formed some interesting conclusions from their confidences and from my own personal experience. The most important is my firm conviction that most people go through life without experiencing sexual pleasure worth the name.[1]

Leonora Eyles, who wrote this in 1933, was a journalist and the author of a sex manual. She had been married twice and had several affairs, and wanted to share what she had learnt. Until the late twentieth century her readers are unlikely to have been surprised that the majority of the population experienced little by way of sexual pleasure, but many would have been taken aback that people would speak frankly to her about their sexual experience.[2] The publication since the 1970s of numerous biographies of radical or literary and highly sexually active individuals, many of whom left generous diaries and letters, and histories of groups to whom

[1] L. Eyles, *Commonsense about Sex* (1933), 77. Recent sexual histories of 20th-century England include that by P. Ferris, who was an observer of events as a journalist in the 1960s. *Sex and the British: A Twentieth Century History* (1994). L. Hall focuses on sexual knowledge. R. Porter and L. Hall, *The Facts of Life: The Creation of Sexual Knowledge in Britain, 1650–1950* (1995). C. Haste makes a quick whip round the usual suspects in C. Haste, *Rules of Desire: Sex in Britain, World War I to the Present* (1992). S. Humphries's useful oral history includes illicit heterosexual activity, *A Secret World of Sex* (1988). J. Weeks provides the only theoretically informed account: *Sex, Politics and Society: The Regulation of Sexuality since 1800* (1981; 1989).

[2] N. E. and V. C. Himes, 'Birth Control for the British Working Classes: A Study of the First Thousand Cases to Visit an English Birth Control Clinic', *Hospital Social Service*, 19 (1929), 588.

sexuality was central may give the impression of a culture in which sexual rebellion, or hidden and forbidden sexual activity, was frequent. These people were often important as they brought new ideas and an insistence on pleasure in the body into twentieth-century English society, but their sexual experiences were unusual. The intention of this chapter is to provide an overview of the sexual behaviour of the majority of people in early to mid-twentieth-century England. These generations continued the struggle that had begun in the early nineteenth century to control fertility by altering sexual response. The sexual culture was shaped by change in three other areas; sexual ignorance and the reshaping of knowledge; the clash between the separate sexual cultures of men and women; and lastly the conflict between an entrenched privacy and the need to talk about sexuality. An individual's sexuality is formed by physical and emotional experiences that take place from infancy to adolescence. Adult experience then shapes the expression of that sexuality.[3] This individual experience takes place within the context of the existing sexual culture. A cultural generation has been defined as a 'vague, ambiguous, and stretchable concept... people of roughly the same age whose shared experience significantly distinguishes them from contemporaries in other age groups'.[4] It is useful to think of sexual generations whose shared experience was distinguished from those who came before or after. It is the young, whose ideas and lives are still in the process of formation, who are powerfully shaped by the new, and, because of this, shifts in sexual mores take place over decades. When we look for changes in, say, the 1900s, we must look at the choices young adults are making and how they are behaving as they form their sexual lives. Then back at the 1880s and 1890s to consider the time in which this generation was formed and how that social context was different from what came before and after.

---

[3] Wyatt et al. found that 'Whatever was learned and practiced in childhood was a strong predictor of how a woman would express her sexuality throughout her life.' G. E. Wyatt, M. D. Newcomb, and M. H. Riederle, *Sexual Abuse and Consensual Sex: Women's Developmental Patterns and Outcomes* (1993), 205. There appears to be no equivalent research into male sexuality, but it seems probable the same is true of men.

[4] A. B. Spitzer, 'The Historical Idea of Generation', *American Historical Review*, 78 (1973), 1353–4.

SEXUAL IGNORANCE

This section examines the sexual culture which made controlling births by abstinence possible. Ignorance about genital sexual activity and reproduction is mentioned frequently in the first half of the century and it must be central to any explanation of the sexual culture. The word ignorance has been used because this was the term chosen by many people during the period to describe their own experience of physical sexuality.[5] Yet, during the course of this research, it has become obvious that many people, including historians, have difficulty in accepting that extreme sexual ignorance could exist. This common-sense perspective is usually not articulated, and so the assumptions underlying it are left unexamined.[6] The problem stems in part from the difficulty of connecting theories of sexuality with the history of physical sexual experience. The ideas of Sigmund Freud (1856–1939) entered popular culture during the middle decades of the twentieth century and have become part of common-sense understandings of behaviour for the generations that came of age since then. Freud gave sexual drives an importance and centrality in human life, human actions, and human behaviour which was new and deeply shocking to many people. He argued that the sexual drives exist and can be discerned in children from birth, giving rise to infantile sexuality, and that sexual energy (libido) is the single most important motivating force in adult life. If the satisfaction of the pleasure drives transgresses sanctions imposed by the ego then the sexual energy may be repressed. The conflicts this causes will be pushed back into the unconscious and deviations and neuroses are likely to occur through the damming up of libidinal energy. Or sublimation may take place, in which case the sexual energy will be

---

[5]   e.g. 'Has one to leave sex alone to be pure? Is it such an evil, ugly thing? No! It must be this dreadful all prevailing ignorance.' From the 1909 diary of Ruth Slate (1884–1953), in T. Thompson (ed.), *Dear Girl: The Diaries and Letters of Two Working Women 1897–1917* (1987), 139.

[6]   e.g. T. Laqueur commented in a book review: 'Similarly, women report not knowing where babies came from until they were married. Perhaps this is true but they learned quickly and it is odd that in such a print saturated culture such ignorance was so widespread.' Laqueur, 'Simply Doing It', *London Review of Books* (22 Feb. 1996). 12. See also the scepticism expressed in K. Fisher, ' "She was Quite Satisfied with the Arrangements I Made": Gender and Birth Control in Britain 1920–1950', *Past and Present*, 169 (2001), 168–9, 173–4. For a thoughtful scepticism, see E. K. Sedgwick who has suggested that we pluralize and specify ignorance. *Epistemology of the Closet* (1990), 7–8.

channelled into the achievement of socially acceptable goals in art or science. Freud encouraged a search for the underlying sexual basis of social behaviour and taught people to be sceptical of persons with an apparent lack of sexual energy. It is still widely believed that an absence of sexual feelings or physical desire is not possible and is merely a sign that sexual feeling had been repressed and denied. Many people born since the 1930s may also find it difficult to accept sexual ignorance as possible because formal sex education is largely irrelevant to the development of sexuality. They have few other memories of acquiring sexual knowledge and they, therefore, perceive their own sexual knowledge as coming naturally. It is necessary to consider how sexuality develops in more detail in order to understand how it was possible for many people in earlier generations to grow up without sexual knowledge.

First, some evidence regarding sexual ignorance. A survey undertaken by Mass Observation in 1949 found sexual ignorance, including ignorance of reproduction, to have been common. The following quotation is one example from a series:

At 26 years of age [in 1914], I was as ignorant as it was possible to be. The funny part is that I can't imagine how I lived to that age without realising. I wasn't helped in the slightest bit. Even when I started my midwifery training I never thought fathers had anything to do with it. (61 year old woman, retired nurse)[7]

In the draft of a book on the Mass Observation survey, Leonard England discussed responses such as this woman's, and the problem of determining the extent of sexual ignorance:

These are not extreme cases, but rather milder instances of prolonged ignorance, and do not appear to be by any means rare. Although discovery of the facts by 'getting married' seems—from the relative elderliness of the majority mentioning it—to be a dying phenomena, it is still mentioned by one in every twenty, usually the less 'well-educated' and generally women. A working-class housewife for instance said: I didn't know until I was married—all my mother said was 'Behave yourself' and none of the details. (39 year old organ grinder's wife)[8]

---

[7] L. Stanley, *Sex Surveyed 1949–1994: From Mass Observation's 'Little Kinsey' to the National Survey and the Hite Reports* (1995), 82.

[8] L. England, 'Little Kinsey', ibid. 83. A brief article on this survey was also published: L. England, 'A British Sex Survey', *International Journal of Sexology*, 3/3 (1950). Other examples:

In 1930, the woman quoted would have been aged around 20. A rate of extreme sexual ignorance of one in twenty suggests that the average level of sexual knowledge in inter-war society was low. The evidence on sexual abstinence presented in the previous chapter reinforces this, and oral historians who have asked about sexual knowledge have consistently found this was the case. It is probable that prolonged ignorance in single people, including a smaller percentage of young men, was relatively common until the early 1930s. This sexual ignorance often included lack of knowledge of how babies were made, that the baby emerged into the world through the vagina, of reproductive processes such as menstruation, of the body of the opposite sex, and of the actual act of coitus. Most importantly, many young people were not aware that mutual genital play and coitus were potentially a source of physical and emotional pleasure. This ignorance of sexual knowledge was closely related to ignorance or 'innocence' of physical sexual desire. Profound sexual ignorance did not necessarily include an absence of flirtation, or of playfulness; it was an absence of knowledge about the potential physical ends of such behaviour. Prior to the First World War such ignorance was common amongst single people in all classes, but during the inter-war decades profound ignorance ceased to exist amongst the sexually progressive or people with extensive formal education. Amongst other groups what passed for sexual knowledge was still very limited even in the 1930s.[9]

How was it possible for profound sexual ignorance to exist? From the last quarter of the late nineteenth century the majority of British parents in all classes had tried to ensure their children did not obtain sexual knowledge. They believed sexual knowledge was something from which children and young people, especially girls, must be protected, and that they must be taught to limit their physical and emotional expression.

C. Chinn, *They Worked All their Lives* (1988), 144–5. M. Llewellyn Davies, *Maternity: Letters from Working Women Collected by the Women's Co-operative Guild* (1915; 1978), 187. M. Llewellyn Davies, *Life as we have Known it*, ed. A. Davin (1931; 1977), 25. D. Gittins, *Fair Sex, Family Size and Structure, 1900–39* (1982), 79, 84–5, 89–90. M. D. Marwick, 'Reminiscence in Retirement', *Family Planning* (Oct. 1965). E. Roberts, *Women and Families: An Oral History, 1940–1970* (1995), 59–60.

[9] E. Chesser, *Love without Fear (A Plain Guide to Sex Technique for Every Married Adult)* (1941), 12. K. Dayus, *Where there's Life* (1985), 151. J. Klein, *Samples of English Culture*, vol. 1 (1965), 38–9, 64–5. E. Roberts, 'The Working Class Extended Family: Functions and Attitudes 1890–1940', *Oral History* (1900), 59.

Respectable men and women were embarrassed and inhibited in their replies to children's questions about topics such as pregnancy and breast feeding. They felt that sexual knowledge would be worrying or frightening to a child and their answers were intended to ensure the processes involved remained mysterious. Children were discouraged from asking adults questions about sexuality and other children usually knew little more. Links between the sexual behaviour of animals and that of human beings, not to mention that of birds and bees, are not obvious or meaningful unless adult comments make them so.

Social learning theory suggests that parental learning endorsement has a strong impact on children. Recent research into the relationship between women's childhood and adult sexual experience found those raised by parents who had, verbally or non-verbally, endorsed body awareness and nudity in childhood and adolescence had more extensive sexual experience and were most likely to have positive sexual experiences as adults.[10] As a child grows up in a sexually relaxed society, they acquire tacit, non-verbalized physical sexual knowledge gradually. Neither the parent nor the child verbally articulates the larger part of this knowledge. The child progresses through a slow process of observing and touching their own body and those of other children, and they have physical contact with adults of both sexes. They can observe adults touch each other with affection and talk generally and lightly about sexual attraction. Enjoying the company of others is part of this. The child will not be routinely chastised for asking questions about sexuality or other matters. They will be allowed to reject unwanted touching (which may occur in the name of hygiene) and adults will not respond to menstruation and wet dreams as if the adolescent had behaved badly.[11] As small children, they are likely to experiment sexually with their own body and with those of other children. As adolescents, they learn about sexual desire and response through masturbating alone and perhaps with others, through

[10] Wyatt et al., *Sexual Abuse*, 117. See also 'Childhood Sexuality: Normal Sexual Behaviour and Development', in J. Rademakers and T. G. M. Sandfort (eds.), *Childhood Sexuality: Normal Sexual Behaviour and Development* (2000). E. J. Roberts (ed.), *Childhood Sexual Learning: The Unwritten Curriculum* (1980).

[11] For menstruation see Ch. 6. Boys could be frightened by wet dreams at puberty, e.g. V. Gollancz, *Reminiscences of Affection* (1968), 198.

holding hands, kissing, and feeling and holding the body of another person. Through all these activities, the growing person gradually becomes aware of the internal physical elements of their own sexual excitement.

Children growing up in the early decades of the century were denied much of this experience. Historian Peter Gay has argued that even if women only found out about sexual intercourse for the first time on their wedding nights, following this experience they then had the knowledge, and therefore, ignorance in unmarried adults was of little importance.[12] Those children who were surrounded by adults who took pleasure in other aspects of the body and were physically affectionate might go on to enjoy physical sexual experience even though they had been refused information actually identified as sexual knowledge. But when a woman or a man had sexual intercourse without having gained this positive embodied knowledge their physical capacity for sexual pleasure was often diminished. This is not only a psychic deficit.[13] Even when such prior learning has taken place, enjoyment of sexual intercourse was (and is) often a learned experience. For example, by 1965 most teenagers acquired basic sexual knowledge. Yet, in a sample of teenagers, less than half of the boys (48 per cent), and under a third (30 per cent) of the girls, said they had liked their first experience of coitus.[14] A young person with prior positive experience of his or her body will be encouraged to persevere and develop an awareness of their own sexual pleasure but people who were already fearful and nervous about sexuality were less likely to persevere in actively seeking enjoyment.

While the consequences of ignorance varied, lack of knowledge did often lead to enduring difficulties. In 1951, Geoffrey Gorer undertook a questionnaire study, which was published as *Exploring English Character*

---

[12] P. Gay has an entire chapter on 'Learned Ignorance'. According to this, 19th-century men and women repressed their 'rousing yet frightening incestuous wishes' twice, first in infancy and then after puberty, and entered marriage in a state of 'factitious ignorance'; this then gave way to happy, sensual marriages. Gay did not explain why this 'psychosexual development, a history . . . shared with all mankind' did not lead to such ignorance before the 19th-century, and does not do so today. P. Gay, *Education of the Senses: The Bourgeois Experience, Victoria to Freud* (1984), 278–9.

[13] Gay, *Education*, 278–94. See Ch. 8 below for physical consequences.

[14] M. Schofield, *The Sexual Behaviour of Young People* (1965; rev. edn. 1968), 67.

(1955).[15] Many of his respondents referred to the difficulty of overcoming initial negative sexual experiences. He commented that his evidence 'strongly suggest[ed] that ignorance, particularly on the part of men, is a major hazard in English marriages'.[16] Naomi Haldane (1897–1999) married Dick Mitchison in 1914. Previously she had shared a bedroom with her mother, suggesting that her parents' sexual relationship was limited. Even before the couple married, she found that she 'couldn't explain that there were words and touches I didn't want . . . Perhaps if it had been possible to take things at a slower tempo I would have been able to respond.'[17] In a poem of this period, she wrote, 'Oh please, you're hurting me! Oh, let me go! You mustn't, mustn't, mustn't kiss me so!' Her biographer, Jenni Calder, suggests that these lines express her difficulty in accepting the transition of Dick from brother/friend to lover. However, Naomi later wrote that she knew 'extremely little about the physical side' when she married and that *Married Love* (1918) by Marie Stopes was a revelation. The central message of this book was that a woman needed to be 'wooed' each and every time that their lover approached them sexually. It seems probable Dick assumed that once engaged it was his right to initiate sexual contact, and he interpreted Naomi's response as the expected female passivity. He appears to have been insensitive to her physical response and her desires, the kind of young man that those who wrote sex manuals were anxious to educate. There were numerous warnings that the young husband risked spoiling the marital relationship forever if he rushed his young and ignorant bride. And, although the couple's sexual relationship improved greatly once Dick too had read *Married Love*, Naomi recorded that she never fully recovered from the couple's early sexual experiences.[18]

[15] G. Gorer, *Exploring English Character* (1955). The research was funded by Odhams Press Ltd. There was a 75% return of the questionnaires sent out by 31 Jan. 1951—but the sample of 5,000 actually coded was skewed for age—only 3% of the sample were over 65 compared to 11% of the population, 8–9.

[16] Gorer, *English Character*, 104–5. Also Roberts, *Women*, 60. Men who did not display sexual interest, e.g. P. Bailey, *An English Madam: The Life and Work of Cynthia Payne* (1982), 151. F. Zweig, *The Worker in an Affluent Society: Family Life and Industry* (1961), cited in Klein, *Samples*, 148. See also Ch. 6.

[17] N. Mitchison, *All Change Here: Girlhood and Marriage* (1975), 106.

[18] J. Calder, *The Nine Lives of Naomi Mitchison* (1997), 42–4, 47–8, 51. Experience helped in interpreting Stopes: 'Dodie [b. 1896] had read Marie Stopes, but she had no idea what the "foothills of sex" entailed.' V. Grove, *Dear Dodie: The Life of Dodie Smith* (1996; 1997), 41.

Dick's insensitivity is reminiscent of that of Edwin Lutyens (1869–1944) but the late Victorian Emily Lutyens was unable to improve her sexual experience,[19] unlike Mitchison, who was not only several decades younger but politically left wing and socially radical, and who, from the 1920s and with the aid of contraception, went on to have sexually satisfying affairs.

In the Freudian model of sexuality denial and repression of sexuality leads to the energy bursting out elsewhere. The actual experience of many people who passed through childhood in a society where sexual stimulation was minimized often appears to have been more analogous to that of a muscle that is not used or a talent that has not been developed. The evidence does not suggest that the absence of physical sexual desire diminished the individual's capacity to love another person nor does the lack of sexual expression seem to have created a need for compensation. Researchers John Gagnon and William Simon explain that in adulthood a low level of sexual activity is usual in the absence of stimulation, as sexuality is usually 'channelled through an existing set of eliciting social situations'. These situations were absent to a considerable extent in prison, and it was found this inhibited sexual responses, resulting in rates of male sexual activity, including masturbation, that were very much lower than occurred outside the institution.[20] Observers commented on the growth of sexual stimulation during the twentieth century. Kenneth Walker (1882–1966) was a surgeon and the author of many books on sexuality. In his biography, he commented that '[m]odern children are also being constantly stimulated by papers, journals, plays ... displaying nude figures in a way in which the children of the Victorian world were never stimulated ... [I]n the future, an increasing number of young people will be unable to sublimate and to control their sexual desires in the way in which their parents and grandparents managed to control them.'[21] In 1951, Gorer commented that 'the absence of of sexual feelings as well as experience, before marriage ... was, and still to a great extent remains, the

---

[19] M. Lutyens, *Edwin Lutyens* (1980), 56, 76. See also Ch. 4.

[20] J. H. Gagnon and W. Simon, *Sexual Conduct: The Social Sources of Human Sexuality* (1974), 240–4, citing A. C. Kinsey et al., *Sexual Behaviour in the Human Male* (1948), *Sexual Behaviour in the Human Female* (1953).

[21] K. M. Walker, *Sexual Behaviour: Creative and Destructive* (1966), 113–4. See also G. Raverat, *Period Piece: A Cambridge Childhood* (1952), 110.

English ideal'. He found that the earlier his respondents' date of birth, the older they were when they 'first started being really interested' in the opposite sex (Table 7.1).[22] This suggests that the generations that did not gain tacit sexual knowledge in childhood and adolescence took longer to feel sexual desire. The timing of the shift Gorer described is consistent with the diminishing levels of sexual ignorance found by Mass Observation.

Few people have described the experience of not feeling sexual desire. However, Margaret Cole (1893–1970) who went on to have an active physical sexual life commented about the pre-First World War period in which she worked with the Guild Socialists:

[They were] about as unconscious of sex and its ramifications as any body of people I have ever known . . . [M]aybe we were just exceptionally undeveloped in a generally undeveloped age. For myself, I know that I had been physically attracted to 'G.D.H.' [her future husband] from almost the time I had met him, though I did not at all recognise the attraction for what it was.[23]

This account suggests that when people who were sexually ignorant felt physically attracted to others, they might not interpret these feelings as sexual. But many men as well as women appear to have had an enduring lower level of physical sexual desire than would now be seen as usual. Margaret Cole described her husband G. D. H. Cole (1889–1959) as a man

Table 7.1. *Age at which people became interested in the opposite sex by date of birth*

Current age of respondent in 1951	Estimated date of birth	Percentage interested in the opposite sex at median age 16
Under 18	1934 or later	83
18–24	1927–33	71
25–34	1917–26	59
35–44	1907–16	55
Over 45	Before 1910	49
All	—	58

Source: Derived from G. Gorer, *Exploring English Character* (1955), 78–9.

[22] Gorer, *English Character*, 80.   [23] M. Cole, *The Life of G. D. H. Cole* (1971), 89, 90.

whose interest in sexual expression was never high. He had some homo-sexual experience. Before marriage, Margaret explained, her husband's 'physical affections, his desire to caress, had been generally directed towards his own sex', but, she added, this had been 'all very mild'.[24] She painted a convincing portrait of a man whose overall interest in, and acceptance of, physical sexual expression of any type was low throughout his life:

> One feels that he would have hardly had the energy for vigorous love-making; and the idea of 'love-play' would have shocked him . . . [H]is sex-life diminished almost to zero for the last twenty years of his life. Concurrently he developed by degrees a positive dislike of, and disgust with, any aspect of sex almost equal to that of the early Christian fathers.[25]

Lack of sexual interest is rarely even considered as a possible explanation for such denial of sexuality. Instead, it is now usual to assume that the answer lies in a denial of homosexuality, and this too is a possibility. But Cole did have access to social circles in which had he wished to it would have been possible for him to have sexual relationships with men, albeit secretly. More importantly, Cole was hardly any closer to fulfilling the demands of genital heterosexuality than he was those of homosexuality. The experience of men and women such as Cole cannot be described in terms of a binary continuum from homosexual through bisexual to heterosexual. They had a different experience of physical sexuality from that presented as natural and inevitable by the Freudian-influenced generations that followed.[26]

Attitudes to lesbianism illuminate the pivotal role played by low levels of genital sexual desire in English sexual culture. Passionate and enduring female friendships were valued during the nineteenth century, but from the early twentieth century such friendships began to come under increasing suspicion. The popularization of the work of Freud and the sexologists is usually offered as the cause of this shift.[27] But the production

---

[24]   Ibid. 92.   [25]   Ibid. 93.

[26]   In other accounts, the low importance of sexual desire is suggested by omissions. e.g. L. Manning, *A Life for Education* (1970), 195. Manning mentions Oscar Wilde and lesbianism but this is probably because she was writing just following homosexual law reform. She specifically rejects the concept of intimate friends, 37, 71–2, 209.

[27]   L. Faderman, *Surpassing the Love of Men: Romantic Friendship and Love between Women from the Renaissance to the Present* (1981; 1985), 243–4, 251. See L. Bland, *Banishing the Beast* (1995), 290–3.

of theory cannot, in itself, be held accountable for the widespread 'recognition' that intense schoolgirl crushes were dangerous, the repulsion directed at spinsters, or the anxiety aroused by fears of lesbianism. Why did this particular theory lend itself at this particular moment to being broadcast to a wider audience, and to arousing such anxiety in that audience? The audience accepted that the sexologists and Freud were correct because of shifts in female sexuality; elements of new emotions and experiences appeared to be more accurately described in these theories than by the existing religious and medical denial of sexuality. What, then, laid the ground for this shift? It has been argued that the fundamental cause was the threat posed by the growing independence and confidence of women, which was creating substantial changes in the dominant heterosexual sexual culture. To this must be added the falling birth rate and growing awareness of contraception.[28] As a result of these shifts the limits of acceptable female sexual expression were widening. However, the growing awareness of women's physical sexual desire and their sexual responsiveness combined with existing strong anxieties, and the fear of sexuality *per se*, to create the need for new rules defining deviance. Rejection of lesbianism rose in parallel with the tentative emergence of positive attitudes to heterosexual female physical sexual desires and pleasure. The rise in prejudice might be described as apparent rather than real because the previous tolerance of physically demonstrative female friendships had been the result of a widespread lack of awareness that genital sexual passion was possible between physically affectionate women.

This new genital orientation was not imposed on women from without but arose because there was an actual change of subjectivity and physical response on the part of many women. The learning process that develops the individual's awareness of their physical sexual potential has been described above. It is equally relevant to lesbian or gay physical sexual

S. Jeffreys, *The Spinster and her Enemies: Feminism and Sexuality, 1880–1930* (1985). M. Vicinus, 'Distance and Desire: English Boarding School Friendships, 1870–1920', in M. Vicinus, M. Bauml Duberman, and G. Chauncey (eds.), *Hidden from History: Reclaiming the Gay and Lesbian Past* (1989; 1991).

[28] Progressive middle-class heterosexual women's discussions are described by Bland, *Banishing*, 145, 285. See also Thompson (ed.), *Dear Girl*, 136, 8–9.

experience as it concerns the individual's relation to their own body, not sexual object choice (though there is a relationship between the two issues). In the early twentieth century, women often expressed affection physically. This included embracing, kissing, sitting close together, and sharing the same bed at night. Women who identified as lesbians (and bisexual women) frequently began by experiencing non-genital physical contact with other women. They then moved to genital sexual activity with women gradually if at all, suggesting that they, like many heterosexual women, did not initially identify their genitals as a source of pleasure in this period.[29] But as new rules defining deviance emerged, some of those who were promoting a more positive attitude to female genital sexuality put all adult women not in heterosexual relationships under suspicion.

Two English sex manuals differentiate between single women who are physically sexually active and those who lack interest in sexuality. In 1931, the Revd Leslie Weatherhead was referring to women who did not feel comfortable with or welcome physical sexuality when he wrote disapprovingly of 'some maiden ladies [who] say . . . "I have no such feelings" '. Elsewhere in the manual, he discusses disapprovingly a lesbian couple who 'slept together, embraced and kissed each other and sexually excited one another'. He was differentiating between those who have no 'feelings' and lesbians.[30] Marie Stopes wrote in 1928 that wives whose husbands were unable to meet their sexual demands 'suffer frightfully in secret', and after discussing masturbation, she then described lesbianism disapprovingly as '[a]nother practical solution which some deprived women find' to the problem of undersexed husbands. Women who lacked sexual desire were discussed elsewhere in her book.[31] Both these writers were clear that there were women who were not interested in physical sexual feelings, and that the term lesbian did not include them but referred to physically, sexually passionate women.

[29] V. Ackland, *For Sylvia: An Honest Account* (1949; 1989), 62, 64, 68, 79. For 'innocent' physical responses, see Calder, *Naomi Mitchison*, 42–4, 47–8, 51. J. Grant, *Time out of Mind* (1956), 123. Thompson (ed.), *Dear Girl*, 193–4, 199.

[30] L. D. Weatherhead, *The Mastery of Sex through Psychology and Religion* (1931), 62, 153.

[31] M. Stopes, *Enduring Passion* (1928; 1931), 40–1; abstinence or refusal, 134–5, 87–94. See also A. Herbert Gray, *Men, Women and God: A Discussion of Sex Questions from the Christian Point of View* (1923; 1947), 31. T. H. van de Velde, *Sex Hostility in Marriage: Its Origin, Prevention and Treatment* (1931), 83–4.

THE SEXUALLY ACTIVE

Historians of sexuality, especially heterosexuality, have tended to disregard people in whose lives sexual expression was unimportant in favour of people who had extensive sexual knowledge and experience. In a society in which speaking, or writing, about physical sexual experience was strongly discouraged, those who have left records of their sexual expression were unusual by definition. From 1900 to the 1940s, sexually knowledgeable and experienced people usually belonged to relatively small sectors of the community such as artists, bohemians, some wealthy businessmen, sexual radicals, sailors, and the non-respectable section of the working class.[32] Male boarding school pupils frequently had adolescent same-sex contacts but on many this appears to have had little impact. The number of unmarried women who were sexually active with men other than their intended spouse was increasing from 1900 but the only substantial group of such women continued to be those who worked as prostitutes.[33] Their numbers diminished as legislation and the intensification of policing introduced pimps into the equation and made prostitution a less acceptable lifestyle for women before the Second World War.[34] Occasional comments reveal the existence of women and men who were otherwise conventional but who had sexual experience and pleasure greater than that suggested as usual by most sources.[35] This category included active but married homosexuals.[36] Taken as a whole all these different groups probably amounted to no more than

[32] e.g. Ackland, *For Sylvia*, 115. M. Holroyd, *Augustus John* (1974). M. Kohn. *Dope Girls: The Birth of the British Drug Underground* (1992). F. MacCarthy, *Eric Gill* (1989). B. Russell, *Marriage and Morals* (1929; 1968), 93. For a summary of Dora and Bertrand's sexual experience see Haste, *Rules*, 81–4. J. Wyndham, *Love is Blue* (1986). J. Wyndham, *Love Lessons* (1986).

[33] For promiscuity and accounts of prostitution, see Bailey, *Cynthia Payne*. S. Cousins, *To Beg I am Ashamed: The Autobiography of a London Prostitute* (1946; 1960). C. Keeler and S. Fawkes, 'Nothing But...Christine Keeler', in *Scandal* (1983). R. Meadley and C. Keeler, *Sex Scandals* (1985). D. Niven, *The Moon's a Balloon* (1972), 11, 36–45, 54, 59, 61–2, 90. M. Parkin, *Moll: The Making of Molly Parkin* (1993).

[34] C. Neville Rolfe, 'Sexual Delinquency', in H. Llewellyn Smith (ed.), *The New Survey of London Life and Labour* (1935).

[35] e.g. Bailey, *Cynthia Payne*, 138.

[36] Hall Carpenter Archives, *Walking after Midnight: Gay Men's Life Histories* (1989). K. Porter and J. Weeks (eds.), *Between the Acts: Lives of Homosexual Men, 1885–1967* (1991). Also W. F. R. Macartney and C. MacKenzie, *Walls have Mouths: A Record of Ten Years Penal Servitude* (1936), ch. XXIII.

around 15 per cent of the population at this time. With the exception of the wealthy businessmen, they tended to be marginal or powerless, and they lived within a sexual culture that silenced them. None of the sources suggest that extensive sexual experience was usual or acceptable to conventional, respectable people before the 1950s. The community as a whole supported and maintained sexual norms. Individuals who openly transgressed sexual boundaries, such as girls who had been sexually assaulted, unmarried mothers, or homosexuals who encountered the police, were usually treated harshly by their families and communities.[37] It was this community support that enabled authorities to uphold rigid sexual mores.

GENDERED SEXUAL CULTURES

Although, for the majority of the population, physical sexual activity involved both men and women, they inhabited almost separate sexual cultures, a male culture and a female culture. Very different, and contradictory, pictures of sexual mores appear depending on which is examined. Gendered sexual cultures were part of a society in which gender segregation was usual in most schooling and in most occupations and remained a common experience up to the 1960s. Discussion of sexuality and of the sexual body in mixed-gender groups including respectable women or in the public sphere was extremely limited until the mid-1960s. Female gossip is characterized as contributing to maintaining rigid sexual mores, but Robert Roberts described how older men also disapproved of the increase in explicit male sexual boastfulness after the First World War.[38] In the 1950s, the authors of *Coal is our Life* found that '[a]ny attempt to discuss sexual problems seriously and frankly with a mixed group was found to be soon acceptable to

[37] For the putting of unmarried mothers into the workhouse or mental hospitals under the Mental Deficiency Act of 1913, see Humphries, *Secret World*, 63–94. For examples of the shocked and punitive response to homosexuality, see P. Higgins, *Heterosexual Dictatorship: Male Homosexuality in Postwar Britain* (1996), ch. 10. Girls who had been sexually assaulted continued to be put in institutions in the 1960s: e.g. M. Lassell, *Wellington Road* (1966), 143, 146–7.

[38] M. Tebbutt, *Women's Talk? A Social History of Gossip in Working-Class Neighbourhoods, 1880– 1960* (1995), 77, 149. N. Dennis, C. Slaughter, and F. D. Henriques, *Coal is our Life* (1956; 1969), 232. Lack of experience: Gorer, *English Character*, 105. R. Hoggart, *The Uses of Literacy* (1957), 83. R. Roberts, *The Classic Slum: Salford Life in the First Quarter of the Century* (1971; 1973), 231–2.

women, who welcomed the opportunity, but the men were embarrassed and almost silent. The only context . . . in which they discussed sex was in a circle of jesting males.'[39] Men in groups used sexual swear words, and shared stories and jokes about sex in order to confirm their status in the group, but participation in such conversations did not necessarily indicate extensive sexual knowledge, or varied experience.[40] In his account of working-class Salford, Robert Roberts (b. 1905) used the phrase 'serious sex talk' for a conversation in which men were discussing their actual sexual activity with their wives.[41] Male conversations about sexual activity were enjoyed as an activity *per se* and a way to display masculinity; for most participants this had little or no relationship to their sexual behaviour.

Heterosexual sexual activity involves women, and greater male sexual knowledge or assertiveness had to be mediated through women. Thus, the tone of societal sexual culture altered in response to the degree of female sexual restraint. Diminishing supervision by their families and employers from the early 1900s left girls responsible for protecting them-selves. Richard Hoggart's (b. 1918) description of working-class social mores offers a good picture of how young men divided young women into categories and how they tested the girls:

The names of the same girls who are willing crop up again and again; the easy ones are soon well known . . . To me the surprising thing is that so many girls are able to remain unaffected, to retain both an ignorance about the facts of sex and an air of inviolability towards its whole atmosphere that would not have been unbecoming in a mid-nineteenth century young lady of the middle-classes. It is wonderful how, without evident prudishness or apparent struggle, many of them can walk through the howling valley of sex-approaches from the local lads and probably of sex-talk at work, and come through to the boy they are going to marry quite untouched physically and mentally.[42]

---

[39] Dennis et al., *Coal*, 218. C. H. Rolph, *Living Twice: An Autobiography* (1974), 58–9.

[40] For male sexual jokes, see Ferris, *Sex*, 217–18. Hoggart gives two explicit sexual jokes describing Jewish genitals but does not give a date when he heard them. R. Hoggart, *A Local Habitation (Life and Times,* i: *1918–1940* (1989), 134–5, 109. G. Legman, *Rationale of the Dirty Joke: An Analysis of Sexual Humour* (1968).

[41] Roberts, *Classic Slum*, 55–6.

[42] Hoggart, *Literacy*, 84. See also Hoggart, *Local Habitation*. Roberts, *Classic Slum*, 50. For more on 'local lads' and young women, see Roberts, *Women*, 64–6, 68. P. Wilmott, *Adolescent Boys of East London* (1966), 56–7.

The 'easy ones', the girls with whom the 'local lads' could have sexual intercourse, were treated with contempt and unkindness, while good girls were admired for their lack of sexual awareness. The 'howling valley of sex-approaches' was a form of hazing, testing the girls and despising those who gave way. Male sexual culture encouraged men to inflate the extent of their sexual experience. However, in *Coal is our Life* (1956), a study carried out in a Yorkshire mining village, amongst the most gender-segregated working-class communities in Britain, the authors report that '[o]pen sexual interest was for the older generations confined to the groups of men and a few girls who were "a bit free"—there always seem to have been a few of these in any village or part of a town'.[43] Gorer undertook a survey of the sexual behaviour of the under-45s (people born after 1924) in 1969, well past the peak of sexual constraint. He found that a quarter of the men who later married had more than three partners but only 2 per cent of women admitted to so many. The wide boys, or men with multiple partners, saw their behaviour as admirable, in sharp contrast to the attitude towards the wide girls.

Many husbands and boyfriends shared Hoggart's admiration of female innocence and they did not want their wives and girlfriends to display sexual knowledge or passion. This reticence was part of a spousal relationship in which other issues, such as money, were also not discussed openly.[44] Specifically in relation to contraception, Woodside and Slater found in the 1940s that shyness and inhibition about expressing dissatisfaction with the method to the spouse were common and even 'characteristic' of the older working-class couples they interviewed, but that this was changing with the younger couples.[45] More generally, they reported that the 'public ignorance of sexual physiology is abysmal. Ordinary men and women have not even the vocabulary with which to frame enquiries and express their puzzlement. Husbands and wives are hampered in

[43] Dennis et al., *Coal*, 232–3.
[44] P. Ayres and J. Lambertz, 'Marriage Relations: Money and Domestic Violence in Working Class Liverpool, 1919–1939', in J. Lewis (ed.), *Labour and Love: Women's Experience of Home and Family 1850–1940* (1986), 196. Roberts, *Women*, 60–1.
[45] E. Slater and M. Woodside, *Patterns of Marriage: A Study of the Marriage Relationships of the Urban Working Classes* (1951), 201.

discussion with each other.'[46] From the 1940s, expanding sales meant sex manuals and other similar sources were providing a new respectable, medicalized language that men and women could share for couples in all classes. Inhibitions about discussing sex eroded slowly, remaining paramount throughout the period.

SUMMARIZING SEXUAL CHANGE

The period from 1900 to 1960 can be divided into three sections; pre-First World War and the war, the inter-war period up to and including the 1940s, and the 1950s. In the period between 1900 and the First World War, there was a relatively homogeneous sexual culture in which respectable people within all classes and age groups in society shared broadly similar, negative attitudes to sexuality.[47] The impression that Victorian sexual mores altered substantially in these decades is misleading. The working classes were becoming more sexually restrained, and while the Bloomsbury group and other rebels contributed to the new openness which was being introduced in novels and magazines, their sexual activity remained limited.[48] In the aftermath of the First World War, historians of masculinity have found that a deeply anti-heroic mood emerged. This further advanced the modification of masculinity set in motion by first-wave feminism, while women's confidence and independence was increased by war work.[49] Nonetheless, the majority of the population remained sexually conservative throughout the inter-war period. The generation that came of age in this period grew up between 1900 and the war, and a high proportion

[46] Ibid. 176, 196. Changing use of language, Calder, *Naomi Mitchison*, 47–8. Chinn, *They worked*, 141, 144. England, 'Sex Survey', 150–1. Gorer, *English Character*, 110. R. D. Laing, *The Facts of Life* (1976), 15–16. Roberts, *Classic Slum*, 48–9. M. Stocks, 'Climate of Opinion', *Family Planning*, 8/3 (1959). Vicinus, 'Distance', 228–9. K. M. Walker and E. B. Strauss, *Sexual Disorders in the Male* (1939; 1954), 172–4, 215.

[47] P. Thompson, *The Edwardians: The Remaking of British Society* (1975; 1977), 77. Weeks, *Sex*, 72–6.

[48] S. Szreter, 'Victorian Britain, 1837–1963: Towards a Social History of Sexuality', *Journal of Victorian Culture*, 1 (1996). See also P. Keating, *The Haunted Study: A Social History of the English Novel, 1875–1914* (1989).

[49] J. Bourke, *Dismembering the Male: Men's Bodies, Britain and the Great War* (1996). M. Roper and J. Tosh (eds.), *Manful Assertions: Masculinity in Britain since 1800* (1991).

remained unmarried or married late. For example, only 59 per cent of women aged 20 to 39 were married in 1931.[50] Fertility rates continued to fall until the 1930s, and the inadequate contraception available ensured that those who did marry continued to focus on sexual restraint. There were considerable changes following the First World War but the impact of these on the sexual knowledge and behaviour of the majority was not felt until the 1930s. By then books on physical sexuality and contraception were becoming more widely available, and such topics could be mentioned in newspapers and magazines, although censorship remained a major constraint.[51] Contraception was being used by all classes. Sexual ignorance was eroding and a recognizably modern sexual culture began to emerge. Children growing up in this period had a very different experience of the body from those who grew up before the First World War. Following the war, clothing, especially that worn by women, became less heavy and tight, more people took recreational exercise, and exposure to sun and air was encouraged.[52] Relevant progressive causes that blossomed in the 1930s included nudism and the free schools movement.[53]

The impact of the Second World War was complex. The existing research into sexuality and the war largely ignores the continuing sexual trends before, during, and after the war.[54] It seems evident that so massive

---

[50] *Marriage and Divorce Statistics*, OPCS Series FM2 no. 7 (1983). Derived from table 1.1 (b).

[51] For books on sexuality, see Chs. 8–10. On censorship, see A. Craig, 'Censorship of Sexual Literature', in A. P. Abarbanel and A. Ellis (eds.), *Encyclopaedia of Sexual Behaviour* (1961). G. Savage, 'Erotic Stories and Public Decency: Newspaper Reporting of Divorce Proceedings in England', *Historical Journal*, 41/2 (1998). A. Travis, *Bound and Gagged: A Secret History of Obscenity in Britain* (2000).

[52] L. Bryder, *Below the Magic Mountain: A Social History of Tuberculosis in Twentieth-Century Britain* (1988). J. J. Matthews, 'They had such a lot of Fun: The Women's League of Health and Beauty between the Wars', *History Workshop*, 30 (1990).

[53] H. Cook, 'Nudism: Sex, Gender and Social Change 1930–1955', unpublished manuscript (1994). F. and M. Merrill, *Among the Nudists* (1931). J. Croall, *Neill of Summerhill: The Permanent Rebel* (1983). W. A. C. Stewart, *Progressives and Radicals in English Education, 1750–1970* (1972).

[54] Costello uses British, American, and European evidence indiscriminately, making his work unhelpful. J. Costello, *Love, Sex and War: Changing values, 1939–45* (1986). Exceptionally, Riley covers trends before and after the Second World War. D. Riley, *War in the Nursery: Theories of the Child and Mother* (1983). Other research is specific to limited groups or periods, e.g. S. O. Rose, 'Girls and GIs: Race, Sex and Diplomacy in Second World War Britain', *International History Review*, 19/1 (1997). P. Summerfield and J. Finch, 'Social Reconstruction and the Emergence of Companionate Marriage, 1945–59', in D. Clark (ed.), *Marriage, Domestic Life, and Social Change: Writings for Jacqueline Burgoyne* (1991).

and unsettling an event should have had a major impact. Yet it is necessary to distinguish between the opportunities and disturbances created in people's day-to-day lives during the war and the consequences of the war victory in the following years. During the war, social dislocation diminished community surveillance and provided opportunities for sexual activity. The bringing together of large numbers of men and women in the forces was particularly important for gay men and women.[55] Evidence of heterosexual women's sexual behaviour during the war is not sufficient to prove the war was a liberalizing force for them. In 1949, Mass-Observation found that one husband in four and one wife in five admitted to extramarital activity.[56] However, women who had extramarital affairs while their husbands were absent for long periods usually saw this as excusable only in an extreme situation, if at all. Women who had premarital sex with a man they believed to be their intended spouse were considerably more likely to wind up with an illegitimate child during the war.[57] Women's guilt regarding their fall from grace would not necessarily translate into future liberality. It is arguable that it did not in the case of the older generation in the 1950s. Eustace Chesser found that over two-thirds of women who had themselves had premarital sex would not wish their daughters to do so.[58] More importantly, men did not return from service tolerant of their wives' sexual activity, although they could dismiss their own peccadilloes as forgivable in men fighting a war.

The 1950s saw the coming together of two streams of change producing contradictory results. The ongoing relaxation of sexual mores endured, but heterosexual male dominance of sexual activity, which had been thrown into question by decades of feminism and by the trauma of the First World War, was reasserted following the Second World War. The inter-war privileging of verbal reticence and self-control endured, but this

---

[55] Service in the armed forces increased the chance of contact with like-minded others, especially for women. Before the war there had been no visible lesbian subculture in London as there was in Paris and Berlin. Bland, *Banishing*, 169. E. Hamer, *Britannia's Glory: A History of Twentieth Century Lesbians* (1996), 141–2. Porter and Weeks, *Between the Acts*, 78, 87, 98, 100–5, 112.

[56] Stanley, *Sex Surveyed*, 134.

[57] See Ch. 12.

[58] E. Chesser, *The Sexual, Marital and Family Relationships of the English Woman* (1956), 342–3. See also Roberts, *Women*, 68.

masked a renewed confidence in masculinity.[59] The outcome in the 1950s and 1960s was a sexual culture more conservative and rigid in gender terms, but less abstinent sexually. The lessening of male sexual restraint required a concomitant lessening of female sexual restraint, which young women often desired, but it was they who bore the costs of relaxed sexual mores in the form of rising rates of illegal abortion, illegitimate babies, and painful adoptions. Middle-class men were starting to want mistresses of their own class, and the increasing availability of contraception and illegal abortion meant conventional middle-class women were more willing to have premarital and extramarital affairs. In spite of the apparent desirability of this from a male perspective, the distress caused to women helped fuel second-wave feminism and the destabilizing of middle-class men's dominant position in the sexual culture.[60]

At the same time, the premarital petting of the 1950s marked a substantial shift back to a more relaxed sexual culture. Women and men were able to learn about each other's bodies and sexual responses before sexual intercourse and commitment to marriage in a similar fashion to that which had existed before the nineteenth century. Many adolescents found that after a little awkward fumbling their body responded with pleasure to new experiences. To many people in this generation sexual pleasure appeared 'natural', not learnt. From the 1920s the more educated, left leaning, and less religious among the middle classes had become increasingly less sexually prudish than the working classes.[61] By the 1960s, class differences were the opposite to those that had existed a century and a half earlier when the religious elements in the emerging middle classes had promulgated a rigid and constricting sexual

---

[59] For post-war masculinity, see S. Brooke, 'Gender and Working Class Identity in Britain during the 1950s', *Journal of Social History* (2001), 784–6. Lynne Segal, *Slow Motion: Changing Masculinities, Changing men* (1990). See also Ch. 10.

[60] See Ch. 15. Also see H. Cook, 'The Long Sexual Revolution: British Women, Sex and Contraception in the Twentieth Century' (Ph.D. thesis, 1999), ch. 16. J. Reger and Shirley Flack, *Janet Reger: Her Story* (1991). Claire Tomalin, *Several Strangers: Writing from Three Decades* (1999).

[61] In 1950, Mass-Observation found that there is a 'noticeable lessening of moral strictness amongst those with more education . . . [This] reflects a completely contrary principle to that shown in the Kinsey Report.' This is yet another difference between US and UK sexual culture. England, 'Sex Survey', 152. See also J. Newson and E. Newson, *Four Years Old in an Urban Community* (1968), 384.

ideology and tried to impose this on the rest of the population. The shared negative perspective on sexuality was breaking down and by the early 1960s accepted standards of sexual behaviour differed widely between classes, by age, and amongst various groups. The gulf between male and female sexual behaviour and attitudes was narrowing in the younger generation.[62] This produced sharp conflict between the generations and, by the end of the 1960s, between men and women. Historians and theorists have raised many important questions about the nature of sexual knowledge, and overthrown earlier triumphalist accounts that argued progress had taken place on the basis of little more than the belief that more sex was automatically better sex. Nonetheless, during the twentieth century there was a dramatic decrease in the anxiety and fear surrounding sexuality, a growth in gender equality, and, from the 1930s, a genuine growth in the acceptance of varied actively sexual lifestyles including homosexuality.

[62] See e.g. G. Gorer, *Sex and Marriage in England Today: A Study of the Views and Experience of the under-45s* (1971), 31.

8

'The Wonderful Tides': Sexual Emotion and Sexual Ignorance in the 1920s

Married Love (1918) by Marie Stopes (1880–1958) transformed the discourse on heterosexual female sexuality and sexual practice. In 1972, *The Joy of Sex* by Alex Comfort (1920–2000) was the last influential text to be published in the discourse Stopes had established, before second-wave feminism once more transformed the terms of the discourse regarding sexuality. In the following chapters the content of all sex manuals found that were published in Britain between these dates is analysed. Sex manuals have been defined for the purposes of this research as legally available books intended for women and/or men to read in order to obtain knowledge about their own body and that of the opposite sex, and about physical sexual practice, primarily sexual intercourse (or coitus). As this suggests, the genre is almost exclusively concerned with heterosexual sexual practice. Some of these manuals contain only a few pages describing the body or discussing physical sexual practice while others consist of little else. This definition includes books ranging from religious texts that delicately skim over the topic of the physical body and its needs to chapters on sexuality in medical health guides. A few texts omit birth control but the majority give the topic considerable space. Sex manuals have been described as marriage manuals by some researchers. While there is considerable overlap between the genres there are also significant differences. Marriage manuals are concerned with the marital relationship, of which sexuality is only a part, and many sex manuals also addressed the unmarried. Appendix A contains a list of the 104 manual authors found and an analysis of their characteristics, including gender, occupation, and so forth. No attempt was made to find all manuals published before 1918 and authors of these are not included in the analysis.

These texts have attracted a deal of academic attention since the mid-1960s. American sociologists Lionel Lewis and Denis Brisset began by examining fifteen of the then current best-sellers. They concluded that the sex manuals presented sex as work, in keeping with the guilt that many people then felt about extended leisure activity.[1] The first study of sex manuals inspired by second-wave feminism was published in the early 1970s. In it Michael Gordon and Penelope Shankweiler argued that the content of the manuals reflected a gendered ideology, which had, they wrote, been created by male experts in a patriarchal society.[2] A new recognition of female sexual desire emerged in the early twentieth-century manuals, they explained, but more important, they felt, was the phallocentric presentation of coitus as the 'real thing'. They typified the texts as sexually conservative because of this and the accompanying belief that men's sexual impulses were more powerful than those of women, which were dormant until marriage, needing to be awakened by the husband.

Influential accounts since then include Jeffrey Weeks's brief discussion, which stressed the apparent social and sexual conservatism of the inter-war manuals, most obvious in the emphasis on sex only in marriage and in the rejection of activities, such as masturbation and homosexuality, which were then understood to be perversions.[3] Margaret Jackson argued that the inter-war period manuals acted to reinforce a 'patriarchal model of sexuality, according to which men's imperious and aggressive sexual "needs" were defined as "natural" '. Jackson followed the lead of Sheila Jeffreys and shares with her a theoretical construction of female sexuality,

[1] L. S. Lewis and D. Brissett, 'Sex as Work', *Social Problems*, 15/8 (1967). D. Brissett and L. S. Lewis, 'Guidelines for Marital Sex: An Analysis of Fifteen Popular Marriage Manuals', *Family Coordinator*, 1 (1970).

[2] M. Gordon and P. J. Shankweiler, 'Different Equals Less: Female Sexuality in Recent Marriage Manuals', *Journal of Marriage and the Family*, 3 (1971). Also see M. Gordon and M. C. Bernstein, 'Mate Choice and Domestic Life in the Nineteenth-Century Marriage Manual', *Journal of Marriage and the Family*, 32 (1970). M. Gordon, 'From an Unfortunate Necessity to a cult of Mutual Orgasm: Sex in American Marital Education Literature, 1830–1940', in J. M. Henslin and E. Sagarin (eds.), *The Sociology of Sex* (1978).

[3] J. Weeks, *Sex, Politics and Society: The Regulation of Sexuality since 1800* (1981; 1989), 206–7.

which emerged in the 1970s in response to male violence against women and predatory male sexuality.[4] In this analysis, the possibility of female sexual pleasure in penetrative penile-vaginal intercourse with men who were not violent, indeed the possibility of men who were not violent *per se*, was rejected, and the evidence that women did experience such pleasure was interpreted as demonstrating their oppression. This is a substantial change from Gordon and Shankweiler's perspective, as even the recognition of female sexual desire is not seen as positive. A different approach was taken by Lesley Hall, who examined the presentation of male sexuality in the major inter-war manuals. She revealed there was an emphasis on men who were timid and fearful, and in her later work has provided much useful information about the English manuals and their authors.[5] The post-Second World War manuals have been woven into accounts of changing sexuality by, for example, the Americans Barbara Ehrenreich, E. Hess, and G. Jacobs, and into the development of sexology in the post-war USA, by Janice Irvine.[6] The emphasis on the manuals as a source of conservative gender ideology continues to dominate the historiography. For example, in a recent article on sex manuals, Jessamyn Neuhaus describes how she 'gathered information with a set of questions about how the author defined male and female sexuality and the role of sex in marriage'.[7] This focus on gender and ideology has provided considerable insights over the last thirty years, but attention also needs to be given to the issues that the manual authors were directly addressing.

Physical sexual experience is the subject of the manuals but in the existing historiography it is assumed that we, the readers, understand what an event such as sexual intercourse, or oral sex, consists of as

[4] M. Jackson, *The Real Facts of Life: Feminism and the Politics of Sexuality, c1850–1940* (1994), 2–3, 129–81. S. Jeffreys, *The Spinster and her Enemies: Feminism and Sexuality, 1880–1930* (1985).

[5] L. A. Hall, *Hidden Anxieties: Male Sexuality, 1900–1950* (1991). R. Porter and L. A. Hall, *The Facts of Life: The Creation of Sexual Knowledge in Britain, 1650–1950* (1995).

[6] B. Ehrenreich, E. Hess, and G. Jacobs, *Re-making Love: The Feminisation of Sex* (1987), 3. J. M. Irvine, *Disorders of Desire: Sex and Gender in Modern American Sexology* (1990), 75. Also see M. S. Weinberg, R. Ganz Swensson, and S. K. Hammersmith, 'Sexual Autonomy and the Status of Women: Models of Female Sexuality in U.S. Sex Manuals from 1950 to 1980', *Social Problems* (1983).

[7] J. Neuhaus, 'The Importance of being Orgasmic: Sexuality, Gender and Marital Sexual Difficulties in the United States, 1920–1963', *Journal of the History of Sexuality*, 9/4 (2000), n. 8, 449.

physical behaviour and what meaning it had for readers in the 1920s or the 1950s. Physical sexual events are inadvertently constructed as natural and unchanging. As a result, substantial shifts in sexual experience have been overlooked. The evidence does not exist on which to base an argument that the manuals did or did not cause sexual change, but the reverse is incontestable; changes in sexual behaviour did cause changes in the content of the sex manuals. The British manual authors were a part of the culture about which they were writing, and they reflected their own time. Before the 1960s many of these authors were more aware of changing physical sexual behaviour than the average person, and more concerned to observe changing attitudes to such behaviour. Many had contacts with their readers through letters, or as patients, or through activities such as giving lectures.[8] Thus their comments on societal sexual mores do provide reliable evidence of change. Foreign authors have been included where their manuals highlight important themes or where they were important influences on British authors.

Current approaches to the manuals build upon arguments developed by sexologists in the 1960s. In 1965, *Newsweek* published an article on sex manuals which quoted several sexologists, and told readers, 'Today's standard manuals are hopelessly dated, medically misleading and potentially harmful.'[9] These standard manuals were, in fact, the major sex manuals of the inter-war era. They had greatly extended a very limited corpus of research on human sexuality and many of the authors also

---

[8] G. C. Beale [pseud.], *Wise Wedlock: The Whole Truth* (1922; 1926), 7. E. Chesser, *Sexual Behaviour: Normal and Abnormal* (1949), 126–7. G. Cox, *Youth, Sex and Life* (1935), p. vi. A. D. Costler and A. Willy, *The Encyclopaedia of Sexual Knowledge*, ed. N. Haire (1934), 9–11. I. E. Hutton, *Memories of a Doctor in War and Peace* (1960), 217. Those who were practising medics included G. Cox, I. Hutton, H. Wright, M. Macaulay, K. Walker, J. Malleson, N. Haire, and C. B. S. Evans. E. Chesser performed illegal abortions for many years, and is unlikely to have obtained only socially acceptable responses. See P. Ferris, *Sex and the British: A Twentieth Century History* (1994), 266. A. H. Gray started, and E. Griffith joined, the NMGC, which was receiving letters 'at the rate of 4,000 a month' in 1945, H. S. Booker and J. H. Wallis, *Marriage Counselling: A Description and Analysis of the Remedial Work of the National Marriage Guidance Council* (1958), 5. Birth control clinic doctors appear to have asked their patients about their sexual experience until well into the 1960s. See L. Secor Florence, *Birth Control on Trial* (1930), 119. M. Macaulay, *The Art of Marriage* (1952; 1957), 12. D. Sanders, *The Woman Book of Love and Sex* (1985), 98. H. Wright, *Sex Fulfilment in Married Women* (1947), 7. Porter and Hall, *Facts*, 283.

[9] 'Sex Manuals: How Not To', *Newsweek* (18 Oct. 1965).

contributed research to the emerging professional journals that were established from the 1930s, but sexologists' contemptuous attitudes have been immensely influential. The development of sexology in the post-Second World War period made the 'tradition' in which the American scientific sexologists placed themselves appear to be an accurate representation of the construction of sexual knowledge in the twentieth century. This largely invented tradition moved from the sexual taxonomists of the nineteenth century, such as Havelock Ellis (1859–1939) and R. Krafft-Ebing (1840–1902), directly to the application of newly developed survey techniques in the inter-war period, and Alfred Kinsey's (1894–1956) research in the 1940s, then on to William Masters (b. 1912) and Virginia Johnson's (b. 1925) use of the laboratory.[10] Initially, the sexologists' version of 'tradition' performed the function of establishing a reputable methodological status for sexology and laying a claim to the place of the discipline within the academy. By using terms such as 'experiential folk wisdom' they were making an implicit claim that producing the sex manuals did not involve research, deploy scientific techniques, or result in 'knowledge'.[11] The claim that survey techniques or laboratory research could produce data that would enable a full understanding of human sexuality exemplifies the post-Second World War mode of thought.

From the viewpoint of the 1970s and after, such judgements appeared valid, because during the post-Second World War period the new manuals had ceased to be innovative. Instead, they drew on the work of previous manual authors, on the new sexology, and on psychoanalysis, which functioned as a normalizing technique, codifying and channelling emotional expression.[12] But the lack of close attention in previous historical analyses of these texts to the original date of publication has obscured the difference between the post-Second World War manuals and the earlier manuals. The former based themselves on what was by then established authority, whereas the inter-war manual authors still accepted their own

[10] e.g. W. H. Masters and V. E. Johnson, *Human Sexual Response* (1966), p. vii. E. M. Brecher, *The Sex Researchers* (1970), ch. 5.

[11] Cited in Irvine, *Disorders*, 75.

[12] Psychoanalysis, see H. Cook, 'The Long Sexual Revolution: British Women, Sex and Contraception in the Twentieth Century' (Ph.D. thesis, 1999); introd. J. H. Gagnon and W. Simon, *Sexual Conduct: The Social Sources of Human Sexuality* (1974), 10, 105.

experience as a valid source of data on the basis of which they could contest authority or create new accounts. This is especially relevant to Stopes whose main contribution was the construction of an autonomous female sexuality, which existed independently of male sexuality, and provided a realistic basis for a more equal interaction with men in the context of her own time. There was no body of theory, or 'tradition', for her to draw upon in the construction of a non-reproductive, non-mercenary, autonomous, and emotionally active female sexual identity, whether marital or otherwise. The major sex manual authors of the 1920s and 1930s can be defended within the terms of 'scientific' research into sexuality, but their work also provides a basis on which to contest this form of knowledge as an adequate perspective from which to seek understanding of human sexuality.

THE SEPARATION OF REPRODUCTION AND SEXUALITY

The first major innovation of Stopes's *Married Love* (1918) was her omission of information about reproduction.[13] Prior to the First World War, manuals, such as those by the nineteenth-century American Russell Thatcher Trall (1812–77) or the English Margaret Stephens, placed sexual activity in a sequence that included reproductive physiology and menstruation, and continued on to pregnancy, birth, and lactation.[14] While occasional manuals published after the First World War still included material on reproduction, the influential manuals reduced their coverage of reproductive events to those that overlapped with physical sexual activity.[15] They included descriptions of, for example, the genitals, of

[13] M. Stopes, *Married Love: A New Contribution to the Solution of Sex Difficulties* (1918). Stopes boasted that she did not include anthropological and zoological details. See Porter and Hall, *Facts*, 261. However, this was also true of M. Stephens, *Women and Marriage: A Handbook* (1910; 1918).

[14] Stephens, *Women*, pp. xv–xvi. Trall was a 19th-century American promoter of hydropathy. There was an English reprint of his manual in 1914, and of a variation of it in 1919. *Sexual Physiology: A Scientific and Popular Exposition of the Fundamental Problems in Sociology* (1866; 1919). R. T. Trall, *Sexual Physiology and Hygiene: An Exposition Practical, Scientific, Moral and Popular, of Some of the Fundamental Problems of Sociology* (1891; 1914).

[15] e.g. manuals by M. Stopes, T. H. van de Velde, and, in the 1930s, H. Wright and E. Chesser.

menstruation, of sexual intercourse, and, from the 1930s, information about birth control. What was occurring was a taxonomic act, a shift in classification that enabled a redefinition of the subject. The result was that sexual intercourse was presented as an isolated event rather than one of a series of events which were integral parts of the life cycle and a developmental sequence that took place over time. The placement of sexual intercourse in the sequence of reproductive events had reflected the lack of separation between sex and reproduction (for women) before the development of effective birth control. The shift to isolating sexual activity resulted from the real physical possibility of the separation between sexual intercourse and reproduction. For this reason, the development of the sex manuals and the improvement in availability and knowledge of birth control occurred in tandem. Stopes's innovative advice manual on birth control, *Wise Parenthood* (1918), was published later in the same year as *Married Love*.[16] Initially these, and the other manuals, were read by middle-class readers who had the resources successfully to use mechanical or artificial methods of birth control such as condoms and caps in the 1920s. A number of the manual writers explicitly made the connection between improved birth control and changing sexual behaviour. For example, Kenneth Walker (1882–1966), a genito-urinary surgeon and author, wrote in 1940 that '[w]hilst methods of limiting childbirth are not entirely new, it is only within the last thirty years that contraceptives have been made reliable and brought within reach of the masses. This . . . has allowed of the sexual relationship being treated quite differently from how it was treated two or three generations ago.'[17]

Stopes included a description of the act of coitus, and descriptions of both male and female physiology and anatomy using scientific terminology. The emergence of texts that described physical sexual activity but not reproduction marked the first time that explicit texts focusing on physical sexual activity were intentionally addressed to respectable middle-class women as well as to men. Birth control was central to this widening readership. Men had been able to separate coitus and reproduction by

[16] M. Stopes, *Wise Parenthood* (1918). R. Hall, *Marie Stopes: A Biography* (1977), 148.

[17] K. M. Walker, *The Physiology of Sex* (1940), 69; on changing status of women, 70–1. See also E. Chesser, *Sex and the Married Woman* (1968; 1970), 35. M. Davis, *The Sexual Responsibility of Woman* (1957; 1964), 15, also 142.

approaches such as recourse to prostitution, but until effective birth control became available this choice had not been open to women (including prostitutes). The inclusion of women readers in the audience enabled the manuals to be addressed to a conventional, respectable *mass* readership. There had been a tiny audience for the sexological works of Ellis prior to the 1930s and an even smaller number who actively sympathized with the progressive aims of such work. For example, Weeks estimated that 250 members was the median size of the British Society for the Study of Sex Psychology from the 1910s to the 1940s.[18] By contrast the manuals sold in very large numbers. Stopes's *Married Love* (1918) had sold 820,000 worldwide by 1937. The more obscure G. Courtenay Beale [pseud.], *Wise Wedlock* (1921), sold 100,000 by 1939. The emphatically Christian manual, Revd L. D. Weatherhead's (1893–1976) *The Mastery of Sex* (1931), had sold 58,000 by 1942.[19]

In *Married Love* the sexual response of the fluid, passionate, physical female body was described by Stopes in an emotional, spiritual language. This text included 'Scientific' descriptions of the genitals and sexual events together with emotional passages such as, 'Welling up in her are the wonderful tides, scented and enriched by the myriad experiences of the human race from its ancient days of leisure and flower-wreathed love-making, urging her to transports and to self-expressions were the man but ready to take the first step in the initiative or to recognise it in her.'[20] This positive model of women's physical sexual desire was very new, and the text presented an attractive young husband to accompany it. In a page picked at random from *Married Love*, Stopes describes the feelings of the young husband to whom the book is dedicated: he strives to please, he has tender feelings, he wants to kiss his bride's fingers and come to her for sweet communion in the dusk, he is aggrieved, he is astonished, he despairs.[21] This list of emotions does not exhaust the descriptions on a single page. Stopes's mixture of emotion and explicit physical detail contravened the categories that were being established to enable a professional and public discourse on birth control and sexuality to occur.[22] In *The*

---

[18]   Weeks, *Sex*, 184.   [19]   See Appendix A.   [20]   Stopes, *Married Love* (1937), 26.

[21]   Ibid. 21.

[22]   See 'We however wish to appeal to reason and we must therefore employ dull neutral phrases such as "extra-marital sexual relations".' B. Russell, *Marriage and Morals* (1929; 1968), ch. 5, 40.

Hygiene of Marriage (1923) Isabel E. Hutton (1887–1960) distanced herself from Stopes's approach, declaring in her introduction, 'The matter has been simply treated . . . it is quite scientific and no attempt has been made to embellish it. Anything of an erotic nature is obviously out of place in a book of this kind and can only appeal to the wrong kind of readers.'[23] For Hutton, sex was made acceptable by a presentation that was divorced from erotic emotion, and she added more medical terminology in later editions of her manual. However, there were obviously more of the 'wrong kind of readers', as *Married Love* was not only the first, it was also the best-selling manual of the inter-war period. In spite of this, Stopes's combination of detailed physical description and emotion was rejected as inappropriate by Dr Norman Haire (1892–1952), who ended a plea for more research into birth control by referring to 'non-medical "doctors" who write erotic treatises on Contraception, conveying misleading information in a sexually-stimulating form'.[24] Dr C. P. Blacker (b. 1895), the eugenicist, was particularly distressed that Stopes was pre-empting the field of birth control with her 'flowery and highly-coloured' books.[25] Historians have been no more comfortable. Paul Ferris, a historian and journalist who has been writing since the 1960s, suggested that Stopes 'was, perhaps, not quite sane'.[26] Writing in a brief moment during the 1970s when heterosexual feminist English women felt confident of their opinions about female sexuality, Ruth Hall wrote in her biography of Stopes that 'it is astonishing that a virgin of thirty eight could talk so much good sense, deplorably flowery though its expression now appears'.[27] Though Hall accepted Stopes's feminism, she still took for granted that the correct, indeed the only, way to give information about the physical sexual body and sexual events was in the unemotional and reductionist language of modern biological science.

---

[23] I. Hutton, *The Hygiene of Marriage* (1923), pp. xi–xii.

[24] N. Haire, *The Comparative Value of Current Contraceptive Methods, Reprinted from the Proceedings of the First International Congress for Sexual Research (Berlin October 10th to 16th, 1926)* (1928), 12.

[25] Quoted in R. A. Soloway, ' "The Perfect Contraceptive": Eugenics and Birth Control Research in Britain and America in the Inter-War Years', *Journal of Contemporary History*, 30 (1996), 643.

[26] Ferris, *Sex*, 109.

[27] Hall, *Stopes*, 131.

In *Ideal Marriage* (1928) the Dutch gynaecologist Theodore van de Velde (1873–1937) also took a positive approach both to sex and to emotional relationships between the sexes. This text was expensive and difficult to obtain during the inter-war period but it greatly influenced other manual writers and became the classic manual of the 1940s and 1950s.[28] While Stopes had several pages of physical descriptions of coitus addressed to young lovers, *Ideal Marriage* contained over 200 pages of detailed and sensitive descriptions of the body and of physical sexual events. There were three 'intermezzos' which consisted of pages of quotations about love and marriage from writers such as Goethe, Stendhal, and Rousseau. The intermezzos have been ignored or dismissed as irrelevant by historians.[29] Dr Margaret Smyth (b. 1937), a British doctor who worked for the Liverpool Family Planning Association, revised the book in 1965. She said, 'I've left all his ideas intact,' but added that she had 'removed some of the gilt from van De Velde's baroque prose', thus moving the text closer to language seen as objective and scientific.[30] This approach was firmly established as the norm well before the 1950s, but judging by sales of both this manual and, in the inter-war period, *Married Love*, many readers wanted manuals that placed their sexual activity in the context of their emotional lives. Sales indicate readers also wanted a positive, reassuring view of sexuality. *The Riddle of Sex* (1930) by the American Joseph Tenenbaum (b. 1887) is not mentioned elsewhere, and does not appear to have sold well. This text included several chapters on venereal disease. In Hutton's manual, the subheadings for chapter 2, 'Before Marriage', read 'Health of Woman, Health of Man, Venereal Disease, Heredity, Insanity, Epilepsy, Alcoholism, Tuberculosis'.[31] The number of deaths from syphilis

[28] e.g. see E. Chesser, *Love without Fear (A Plain Guide to Sex Technique for Every Married Adult)* (1941), 67. H. Wright, *The Sex Factor in Marriage* (1930; 1940), 5.

[29] Porter and Hall, *Facts*, 212.

[30] 'Sex manuals: how not to . . . '.

[31] J. Tenenbaum, *The Riddle of Sex: The Medical and Social Aspects of Sex, Love and Marriage* (1930), pp. x. Hutton, *Hygiene*. Other negative manuals include C. S. Whitehead and C. A. Hoff, *Sex Revelations and the New Eugenics: A Safe Guide for Young Men—Young Women* (1936). M. Sanger, *Happiness in Marriage* (1927). Some of the better-selling manuals did have a little information on VD. The Revd L. Weatherhead suggested that syphilis could be caught from toilet seats in his manual *The Mastery of Sex through Psychology and Religion* (1931), 22, 187. R. Macandrew [pseud.] wrote that women who engage in premarital genital play should check for 'syphilitic lesions' on the man's fingers. *Friendship, Love Affairs and Marriage* (1939), 89.

was higher than that from either cancer or tuberculosis in 1924.[32] In this context fears about venereal disease and physical sexual activity were not irrational; however, Stopes included no such information in *Married Love*. In 1923, the Revd A. Herbert Gray (b. 1868), who published a popular religious text which contained a brief description of the genitals and sexual intercourse, wrote that:

I have deliberately omitted from these pages any reference to disease. I do that not because I am not impressed by the terrible penalties with which nature visits certain sins, but because I do not believe in the power of fear to deliver us. Though there were no such things as venereal disease, immorality would still be a way of death and morality would still be the way of life and joy.[33]

The very successful manuals presented sexual activity as pure, clean, and a physical source of love between a man and a woman. They wanted their readers to feel confident and to experience mutual sexual pleasure.

RECONSTRUCTING FEMALE SEXUALITY

Without exception the manual authors were most concerned about young newly married women, who were thought to be more vulnerable than young men:

In every healthy young man the instinct of sex is present, controlled or allowed to run riot according to his strength of self-control and elevation of mind. Some young women possess it in as great, and in rare cases even a greater degree; but in the majority of average healthy women before marriage it lies in a more or less dormant condition, and occasionally is altogether absent.[34]

This writer, an English female poet, carefully explains that women's sexual 'instinct' encompasses a full range of responses, but, writing in 1910, says that in the majority of young women sexual feeling is dormant until marriage. Most manual authors agree with this assessment of female sexuality until the 1940s, from which point the authors tend to modify

---

[32] R. Davenport-Hines, *Sex, Death and Punishment* (1991), 246.

[33] A. H. Gray, *Men, Women and God: A Discussion of Sex Questions from the Christian Point of View* (1923; 17th edn. 1947), 7.

[34] Stephens, *Women*, 40.

their stance and suggest that though this is still true of some women, there are many who are aware of sexual desires before marriage. This statement should be treated not as an attempt by the authors to construct gendered sexuality but as a reflection of the existing socially constructed sexual experience of many women in English society in this period. Why might women's sexuality have been dormant until marriage? In earlier chapters it has been explained that every effort was made to prevent girls and young women from gaining knowledge associated with sex or reproduction. As girls, most women did not learn to express sexuality or to feel pleasure in their genitals in this period.

Even where young women felt intense desire for a man this did not mean that they expected or understood what sexual intercourse entailed. A young middle-class woman named Joan Grant, who had shared a bed overnight but not had sexual intercourse with her fiancé, decided this meant she was no longer a virgin. Her horrified parents accepted her at her word. She explained in her autobiography: 'Books! Scientific books! . . . words like fallopian tubes and spermatozoa—just words! I thought spermatozoa crept out and crept in while both parties were asleep.'[35] Manuals published before 1918 avoided describing intercourse directly and lent themselves to such misunderstandings.[36] Stopes's description of the genitals and of coitus included the erection of the penis and insertion into the vagina, but other British-authored manuals continued to be indirect and confused in the 1920s. In 1923, Isabel Hutton (1887–1960) wrote that the 'husband and wife should be close together in a comfortable and easy horizontal position. They are thus face to face, their bodies in contact and in the most natural way reflex sexual processes take place almost without their being aware of it.'[37] This description would lend itself to fundamental misunderstandings of sexual intercourse, such as are revealed by Grant and by oral history respondents.

Beale suggested that less than complete ignorance still created major problems for young women: 'More probably, however, she will have arrived at the marriageable age not indeed without all knowledge of sex,

---

[35] J. Grant, *Time out of Mind* (1956), 123.

[36] e.g. Stephens, *Women*, 35–7. Trall, *Sexual Physiology*, (1866).

[37] Hutton, *Hygiene*, ch. 3. See also Gray, *Men*, 143. Weatherhead, *Mastery*, 222–34. Beale, *Wise Wedlock*, 71–5.

but with a woefully incomplete and inaccurate knowledge, distorted and sullied by the belief that sex is a thing to be ashamed of and the exercise of the marital function a descent from the heights of virgin purity to a lower level.'[38] Considerable numbers of men also lacked sexual knowledge. As a result of shared ignorance, and not infrequent male insensitivity, women's first experience of intercourse was a potentially frightening experience. These fears were not baseless. Breaking the hymen was, and still is today, a painful experience for some women. More importantly, if haste on the part of the husband or lack of desire on the part of the wife meant she was not sexually aroused, her vagina would not be lubricated and intercourse would be quite straightforwardly painful.[39] Where their first experience of intercourse was an unpleasant shock, women with little expectation of pleasure would have been provided with no reason to become physically aroused and produce vaginal lubrication on future occasions, increasing the likelihood of further unpleasant physical experiences.

Stopes argued that 'no union should ever take place unless the woman also desires it and is made physically ready for it'. Her insistence that the woman must be courted (or persuaded, seduced, wooed, etc.) before sexual intercourse in order that she will enjoy the experience provided the woman with a veto, if she still did not wish to have intercourse. Thus accepting Stopes's advice necessitated the rejection of the male conjugal right, which the husband acquired on marriage, to have sexual intercourse with his wife whenever he desired it. Nineteenth-century feminists in Britain and America had argued that marriage should not give the husband the right to have sexual intercourse with his wife on demand.[40] The rejection of these 'conjugal rights' was well established in the radical, nineteenth-century American discourse on sexuality of which some of the sex manuals had been a part. In 1866, the American Trall wrote: 'what I mean is, that sexual intercourse, for any purpose, should be, under all

---

[38] Beale, *Wise Wedlock*, 48. See also H. W. Long, *Sane Sex Life and Sane Sex Living* (1919), 72.

[39] Stopes, *Married Love*, 62. It was then believed that the mucus was produced by the Bartholin's glands in the labia minora e.g. Weatherhead, *Mastery*, 243. M. J. Exner, *The Sexual Side of Marriage* (1932; 1951), 43, 70.

[40] L. Bland, 'Marriage Laid Bare: Middle-Class Women and Marital Sex c.1880–1914', in J. Lewis (ed), *Labour and Love: Women's Experience of Home and Family 1850–1940* (1986), 127–30, 135. S. K. Kent, *Sex and Suffrage in Britain, 1860–1914* (1987; 1990).

circumstances, for the female to accept or refuse, and not for the male to dictate or enforce.'[41] However, the rejection of the concept of conjugal rights was reinforced by feminist acceptance of the societal belief that women were passionless. According to nineteenth-century feminism, advance would come from men learning to control themselves, not from women discovering their capacity for sexual passion. In 1918, Stopes explained that 'the trend of social feeling has largely been in the direction of freeing her from [being used as man's instrument], and thus mistakenly encouraging the idea that sex-life is a low, physical and degrading necessity which a pure woman is above enjoying'.[42] Instead Stopes constructed the female body as actively sexual at a physiological level.

In *Married Love* (1918) she explained that women had a fortnightly cycle, relating to their menstrual cycle, during which sexual desire welled up and ebbed away. This gave a biological mandate both to women's rejection of a husband's demands for intercourse and to Stopes's new insistence on women's desire for physical sexual pleasure. The existence of this cycle meant that women did desire sex at times determined by themselves and could say yes without being 'lowered', while still maintaining the right to say no on other occasions. Physiological detail about male sexual function was also employed to support Stopes's beliefs about behaviour. For example, in the course of explaining that the penis was made erect by the filling of venous cavities with blood and not with sperm, she rejected one of the arguments in support of conjugal rights, adding that 'if this is clear, it will be realised that the stiffening and erection does not *necessarily* call for relief in the ejaculation of sperm [italics in original].'[43] Beale also rejected the idea of conjugal rights and accepted that males must control their sexual desires, but he still argued that the 'continuous accumulation of the sperm cells...create[d] the male desire', thus leaving open the

[41] Trall, *Sexual Physiology*, (1866)., p. xi, also 201. The pre-First World War Trall and Stephens relate conjugal rights to enforced maternity as well as to coitus: Trall, chapter heading 12, p. vii. Stephens, *Women*, 45. See also B. G. Jefferis and J. L. Nichols, *Search Lights on Health: Light on Dark Corners* (1894), 262–6. J. Guyot, *A Ritual for Married Lovers* (1859), 56–9. Long, *Sane Sex*, 56–7, 61, 73, 93. A. B. Stockham, *Tokology: A Book for every Woman* (1883; 1897). T. H. van de Velde, *Ideal Marriage* (1928; reset 1943), 255.

[42] Stopes, *Married Love* (1937), 32. See T. Laqueur, *Making Sex: Body and Gender from the Greeks to Freud* (1990), 206–7.

[43] Stopes, *Married Love* (1937), 54.

possibility that the male had a biological need for relief.[44] Van de Velde stated that conjugal rights must be mutual, not based on only the wife's desires, as Stopes suggested. He called this mutuality 'sexual altruism', but as coitus cannot occur when the man does not feel desire, such altruism must be one sided in practice.[45] Dr Edward Griffith (1895–1988) was almost unique amongst the post-war male authors in arguing unequivocally that 'Sex union is only permissible—is only morally right—when it is mutually desired.'[46] The resistance to the erosion of conjugal rights highlights the importance of male domination of sexual activity to men.

Stopes's support for an existing theory that semen was absorbed through the walls of the vagina provided her with a rationale for claiming that sexual intercourse was important for women's health.[47] Sir Arbuthnot Lane, a prominent London surgeon, supported her in her belief that the absorption of semen did occur, and other authors, including van de Velde, also accepted this.[48] It has been suggested that 'Stopes was forced to invent a mythical dependence of women on sexual intercourse for their physical health for want of any more cogent arguments against lesbianism.'[49] Alternative physical sexual practices, whether with men or between women, do not appear to have been of such importance to Stopes that she would *develop* an argument defending the primacy of coitus in order to reject them. Rather her ideas about the female sexual body derived from her focus on the importance of physical sexual pleasure (provided by

[44] Beale, *Wise Wedlock*, 47–9, 84. also Exner, *Sexual Side*, 56. G. R. Scott, *The New Art of Love* (1934), 75.

[45] van de Velde, *Ideal Marriage*, 255.

[46] E. F. Griffith, *Modern Marriage* (1935; 1947), 98. He retained this statement in the post-Second World War edition quoted here.

[47] Stopes, *Married Love* (1926), 71–2. M. Stopes, *Enduring Passion* (1928; 1931), 43–4.

[48] For absorption as an 18th-century belief, see T. Hitchcock, *English Sexualities: 1700–1800* (1997), 80. Absorption was mentioned as a reason why withdrawal was unsuccessful by C. Knowlton, 'Fruits of Philosophy' (1832), repr. in S. Chandrasekhar (ed.), *'A Dirty, Filthy Book': The Writings of Charles Knowlton and Annie Besant* (1981), 114, 116–18. As part of mutual communion by E. Carpenter, *Love's Coming-of-Age* (1896; 1923), 29–30. Also see van de Velde, *Ideal Marriage*, 121. Long, *Sane Sex*, 86. On A. W. Lane see J. C. Whorton, 'Inner Hygiene: The Philosophy and Practice of Intestinal Purity in Western Civilization', in Y. Kawakita, S. Sakai, and Y. Otsuka (eds.), *History of Hygiene: Proceedings of the 12th International Symposium on the Comparative History of Medicine—East and West* (1991). A. Comfort, *The Anxiety Makers* (1967), 124–34.

[49] Jeffreys, *Spinster*, 120–1. Jackson, *Real Facts*, 136–9.

intercourse) for women in a society in which the accepted ideal was a lack of such physical sexual feeling. Absorption also complemented Stopes's rejection of methods of birth control that lessened female sexual pleasure, such as abstinence, early condoms, and withdrawal.

RESHAPING MALE SEXUALITY

The authors assumed that healthy men initiated physical sexual activity and determined the timing of sexual events. Following Stopes, the manuals also addressed the contribution husbands made to women's physical sexual pleasure.[50] In van de Velde's writing there is an insistence on the importance of female sexual pleasure, albeit certainly not independent female sexual pleasure. It is because of this absence of female sexual autonomy that it has been argued that these texts are constructing a phallocentric, heterosexist, and anti-feminist approach to sexuality. There is no evidence suggesting that an alternative construction of heterosexual physical sexual activity existed. These texts should be read as revealing that gender roles in physical sexual practice were rigidly constructed, not treated as causal.[51] These inter-war period authors were largely concerned with presenting a vision of idealized but attainable sexual practice, and thus the first-wave feminist emphasis on male sexual domination, predatory sexual behaviour, and sexual violence had no place in their texts. They do not appear to have been aware of any utopian visions of gender equality in *physical* sexual practice, nor have I encountered any such visions elsewhere in the writing of this period. Yet men were almost invariably presented by these authors as either timid and in need of encouragement, or gentlemanly and concerned to take care of their wife's sexual needs; at worst men were selfish only because they were unaware of their wife's desires.[52] This itself could be considered almost utopian; it is certainly idealized. But the means by which men were to satisfy their wife's sexual needs were quite specific. As Stopes explained in

[50] The American Long discusses this in 1919, probably before seeing Stopes's manual. Long, *Sane Sex*.

[51] For this claim see Jackson, *Real Facts*, 185; see also 75.

[52] Timid men, see Hall, *Hidden Anxieties*.

1918, women took longer to reach orgasm from intercourse than did men; therefore if husbands delayed their own orgasms this would ensure female satisfaction:

Married women . . . are deprived of the full orgasm through the excessive speed of the husband's reactions . . . [I]t may even take as much as from ten to twenty minutes of actual physical union to consummate her feeling, while two to three minutes often completes the union for a man who is ignorant of the need to control his reactions so that both may experience the added benefit of a mutual crisis to love.[53]

This argument that husbands must alter their sexual behaviour to be more aware of their wife's sexual needs was one of the points most widely accepted by other manual authors. Husbands were told repeatedly in manuals that their wives' sexual pleasure was vital to their own, and that they must learn how to delay their own orgasm to extend the duration of intercourse.

However, for most men to continue intercourse for as long as ten to twenty minutes seems to have been a considerable demand. Stopes repeated the estimate of two to three minutes, average duration of intercourse in *Enduring Passion* (1928) but mentioned that use of different positions had enabled some men to continue for much longer periods of time, such as forty-five minutes.[54] Dr Eustace Chesser (1902–73), who was not a sexually conservative author, estimated in 1941 that the 'average duration of the stay of the penis in the vagina is about five minutes. Many regularly exceed that time. The actual union sometimes lasts between five and ten minutes. Extreme cases of longer duration also occur.'[55] Durations of intercourse over ten minutes would not now be considered extreme but they evidently were in the early twentieth century, as all the authors who discuss the topic assume that the duration of intercourse is usually brief. Before 1918 the manuals had focused on the appropriate

---

[53] Stopes, *Married Love*, (1937), 69–70. Also see van de Velde, *Ideal Marriage*, 6, 152. Gray, *Men*, 147. Beale, *Wise Wedlock*, 86. Weatherhead, *Mastery*, 243–4. E. F. Griffith, *Modern Marriage and Birth Control* (1935), 123. Exner, *Sexual Side*, 57. Chesser, *Love*, 43.

[54] M. Stopes, *Enduring Passion*, 145.

[55] Chesser, *Love*, 129–30. Also E. Bergler, 'Short Genetic Survey of Psychic Impotence', *Psychiatric Quarterly*, 1/19 (1945), 412–437. Medica [pseud. J. Malleson], *Any Wife or Any Husband* (1951; 1955), 72–3, 34.

frequency of intercourse, and duration had gone unmentioned, except in relation to methods of birth control that depended on avoiding orgasm altogether.[56] The new emphasis on a longer duration of intercourse as the answer to the problem of women's lack of sexual satisfaction is testimony to a new view of women's importance, as well as to the focus on sexual intercourse. Asking men to control, by delaying, their orgasms required a transformation of the existing male approach to intercourse. Beale makes his discomfort clear: there 'is plenty of room . . . [for male] sexual restraint, even within married life, but hardly in the conjugal act itself, where spontaneity is of the essence of the function's wholesome performance; to hold up the climax . . . means the imposing of a severe and probably injurious strain upon the nerves and emotions alike.'[57] Thus the process from arousal through to orgasm was experienced as a spontaneous act that could not be controlled without severe strain on the man. Even so, Beale recommended that men continue intercourse after reaching their orgasm, revealing that he accepted the necessity for female sexual satisfaction.[58] The German manual authors Abraham Buschke (b. 1868) and Friedrich Jacobsohn (b. 1894) did not. They directly addressed the conflict between men's and women's sexual needs. Extending the duration of intercourse might further sexual pleasure in women, they wrote, but this was not an adequate reason to undertake the procedure, as it would make sexual neurasthenics of men. Instead men were advised to 'enjoy sexual intercourse in normal fashion, without extensive preliminaries, without any attempt at artificial prolongation, but proceeding as quickly as may be to orgasm and ejaculation'.[59] This lack of concern for female pleasure was exceptional. The continuing influence of feminism, combined with the progressive preference for a sexually responsive partner, resulted in other manual authors following the example of Stopes and van de Velde. Through the 1920s and 1930s manuals repeatedly counselled men to extend the duration of intercourse so their wives could reach orgasm.

[56] e.g. Duration of intercourse is not mentioned in the section on impotence in Jefferis and Nichols, *Search Lights*, 252–5. Avoidance of orgasm, see Stockham, *Tokology*.

[57] Beale, *Wise Wedlock*, 86–7.

[58] Ibid. 87. None of the other manual authors suggests this approach but the bitter fictional account of its use by D. H. Lawrence is discussed in Ch. 9.

[59] A Buschke and F. Jacobsohn, *Sex Habits: A Vital Factor in Well-Being*, trans. E. Paul and C. Paul (1932), 148.

THE MODERNIZATION OF PHYSICAL
SEXUAL BEHAVIOUR

This change in male sexual behaviour is central to the modernization of physical sexual behaviour. In *Sex in the Human Male* (1948) Kinsey drew from his evidence the concept of two distinct 'systems of mores' or behavioural patterns. His findings cannot be applied directly to Britain as his research was based on the very different American population,[60] but his two patterns are a useful way to understand the shift that was taking place:

In the last two decades, marriage manuals have more or less uniformly emphasized the value of variety in coital techniques, and have probably encouraged an increasing proportion of the population to experiment . . . There is, however, a considerable portion of the population . . . which is not interested in prolonging a sexual relationship. This is true, for the most part, of the more poorly educated portions of the population, although there are not a few upper level individuals who react similarly. It is a mistake to assume that a sophistication [*sic*] of techniques would be equally significant to all persons. For most of the population, the satisfaction to be secured in orgasm is the goal of the sex act, and the more quickly that satisfaction is attained, the more effective the performance is judged to be.[61]

In Kinsey's second pattern of sexual behaviour speed is a desired goal and varied techniques are not valued. The notion that greater satisfaction is to be gained from this approach is now all but incomprehensible to most people, at least in theory, so completely has this society been convinced that variety and extended duration is the acme of sexual experience. Yet the evidence suggests that for the vast majority of couples in the late nineteenth and early twentieth centuries sexual activity consisted almost exclusively of brief episodes of sexual intercourse. Thus substantial change has taken place in perceptions of desirable and 'natural' sexual activity. There were two relevant developments. The impact of birth control

---

[60] In the early 20th century the demographic profile of the US population was younger and there was a high proportion of first-generation immigrants, many from cultures with more liberal attitudes to sexuality. Greater sexual liberalization occurred in the 1920s than in England. The age at marriage fell faster and more people married during the early 20th century.

[61] A. C. Kinsey, W. B. Pomeroy, P. H. Gebhard, and C. E. Martin, *Sexual Behaviour in the Human Male* (1948), 572.

methods on sexual practice has been described in the first section of the book. The spontaneity that men like Beale claimed was essential to the performance of intercourse was already undermined by the control necessary for effective use of contraception. Those who recommended birth control were aware of this and saw it as a gain because they valued female sexual pleasure and greater sexual sophistication.[62] The second change was only just beginning to take place; the widening out of acceptable physical sexual activity beyond sexual intercourse. For this to occur, substantial changes in women and men's attitudes to the genitals and masturbation had to take place. The next chapter looks at new ideas about masturbation and other sexual practices during the 1930s.

[62] e.g. H. G. Wells, preface to M. Fielding, *Parenthood: Design or Accident? A Manual of Birth Control* (1928), 10. Th. H. van de Velde, *Fertility and Sterility in Marriage: Their Voluntary Promotion and Limitation* (1931), 286–9, also 339.

9

'The Spontaneous Feeling of Shame': Masturbation and Freud 1930–1940

In the 1920s and 1930s, British sexual culture was shaped by an almost abstract perception of sexuality as a negative force that had to be restricted and controlled in whatever form it occurred. The genitals were not primarily a source of pleasure but a part of the body to avoid and think about as little as possible. The major shift that occurred in the sex manuals of the 1930s was a move away from acceptance of this feeling of shame and fear to promotion of a more positive conception of the body and sexuality. While the manuals do challenge male control of sexual activity in new ways during the 1930s, the challenge is largely indirect, and it comes about from the desire of both men and women that women should experience sexual pleasure. The redefinition of masturbation which took place during the inter-war decades had more impact than any direct challenge to gender relations on sexual practice in the 1930s. Attitudes to masturbation concerned not only the relation of the individual to their own body but their approach to the body of a sexual partner. The limits that these inhibitions about the body placed on physical sexual practice were severe.

CLITORAL STIMULATION

The previous chapter described how first Marie Stopes, and then the manual authors that came after her, told husbands that they must court or woo their wife on each and every occasion they had intercourse. In other words, their wife too must be aroused and desire to have intercourse. Then, during intercourse, men were told to delay their own orgasms in order that she received sufficient duration of stimulation to reach orgasm. Letters and contact with patients quickly revealed that a woman might well not have an orgasm even if her partner had sufficient control to delay his orgasm, and that, in any event, many men were not capable of such control. Clitoral stimulation appears to be the obvious solution to this dilemma. However, the generation that came of age in the 1920s was shaped by the peak of anxiety about masturbation, which occurred from the late Victorian period until the First World War.[1] The majority of inter-war authors and their readers believed women and men should experience orgasms during coitus because handling of the genitals to produce pleasure by either partner was deeply discomforting to them. There was no word or term for touching your wife's clitoris (or your husband's penis) although it was sometimes labelled as masturbation. Most individuals internalized prohibitions against touching the genitals in infancy, and the experiences of childhood and adolescence reinforced their discomfort. The taboo against masturbation provided an intellectual justification for feelings that this generation experienced as natural and inevitable. Some couples were unaware that the clitoris even existed, but even couples that realized clitoral stimulation was possible often felt unhappy and uncomfortable about producing orgasm in this way.[2] The English sexologist Havelock Ellis had written in the 1890s that masturbation would not cause physical damage although it might result in slight nervous disorders and that extensive masturbation in youth might lead to the divorce of sexuality from affection.[3] In the 1920s and 1930s, many of

---

[1] L. A. Hall, 'Forbidden by God, Despised by Men: Masturbation, Medical Warnings, Moral Panic, and Manhood in Great Britain, 1850–1950', *Journal of the History of Sexuality*, 2/3 (1992), 385.

[2] Ibid, E. M. Holtzman, 'The Pursuit of Married Love: Women's Attitudes toward Sexuality and Marriage in Great Britain, 1918–1939', *Journal of Social History*, 16/2 (1982), 45–6. See also H. Wright, *Sex Fulfilment in Married Women* (1947), 17–18. Medica [pseud. J. Malleson], *Any Wife or Any Husband* (1951; 1955), 54. M. Stopes, *Enduring Passion* (1931 4th edn. 1931), 145–6.

[3] See P. Robinson, *The Modernization of Sex* (1976), 12–14. Ellis greatly influenced those writing manuals. Though it was initially banned in England there were American editions of his six-volume *Studies in the Psychology of Sex* published before the First World War and he published many essays. His sexological work was not available to the general reader in England until the mid-1930s. *Sex in Relation to Society* was published in 1937, in a new edition 'intended for a wider public', and the *Psychology of Sex: A Manual for Students* was published in 1933, with a Pan paperback edition in 1959.

the manual authors who read and admired Ellis struggled against their own inhibitions to accept this liberal position. However, both male and female manual readers wanted women to gain sexual satisfaction, and the manual authors realized that clitoral stimulation was the next expedient. In 1926, Theodore van de Velde suggested that if 'the man should be unable to produce his wife's orgasm by genital friction [coitus], autotherapeutic measures are probably better than none at all, although the objections, on many counts, to such expedients, are far from trivial.'[4] Autotherapeutic measures were stimulation of the clitoris by hand. His pseudoscientific language reinforces the sense of unease he is expressing. Other manual authors described this as digital or manual stimulation, or as masturbation.[5]

The next major innovation in the sex manuals, after those of Stopes and van de Velde, came from Helena Wright (1887–1982), a woman who was notably direct and confident. She expressed more scepticism about conventional heterosexual masculine and feminine roles than any other manual writer.[6] In 1930, Wright published a short, clear manual, in which she suggested that in 'the first few days of marriage . . . an orgasm induced by the husband's hand, and entirely by way of clitoris sensation, may be a kind and gentle way of introducing a timid and perhaps frightened girl to a happy sex-life'.[7] Even Wright suggested this expedient only for the first few days. In the same book, she wrote that:

[I]t is very difficult even for an adventurous-minded person to find and hold a reasonable point of view on this subject . . . It is, perhaps . . . the fact that masturbation is purely selfish that is at the root of the *spontaneous* feeling of shame experienced by most masturbators. (my italics)[8]

---

[4] Th. H. van de Velde, *Ideal Marriage: Its Physiology and Technique* (1928; reset 1943), 169.

[5] R. Macandrew [pseud.], *Friendship, Love Affairs and Marriage* (1939), 87. Stopes, *Enduring Passion*, 146. One later author referred to 'self-masturbation' to avoid confusion. M. N. Robinson, *The Power of Sexual Surrender* (1960), 43. W. H. Long, if still somewhat given to Victorian alarmism, was notably relaxed and elegantly erotic on this topic when compared to other authors but his manual seems to have had little circulation. H. W. Long, *Sane Sex Life and Sane Sex Living* (1919), 113, 122–7, 131–2.

[6] Wright, *The Sex Factor in Marriage* (1930; 1940), 34, 76, 86, 95–6.

[7] Ibid. 95–6.

[8] Ibid. 91–2.

Wright's belief that such shame was spontaneous highlights the impossibility of simply casting off such socially constructed beliefs. Her background was very different from the prudent middle-class, provincial roots from which much of nineteenth-century British feminism sprang.[9] Wright's father was a Polish immigrant who became a wealthy businessman. He openly took a new mistress every year, for a year, in order to ensure the woman never became a threat to his family. In spite of this precaution, his wife divorced him when Helena was a teenager. Helena herself had an open marriage and enjoyed affairs with younger men.[10] She showed her patients where their clitoris was and encouraged them to recognize clitoral sensation. If she believed that shame at masturbation was spontaneous there was little hope that more conventional people could easily overcome their anxieties.

By the late 1930s, the more progressive authors began to adopt Sigmund Freud's (1856–1939) argument that masturbation in infancy and adolescence was a phase through which the vast majority of the population passed. Freud's analysis of masturbation provided an explanation for the observed fact that the practice was too frequent to cause the alleged ill effects. A new rationale was used to explain why adult masturbation was unacceptable: 'It is a solitary vice; it conduces to egoistic pleasure. It is an anti-social and selfish act. The doer is in love with himself; he does not share his pleasure with another. Biologically, it is in opposition to the law of mating.'[11] The concept of a social act was made necessary by the introduction of birth control. Unacceptable sexual activity could no longer be defined by the fact that it did not result in reproduction. Men who did not care about female pleasure and women who did not want sexual intercourse were also both described as selfish. However, some authors extended this interpretation of masturbation using it as the basis for a more tolerant attitude to other sexual practices, including homosexuality. Eustace Chesser (1902–73) placed these 'other deviations' in the same category as masturbation in 1949:

---

[9] For the backgrounds of British feminists, see O. Banks, *Becoming a Feminist: The Social Origins of First Wave Feminism* (1986). R. Hall, *Marie Stopes: A Biography* (1977).

[10] B. Evans, *Freedom to Choose: The Life and Work of Dr Helena Wright, Pioneer of Contraception* (1982).

[11] E. Cole, *Education for Marriage* (1938), 43. See also A. Craig, *Sex and Revolution* (1934), 136–7.

Nowadays the term auto-erotism is used to cover a number of deviations from normality, all of which have one characteristic which brings them within the auto-erotic sphere-that they involve concentration upon the self instead of a love objective outside of the self, and normally a person of the opposite sex. At one time the term was used synonomously with masturbation ... Most sexual abnormalities are substitutes for normal adult sexual activity; they represent a turning away from the real thing.[12]

For this generation, heterosexual coitus was the 'real thing', but the presentation of sexuality as positive that this entailed was itself a shift. Discussions such as this were part of the process of gradually extending the boundaries of permissible sexual behaviour amongst conventional, respectable couples. Kenneth Walker (1882–1966) wrote in 1940 that 'No one can claim complete normality for his own particular pattern of sexuality,' and Chesser expressed a similar sentiment.[13] The linking of masturbation with 'sexual abnormalities' highlights both the importance of the practice and the extent to which it was seen as unacceptable. These authors were writing for an audience that were still uncomfortable with their own sexuality, and the authors themselves had barriers to overcome.[14] Such tentative attempts at promoting tolerance were as far as they were able to go at this time.

The manual authors were subject to considerable legal constraints, and it is arguable that the law imposed such conservative attitudes to masturbation upon them. The sex radical and historian of English censorship, Alec Craig, wrote that Stopes, who did not even mention masturbation, had gone to the edge of what was legal in 1918.[15] Wright's publishers feared police might confiscate all copies of her book on publication in 1930 and the courts had a sex manual destroyed in 1936. Not until the attempt to ban Chesser's manual *Love without Fear* (1940) in 1941 failed did the situation ease substantially.[16] Nonetheless the gradual evolution of attitudes in their

[12] E. Chesser, *Sexual Behaviour: Normal and Abnormal* (1949), 122, 124, 127. See also R. Macandrew [pseud.], *Encyclopedia of Sex and Love Technique* (1941; 1951), 32–9, 205. A. D. Costler and A. Willy, *The Encyclopaedia of Sex Practice*, ed. N. Haire (1938), 117.

[13] K. M. Walker, *The Physiology of Sex* (1940), pp. vi–vii. E. Chesser, *Love without Fear (A Plain Guide to Sex Technique for Every Married Adult)* (1941), 105.

[14] See K. M. Walker, *I Talk of Dreams* (1946).

[15] A. Craig. 'Censorship of Sexual Literature', in A. P. Abarbanel and A. Ellis (eds.), *Encyclopaedia of Sexual Behaviour* (1961), 235–46.

[16] For a description of Chesser's trial see R. Porter and L. A. Hall, *The Facts of Life: The Creation of Sexual Knowledge in Britain, 1650–1950* (1995), 261–2. Evans, *Freedom*, 153.

work suggests that the law was not the sole problem. As early as 1934 it was possible to publish a translation of the French sex theorist René Guyon's lengthy defence of 'mutual' and solitary masturbation as a 'natural form of sexual pleasure', showing that the law had limits.[17] Alec Craig, although he was a practising nudist who wrote about censorship, and a man of similar class and type to the more liberal manual authors, specifically rejected Guyon's liberal approach in 1936.[18] Dr Edward Griffith included a ten-page stricture on avoidance of masturbation by use of self-control in his 1935 sex manual.[19] Censorship law was liberalized in 1959. In his substantially revised 1963 edition, Griffith initially declared masturbation was not harmful, but only two pages later he wrote that 'the sex act is really intended to be used between two persons for their mutual benefit'.[20] He still felt the need to emphasize that acceptable sex was a social act. Thus even after the law ceased to be an obstacle he still expressed reservations about masturbation, confirming that his anxieties were genuinely felt. Kenneth Walker's attitudes had been, and appear to have remained, even more ambivalent. In 1954, he still included masturbation (and oral sex) in a list of 'Deviations of Aim', which also included coprophagia, that is, eating faeces.[21]

MASTURBATION AND MALE DOMINANCE

In 1935, the publishers of Edward Charles's *The Sexual Impulse* (1935) were prosecuted successfully for publishing an obscene book. Charles (b.1898), an English novelist and academic, whose book 'aimed to produce an enlightened intelligentsia', was elitist and racist.[22] He despised the working

---

[17] R. Guyon, *Sex Life and Sex Ethics* (1934), 290–5.

[18] Craig, *Sex and Revolution*, 136.

[19] E. F. Griffith, *Modern Marriage and Birth Control* (1935), 157–68. This was reprinted from L. D. Weatherhead, *The Mastery of Sex through Psychology and Religion* (1931).

[20] E. F. Griffith, *Modern Marriage* (1935; 1963), 250, 253.

[21] K. M. Walker and E. B. Strauss, *Sexual Disorders in the Male* (1939; 1954), 172–4.

[22] E. Charles, *The Sexual Impulse: An Introduction to the Study of the Psychology, Physiology and Bio-chemistry of the Sexual Impulse Among Adults in Mental and Bodily Health* (1935), 155, 207. In keeping with his ambivalent modernity, Charles does include reproduction—but he explicitly separates the two sections. See 119–20.

class and Indians and believed ardently in the subordination of women. The defence presented a parade of eminent witnesses, and had agreed that the chapter on 'Sexual union' be removed, but in his summing up the judge concluded:

I see a most disgusting reference to a beautiful building on page 68, and I find coarse language elsewhere...And there is no question that the author is sniggering at pre-marital chastity among women. I am afraid there would be much to be picked out...Therefore I shall order it to be destroyed.[23]

The 'disgusting reference' read, 'the building of the Taj Mahal...was presumably a masturbatory act...since it was a tomb for a dead mistress and a dead queen'.[24] The judge's response indicates the strength of feeling against masturbation. In a convoluted argument of theological complexity, Charles revealed that male masturbation as usually understood was acceptable to him:

Masturbation for a male may occur within the female vagina just as easily and as frequently as elsewhere...The act of sexual union being performed, where there is no spontaneous mutual desire, is definitely masturbation...Handling of the genitals by an individual, during a period of enforced abstinence, to secure his own fidelity or to secure sleep...is not masturbation.[25]

In this passage Charles was redefining masturbation to include only so-called selfish acts. Sexual acts were acceptable if they were social acts (usually coitus), and selfishness in sexual pleasure was unacceptable, so he redefined as masturbation all sexual acts that have selfish pleasure as their aim. Thus handling of the genitals with the aim of sleep was acceptable to him but coitus where the woman did not feel desire was not. Charles had to go to considerable lengths to justify masturbation; like Wright and others of this generation he could not simply throw off his inhibitions.

Although Charles wanted women to enjoy sex, he rejected Stopes and her ideas utterly. In 1928, he wrote that when he saw her book he thought

---

[23] A. Craig, 'Report of Police Action and Proceedings Regarding "*An Introduction to the Study of the Psychology, Physiology and Bio-chemistry of the Sexual Impulse among Adults in Mental and Bodily Health*": A Study by E. Charles, Published on the 7th of February, 1935', unpublished, British Library, 2–3.

[24] Charles, *Sexual Impulse*, 68–9.

[25] Ibid. 64–5.

of 'the big green mantis sitting up on her hind legs and eating husband after husband as soon as he has satisfied her biological needs'.[26] Stopes had in fact suggested only a relatively minor degree of greater sexual equality, and certainly not dominance by the woman. It was vital to Charles that sexual activity be male dominated and centred on the phallus and, unlike other inter-war manual authors, he saw clitoral orgasms as threatening this:

Dr Marie Stopes has 'discovered', by which I mean popularized . . . the half-truth that woman enjoys two distinct types of orgasm, with physiological differences, the one clitoridal, the other vaginal or cervical . . . [but] woman may be equally psychically versatile, and, what is far, far more important, that man may be her equal.[27]

The difference, he told his readers, between vaginal and clitoral orgasms was the same as the difference between masturbatory and non-masturbatory sex, which men could also experience. In the case of women's orgasms it was the man's penis that defined the act as masturbatory or not:

The truth is that the distinction in women is psychic far more than physical. The stimulation of the cervix by artificial means [i.e. vaginal masturbation] will produce in women an orgasm, spiritually no different (and physically very slightly different) from the orgasm produced by the artificial stimulation of the clitoris. It happens, of course, that a woman is far more often clitoridally stimulated in mean and unnatural circumstances, whereas she is more usually cervically stimulated in the lovely and healthy satisfaction of her sexual impulse with her dear and practised lover [i.e. coitus]. And the difference between the woman's 'two' orgasms is exactly the difference between masturbation and the satisfaction of the sexual impulse.[28]

In other words, clitoral orgasms were masturbation and vaginal orgasms produced in coitus by the man's penis were not.[29] Charles was a harbinger of the liberal manuals of the 1950s and 1960s, with their relaxed attitude to sexual practice coupled with intense anxiety about the possibility of

---

[26] E. Charles, *An Indian Patchwork* (1934), 283.

[27] Charles, *Sexual Impulse*, 9. e.g. Stopes, *Enduring Passian*, 90.

[28] Charles, *Sexual Impulse*, 10.

[29] Ibid. 141–2.

female domination. The other manual authors of his time were concerned to improve sexual experience. Most were unaware or, albeit subtly, actively pleased that this would erode male domination of sexual practice. Like Stopes, Charles was moving on from the first-wave feminist rejection of conjugal rights, but the argument he constructs enables him simultaneously to promote the modernization of many aspects of sexual practice and to reassert male domination as central to sexual activity. To achieve this he abandons all other aspects of the taboo against masturbation while introducing Freud's prohibition against clitoral masturbation as an expression of active adult female sexuality.

Freud's theory of human development described internal psychic structures but related these to the body and its sensations. He argued that infantile masturbation was a universal experience, thus giving permission for such behaviour: if everyone masturbated as an infant then infantile masturbation must be acceptable. At one level this contributed to the erosion of the prohibition against adult masturbation, but Freud transposed it into a specific prohibition against adult women's clitoral orgasms. In 1905, he explained that the sole task of the clitoris in the adult woman is to transmit excitement to the vagina. Initially the young woman is 'anaesthetic', that is, she has no sexual sensations in her vagina. He goes on to explain that this 'anaesthesia may become permanent if the clitoridal zone refuses to abandon its excitability', that is, if the woman still experienced clitoral orgasms.[30] Anaesthesia was synonymous with frigidity and an indication of immaturity. Freud's ideas about female sexuality enabled men such as Charles to legitimize male-dominated sexual practice while accepting a more sexually passionate role for women. This shift was away from regulating sexuality *per se* towards regulating gender power relations in order to maintain male domination. Sexuality ceases to be seen as a negative force but sexual activity is now to be restricted and controlled in a new way.

D. H. Lawrence's (1885–1930) descriptions of sexual intercourse were influenced by these ideas, and in turn influenced, the development of English sexual culture strongly. He incorporated the rejection of

---

[30] S. Freud, *On Sexuality: Three Essays on the Theory of Sexuality and Other Works*, ed. J. Strachey (1962; 1977), 143.

masturbation as self-directed sexuality, and of clitoral stimulation as a form of masturbation. His last and most relevant novel, *Lady Chatterley's Lover* (1928), was not published in England in an unexpurgated version until 1960, but it was widely read by middle-class men before this. The novel tells the story of an adulterous relationship between Lady Chatterley and Mellors, the gamekeeper of her crippled and impotent husband. Lawrence rewrote the novel three times, and his wife, Frieda Lawrence, commented that: 'The First Lady Chatterley he wrote as she came out of him, out of his own immediate self. In the third version he was also aware of his contemporaries' minds.'[31] One of those contemporaries was Stopes. In an essay in the late 1920s Lawrence fulminated against Stopes, who, he wrote, had taken out the 'dirty little secret [of sex] and thoroughly disinfected it with scientific words'. Sex had been 'mentalized', it was all 'cerebral reaction', and 'not a bit of phallic insouciance and spontaneity'.[32] We have seen in the previous chapter that spontaneity, or absence of control, had been central to the male experience of coitus. Frieda, who was German, had introduced Lawrence to Freud's ideas as early as 1912. Between the first and the third and final draft of the novel, he inserted lengthy descriptions of physical sexual events. Freud's ideas and Stopes's manual influenced the novel, and it in turn influenced ideas about the conduct of physical sexual activity.[33]

In the novel, Lawrence attaches enormous importance to the difference between clitoral and vaginal orgasms. He accepted that some men were to blame for women's lack of sexual pleasure because they reached orgasm too quickly (as Stopes had written). However, his male characters condemned active participation by the woman to ensure that she also had an orgasm during coitus. In this quotation, Michaelis, the lover of Connie, Lady Chatterley, was reproaching her for being active and reaching her orgasm through clitoral stimulation, albeit from his penis:

'You couldn't go off at the same time as a man, could you? You'd have to bring yourself off! You'd have to run the show!' ... 'What do you mean?' she said. 'You know what I mean. You keep on for hours after I've gone off ... and I have to

    [31] F. Lawrence, introd. to D. H. Lawrence, *The First Lady Chatterley* (1944; 1973), 10.

    [32] D. H. Lawrence, *Sex, Literature and Censorship*, ed. H. T. Moore (1955), 76.

    [33] K. Sagar, *D. H. Lawrence: Life into Art* (1985), 91–3. For Lawrence's own sexuality, see D. Britton, *Lady Chatterley: The Making of the Novel* (1988).

hang on with my teeth till you bring yourself off by your own exertions.' [punctuation as original] She was stunned by this unexpected piece of brutality, at the moment when she was glowing with a sort of pleasure beyond words and a sort of love for him. Because, after all, like so many modern men, he was finished almost before he had begun. And that forced the woman to be active.[34]

The manual writers had usually recommended that the man delay coming. Instead in this quotation, the man maintained his erection after orgasm, and was depicted as having to share control of intercourse with the woman; that is, her orgasm determined when coitus ended. Lawrence's novel portrays the woman's desire for orgasm as a conscious struggle for power between the man and the woman. A later passage, in which Mellors, describing the same mode of intercourse, after repeatedly referring to his first wife's clitoris as a 'beak' that 'tears' at him, underlined the point:

I had to stop inside her till she brought herself off, wriggling and shouting... Self! Self! Self! all Self! tearing and shouting!... Like an old trull [prostitute]... I told her how I hated it. And she'd even try. She'd try to lie still and let me work the business. She'd try. But it was no good ... She had to work the thing herself, grind her own coffee.[35]

The association of clitoral stimulation with self and thus with masturbation is made powerfully negative. The character Mellors can then use this to legitimize male preferences and regulate women's sexual behaviour. Self-directed, female desire for sexual pleasure also led him to accuse the woman of similarity to a prostitute, a powerful negative association. Charles and Lawrence were constructing a male-controlled sexual event that still centred on the male orgasm but incorporated a sexually passionate woman.

Amongst such men, male domination was combined with a more spontaneous vision of physical sexual activity. This emphasis on spontaneity was a rejection of the demand for male control in Stopes's work and that of the manual authors she had influenced and the first-wave feminism that had influenced her. Charles rejected Stopes's insistence that women should be wooed before each episode of coitus, insisting that coitus should only occur when there was not just mutual desire but

---

[34] D. H. Lawrence, *Lady Chatterley's Lover* (1928; 1990), 57.
[35] Lawrence, *Lady Chatterley*, 210.

'spontaneous mutual desire'.[36] He did not want a return to Victorian female passivity and lack of sexual response; instead he wanted his partner to produce sexual desire whenever he desired her. Charles associated spontaneous sex strongly with nature, as did Lawrence. The chapter on 'Sexual Union' in Charles's manual (which the judge wished to have removed in its entirety) began by suggesting that coitus should be an emotional experience, and involve a variety of positions. It should happen under beech trees, on grassy banks, on chairs, in front of a fire, anywhere but in a bed on an inner spring mattress. In the context of the 1930s, this demand for spontaneity was in part a demand that women be more like a man and, as was so often the case, such a demand could not be accommodated without eventually undermining male control.

The assumption of male management and control of physical sexual events in the manuals makes it plain that male sexual domination was the sexual norm. Once conventional couples accepted female sexual desire, then the norm of male control came into question. This was especially so if the woman did not reach orgasm in coitus, thus necessitating clitoral stimulation, or if the woman sat astride the man during coitus. More active female participation and more varied sexual activity potentially heightened male sexual anxiety.[37] The accounts assumed that either men or women were active and initiated controlled sexual activity; thus if women were active, men must become passive.[38] The notion of shared activity in which neither partner dominated was completely absent from the discourse. Historians of homosexuality have found that in the early twentieth century a man who took only the active, dominant, penetrating role in male homosexual physical sexual activity often considered himself 'normal', what would now be called heterosexual.[39] The manuals

[36] Charles, *Sexual Impulse*, 64–5.

[37] For the anxieties this aroused, see e.g. van de Velde, *Ideal Marriage*, 195–7. For the opposite attitude, Chesser, *Love*, 55–6.

[38] Ellis, *Psychology*, 347. L. Eyles, *Commonsense about Sex* (1933), 49, 66. I. Hutton, *The Hygiene of Marriage* (1923), chs. 3 and 4. K. M. Walker, *Sexual Behaviour: Creative and Destructive*, (1966), 185. Wright, *Sex Factor*, 76, 86.

[39] M. Vicinus, M. B. Duberman, and G. Chauncey (eds.), 'Hidden from History: Reclaiming the Gay and Lesbian Past', introd. in *Hidden from History: Reclaiming the Gay and Lesbian Past* (1989; 1991), 10. J. H. Gagnon and W. Simon, *Sexual Conduct: The Social Sources of Human Sexuality* (1974), 247.

suggest that at this historical juncture a man might feel his masculinity was threatened even when having coitus with a woman if he was not dominant. This rigid role was not fully compatible with producing female sexual pleasure. For example there was no pre-existing active/dominant role and passive/subordinate role in masturbatory techniques. Helena Wright's books show that women often needed to demonstrate to their husbands what gave them sexual pleasure, thus undermining the notion that it was men who had sexual knowledge and produced sexual pleasure in women and forcing a small shift away from female passivity.[40]

LIBERTINE SEXUALITY

The male manual writers mentioned so far did largely share a progressive vision of masculinity in one important respect. They believed that ideal sexual activity involved an emotional (and often spiritual) bond between the couple, and to this extent, they rejected the double standard of sexual behaviour. Crucially, these authors usually rejected prostitution, as did feminists.[41] Amongst those men who accepted prostitution, female sexual pleasure was just one more element in what they were paying for.[42] George Ryley Scott's (b. 1886) *Sex and its Mysteries* (1929) was the first sex manual that took a non-feminist, libertine male approach to sexuality. He considered that considerable change in sexual mores had taken place and that this had not made sexual relations easier. In *The New Art of Love* (1934) he wrote:

Up to as recently as ten years ago sex was a most one-sided affair. It was pre-eminently a male affair. The woman, at any rate the woman of respectability, went to the altar a virgin in both fact and thought... With the rise of women's emancipation has gone her reputed sexual anaesthesia... (which, as regards

[40] Wright, *Sex Factor*, 1930. 58. Wright, *Sex Fulfilment*, 1947. 81.

[41] Beale, *Wise Wedlock*, 16. A. H. Gray, *Men, Women and God* (1923; 17th edn. 1947), 133. J. Tenenbaum, *The Riddle of Sex* (1930), 213. For van de Velde's attitudes, see E. M. Brecher, *The Sex Researchers* (1970), 89–90. Weatherhead, *Mastery*, 97, 188. Charles supported 'union by a male with a prostitute' if it enabled the man to improve sex with his wife or mistress. Charles, *Sexual Impulse*, 65.

[42] See Stopes, *Enduring Passion* (1931), 6.

married women, was greatly exaggerated)...This emergence of woman into a position, on the eve of marriage, somewhat analogous to man, has *greatly extended* the possibilities of marital sexual *disharmony*. (italics added)[43]

Scott believed that marital harmony had been greater when sex was a one-sided affair. He was not anti-feminist in the sense of Charles, Freud, or Lawrence; rather in his manuals he simply did not engage intellectually or emotionally with feminist arguments. Instead he took advantage of the publishing opportunity that had arisen as a result of the new, albeit very partial, respectability of sex. Scott's two texts interspersed the conventional wisdom of the 1920s sex manuals with fragments of anthropology and libertine sexual beliefs. In strong contrast to other authors quoted thus far, he placed examples of the behaviour of prostitutes side by side with that of other women, effectively placing all women on a continuum. For example:

The woman is in an altogether different street. Only in the case of passionate orgasm is coitus in any way exhausting. Prostitutes regularly receive as many as a dozen men a night.[44]

[A] woman can and often does rape a man.[45]

Pederasty is a common contraceptive practice; bestiality, like intercourse with a virgin, has a widespread reputation as a cure for venereal disease.[46]

Scott's work appears to have sold consistently but not in large numbers. Given the emphasis on female ignorance and the rejection of prostitution in the manuals that sold well, and in manuals by women, it is probable that female readers did not wish to entertain Scott's view of their sex. In his third manual, he abandoned this type of material.[47] An examination of Scott's work re-emphasizes the extent to which most sex manuals aimed at a conventional middle-class readership. The manuals might be titillating, arousing, or even erotic, but they were not pornography. They consistently presented readers with an ideal of sexual activity involving an emotional bond between the couple and combined this with the

---

[43] G. R. Scott, *The New Art of Love* (1934), 12–13.
[44] G. R. Scott, *Sex and its Mysteries* (1929; 2nd edn. 1948) 79.
[45] Ibid. 77.
[46] Scott, *New Art*, 110.
[47] G. R. Scott, *Sex in Married Life* (1938).

use of unemotional, medicalized language when describing actual sexual events.

Scott's work can be contrasted with Eustace Chesser's *Love without Fear* (1940), which was one of the highest-selling manuals. It was also packed with racy, and sometimes funny, little anecdotes, and, like Scott, suggested that not all women were ignorant of sex. Unlike Scott, Chesser was as reassuring and positive about sexuality as earlier best-selling manuals had been. Chesser tried hard not to be didactic or patronizing and suggested that individual variation was important and should be accepted. In the second edition he added a little saying, which read: 'Happiness is the true test...Never mind what books—including this one—say you should do. If you are happy, and your partner is, too, leave well enough alone.'[48] Chesser's high sales compared to Scott reinforce the argument that the high sales enjoyed by Stopes and van de Velde's manuals reveal that readers wanted manuals to present a positive view of sexuality as joyous and loving. However by the 1940s a new generation had grown up with greater awareness of the body and access to sexual knowledge. They were growing in confidence and many wanted sex to be light-hearted as well as romantic. Chesser provided this, and his original contribution lay in the new tone he struck as much as anything else.

REPRESSION AND THE IMPOSITION OF SEXUAL NORMS

The introduction of Freudian psychoanalytic theory into the manuals, from the mid-1930s, reflected the intense interest in Freud's ideas and those of his followers amongst socially progressive people. They perceived Victorian society as having been riddled with sexual hypocrisy, and they treated as axiomatic Freud's claim that individuals did not always reveal what was most important, or tell the truth, even to themselves.[49] Increasingly they accepted the claims of psychoanalysis to define normal sexual behaviour. The influence of Freud was both repressive and liberalizing. He

[48] Chesser, *Love*, 94.
[49] For Freud's influence, see C. E. M. Joad, *Guide to Modern Thought* (1933), 192–221.

had stated that 'scarcely a single individual escapes [early infantile masturbation]'.[50] His definition of masturbation included any pleasurable contact with the genitals however minor and whether accidental, for the purposes of hygiene, or for any other reason. Only in his claim that this behaviour was universal in infancy did Freud's definition, or indeed his attitude, differ substantially from others of his generation.[51] However, many people in the inter-war decades did not believe that they had masturbated at any point in their lives. In 1933, manual author Leonora Eyles (1889–1960) wrote that:

A psychoanalyst once said to me that ninety-nine per cent of people would admit to having at some time or other been addicted to masturbation and the other one per cent would lie about it. But I find my own experience and observation does not coincide with this. Discussing the subject once with some young people, I found that two out of the seven had, like myself, first heard of it by reading books about sex.[52]

Psychoanalysts simply asserted that testimony such as that of Eyles was based on repression of unacceptable sexual memories. This made Freud's theories a powerful weapon against those sectors of society who insisted that sexual impulses could be denied and repressed and that it was more honourable and made one a better person to do so. The insistence that all people had sexual desires was liberal in its immediate impact but psychoanalysis also reinforced the move away from a tentative pluralism to an authoritarian insistence on norms in the manuals. As we shall see in the next chapter, this trend peaked in the 1950s and 1960s. Freud's vision of the polymorphously perverse condition of infancy implied an inherent sexual pluralism but this was easily dismissed because the psyche was conceived of in essentialist terms. The libido, which was the source of sexual energy, according to Freud, was not limited to the observable behaviour of the infant or, for that matter, anyone else. It was a hypothetical instinct that, Freud theorized, underlay all human sexuality but which could never be observed in itself. This, then, was a force which provided 'man' with a sexual nature that society modified and controlled, but which itself

---

[50] Freud, *Three Essays*, 1962. 105.

[51] J. Mitchell, *Psychoanalysis and Feminism* (1974; 1990), 421.

[52] Eyles, *Commonsense*, 34. See also Gray, *Men*, 21. P. Makin, *The Evelyn Home Story* (1975), 140.

remained hidden, and about which assertions could be made that were not falsifiable on the basis of lived experience. Thus people who claimed not to masturbate or women who had only clitoral orgasms, could simply be told they were wrong. They did not remember or they were immature. This was a redrawing of the boundaries of deviance away from sexuality *per se*, which became acceptable, and towards a restatement of gender power relations. It was acceptable to have sexual desires and sensations, but not autonomous female sexual desires and sensations (or those directed toward the same-sex).

In 1938, a 'medical psychologist' named Estelle Cole published a manual. She reveals attitudes that the manual authors were to take up in the 1950s as they became more sexually and socially conservative. She based her manual on 'simple talks' she had given to the 'most varied types from young women just down from university to girls in offices and shops'.[53] This probably included women in their twenties rather than those in their teens. Cole intended the talks to overcome ignorance and, by so doing, lower the divorce rate. She wrote that the wife's sexual satisfaction was the 'basis of a successful marriage, and of a happy family life, which [led] to worthy and competent citizenship'.[54] The use of such language demonstrated the growing acceptance of a respectable female genital sexuality and reinforced the male's responsibility to 'give' his wife orgasms. In Cole's manual, the association of masturbation with clitoral stimulation has become explicit and extended to include frigidity: 'A frigid woman is interested in the sensations derived from the stimulation of the clitoris; the vaginal sensations, so necessary for normal and satisfactory intercourse are absent. She has probably been a masturbator and may be unable to rid herself of the habit.'[55] She follows Freud's assertion that clitoral orgasm in women was a sign of immaturity, and that mature adult women who accepted their female role experienced only vaginal orgasms. This is a more conservative approach than that of Wright whose manual had been published nearly a decade previously. Cole rejected masturbation and Freud's ideas reinforced this belief. His assertion that vaginal orgasms were mature would probably have appeared self-evident to Cole, given that they did not entail masturbation. This was the first manual to

---

[53] Cole, *Education*, 9.   [54] Ibid. 10.   [55] Ibid. 71.

present Freud's ideas confidently to a female audience. From the end of the 1940s, manual authors used Freudian theory to direct women back to the home and marital duty that many women had rejected in previous decades, and they often encouraged men to take a more libertine approach to women. However, while the gender ideology promoted by these manuals became more restrictive, the physical sexual confidence promoted so diffidently by the inter-war manual authors developed. The new generation of authors and readers increasingly accepted that touching their partner's genitals and their own was an enjoyable part of physical sexual activity.

10

'Thought Control': Conjugal Rights and Vaginal Orgasms 1940s–1960s

Legal and social attitudes had loosened considerably by the end of the 1930s. The trends toward sexual liberalization and libertinism and reassertion of male domination within the discourse on sexuality, which were to shape the post-war decades, were also well established. Nonetheless, many of the individuals who produced the inter-war sex manuals were progressive and strongly influenced by feminism. In the mid-1940s, there was a hiatus caused by the Second World War, during which no new manuals came out. Following this pause, manuals became considerably easier to obtain than had been the case before the war, but the content of the manuals gives no indication that the actual wartime experience caused any substantial change in sexual attitudes. However, more of the new post-war authors were professional writers motivated by the growing profits to be made, and the ideas and attitudes toward sexuality these authors expressed were less idealistic than those of the inter-war authors.

American manuals appear more frequently in this chapter than the previous two because they had a greater influence in this period. The increasing availability of American material was a major development following the Second World War. Peggy Makin, a well-known agony aunt called Evelyn Home, who had been working as a magazine journalist since the early 1930s, described the effect of this:

[J]ust after the war . . . the load of imported literature from all over the world, especially the United States, had begun to soften up our publishing conventions American women's magazines were running whole articles on taboo topics such as masturbation and its morals; our readers were buying these publications on the bookstalls ... and they were asking us why we were depriving them of such hot knowledge.[1]

This imported literature included cheap paperback editions of the more physically explicit American sex manuals. The American tendency to-wards a more relaxed style, along with a less cautious approach to sexual subjects, reflected a different sexual and physical culture. Compared to the English manuals, they revealed a less inhibited approach to the body, and in many instances a stronger emphasis on the need for women to accept a feminine role. This is probably because male control of sexual activity was more highly contested in the USA and not because American women were more supine. Indirect evidence of greater confidence amongst American women in 1950s USA includes the higher proportion of women in the paid workforce, higher levels of female education, and the earlier arrival of second-wave feminism. In the post-Second World War years, 'scientific' sexology also played an increasing part in shaping new attitudes to sex. The publication of Alfred Kinsey's *Sex in the Human Male* (1948) and *Sex in the Human Female* (1953) was front-page news in the British popular press, and experts in fields such as sex education or family planning read them eagerly.[2] Perhaps most important were the findings that between 92 and 97 per cent of all American males had masturbated and that 37 per cent had had sexual contact to orgasm with other men.

There was a sharp swing upward in the sales figures for manuals. For example, by 1938 the worldwide sales figure for *Married Love* (1918) was 820,000, which averages out at 41,000 copies a year. But *Love without Fear* (1940) by Dr Eustace Chesser (1902–73) had sold 720,000 by 1951, which averages out at 72,000 a year. By 1964, Chesser's book had sold three million, an average of 231,000 a year.[3] Yet this manual was of much less importance in its own time than *Married Love* had been during the inter-war decades. Stopes had involved herself in highly controversial legal cases and in birth control activities, all of which received huge publicity. Chesser, whose peak period was after the war, was prolific and involved in research and in commenting on controversial issues, but he and his

---

[1] P. Makin, *The Evelyn Home Story* (1975), 140–1.

[2] H. Hopkins, *The New Look: A Social History of the Forties and Fifties in Britain* (1964), 194–5. Reading, e.g. K. M. Walker, *Love, Marriage and the Family* (1957), 274, 276, 279.

[3] All information found on sales figures is given in Appendix A.

work had nothing like the same influence Stopes had. His manual was one amongst many, and the substantial sales figures reflect the relaxing of prohibitions on sexual material combined with the growing demand for information. The price of manuals in relation to real wages fell consistently until the end of the 1960s.[4] They went from being relatively expensive to being easily affordable and the readership broadened out accordingly beyond the middle classes.[5] Nonetheless, the new manuals continued to reflect the attitudes and emerging contradictions of sexual practice amongst the middle-class authors and the sexually progressive rather than the working class or the large socially conservative sections of the middle class. The manuals of the inter-war years continued to sell in large numbers throughout the 1940s and 1950s, with some appearing in new revised editions well into the 1970s.[6] The limited, albeit varied, evidence suggests that from the 1940s to the 1960s working-class people were most likely to encounter the early manuals, and possibly the cheaper, simply written British manuals of the late 1940s. The relaxation of the law on censorship in 1959 led to a sharp increase in the number and variety of cheap books containing sexual material. These included numerous paperback editions of 'erotic' classics and, thanks to the improving print technology, illustrated manuals.[7]

THE CREATION OF INSTITUTIONS

By the late 1940s, groups had been formed to support the dissemination of information on sexuality. Over a quarter of the manual authors belonged to the National Marriage Guidance Council (NMGC), the Family Planning Association (FPA), or the equivalents abroad. The NMGC's goal was

[4] Prices include: paperbacks: Exner 1951, 1s. 6d.; Macaulay 1957, 2s. 6d.; Walker and Fletcher 1962, 4s.; Barnes 1962, 3s. 6d.; hardbacks: Stopes 23rd edn. 1937, 6s.; Wright 1947, 5s.

[5] For some of the survey findings on readership, see R. Porter and L. A. Hall, *The Facts of Life: The Creation of Sexual Knowledge in Britain, 1650–1950* (1995), 256.

[6] e.g. I. E. Hutton, *The Hygiene of Marriage* (1923). E. F. Griffith, *Modern Marriage* (1973). Th. H. van de Velde, *Ideal Marriage: Its Physiology and Technique* (1928; reset 1943). A. Stone and H. Stone, *A Marriage Manual. A Practical Guide Book to Sex and Marriage* (1936; 1954).

[7] e.g. T. Hendrickson, *Variations on a Sexual Theme* (1969). M. Toft, *Sexual Techniques: An Illustrated Guide* (1969).

preserving marriages and so it emphasized the marital relationship, rather than the sexual satisfaction of the individual.[8] Invariably this meant that it advised women to accommodate themselves to their husband's sexual needs and avoided discussion of varied sexual practices. *The Art of Marriage* (1952) was written by Dr Mary Macaulay (b. 1902) who had been the medical officer for the Liverpool branch of the FPA from 1930 to 1956. She was also the founder and vice president of the Merseyside MGC. The FPA continued to recommend Macaulay's marriage and sex manual to engaged and newly wed women until the early 1970s.[9] The husband's responsibility to educate his new bride in order that she should learn to enjoy sex was still emphasized. But combined with the insistence that the wife should accommodate the husband's sexual needs in return, this took on the overtones of a marital duty, which citizens owed to society as much as to their partner.[10] This language can be placed in the context of the late 1940s and 1950s when there was a tremendous sense of optimism about belonging to society and citizenship. However Macaulay elided physical and emotional satisfaction. She suggested that a woman should be utterly satisfied with the 'free gift of love' she received from her husband in intercourse rather than make the mistake of seeking mere physical thrills. Books on sex and marriage were partly to blame for this mistake because they laid too much emphasis on the woman sharing her husband's sexual satisfaction, Macaulay explained. She accepted the husband's conjugal rights, commenting that it 'is a shocking thing to hear a woman say that she has not had any intercourse for years because she will not be raped even by her husband'.[11] A wife's rights were limited to saying no occasionally and to the insistence that her husband must ensure that she too was experiencing pleasure, evidently regardless of whether she felt desire.[12] These ideas about sexual practice, including the acceptance of

[8] See J. Lewis, D. Clark, and D. Morgan, *Whom God hath Joined: The Work of Marriage Guidance* (1992).

[9] *SHE* magazine (Aug. 1964). See also A. Giles, review of *The Art of Marriage*, by M. Macaulay, *Family Planning*, 19/4 (1971).

[10] M. Macaulay, *The Art of Marriage* (1952; 1957), 16–17, 72. Medica [pseud. of J. Malleson], *Any Wife or Any Husband* (1951; 1955), 53. See also R. Hacker, 'Love Without Tears', *Sunday Pictorial* (25 Nov. 1956). E. Mears, *Marriage: A Continuing Relationship* (1960).

[11] Macaulay, *Art*, 80.

[12] Ibid. 42–4, 112. See also Medica, *Any Wife*, 85–8.

male conjugal rights, are common to almost all the manuals written in this period.[13] They reinforce other evidence that suggests many women in all classes were still resisting sexual intercourse.

Many of those involved in the NMGC were practising Christians. Their rejection of a negative Christian tradition was an important aspect of changing societal sexual mores. Macaulay used the phrase 'one flesh' from the marriage service to describe the union that created the ideal sexual experience. She may have been drawing on the work of theologians, such as Dr Derrick Sherwin Bailey, who were integrating new sexual attitudes into the Anglican vision of marriage. In 1952, Bailey discussed the duties that husband and wife owe to one another in marital sex relations. He explained that to 'refrain [from sexual intercourse] except temporarily by mutual agreement . . . is to deprive the partner of a benefit to which he or she is entitled'. Thus 'only in special circumstances . . . may she [the wife] refuse a reasonable request for intercourse'.[14] The extent to which Bailey considered the husband and wife to be equal sheds further light. He took as his text the verse from St Paul 'Wives be in subjection unto your own husbands, as unto the Lord,' and told the reader that these words, 'misunderstood and judged from the standpoint of modern feminism or sentimentality, are repugnant to many, but they embody nevertheless an important and fundamental truth'.[15] This was that there was a 'principle of subordination which finds expression wherever human community exists'. '[T]he principle of subordination operates in a multitude of ways to differentiate between ruler and ruled, employer and employed . . . Without it, social stability is precarious, and equalitarian or communistic groups abolish it in a traditional form only to renew it in a fresh guise. Authority and obedience are essential . . . subordination is the only alternative to anarchy.'[16] Seven years later, Bailey explained to his readers that he had reversed his position; 'there remains the critical question of the status of woman . . . In [1952] . . . I attempted (not without misgiving) to

---

[13] Chesser was an honourable exception. By 1968 he had reversed several opinions he held in 1941 and a woman's right to say no to sexual activity is discussed at length in *Sex and the Married Woman* (1968; 1970), 118, 240–1.

[14] S. D. Bailey, *The Mystery of Love* (1952), 63.

[15] Ibid. 129. Eph. 5: 22–4 (St Paul), Authorized Version.

[16] Bailey, *Mystery*, 130.

justify the traditional theological view that woman is subordinate to man
... the pages which follow are, therefore, in the nature of a retraction.'[17]
His uncertainty reflected the existence of debate about women, feminism,
and sexual values *and* the strength of the consensus in support of conjugal
rights in the 1950s.

PSYCHOANALYSIS AND WOMEN'S PHYSICAL RESPONSE

Other authors were moving in a different direction. By the 1940s, all the
English manual authors were aware that extreme sexual ignorance had
declined. Young, respectable, unmarried women were the group who had
been most ignorant of sexuality. Comments that described a range of
responses and suggested that sexual awareness, or even sexual experience,
was not unknown amongst these women began to appear at the end of
the 1930s. The English author Rennie Macandrew (b. 1907) recommended
'flirting' before marriage. He wrote that 'I see no harm at all in two
unmarried lovers going the length of mutual digital masturbation, or
for the man to caress or kiss the woman's breasts.'[18] In 1941, discussing the
wedding night, Chesser had told husbands that clitoral stimulation of
their new bride was not desirable: 'It is safe to say', he wrote, 'that in *a very
large* number of cases, the inexperienced bride will not be pleasurably
moved by attempts to stimulate the clitoris. She is apt to experience no
other sensation than shock, the very thing which should be avoided'
(italics added).[19] In the 1948 edition of the manual, Chesser altered the
'very large' to simply a 'large number of cases'. He continued:

The genital kiss, too, sometimes indicated as an invaluable help in bringing an
inexperienced bride to the highly stimulated state where penetration is sought,
must be ruled out for much the same reason. On the other hand if she happens

[17] S. D. Bailey, *The Man–Woman Relation in Christian Thought* (1959), 293.

[18] Macandrew warned against premarital coitus because of venereal disease, possible
pregnancy, and the double standard. He may have felt vulnerable to censorship as the judge
who condemned E. Charles's manual to be destroyed only four years previously had
mentioned 'sniggering at pre-marital chastity among women' in his decision. R. Macandrew
[pseud.], *Friendship, Love Affairs and Marriage* (1939), 61, 87, also 80–9. For an earlier idealism, see
L. D. Weatherhead, *The Mastery of Sex through Psychology and Religion* (1931), 39–42.

[19] Chesser, *Love without fear* (1941), 67.

to be 'virgin in body only'—that is one who has had much experience short of actual defloration, and who is well familiar, through reading and discussion with such stimulating measures as the genital kiss—full use can be made of this aid.[20]

Women, or couples, who were unable to countenance clitoral stimulation would obviously not have been comfortable with oral sex, the 'genital kiss' which van de Velde had recommended in 1928. But, like Macandrew, Chesser thought there were a growing number of women who had sexual experience before marriage, and he assumed that men were sexually knowledgeable.

Sex manuals were increasingly aimed at particular audiences, but those addressed to younger people still emphasized that that it often took some time after marriage before women enjoyed intercourse.[21] The delay had been reinterpreted by some authors as the period of latency during which Freud had claimed sensation was transferred from clitoris to the vagina.[22] Macandrew explained how women who were 'frigid' could learn to have vaginal orgasms. He used 'externally' and the 'outer lips' to refer to the clitoris:

[Some women] may perhaps prefer to be stimulated externally rather than internally. This can largely be corrected by thought control, and the lining of the vagina must be trained to register stimulation. During intercourse, therefore, such women must force themselves to believe that stimulation inside the vagina is preferable to around the outer lips. The transfer of an erotic zone from one focul [sic] point to another may occupy months, but with perseverance, it can be attained.[23]

Unsurprisingly 'thought control' failed to produce the desired sexual pleasure for many women. The delivery was often more sophisticated but Freud's ideas underlay most descriptions of female sexuality by the late 1940s. The incompatibility of this account of sexual development with women's actual physical experience can only have contributed to the growing perception of women's sexuality as a problem.

---

[20] E. Chesser, *Love without Fear* (1948), 68. See also R. Macandrew [pseud.], *Encyclopedia of Sex and Love Technique* (1941; 1951), 217.

[21] e.g. K. C. Barnes, *He and She* (1958; 1962), 155. Macaulay, *Art*, 70–1.

[22] See Ch. 9.   [23] Macandrew, *Encyclopedia*, 218.

Nonetheless, there were reasons for the acceptance of vaginal orgasm by female manual authors. The strong resistance to masturbatory activities reveals that such women were not internalizing a new prohibition in rejecting clitoral stimulation but extending an existing one. Manuals by women (and the evidence on behaviour) also suggest that English women were generally less comfortable with varied sexual practices than were men. For many married women of this generation their sexual aspirations lay in a different direction. Although the theme had been present in the manuals throughout the inter-war period, the 1950s saw the peak of the insistence on vaginal orgasm for women and the peak of the glorification of sexual intercourse as a transcendent, shared emotional experience for the couple. Authors used phrases such as 'their spirits as well as their bodies seem to rise together to a flame of ecstasy which is quite indescribable' or 'total emotional surrender'.[24] Definitions of marital sexual pleasure incorporated emotion. In *The Golden Notebook* (1962) the Rhodesian-born novelist Doris Lessing (b. 1919) made a frequently quoted, classic statement of support for the vaginal orgasm. She wrote that a 'vaginal orgasm is emotion and nothing else, felt as emotion and expressed in sensations that are indistinguishable from emotion'.[25] In her 1995 autobiography she also commented that 'when I masturbated in my adolescence it was the vagina and its amazing possibilities I learned about. The clitoris was only part of the whole ensemble.'[26] In the 1950s, there were many articulate middle-class women who agreed with Doris Lessing and her perception of female sexual experience. They experienced coitus and vaginal orgasm as an emotional experience and they wanted men to participate emotionally also. Men had to alter their attitude to marital sexuality if they were to accommodate this demand, as a shared emotional experience was incompatible with the exercise of conjugal rights. Thus, in a context where male initiation and management of physical sexual activity was still the norm, the vaginal orgasm involved a further step toward the destruction of the double standard.

[24] M. Macaulay, *The Art of Marriage* (1952; 1957), 42. J. R. G. Rainer and J. Rainer, *Sexual Pleasure in Marriage* (1959), 223. See also A. Ellis, *The Sensuous Person* (1972), 182. O. Schwarz, *The Psychology of Sex* (1949), 167. R. D. von Urban, *Sex Perfection* (1952; 1969), 37. H. Wright. *Sex Fulfilment in Married Women* (1947). 78.

[25] D. Lessing, *The Golden Notebook* (1962; 1973), 220.

[26] Doris Lessing, *Under my Skin: Volume One of my Autobiography, to 1949* (1995), 265–7.

It was because vaginal orgasm addressed some female desires that the response to the concept was one of confused acceptance, not rejection. Joan Malleson (1900–56) was a gynaecologist with twenty years' experience of running sexual problem clinics for the Family Planning Association. In 1951, she wrote that:

Possibly about a third of civilised women get their climax externally [clitorally]; perhaps another third achieve it mainly in the vaginal passage, and another third achieve it seldom or never. Of women who can reach it from either area it is found that the inner climax is generally—but not quite always—the one most valued. It is held by psychiatrists that the emotional content of the two types of orgasm is different. Most women will confirm this, though there can be no question of the significance being identical for everybody.[27]

This revealed considerable problems. According to Malleson, two-thirds of women were not achieving the vaginal orgasms held to be most desirable by Freud, by most sex manual authors, and frequently by women themselves. Less specifically, Helena Wright, who saw London women through her private medical practice and in Family Planning clinics, wrote in 1947 that she had kept careful records of her patients' experiences since 1928, and that 'sexual satisfaction is not obtained by more than 50 per cent of married women'.[28] Unsurprisingly Macaulay, who advised women to lower their expectations, was more sanguine about female sexual pleasure: 'The answers I have received on questioning my patients about their sexual life are in complete contrast to the somewhat gloomy figures published by other writers.'[29] In her second sex manual, published in 1947, Wright commented that 'Fifteen years ago most workers along this line thought that the main problem [for women] was ignorance.'[30] This, Wright felt, had changed, revealing another problem, which was that both men and women expected female sexual response to conform to a male pattern:

[Men] discover very early in their sexual experiences that . . . a comparatively short time of rhythmic movements of the penis in the vagina produces an orgasm and ejaculation easily and completely . . . men, therefore, expect that

---

[27] Medica, *Any Wife*, 66. Also see J. Marmor. 'Some Considerations Concerning Orgasm in the Female', *Psychosomatic Medicine*, 16 (1954), 22.

[28] Wright, *Sex Fulfilment*, 7.

[29] Macaulay, *Art*, 12–3.   [30] Wright, *Sex Fulfilment*, 9.

woman will have an answering orgasm felt in the vagina induced by the movements of the penis, with similar speed and easiness.[31]

While the manuals had been placing the responsibility for female sexual response on men, Wright's comment on couples' 'amusingly different' response to this problem reveals that many men did not accept this:

The wife when she finds . . . that her vagina continues to be lacking in sensation, almost invariably blames herself. She feels inferior, she says to herself that she's a failure . . . The husband, with nothing to complain of in his own sensations, has no inclination to criticize himself; instead he agrees with his wife, and thinks, with her, that she is the one to blame and that she must be unusually lacking in sex-capacity![32]

In 1931, Stopes had also commented that, where a difference existed, both husband and wife assumed him to be the norm and her to be the exception.[33] This was an old problem in new guise. Wright and Malleson's acceptance of varied female responses was exceptional.[34] Increasingly new manuals strongly encouraged women to feel that not having vaginal orgasms was a 'failure' on their part.

Psychoanalysts greatly encouraged this attitude. Marie N. Robinson (b. 1919), an American, produced a popularization of Freudian ideas called *The Power of Sexual Surrender* (1960). Robinson explained that women were at fault if they lacked sexual satisfaction. 'In saying that the husband is rarely if ever to blame for a frigidity problem I am running counter to a vast body of information . . . [B]ook after book appeared, each showing conclusively that a happily married sexual life depended on the male's skill at arousing the woman . . . This is simply not true.'[35] According to Robinson 'frigid' women needed help to overcome their competitiveness, their resentment of male insensitivity, their fear of the male's 'sometimes violent thrusting' during intercourse, their desire to take the masculine position in inter-course, and so on.[36] She had a chapter on the behaviour of the ideal

---

[31] Wright, *Sex Fulfilment*, 47.   [32] Ibid. 48–9.

[33] M. Stopes, *Enduring Passion* (1928; 1931), 129.

[34] See also W. de Kok, 'Woman and Sex', in Lord Horder, J. Malleson, and G. Cox (eds.), *The Modern Woman's Medical Guide* (1949; 1955), 135.

[35] M. N. Robinson, *The Power of Sexual Surrender* (1960), 17.

[36] Ibid. 199. The phrase 'violent thrusting' probably originated with Marie Bonaparte. See M. Bonaparte, *Female Sexuality* (1953), 85–6.

woman, in which she repeatedly told women that they must never reject their husbands' requests for sex:

Her eternal acquiescence, her ever-readiness, never lets her in for a painful sexual experience however. She knows that ninety-nine times out of one hundred even negative sexual feelings in herself will soon turn to eagerness, and eagerness to desire. And even if that one in a hundred times occurs, she will still get a profound satisfaction from the pleasure she is able to give her husband, the very obvious pleasure. Once more that deep altruism.[37]

Robinson insisted that the woman must not only perform sex on demand but that she must enjoy the experience. She insisted the woman must insert her diaphragm every night as the ideal woman 'should always be prepared for intercourse whenever it is even remotely possible'.[38] In 1965, Alexander Lowen (b. 1910), an American Reichian psychoanalyst, who was part of the US human potential or growth movement, explained why vaginal orgasms were preferable:

Most men, however, feel that the need to bring a woman to climax through clitoral stimulation is a burden. If it is done before intercourse but after the man is excited and ready to penetrate, it imposes a restraint upon his natural desire for closeness and intimacy . . . Clitoral stimulation during the act of intercourse . . . distracts the man from the perception of his genital sensations . . . The need to bring a woman to climax through clitoral stimulation after the act of intercourse has been completed and the man has reached his climax is burdensome, since it prevents him from enjoying the relaxation and peace that are the rewards of sexuality. Most men to whom I have spoken who engaged in this practice resented it.[39]

Lowen's rejection of clitoral stimulation is very close to that quoted earlier by the male characters in D. H. Lawrence's *Lady Chatterley's Lover* (1928). It reveals the conflict between the desire for a sexually responsive woman, and resentment (or anxiety) at having to make any sexual effort on her behalf. The psychoanalytic vision of female sexuality was highly contested

---

[37] Robinson, *Power*, 45.

[38] Ibid. 46, 253. See also M. Davis, *The Sexual Responsibility of Woman* (1957; 1966), 142, 155. M. Macaulay, *Marriage for the Married* (1964), 206.

[39] A. M. Lowen, *Love and Orgasm: A Revolutionary Guide to Sexual Fulfillment* (1965), 232. For Lowen and the growth movement, see J. Howard, *Please Touch* (1970; 1971), 170–1.

but by the 1960s the notion that women who were not sexually interested in men, or at all, were frigid and that this meant they were at fault and inadequate was widely accepted by younger people. In 1960, most psycho-analysts still argued fiercely that normal, mature women came solely through vaginal sensations, and those within the profession who disputed this were regarded as 'uncommonly courageous'.[40]

MALE SEXUAL NEEDS

However, male authors increasingly rejected psychoanalytic interpret-ations of physical sexual activity. For these men the emphasis on vaginal orgasm was increasingly inconvenient because of the stress on a mutual emotional experience and the limits it placed on sexual practice. Many abandoned the notion. By the 1950s, a group of American manuals had appeared which assumed that far greater sexual demands could be made of the wife than manuals had previously. In 1961, Joseph Kaufman (b. 1931) and Griffith Borgeson commented that '*Ideal Marriage* by T. H. van de Velde, M.D. is noteworthy... for its severely condemnatory attitude toward the male in the heterosexual relationship.'[41] This is an astonishing judgement in comparison to those made by feminist historians, who have described van de Velde as a misogynist who believed male dominance in sex was natural.[42] Van de Velde, like Stopes, had an idealistic view of marriage, which he based on a construction of marital physical sexual pleasure as a mutual emotional experience. He held men responsible for the lack of female sexual pleasure and insisted that husbands should go to considerable effort and use a variety of techniques to ensure that their wives learned to enjoy sex. In his text, the male was dominant but the wife was both idealized and sexual. In the manuals by new male authors during

[40] M. J. Sherfey, The *Nature and Evolution of Female Sexuality* (1966; 1973), 24, citing E. B. Moore, 'Panel Report: Frigidity in Women', *Journal of the American Psychoanalytic Association* (1961).

[41] J. J. Kaufman and G. Borgeson, *Man and Sex* (1961; 1964), 33.

[42] B. Ehrenreich, E. Hess, and G. Jacobs, *Re-making Love: The Feminisation of Sex* (1987), 49–50. L. A. Hall, *Hidden Anxieties: Male Sexuality, 1900–1950* (1991), 68. M. Jackson, *The Real Facts of Life: Feminism and the Politics of Sexuality, c1850–1940* (1994), 164–8. S. Jeffreys, *The Spinster and her Enemies: Feminism and Sexuality, 1880–1930* (1985). L. Segal, *Straight Sex: The Politics of Pleasure* (1994), 86.

the 1950s and 1960s, the (Victorian) wife, whom the husband dominated but also respected and loved, had disappeared and the new wife was a sexualized woman. The insistence on male conjugal rights meant that in these manuals, her sexual role increasingly corresponded to that of the other woman who existed to meet male demands for sexual services, the prostitute. The growing acceptance of sexuality resulted in a new openness about men's control of sexual activity, and men's perception of their sexual needs. These new manuals make the extent of the feminist influence on the earlier manuals evident. The American Dr John Eichenlaub (b. 1922) directly addressed the issue of conjugal rights:

Perhaps the biggest problem centers on a wife's participation in sex when she has no sensual desire. Unless she makes her willingness entirely clear, her husband often finds these incidents tainting his attitudes toward sex with quite unpleasant feelings . . . [These include] indignation if rebuffs and hesitations seem to violate his rightful privileges (which in point of law and religion they always do, although the prevailing attitudes in our society might deny this position).[43]

Eichenlaub suggested that if the wife fears for 'her human dignity, integrity and independence' as a result of her husband's insistence on his conjugal rights, the husband should compliment his wife's achievements in other areas, such as her management of the household budget or her hobbies.[44] Note that Eichenlaub acknowledged that this was highly contested: 'prevailing attitudes' now denied the husband's right to intercourse on demand, although, as he correctly claimed, it was a legal right. According to the cover, this manual had sold one and a half million copies in the USA by 1961 and was in its eleventh UK reprint by 1966. In 1955, the Americans Dr Louis Berg (b. 1901) and Robert Street, a professional writer, explained that:

The female has very definite duties apart from her obligation to render normal sexual service to her husband . . . Should her period run five, six, seven, or eight days, this is a lengthy interval for the man to practice self-control. Of course, he should be able to do it, but there is no reason to force it upon him when the simple expedient of the female hand or oral connection can remove the necessity. Since many men are reluctant to force any type of relationship upon

---

[43] J. E. Eichenlaub, *The Marriage Art* (1961; 1964), 174.   [44] Ibid. 176–7.

their wives during this period, the woman herself should take the initiative ... It might be added also, that in conducting sexual intimacy, it is equally the duty of the wife to excite her partner by engaging in genital stimulation. The woman who lies passively and overlooks these essentials is as guilty of neglect in her way as the husband who fails to satisfy her.[45]

These writers were confidently demanding 'sexual services' from the wife, which would have been unthinkable in the manuals of the inter-war period. As is obvious, the new writers suggested a wide range of sexual practices, and the concept of masturbatory techniques had ceased to be relevant to them. They also did not insist on vaginal orgasms, though they continued to accuse non-compliant women of frigidity.[46] For most English men these manuals were fantasy literature, as there was no possibility that their wives would behave accordingly. But the texts reinforced beliefs that women were a function of their husbands' needs, objects, not subjects with legitimate needs and desires of their own.

These authors were reflecting the breaking down of boundaries that had demarcated women's sexual roles. During the inter-war years the behaviour of young middle-class women changed. Men began to take women who were not married out alone to public places such as restaurants, the theatre, and clubs.[47] They became increasingly likely to agree to sexual activity and the boundary between these women and mistresses or prostitutes became blurred.[48] From the 1940s, there was also increasingly open acceptance of actual prostitution on the part of male authors. The expectation of male emotional involvement in physical sexual activity had

---

[45] L. M. Berg and R. Street, *The Basis of Happy Marriage* (1955; 1969), 179–80. Also see R. Chartham, *Sex Manners for Women* (1964), 22–3, 26, 50. Eichenlaub, *Marriage Art*, 71. Rainer and Rainer, *Sexual Pleasure*, 48–9.

[46] R. Chartham, *Mainly for Women: A Practical Guide to Love-Making in Marriage* (1964; 1966), 97. Kaufman and Borgeson, *Man*, 24–9. S. and I. Hegeler, *An ABZ of Love* (1963; 1969), 140.

[47] These changes had taken place faster in the USA, e.g. J. Tenenbaum, *The Riddle of Sex: The Medical and Social Aspects of Sex, Love and Marriage* (1930), 211–13.

[48] A. Comfort, *Barbarism and Sexual Freedom* (1948), 58–9. A. Havil, *The Technique of Sex: Towards a Better Understanding of Sexual Relationship* (1939; 1959), 97, 105. Macandrew, *Friendship*. Macandrew, *Encyclopedia*, 359–86. K. M. Walker and P. Fletcher, *Sex and Society* (1955), 128. Medica, *Any Wife*, 39, 41. G. R. Scott, *The History of Prostitution: From Antiquity to the Present Day* (1936; 1996), 154–8.

been intimately tied into the rejection of prostitution. In 1949, Oswald Schwarz argued that:

According to Roman law, for instance, a prostitute was a woman who offered herself *passim et sine delectu* (everywhere and without pleasure). Observe how much more human than ours this concept is, because it stresses just that lack of emotional participation which lowers the sexual act to a mere genital function and thus constitutes the essential, as distinct from the conventional immorality of prostitution. Incidentally, the men who frequent prostitutes make themselves guilty of the same offence.[49]

Except in unusual circumstances such as wartime, emotional involvement (or romantic love) entailed the risk of commitment over a period of time for men (as pregnancy did for women). In *The Golden Notebook* (1962) Lessing was describing vaginal orgasm in the context of a love affair between two characters. She explains how the woman, Ella, perceived the emotional demand this made on her married male lover Paul:

[S]he could not have experienced [vaginal orgasm] if she had not loved him ... As time went on ... Paul began to rely on manipulating her externally, on giving Ella clitoral orgasms. Very exciting. Yet there was always a part of her that resented it. Because she felt that the fact he wanted to was an expression of his instinctive desire not to commit himself to her. She felt that without knowing it or being conscious of it (though perhaps he was conscious of it) he was afraid of the emotion.[50]

Ella's perspective has been treated as meaningless except as part of a masochistic relationship. Yet the link Ella makes between emotional involvement and commitment is correct. Women's demand for emotion put coitus back into a sequence of events involving male obligations, unlike an encounter with a prostitute. The separation of recreational coitus from reproductive coitus was crucially about removing sex from such a sequence. The character Ella was enjoying sexual pleasure while rejecting the role of a wife. For her generation that was a risky stance. It was not until the mid-1960s that a new generation of British female novelists began to describe women taking such pleasure without it

---

[49] Schwarz, *Psychology* 1949. 74–5. See also Kaufman and Borgeson, *Man*, 44.
[50] Lessing, *Golden Notebook*, 220.

resulting in intense distress.[51] The American Terry Garrity or 'J.' who wrote *The Sensuous Woman* (1969) was the only woman to produce a manual along these lines. Garrity later revealed that she felt sexually and personally exploited by Lyle Stuart, her publisher, who suggested she write the book.[52]

English male manual authors insisted women were not just unwilling but unable to separate sex from emotional commitment. Alex Comfort (b. 1920) explained that '[The girl] can never feel exactly the same towards a man who has "known" her thus, even if only once—many boys are staggered by the change in her attitude which one act of intercourse can bring about, and her intensity may scare them off.'[53] It is possible that this had been true for some, perhaps many, women in the inter-war period. Sexually libertine men insisted that it would be preferable if this were not the case. In 1939, Macandrew remarked, 'for their own sakes I wish girls could take love affairs less seriously'.[54] However, those young women who did take things less seriously were stigmatized as cold hearted and mercenary in his manuals. Surveys of English sexual attitudes in the post-Second World War era found that men supposedly rejected the sexual double standard. For example, in 1969, Geoffrey Gorer found that:

[T]he double standard of sexual morality, by which men are allowed license which is denied to women, still has fairly wide currency and, it would appear, it is predominately women who maintain this double standard...Women who support the double standard are liable to invoke generalisations about the differing nature of men and women...whereas men tend to invoke abstract

---

[51] e.g. M. Forster, *Georgy Girl* (1965; 1978), 34. J. Collins, *The World is Full of Married Men* (1968; 1969). F. Weldon, *The Fat Woman's Joke* (1967; 1982), 96, 117–19. For an extended discussion of sexuality in novels by British women 1955–75, see H. Cook, 'The Long Sexual Revolution: British Women, Sex and Contraception in the Twentieth Century' (Ph.D. thesis, 1999), ch. 16.

[52] See L. Grant, *Sexing the Millennium* (1993), 121–4. H. Gurley Brown, *Sex and the Single Girl* (1962) has been included as a manual elsewhere. Physical sexual anatomy and activity are not discussed so it has not been included in this research, but J.'s book was part of a discourse about single women and sexuality introduced by Brown. M. Gordon and P. Shankweiler, 'Different Equals Less: Female Sexuality in Recent Marriage Manuals', *Journal of Marriage and the Family*, 3 (1971). See also Ehrenreich et al., *Re-making Love*.

[53] A. Comfort, *Sex in Society* (1963; 1964), 103. See also E. Chesser, *Is Chastity Outmoded?* (1960; 1961), 118.

[54] Macandrew, *Friendship*, 61.

principles of justice, typically with the adage: 'What is sauce for the goose, is sauce for the gander.'[55]

Support for abstract principles of justice and equality between the sexes does not appear to have dictated male sexual behaviour. This finding is an indication that the shift in content in the manuals reflected changes taking place in societal attitudes and that men were more eager for sexual liberalization than women.

Resistance to male sexual exploitation and abuse by women in England during the post-war decades was hampered by the existing sexual ethos. Sexually progressive women had rejected the Victorian and Edwardian belief, shared by first-wave feminists, that sexual desire should be controlled and contained.[56] They wanted to present sexual experience as positive and healthy, perhaps to themselves as well as to their readers. As the evidence on sexual behaviour in earlier chapters has shown, for much of the population, the discourse on sexuality in the manuals had far outpaced the changes in behaviour. Authors who were also medical practitioners were aware that many couples had fundamental problems. The experience of helping couples who were often timid and inhibited by anxieties, or unaware of the need to display affection, shaped their manuals. They saw encouraging people to become more sexually confident and spontaneous as part of their task. In the 1950s, Joan Malleson wrote that it 'has been repeatedly said that every woman in her heart wishes to be raped, and although this extreme may not be true, a husband should remember that a wife's self-esteem is enhanced by being wanted'.[57] Although she hints that readers should not take this approach to rape literally, this statement places rape on a continuum with expressing male sexual desire. But from Malleson's perspective, the last thing the sexually constricted men and women she saw needed was encouragement to control themselves

[55] G. Gorer, *Sex and Marriage in England Today* (1971), 36. G. Gorer, *Exploring English Character* (1955), 94, 114–15. See also Chesser, *Chastity*, 108. M. Schofield, *The Sexual Behaviour of Young People* (1965; 1968), 108–10.

[56] B. Caine, *English Feminism, 1780–1980* (1997), 183–9; 214–15. J. Alberti, *Beyond Suffrage: Feminists in War and Peace, 1914–28* (1989), 103–12.

[57] Medica [Malleson], *Any Wife*, 65. See also Macaulay, *Art*, 80. Barnes, *He and She*, 99–100. For timid men, see L. J. Friedman, *Virgin Wives: A Study of Unconsummated Marriages* (1962). Hall, *Hidden Anxieties*. K. M. Walker and E. B. Strauss, *Sexual Disorders in the Male* (1939; 1954).

sexually. The manuals acknowledged that male demands for over-frequent intercourse (e.g. nightly) were a possible problem, but their efforts to present a positive perspective meant that they made almost no comments on sexual harassment or abuse. Non-feminist men of the type who accepted prostitution and premarital sex were more likely to make comments on sexual abuse in their manuals. They reflect prevailing medical and social beliefs about sexual violence. Macandrew (b. 1907) wrote that 'It is a well known fact that in cases of attempted rape, the man very rarely gains entry.' Later he added that sexual harassment did not provide an explanation for female sexual coldness because 'nearly all women have at some time or other been frightened in such a way'.[58] In this period progressive discourses on sexuality encouraged men who engaged in abusive or predatory sexual behaviour to see themselves as normal and women who objected as abnormal.

For example, in 1956, Rose Hacker (b. 1904), a liberal and progressive senior member of the National Marriage Guidance Council, who had also written a sex manual for older unmarried teenagers, explained in a newspaper article that:

Unfortunately few girls realise the force of the glandular processes they themselves have aroused in boys . . . Nor do they see how boys are impelled beyond their control to use any means to reach their objective . . . . The main causes of worry in a courtship occur because girls do not understand that when a man is stimulated to the point of readiness for sexual activity, the strength of his feelings will cause him to say many things that he does not really mean.[59]

Girls or women were seen as wholly responsible for controlling sexual activity and men's glandular processes provided them with a licence to lie. Women like Hacker saw themselves as enabling young women to protect themselves from the reality of male sexuality. In 1969, almost the peak of male sexual liberalism, a pseudonymous doctor, published in England, John James, wrote a sex manual intended for young people. He explained, 'These days it is as often as not the girl who makes the advances; and this is quite a new thing.'[60] A girl had to do very little in order for men to tell her she was making advances. James continued:

---

[58] Macandrew, *Encyclopedia*, 215–16, 28–9.   [59] R. Hacker, *Sunday Pictorial* (4 Nov. 1956).
[60] J. James [pseud.], *The Facts of Sex* (1969), 30–1.

One great difficulty has only lately been admitted; there has always been great natural indignation when adult or elderly men have been found to have interfered sexually with young girls. Unfortunately as has been shown the 'seducer' is quite often the young girl, who in all innocence perhaps, has introduced the sexual element... the novel Lolita... caused a great deal of anger in those... reminded of facts.[61]

This quotation demonstrates the belief that men were not responsible for their sexual actions. A young girl who acted 'in all innocence' was not culpable in the usual sense, but females were responsible because sex desire was an overwhelming force which men could not resist. Many men in this period utterly rejected the late Victorian belief that men could and should control themselves sexually. Progressive women were unable to rebut this at an ideological level because they did not want women to have to control and repress their sexual desires, as the Victorians had assumed they should.

Over the period from 1918 to the 1970s, the changing structure of the manuals reflected the changes occurring in ideas about sexuality and marriage. *Married Love* (1918) was intended for the newly married couple and *Ideal Marriage* (1928) for the couple throughout their marriage. By the end of the inter-war period many of the manuals loosely followed a life course format. This went through courtship, the wedding night, physical descriptions of the genitals, satisfaction in marriage, problems that might occur such as frigidity and impotence, birth control, and sex for the older couple. Authors included varying material on topics such as coital positions, physiology and hormones, marital behaviour aside from sexual events, 'deviations', and morality. This format depended on a rigid approach to normative socio-sexual behaviour for its effectiveness as an organizing principle, placing physical sexual activity in the context of the emotional development of the marriage and of the family. Although birth control meant that sexual intercourse need not have reproductive consequences, this format continued to structure coitus as an act with lasting consequences. There had been a scattering of sexual encyclopedias, question and answer formats, and alphabetical lists from the 1930s.[62] Alex

---

[61] Ibid. 30–1.

[62] e.g. A. D. Costler and A. Willy, *The Encyclopaedia of Sex Practice*, ed. N. Haire (1938; 1951). Macandrew, *Encyclopedia*. Hegeler and Hegeler, *An ABZ*.

Comfort's *The Joy of Sex*, published in 1972, was the last sex manual of major significance in the tradition described here. This consisted of descriptions of sexual events organized as if on a menu, and illustrated by copious drawings of a heterosexual couple engaged in sexual activities. Although Comfort was concerned to reassure people about the acceptability of themselves and their desires, heterosexual coitus remained the main dish. The menu format of this manual reflected the decontextualizing of sex just as the earlier life course format manuals reflected the social framework. This shift reflected an intellectual reconceptualization of sexuality, and the genuine and substantial alteration in sexual behaviour that was occurring by the late 1960s.

To conclude, the manuals written in these decades fit into two main strands. There was the creation of the female citizen who valued her emotionally intense vaginal orgasm, and accepted her marital duty, previously her husband's conjugal right. Often the authors had been involved in the growing marriage guidance movement or the Family Planning Association, and many had strong religious convictions. The second strand was the increasingly confident emergence of a libertine male sexual ethos. More varied sexual practice, including short-term sexual affairs, was promoted as natural, and emotional involvement was omitted. Amongst both groups female lack of sexual satisfaction was recognized as a problem but increasingly this was seen as her responsibility, not his. In the second half of the century writing sex manuals became more acceptable (as well as profitable). Compared to the previous decades there is a shift in tone, with authors less likely to make suggestions and more likely to state norms. The next and final chapter in this part of the book considers research into women's genital sexuality and the response of the new second-wave feminists.

11

'The Vagina too, Responds':
Vaginal Orgasms, Clitoral Masturbation,
Feminism, and Sex Research 1920–1975

THE ACTIVE VAGINA

Debates on female sexuality throughout the twentieth century assumed the existence of a transhistorical, unchanging body which provided a secure basis for knowledge. Questions about how the female orgasm occurs and what it consists of directly related to the issue of whether the female vagina is an active organ, or an inert canal which forms a passive receptacle for the penis during heterosexual intercourse. Marie Stopes described the female genitals and the act of coitus in detail in *Contraception* (1923). She understood sexual intercourse as an activity in which both partners were active, arguing that 'the coital act is an extremely complex social function in which the woman (as well as the man) is an *active* partner' (italics in original). According to her the female orgasm entailed a corresponding action of the vagina to that of the penis:

[I]n the fully excited uterus the cervix may spontaneously open and inter-lock with the glans penis which thus discharges directly into the uterus... I have formerly hinted at this active co-operation of the cervix, but received critical comment or denial of the possibility of the action. Such criticism is, however, due to the rarity of the persons in whom this happens and the impossibility of demonstrating it, as it can *only* take place at the height of sexual excitement. There is no doubt whatever, that some fully sexed and roused women do experience the interlocking of the glans penis with the cervical canal, and such a woman does aspirate some of the seminal ejaculate into the uterus.[1]

The notion that the cervix might not just move, but move in response to female sexual pleasure, appeared so outlandish that it was ignored. It is possible to respond to this as historians have done to the notion of the absorption of semen by the vaginal walls, that is, as if such ideas were self-evidently incorrect or with an uncritical acceptance that Stopes was wrong to contest 'expert' opinions.[2] There was little medical knowledge of physical sexual events and no instruments adequate to testing such theories existed throughout the period covered in this study. For example, until recently it was impossible to observe the inside of the vagina during intercourse. As late as the 1960s sex researchers used what they themselves saw as crude and limited instruments.[3] This is not to say that 'coital interlocking' occurred, rather that Stopes was presenting a legitimate hypothesis within the framework of the existing knowledge.

Stopes's theories were certainly sounder anatomically than Freud's theory of the transferral of clitoral sensation to the vagina, which dominated Western understanding of female sexuality throughout the mid-twentieth century. Some authors accepted that the more limited 'uterine suction' of the sperm during female orgasm did occur. This transformed the female response from a sexual impulse to a reproductive response, which probably made it acceptable.[4] In *Ideal Marriage* (1928) van de Velde also attributed importance to the cervix as a source of sensation; however,

[1] M. Stopes, *Contraception: Theory, History and Practice* (1923; 1925), 12, 139. Similar ideas were expressed in E. H. Kisch, *The Sexual Life of Woman in its Physiological, Pathological and Hygienic Aspects* (1910; 1926).

[2] e.g. R. A. Soloway, ' "The Perfect Contraceptive": Eugenics and Birth Control Research in Britain and America in the Inter-War Years', *Journal of Contemporary History*, 30 (1996), 643. M. Jackson, *The Real Facts of Life: Feminism and the Politics of Sexuality, c1850–1940* (1994), 148–9.

[3] A. C. Kinsey, W. B. Pomeroy, P. H. Gebhard, and C. E. Martin, *Sexual Behaviour in the Human Female* (1953), 577, 580. Also see W. Masters cited in J. M. Irvine, *Disorders of Desire: Sex and Gender in Modern American Sexology* (1990), 78.

[4] N. Haire, *The Comparative Value of Current Contraceptive Methods, Reprinted from the Proceedings of the First International Congress for Sexual Research (Berlin October 10th to 16th, 1926)* (1928), 5. I. Singer, *The Goals of Human Sexuality* (1973; 1974), 161–75. See also Kate Millet, *Sexual Politics* (1969; 1971), 190.

he suggested this was because the woman can feel the man ejaculating onto the cervix. This was another instance in which a subtle adjustment of physical detail shifted the account of physical sexual activity away from Stopes's active female sexual body during the 1920s and 1930s.[5] The differing reception of the ideas of Stopes and of van de Velde reflected the societal construction of gender. Stopes's conception was ignored in this instance while van de Velde's notion, which reduced the woman to a passive recipient of sensation, was repeated for the next fifty years by manual authors.[6]

There is another aspect to the debate on vaginal movement. Marie Stopes had championed her 'Pro-Race' version of the rubber cervical cap because the diaphragm 'must be worn so as to cover the whole of the end of the vagina and depends on stretching the vaginal walls to stay in position…[so] certain movements of physiological value (particularly to the man) which ideally the woman should make are then impossible'.[7] Van de Velde agreed with Stopes that the diaphragm limited vaginal movements but he commented dismissively that most 'women to-day are not able to operate their pelvic muscles voluntarily to the best advantage in coitus; so the *inability* to do so would not represent any appreciable loss to them'.[8] It is possible that the sexual upbringing of women over generations ensured they were unaware of the range of movement the muscles associated with vagina were capable of, and that this contributed to the lack of

[5] Th. H. van de Velde, *Ideal Marriage* (1926; reset 1943), 161.

[6] e.g. J. E. Eichenlaub, *The Marriage Art* (1961; 1964), 27. T. Hendrickson, *Variations on a Sexual Theme* (1969), 17.

[7] Stopes, *Contraception*, 162.

[8] Th. H. van de Velde, *Fertility and Sterility in Marriage* (1931) 334. In 1977, Ruth Hall felt there was 'little evidence to support Stopes' belief that the vaginal pessary [diaphragm] would stretch vaginal walls'. Yet diaphragms came in sizes ranging from 5 to 9 centimetres in diameter and there was no consensus as to whether the use of larger sizes was more or less uncomfortable for users. As vaginas vary in size, the larger sizes must have stretched the vaginal walls and, in some women, pressed on the bladder or otherwise caused discomfort. This is another example of the willingness to see the vagina as inactive. R. Hall, *Marie Stopes: A Biography* (1977), 198. M. Sanger and H. Stone, *The Practice of Contraception: An International Symposium and Survey. From the Proceedings of the Seventh International Birth Control Congress, Zurich, Switzerland, September 1930* (1931), 3–30. See also Haire, *Comparative Value*, 11. L. S. Florence, *Birth Control on Trial* (1930). Size of pessaries, 44–5.

sexual pleasure experienced by so many women during the twentieth century.[9]

In the 1930s, practitioners began trying to relate the physical sexual experience described by women to Freud's concept of the vaginal orgasm and it became apparent that the distinction between the vaginal and clitoral orgasms was unclear. Debate over this issue occurred in the burgeoning professional journals. Those involved in clinical work found that some women when asked were unsure as to whether they had orgasms or not, or researchers felt that perhaps they had not, though the women felt that they had. Researchers found it difficult to identify any female orgasm with certainty. In 1935, a female psychologist wrote in a British journal that 'orgasm of the vagina...may include muscular contraction of the uterus...and has a sucking characteristic and in some cases the uterus may definitely retract up slightly into the pelvis. Clitoral orgasm is a discharging orgasm and is more like the male orgasm.'[10] What was a 'discharging orgasm'? In 1948, Lena Levine (b. 1903), an American psychiatrist and sex researcher, suggested that perineal contractions provided criteria:

Where the involuntary perineal contractions occur, they are definite and are observable by the woman if her attention is directed to them...By accepting involuntary perineal contractions as the criterion for the female orgasm, we would have a definite standard for evaluation of the reaction of the female, which can be used in diagnoses and in treatment.[11]

[9] Some later manuals did recommend vaginal exercises. See Th. H. van de Velde, *Sex Efficiency through Exercises: Special Physical Culture for Women* (1933). The likely most influential source was concerned with curing incontinence: A. Kegel, 'Early Genital Relaxation: New Technic of Diagnosis and Nonsurgical Treatment', *Obstetrics and Gynaecology* (1956). See M. Davis, *Sexual Responsibility in Marriage* (1964; 1966), 182. P. Davis [pseud.], *Handbook for Husbands (and Wives)* (1949), 20. M. Davis, *The Sexual Responsibility of Woman* (1957; 1964), 94–6. L. and J. Lopiccolo and J. Heiman, *Becoming Orgasmic: A Sexual Growth Program for Women* (1976). J. and J. Rainer [pseuds.], *Sexual Pleasure in Marriage* (1959), 159–60.

[10] Sylvia M. Payne, 'A Conception of Femininity', *British Journal of Medical Psychology*, 15 (1935).

[11] L. Levine (an exchange with J. Malleson), 'A Criterion for Orgasm in the Female', *Marriage Hygiene* 1 (1948), 173–4. Levine was a major figure in the US Planned Parenthood Federation. See Linda Gordon, *Woman's Body, Woman's Right: A Social History of Birth Control in America* (1976).

Perineal contractions occurred in the third of the vagina closest to the entrance. Joan Malleson responded that these contractions, which she referred to as 'vulval', were:

only a proof of clitoral orgasm... I wish I could be more specific about vaginal orgasm. I do not myself believe that there are 'measurements' that can be observed *always*, and assessed and I do not think these vulval contractions are necessarily found with a true vaginal orgasm. Such movement as there is, I should say, is confined much more to the levator and the upper vaginal musculature. (italics in original)[12]

The levator is a muscle that circumnavigates the vagina. The problem with this explanation was that researchers had supposedly proven that the vagina was a relatively insensitive and nerve-deficient organ. The clitoris, on the other hand, was packed with nerve endings. The American findings of Alfred Kinsey et al. in *Sex in the Human Male* (1948) reinforced existing beliefs: 'In most females the walls of the vagina are devoid of end organs of touch... Among the women who were tested in our gyneco-logic sample, less than 14 per cent were at all conscious that they had been touched.'[13] The 1953 Kinsey report *Sex in the Human Female* followed this up with the first detailed attack on the physiology of the vaginal orgasm. Kinsey stated that while many women, and perhaps even a majority of them, distinguished between a type of satisfaction that results from coitus involving deep vaginal penetration and one that results from the stimu-lation of the labia or clitoris alone, he considered the vaginal orgasm to be a 'biologic impossibility'.[14]

Malleson had already disputed the statement made in the 1948 report on the male, arguing that:

I would disagree entirely with [Kinsey's] assumption that because the vagina is anatomically 'less supplied with nerves' than the clitoris that its qualitative and quantitative sensation must therefore be less. One can cut the intestine of a sentient patient without hurting him; but stretch it and you have agony. You can cut or cauterize the cervix with little pain, but stretch it No: or give it friction

[12] J. Malleson (an exchange with L. Levine) 'Criterion', 174.
[13] A. C. Kinsey, W. B. Pomeroy, P. H. Gebhard, and C. E. Martin, *Sexual Behaviour in the Human Male* (1948), 580.
[14] Kinsey et al., *Female*, 582–3.

under emotional circumstances and quite another type of sensation will be engendered.[15]

An American gynaecological surgeon, LeMon Clark, suggested in 1949 that the source of the sensations felt when the penis stimulated the vagina might be the peritoneum, a sensitive membranous lining which surrounds the intestines, uterus, and other abdominal viscera.[16]

Clark believed there must some source of sensation relating to the vagina because he was aware that many women found that a total hysterectomy had a negative impact on their sexual response. Kinsey had commented in 1948 that the satisfaction experienced from deep penetration in anal intercourse was anatomically confusing. Much later, in 1973, the American Irving Singer commented that stimulation of the peritoneum might also explain this. However, in 1950, Ernest Grafenberg, an American researcher, wrote that: 'an erotic zone always could be demonstrated on the anterior wall of the vagina along the course of the urethra [proximate to the back of the clitoris].'[17] This was another candidate for vaginal sensations aside from the peritoneum. Grafenberg suggested that removal of this erotogenic zone in the anterior wall of the vagina would cause the loss of sexual response reported by LeMon Clark's patients following total hysterectomies. Swelling of this area also occurred more frequently during orgasm than the contractions described by Levine, Grafenberg claimed. Kinsey and others found variation in physical responses and actual anatomical variation in the area described first by Grafenberg.[18] Closer examination of the body and its organs and orifices was not revealing simple truths of the kind still assumed to exist by those sex researchers and historians who rely on a transhistorical body. These debates continue and have extended into the area of female ejaculation, which is associated with intense sexual pleasure. There is increasing evidence that such a physical response can occur although it very

---

[15] J. Malleson, 'Vaginal Orgasm', *International Journal of Sexology*, 2 (1949), 255.

[16] L. Clark, 'Notes and Comments', *International Journal of Sexology*, 2 (1949), 254–5.

[17] E. Grafenberg, 'The Role of the Urethra in Female Orgasm', *International Journal of Sexology*, 3/3 (1950), 146.

[18] H. Desmond, 'An Investigation into a Copious Vaginal Discharge during Intercourse: "Enough to Wet the Bed"—that "is not Urine" ', *Journal of Sex Research*, 20/2 (1984), 199, 201, 203, 205. Also citing Kinsey, *Female*, 580.

frequently does not. Recent research reveals that the vagina and the urethral passage have an extremely complex physical structure and suggests that Skene's glands may be a female prostatic homologue. Josephine Seveley argues that in arousal there is an increased flow of blood and a process of swelling and expansion takes place, as a result of which the clitoris, the urethra, the vagina, and their related structures are transformed into a functional unit.[19]

HUMAN SEXUAL RESPONSE AND FEMINISM

During the second half of the 1960s, a combination of sexology and feminism transformed conceptions of female sexuality. The precipitating event was the simultaneous US and UK publication of *Human Sexual Response* by the American researchers William Masters and Virginia Johnson in 1966. As the discussion above and in the previous chapter has revealed, there was nothing new about questioning or even rejecting the Freudian female orgasm by this date. But in the mid-1960s it was possible to publicize new research into the female orgasm through the mass media, research that necessitated discussing female genitals, which would not have been possible in the 1950s. Although they produced a report on laboratory research, not a sex manual, large numbers of people ploughed through the intentionally obscurantist text or the books and manuals in which the research was discussed and applied the findings to their own sexual behaviour and their interpretations of the behaviour of others.[20] The following discussion is based on Ruth and Edward Brecher's *An Analysis of 'Human Sexual Response'* (1966) 'interpreted and considered in non-technical language', as this was intended for, and reached, a wide audience.[21]

[19] J. L. Sevely, *Eve's Secrets: A New Perspective on Human Sexuality* (1987), 138. For a description of the musculature of the female pelvis, see M. J. Sherfey, *The Nature and Evolution of Female Sexuality* (1966; 1973). For a summary of ideas about female genital sexuality today, see R. Chalker, *The Clitoral Truth: The World at your Fingertips* (2000).

[20] For an entertaining assessment of the prose style, see P. Robinson, *The Modernization of Sex* (1976).

[21] E. M. Brecher and R. E. Brecher, *An Analysis of Human Sexual Response*, (1967; 1968).

Masters and Johnson's methods as much as the actual findings contributed to the debate taking place about female sexuality and sexual morality. A total of 1,273 people were interviewed and of these 694 people, including 276 married couples, participated in the laboratory stage of the research.[22] The research was presented as scientific and rigorous. Here is a description of a 'fully controlled experimental session', described as part of a series intended to determine the relative pH level in the vagina. The experimental subjects Mr and Mrs K. had been requested to refrain from either masturbation or intercourse for three days previously. A glass slide with a sample of Mrs K.'s vaginal secretion was examined under a microscope to confirm that she had not yet ovulated. Following this:

An electronic probe or electrode sheathed in glass was inserted into Mrs K.'s vagina. It was attached by wires to a standard pH meter which determined the relative pH of any region of the vaginal lining touched by the probe. The pH at five points was recorded in succession ... After this first or baseline reading, Mrs K. was requested to masturbate. The electronic probe was reinserted $2\frac{1}{2}$ minutes later and another set of five pH readings was recorded. At this time too, Dr Masters and Mrs Johnson checked the interior of the vagina to gauge the amount of lubricating moisture secreted ... Three additional sets of pH readings and of lubrication observations were taken 5 minutes, $7\frac{1}{2}$ minutes, and 10 minutes after Mrs K. had started masturbating. During Mrs K.'s next menstrual cycle, [Mr K.] ... joined Mrs K. wearing a condom so that his semen would not affect pH measurements. Sex play began, followed by sexual intercourse. The intercourse was interrupted when Mrs K. reported she was fully aroused sexually ... [etc, etc].[23]

This description continued for a further three pages. The relative amount of space given to Mr and Mrs K. in this quote is representative of that in the research as a whole.[24] As in the manuals, it was female sexuality which was problematized. The reported discoveries about male sexuality amounted to little more than the finding that different-sized non-erect penises expand to differing extents and so the size range of erect penises is much less. The relation of this information to men's insecurities about the

[22] E. M. Brecher and R. E. Brecher, *An Analysis of Human Sexual Response*, (1967; 1968) 63.
[23] Ibid. 85–7.
[24] In *Human Sexual Response*, the section on women is 167 pages and that on men 75 pages long.

size of their own individual penis is obvious. Nevertheless, the reader was not treated to a lengthy description of Dr Masters and Mrs Johnson measuring several hundred penises. It was the female body which was described surrounded by laboratory instruments, white coats, and medical titles.

Masters and Johnson's research methods deeply offended many people. In 1969, Leslie Paul, an English Catholic academic, expressed the following view:

The goal may be the lofty one of human knowledge but there does remain the question of the entitlement of any one individual to so deep an invasion of the privacy of another as the Kinsey—or the Masters and Johnson investigation demanded. [The latter had] an insolence of which only the most humble scientists are truly capable... as though their own motives could never be suspect even to themselves... and the value... of their knowledge is beyond question.[25]

For Paul the scientific invasion of sexual privacy by 'non-sexual values' was in itself so negative that no knowledge gained by this method could be worthwhile. Non-sexual values included social interests, individual pleasure, privacy, freedom, and living space. Paul prioritized emotional control and reticence, an attitude that was central to English culture during the 1950s. Privacy and emotional reticence were necessary to genuine love, he felt, and it was right that many aspects of life should not be understood; acceptance of this was part of the human condition. Love was in direct opposition to an emphasis on genital sex. Paul saw this as an either/or inevitable opposition; sex as love or genital sex. Only within the privacy of lifetime monogamous marriage could this be resolved and sex be a valid expression of love. Other Christian conservatives writing in opposition to new approaches to sexuality held similar positions.[26] Most such people also rejected other social innovations such as a more equal role for women and a less deferential society.

In contrast to the likes of Lesley Paul, the response of young female thinkers to Masters and Johnson's findings was extremely positive.

[25] L. Paul, *Coming to Terms with Sex* (1969), 91–3.
[26] e.g. A. Lunn and G. Lean, *The New Morality* (1964). R. Sadler, R. S. Acland, and G. B. Bentley, *Sexual Morality: Three Views*, ed. C. L. Gough (1965).

Masters and Johnson's major conclusion was that there was only one female orgasm and that it originated in the clitoris regardless of where it was felt. This was in spite of their description of the vaginal response to erotic stimulation, explained here by the Brechers:

The vagina too, responds. It can be thought of as a cylinder or 'barrel', which remains in a collapsed state in the absence of erotic stimulation. The Masters–Johnson studies have established that the outer third of this barrel reacts in one way and the inner two-thirds in a very different way during the successive phases of sexual response. As sexual tension mounts during the excitement phase . . . [t]he cervix and the uterus are pulled back and up . . . producing a 'tenting' of the vaginal walls surrounding the cervix. The net result of these and other changes is a dramatic 'ballooning' of the inner two thirds of the vagina. The diameter at the widest point of the ballooning may be three times the diameter of the erotically unstimulated vagina; and the total length of the vaginal barrel may be increased as much as a full inch.[27]

Given this physical response the vagina cannot be described as inactive or even passive. However, Masters and Johnson assumed this to be the case, and their findings focused on what they called clitoral orgasms. The female research subjects were chosen on the basis of their capacity to produce orgasms in the laboratory while under observation. Regarding these women, Masters and Johnson found that as 'contrasted with the male's usual inability to have more than one orgasm in a short period, many females, especially when clitorally stimulated can regularly have five or six full orgasms within a matter of minutes'.[28] In this context, with these female subjects, it was found that the most intense orgasms on a physiological level occurred as a result of masturbation, not while engaging in penile-vaginal intercourse. In response to these findings, Dr Mary Jane Sherfey, an American psychoanalyst, concluded in 1966 that 'biology gives to women an inordinate sexual drive and capacity which had to be suppressed in the interests of maternal responsibility and male property rights with the rise of modern civilisation'.[29] Sherfey was revers-

---

[27] Brecher and Brecher, *An Analysis*, 27–8.

[28] W. H. Masters and V. E. Johnson, 'Orgasm, Anatomy of the Female', in A. P. Abarbanel and A. Ellis (eds.), *The Encyclopaedia of Sexual Behaviour* (1961), 792.

[29] Sherfey, *nature* 1966. 112–3. For responses to Sherfey also see Millet, *Sexual Politics* 117–19. S. Firestone, *The Dialectic of Sex* (1970; 1971), 48.

ing cultural assumptions that women were naturally monogamous and less interested in sex than men. For example, the English agony aunt and writer Claire Rayner had written a manual called *People in Love: A Modern Guide to Sex in Marriage* (1968). She explained that 'few would be willing to see the strongly sexual man as one mentally ill, while almost everyone sees nymphomania as a decided aberration . . . Women are passive because for them, sex is really baby-making . . . Since their sex drive is different, fewer women than men seem to need success in careers.'[30] As popularized by female writers such as the American Barbara Seaman, Sherfey's work was used to support an exercise in turning the tables. Rather than women being frigid and cold:

[T]he latest scientific evidence indicates that, sexually, the male is but a pale imitation—of *us*. His capacity, which compared to ours, was not much to start with, peaks at a ridiculously early age, and after that, it's downhill all the way. Our capacity continues to grow throughout much of our adult lifetime, *if* the world we inhabit and the men we consort with do not cruelly abort it.[31]

It was because Masters and Johnson decontextualized sexuality, and presented the (transhistorical) body as a source of empirical scientific truth, that so radical a redefinition of female sexuality could gain credence. Sherfey and Seaman were part of an explosion of mainly American feminist writing about heterosexual female sexuality, and women's capacity for sexual pleasure, which took place over the five years following the publication of *Human Sexual Response* (1966). This excited and angry work received an enthusiastic reception from young educated women, demonstrating the impact of the Freudian insistence that women who did not have vaginal orgasms through penile penetration were frigid and inadequate.[32]

---

[30] C. Rayner, *People in Love: A Modern Guide to Sex in Marriage* (1968), 26. See also (the inaccurate and anxiety-creating best-selling manual) D. Reuben, *Everything you Always Wanted to Know about Sex* but were Afraid to Ask* (1970).

[31] B. Seaman, *Free and Female* (1972), 32, 42.

[32] For English responses see e.g. P. Whiting, 'Female Sexuality: Its Political Implications', in M. Wandor (ed.), *The Body Politic: Women's Liberation in Britain 1969–1972* (1972), 190. E. Phillips (ed.), 'Introduction: Libertarianism, "Egotism", and Liberation', in *The Left and the Erotic* (1983). Male manual writers also accepted that the vagina was inert: e.g. J. James [pseud.], *The Facts of Sex* (1969), 40.

Young feminists used the notion that the vagina was largely inert to their own ends. In *Sexual Politics* (1969), Kate Millet used Masters and Johnson's findings as sources to explain that the 'clitoris is the organ specific to sexuality in the human female, the vagina being an organ of reproduction as well as of sexuality'.[33] In an influential 1970 article called 'The Myth of Vaginal Orgasm' the American feminist Anna Koedt argued that 'Men have orgasms essentially by friction with the vagina, not the clitoral area, which is external and not able to cause friction the way penetration does. Women have thus been defined sexually in terms of what pleases men; our own biology has not been properly analysed.'[34] The vestiges of the prohibition against masturbation led to an absolute association of vaginal sensation with the penis. For example, in 1970 when the Australian feminist Germaine Greer was trying to make the point that the vagina was responsive to stimulation she assumed the stimulus would be a penis. 'It is nonsense to say that a woman feels nothing when a man is moving his penis in her vagina. The orgasm is qualitatively different when the vagina can undulate around the penis instead of vacancy.'[35] This association between vaginal sensation and the penis meant that at this time it was not possible to argue that the vagina was a sexually responsive organ without appearing to accept the norm of male-dominated sexual practice. Conversely, those women who rejected the vagina as a site of erotic sensation were also rejecting the idea that women were dependent on men. Koedt believed that 'Men fear they will become sexually expendable if the clitoris is substituted for the vagina as the centre of pleasure for women.'[36]

Sexuality was considered entirely in the context of gender power relations. By the mid-1960s, the pre-Second World War societal rejection of sexual expression *per se* and the relation of masturbation to clitoral stimulation had become irrelevant. As a result of the introduction of effective contraception, primarily the pill, reproduction could be treated as entirely separate from and irrelevant to female sexual pleasure. Female

---

[33]   Millet, *Sexual Politics*, 117. See also M. Ejlersen, *I Accuse!* (1969), 45.

[34]   A. Koedt, 'The Myth of Vaginal orgasm', repr. in Sneja Gunew (ed.), *A Reader in Feminist Knowledge* (1970; 1991), 326.

[35]   G. Greer, *The Female Eunuch* (1970; 1971), 52–3.

[36]   Koedt, 'Myth', 333.

sexuality was now understood as being constrained by the male desire for vaginal intercourse—labelled phallocentric heterosexuality. Koedt believed that the 'recognition of clitoral orgasm as fact would threaten the heterosexual *institution*. For it would indicate that sexual pleasure was obtainable from either men *or* women thus making heterosexuality not an absolute, but an option.'[37] This stance evolved very rapidly into a rejection of vaginal sensation. Some lesbian-separatist feminists concluded that they should reject heterosexual intercourse and vaginal stimulation altogether, arguing that 'Our personality alters as we become less penetrable (vaginal) and increasingly self-contained (clitoral).'[38] This position was taken up by a numerically small number of women, but because many women felt deeply ambivalent about male-dominated societal attitudes to sexuality, and the problem of male violence, those who held it played a major role in refocusing the discourse on sexuality during the late 1970s and 1980s.

American clinical psychologist Leonore Teifer has explained that in the medical model, on which Masters and Johnson's research was based, the body has its own empirical laws and processes, which operate independently of mental or social life. Sexuality is a natural property, or set of properties, of individuals expressed in acts which require properly functioning organ systems.[39] The complex interaction between physical and emotional responses, which women describe and which the earlier sex researchers acknowledged to be confusing, could not be explained by the use of such a reductive model. But the lived experience of an older generation of women who did experience vaginal orgasms was rejected on this basis. For example, in 1974 academic literary critic Rosalind Miles wrote patronizingly that in 'defiance of modern biological discovery, Doris Lessing clings to the old notion of there being two types of orgasm

---

[37] Ibid.

[38] A. Coote and B. Campbell, *Sweet Freedom: The Struggle for Women's Liberation* (1982), 224, also 226–7. Quoted from 'Thoughts on Feminism', a paper published in 1971 for the November national women's liberation conference in London. Later reprinted as Leeds Revolutionary Feminist Group, *Love your Enemy: Political Lesbianism: The Case against Heterosexuality* (1979). J. Dixon, 'Separatism: A Look Back at Anger', in S. Hemmings and B. Cant (eds.), *Radical Records: Thirty Years of Lesbian and Gay History, 1957–1987* (1988), 79.

[39] L. Teifer, 'Medicine, Morality and the Public Management of Sexual Matters', in L. Segal (ed.), *New Sexual Agendas* (1997), 106–8.

in female sexual response, the vaginal and the clitoral'.[40] Miles was probably following Koedt who asserted:

Because of the lack of knowledge of their own anatomy, some women accept the idea that an orgasm felt during 'normal' intercourse was vaginally caused. This confusion is caused by a combination of two factors. One, failing to locate the centre of the orgasm, and two, by a desire to fit her experience to the male-defined idea of sexual normalcy.[41]

Yet even in the 1970s, some women continued to insist that they experienced vaginal orgasms. In the 1940s, Robert Latou Dickinson, an American gynaecologist and sex researcher, had already concluded that women might *feel, think,* or *believe* that they were having two different orgasms, but the biological base proved there were not two orgasms.[42] These words can be used ambiguously. They could mean women feel; they have an experience, something actually happens to them. Or 'feel' could mean women imagine a sensation. A difference seems or appears to exist, but women are wrong, the event does not actually happen. In their haste to reject the existing controlling and misogynistic approach to female sexuality young feminists stood alongside sex researchers and male sex manual authors and asserted the vagina was passive and inert in the 1970s.[43] Those women who had vaginal orgasms (or even just vaginal sensation) were denied the right to define their own desire as had been women who had an absence of sexual desire.[44] Doris Lessing's comments made it quite clear that she did not accept this interpretation of her experience. In 1995, she commented in her autobiography:

[T]he clitoris was far from the big deal it is at the moment of writing...when I masturbated in my adolescence it was the vagina and its amazing possibilities I learned about...A clitoral orgasm by itself was a secondary and inferior

---

[40] R. Miles, *The Fiction of Sex* (1974), 166.

[41] Koedt, 'Myth', 330.

[42] Irvine also comments on how this discourse fostered women's mistrust of their own physical experiences. She analyses the development of sexology and concepts of female sexuality during the 1970s and 1980s. *Disorders*, 226.

[43] M. McIntosh, 'Who Needs Prostitutes? The Ideology of Male Sexual Needs', in C. Smart and B. Smart (eds.), *Women, Sexuality and Social Control* (1978), 61. Citing S. Fisher, *Understanding the Female Orgasm* [paperback summary of *The Female Orgasm*, 1973] (1973).

[44] See Ch. 6.

pleasure. If I had been told that clitoral and vaginal orgasms would within a few decades become ideological enemies, or that people would say vaginal orgasms did not exist, I'd have thought it a joke.[45]

Lessing, and other intellectual women of her generation, described sexual relationships that were profoundly exploitative and misogynistic. However, many young feminists took the part for the whole; in an act of intellectual metonymy, the vaginal sensation was treated as the misogynistic relationship, as if by rejecting the vagina, the system of gender power relations could be reshaped. Vaginal orgasm was identified not with but *as* the misogynist, phallocentric vision of female sexuality created by Freud and made central to the modernization of female submission. The female part, the vagina, was taken for the whole psychic structure of male-dominated sexuality, as if female submission did not exist when sexual activity was confined to, for example, oral sex.

Young feminists articulated the rejection by young women (revealed in their growing levels of sexual activity) of a model of female sexuality allegedly based on the biological demands of reproduction, which included monogamy and acceptance of male needs. These biological 'facts' were being used as a reason to continue imposing sexual control upon young women by an older generation faced with the challenge posed by female financial independence and contraception. However, the substitution of a norm of sex divorced from emotion would have left heterosexual women of an earlier generation with no arguments against a male libertine perspective on sexuality.[46]

Vaginal sensations are emphasized in this research because of the period it covers. For the younger generation of women who grew up in the 1950s and 1960s, clitoral sensation was often more important, as feminists argued. Although these women often were, as most young girls still are today, brought up to perceive their genitals as ugly and a source of embarrassment, inhibitions about touching the genitals had become far less intense and awareness of the clitoris as a source of pleasure was usual. By the 1960s, most young heterosexual women were likely to engage in

---

[45] D. Lessing, *Under my Skin: Volume One of my Autobiography, to 1949* (1995), 265–7.

[46] P. Diggs, *BMJ* (1 July 1972), 46. K. Leech, *Youthquake: The Growth of a Counter-Culture through Two Decades* (1973), 25. R. Neville, *Play Power* (1971). C. Wilson, *Sex and the Intelligent Teenager* (1966), 183, 192. Phillips, 'Introduction', 15, 32.

petting, unlike women of earlier generations. A woman aged only 40 in 1960 was born in 1920 and had been brought up in a culture with very different attitudes to her genitals and her sexuality, from a woman who was 20 that same year. There was little opportunity for women to appreciate the huge differences in their physical experiences, as it was usually unacceptable to discuss this in detail. In any event, the older generation of women often intensely disapproved of the relatively casual sexual activity which was becoming usual among the younger generation of women, especially those who were highly educated and socially unconventional. Furthermore, embodied sexuality was seen as natural, a set of physical sensations that might be expressed or repressed, a capacity which was present from infancy and emerged in puberty, and certainly not an attribute which could change from one generation to another. Therefore, arguments about sexual response assumed that any conclusions reached, and the social implications of these, applied to all women. As this research has shown, that belief was not correct.

PART III

The English Sexual Revolution

Sexual Pleasure, Contraception, and Fertility Decline

In Parts I and II of this book major shifts in sexual mores from around 1800 to around the 1960s have been charted. In Part III the impact of oral contraception, that is, the pill, is described. In this introductory chapter the path of fertility from the low point, which was reached in 1933, to a new low point in 1976 is analysed. The availability of contraception altered the impact of demographic changes from the middle half of the twentieth century. The median age at marriage was at a low of around 21 in 1800, and returned to much the same figure in 1971, after rising to a high of 24 years around the First World War. This low age of marriage produced large families in 1800 when contraception was almost unknown but, by 1971, people were able to marry at the same low age and control their fertility by use of contraception. Hence the apparent paradox that relaxed sexual mores resulted in large families in 1800 but in 1971 small families accompanied the loosening of sexual restraint.[1]

Initially, however, the relaxation of sexual restraint was probably the major cause of the rise in marital fertility rates that took place from the mid-1930s to the early 1960s. Part of the increase in the numbers of babies born resulted from more people marrying. In 1931 only 54 per cent, that is just over half of women aged between 16 and 44, were married; by 1971, the percentage had risen to 73 per cent, nearly three-quarters.[2] Of that 19

---

[1] M. Anderson, 'The Emergence of the Modern Life Cycle in Britain', *Social History*, 10 (1985), fig. 3, 73, 74.

[2] *Marriage and Divorce Statistics: Review of the Registrar General on Marriages and Divorces in England and Wales, 1980*, OPCS Series FM2 no. 7 (1983), derived from table 1.1(B), proportions per thousand married by sex and age: women ever married, aged 16–44, 1931 54%, 1951 65%, 1961 70%, 1971 73%.

per cent increase, 11 per cent occurred between 1931 and 1951, and the other 8 per cent from then until 1971. More people were able to marry and engage in sexual activity. Throughout the nineteenth and early twentieth centuries, many people who wanted to marry were unable to do so and it is also probable that many women and men did not want to marry. Attitudes to marriage changed and, by the 1950s, it was unusual (and often unacceptable) for young people to choose not to marry or to abjure sexual expression.

However, the marital fertility rate also rose. This is the number of children women have at given durations of marriage and use of this rate makes it possible to compare the fertility of women who have been married for the same number of years in different eras. After four years of marriage, the average number of children born per woman in the cohort of women who got married 1931–5 was 0.95. In the cohort who married in 1956–60, the average was 1.15.[3] Thus, there was a rise in women's fertility that cannot be explained by greater numbers of women marrying. A small part of this rise can be accounted for by the fall in the mean age of women at first marriage, which fell from 25.5 in the early 1930s to 22.5 in the late 1960s, as younger women are more fertile.[4] The total fertility rate is another way of measuring this increase. It shows the family size a woman would have if she experienced current age-specific fertility rates throughout her lifetime. By 1933 English fertility had fallen to a low point of 1.72 TFR.[5] If the Second World War is disregarded there is then a slow rise until a high of 2.93 is reached in 1964. In contrast to this, rates of use of contraception increased from the 1890s to the 1970s.

The explanation for this rise in fertility is the mirror of that for the fall in marital fertility that took place from around 1870 to 1933. In the first part of this book, it was explained that a rising age at marriage and partial abstinence in the form of low coital frequencies were the crucial factors in

---

[3] C. M. Langford, 'Birth Control Practice in Great Britain: A Review of the Evidence from Cross-Sectional Surveys', in M. Murphy and J. Hobcraft (eds.), *Population Research in Britain: A Supplement to Population Studies*, 45 (1991), table 3.6, 61.

[4] OPCS Series FM2 no. 7, 1983. table 1.1 (B).

[5] The TFR shows the family size a woman would have if she experienced current age-specific fertility rates throughout her lifetime.

the driving down of fertility from the 1870s to the 1930s. This was achieved in the context of considerable anxiety regarding unwanted pregnancies and venereal disease and a broad social acceptance of emotional and sexual self-control as an ideal to be aimed for. The women and men who came of age in the 1940s and 1950s were exposed to increasingly positive information about sexuality, and encouraged to believe that use of birth control methods would prevent pregnancy. This gradually eroded the emotional and sexual control that had produced low frequencies of intercourse. The war brought rising real wages and full employment, and improved provision of services by the welfare state followed, all of which also contributed to improving marital relationships from the late 1940s. In such conditions, couples were also more willing to risk a further child rather than abstain. However, while some middle-class women returned to having large families by choice in the 1950s,[6] most women who had large families in the 1950s did not plan to do so and they had them because they could not control their fertility. A survey in 1967, by Myra Woolf, found that 73 per cent of women with completed family sizes of four or more children said they had more children than they considered ideal for families 'like themselves'.[7] The results of the introduction of the pill, an almost 100 per cent effective female-controlled method of contraception, confirm this interpretation. By 1970–5, following the introduction of the pill and the fall in the TFR, there had been a fall in the number of pregnancies reported as unwanted or mistimed in every social class and a sharp fall in fertility.[8]

There is no way of directly measuring coital frequencies in this period but changes in the sexual culture suggest that couples were having more sexual intercourse. Unfortunately for these generations, their rising coital frequencies would have reduced the contraceptive efficiency of the available methods sharply. This is because coital frequency alters the risk of contraceptive failure. For example, if one group of women has sexual

---

[6] See V. Grove, *The Compleat Woman: Marriage, Motherhood, Career: Can she Have it All?* (1987; 1988).

[7] M. Woolf, *Family Intentions* (1971), table 2.18, 35, 37, 74–6. A randomly selected national sample of 6,300 married women under the age of 45 was interviewed for the survey in July–Dec. 1967.

[8] Ibid. 37. M. Bone, *The Family Planning Service: Changes and Effects (1970–1975)* (1978), 64.

intercourse twice as often as another group of women, the contraceptive failure rate will be the same for each act of intercourse, but the cumulative method failure rate in the first group will be twice that of the second group. Therefore the *rise* in marital fertility from 1933 until 1964 was almost certainly caused by increasing rates of coitus, which meant that couples' increasing use of contraception was not sufficient to maintain their fertility at the low level reached in the 1930s. Sex was not openly discussed and few people could have gauged the extent to which their coital frequencies differed from those of previous generations. Nor, even had they done so, would they have known how substantial a difference this made to their risk of pregnancy, as this was not understood until the 1960s.[9]

There is a counter-argument that there was no trend rise in the birth rate 1931–64. Instead, this argument goes, there were two small baby booms, one after the Second World War and one after the end of rationing and national service. These can be misread as a long-term rise when combined with the fall in the age of marriage as this resulted in women marrying at an age when their fertility was higher. The detailed statistical work required to rebut this argument definitively is beyond the scope of this book; however, this explanation does not adequately explain the rise. The increase in fertility rates began before the war and the rates never returned to pre-war levels. There was a plateau in the mid-1950s but the rise from 1956 ended only when pill use rose to sufficient heights in 1964 (see below). This suggests an underlying long-term trend that can be found in the shift toward a more sexually liberal society of which the falling age at marriage is a part. The falling age at marriage results in higher coital frequencies, as well as higher fecundity, because younger women have higher rates of both.[10]

International comparisons suggest that British rates of coitus were low relative to other Anglo cultures throughout this period. Demographers L. T. Ruzicka and John Caldwell found in 1977 that there had been an 'astonishing similarity' between the reproductive behaviour of Britain, Australia, and the USA from the 1930s, including falls in the average age

[9] S. Szreter, *Fertility, Class and Gender in Britain, 1860–1940* (1996), 395.
[10] J. Trussell and K. Kost, 'Contraceptive Failure in the United States: A Critical Review of the Literature', *Studies in Family Planning*, 18 (1987), 244.

at marriage and more women marrying.[11] American and British marital fertility levels were very close.[12] However, in 1961 Griselda Rowntree and Rachel Pierce found that only 67 per cent of the British women married in the 1940s admitted to using birth control as compared with 74 per cent of the American women married at a similar time. They commented that an explanation for this discrepancy was needed 'since there is much evidence that fertility aspirations and achievements are lower in Britain than in the U.S.A.'[13] It is possible that the level of concealment of use of birth control was higher in Britain than that in the USA as this would be consistent with enduring cultural differences between the two nations. Thus, the 7 per cent shortfall in birth control use could have been illusory. However, British couples also chose less effective methods than those used by American couples. In the 1950s, only 14 percent of British women used female-controlled methods compared to nearly two-thirds of white American women.[14] Withdrawal, a less effective method, was favoured in Britain compared to the USA (and Australia). There continued to be no British government quality control of condoms until 1964, whereas condoms were brought under the control of the American Food and Drug Administration in 1938, so this method also would have been less effective.[15] This suggests

[11] L. T. Ruzicka and J. C. Caldwell, *The End of the Demographic Transition in Australia* (1977), 5.

[12] Ibid. 6. J. C. Caldwell, P. F. McDonald, and L. T. Ruzicka, 'Nuptiality and Fertility in Australia, 1921–1976', in L. T. Ruzicka (ed.), *Nuptiality and Fertility: Proceedings of a Seminar Held in Bruges (Belgium), 8–11 January 1979* (1979), 211–13.

[13] G. Rowntree and R. M. Pierce, 'Birth Control in Britain: Part One', *Population Studies*, 15/1 (1961), 17.

[14] The percentage of women using the diaphragm is combined with the use of the less effective douche to give a total use of female methods of contraception by white American women of 64%, compared to a total use of female methods by British women of 14%. British couples married 1950–60: diaphragm 12.5%, douche 1.5%. White, married American women aged 18–39 in 1955: diaphragm 36%, douche 28%. The British couples had not been married as long as some of the American couples. This probably produces a slightly higher difference in levels of use, as diaphragm use increased with duration of marriage. F. Lafitte, *Family Planning in the Sixties: The Report of the Family Planning Association Working Party* (1963), ch. 2.10, citing P. K. Whelpton, A. C. Campbell, and R. Freedon, *Family Planning, Sterility and Population Growth* (1959) and G. Rowntree and R. M. Pierce, 'Birth Control in Britain: Part Two', *Population Studies*, 15/2 (1961), table 1.

[15] The US legislation did not apply to exports. C. Tietze, 'The Use-Effectiveness of Contraceptive Methods', in Clyde V. Kiser (ed.), *Research in Family Planning* (1962), 367. Citing C. Tietze, *The Condom as a Contraceptive* (1960). H. Wright, review of *The Condom as a Contraceptive*, by C. Tietze, *Family Planning*, 9/3 (1960).

that lower coital frequencies would have been necessary to produce a level of marital fertility in Britain as low as that in the USA. In Australia those women born in Britain in each cohort also had on average 10 per cent lower fertility than that of people born in Australia. This difference persisted at least until the 1970s. Reported contraceptive use does not account for this and again it is difficult to find an explanation other than lower coital frequencies.[16] The comparison reinforces the argument that British coital frequencies had been particularly low and were perhaps more likely to rise in response to social change.

The pill was introduced in late 1961, and by 1964 an estimated 480,000 women were taking the drug. Previously unpublished data from the Medical Research Council's National Survey of Health and Development on women's use of the pill provides a revealing picture of pill use by young women. The women in the sample were engaging in sexual activity, using contraceptives, and getting married in the years when the pill first became widely available.[17] Fig. 12.1 shows the cumulative incidence of their first use of the pill. The cohort were aged 20 in 1966, and the data shows that by 1969 48 per cent of all women then aged 23 had used the drug. This was 62 per cent of the total group who used the pill at any stage in their life, showing that the pill was widely available and widely used by young women in the second half of the 1960s. By 1989, over 80 per cent of women born 1950–9 had used the pill as a contraceptive method.[18] In 1985, social scientist Margaret Bone commented that in Scotland 'between 1964 and 1981, the course described by fertility . . . was virtually a mirror image of the trend in prevalence of oral contraception'. In spite of the coincidence of the rising use of the pill with the falling TFR, which was also occurring in the rest of Britain, demographers continued to argue that the pill did not cause the decline until the demographer Michael Murphy demonstrated

---

[16] J. C. Caldwell, *Theory of Fertility Decline* (1983), 190.

[17] This longitudinal cohort study is a socially stratified sample of all the births in England, Scotland, and Wales in the first week of March 1946. In 1989, the 1,628 women in the sample were asked, 'Are you currently taking the pill?', 'Have you ever taken the pill?', 'How old were you when you first took the pill?', and 'For how long in total have you taken the pill?' The base used is the 1,622 women for whom full information is available.

[18] M. Thorogood and M. P. Vessey, 'Trends in Use of Oral Contraceptives in Britain', *British Journal of Family Planning*, 16 (1990), 48.

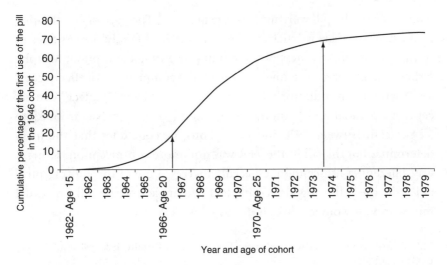

Fig. 12.1 The cumulative percentage of the first use of the pill by the MRC 1946 cohort

Source: MRC 1946 cohort.

statistically in 1993 that the bulk of the fall in fertility in the 1970s, and by implication the fall from 1964, did result from pill use.[19]

Murphy shows that although the proportions of married couples using contraception changed very little during the years 1970 and 1976, total fertility in the years 1971 and 1977 fell by 30 per cent. That is, although the level of use of all methods of contraception did not change, 30 per cent fewer conceptions occurred in 1976 than had done in 1970. This meant that births fell by 30 per cent in 1977 as compared to 1971. What did change between 1970 and 1976 were the proportions of women in the first five years of marriage using the pill as contraception. Under a third of these women were using the pill in 1967–8 but by 1976 around 80 per cent were.[20] These age-specific marital fertility rates had begun to fall from 1964. For women aged 20–4 the rate fell from 291.9 in 1964 to 250.7 in 1969, for women aged 25–9 it fell from 212.5 to 177.8. The highest levels of

---

[19] M. Murphy, 'The Contraceptive Pill and Women's employment as Factors in Fertility Change in Britain 1963–1980', *Population Studies*, 47 (1993), 223.

[20] Murphy citing Langford, 'Birth Control in Great Britain', table 3.3.

women using the pill were in these age groups.[21] The pace of childbearing in the first five years is crucial in determining final family size. As a result of the greater effectiveness of the pill in preventing conception, Murphy writes that '[A]verage use-ineffectiveness (the complement of effectiveness and therefore an indicator which shows how far from "perfect" contraception a population is) among contracepting couples halved from 6.2 to 3.2 per cent between 1970 and 1976.' Thus, he concludes that the main determinant of the fall in the TFR was not 'more contraception, rather it was different contraception, especially increased use of the contraceptive pill'.[22] In the following three chapters the impact of the pill on sexual mores and on women's lives is discussed in detail.

[21] M. Kirk, M. Murphy, and J. Hobcraft, 'The Problem of Fertility, 1936–1986', in Murphy and Hobcraft (eds.), *Population Research*, 37.

[22] Murphy, 'Contraceptive Pill', 223.

13

'Truly it Felt Like Year One':
The English Sexual Revolution

In the late 1960s, many young women believed that a sexual revolution was taking place. The novelist Angela Carter wrote that by 1969 'the introduction of more or less 100 per cent effective methods of birth control, combined with the relaxation of manners that may have derived from this technological innovation or else came from God knows where, changed, well, everything'.[1] Margaret Drabble, another novelist, said in the *Guardian* that 'we face the certainty of a sexual revolution, and [this]...is caused largely by the development of contraceptive techniques...This freedom is evidently connected to that other major revolution of our society, the emancipation of women.'[2] But, by the early 1980s, the idea that a sexual revolution had taken place was being treated with scepticism, and historians including, for example, Jeffrey Weeks and Jane Lewis have consistently argued that heterosexual sexual behaviour remained conservative during the 1960s.[3] The only measurable change occurring in sexual behaviour was the rising incidence of premarital

---

[1] A. Carter, 'Truly, It Felt like Year One', in S. Maitland (ed.), *Very Heaven: Looking Back at the 1960s* (1988), 213–14.

[2] M. Drabble, *Guardian* (10 Nov. 1967). See also C. White, *Women's Magazines 1693–1968* (1970), 163.

[3] J. Weeks, *Sex, Politics and Society: The Regulation of Sexuality since 1800* (1981; 1989), 254. J. Lewis, *Women in Britain since 1945* (1992), 48. See also L. V. Marks, *Sexual Chemistry: A History of the Contraceptive Pill* (2001), 3. E. R. Watkins has argued that the pill did not cause the sexual revolution in the USA. She used a limited range of sources and did not look at young women's behaviour in detail; however, the argument made here would have to be considered in the light of the specific US circumstances. E. R. Watkins, *On the Pill: A Social History of Oral Contraceptives in America, 1950–1970* (1998).

sexual intercourse and, on the basis of the ample evidence that the unmarried insisted they were having sexual intercourse only with their intended spouse, they dismiss this as the continuation of an existing trend. Indeed, outside the middle classes, premarital sex was almost certainly a frequent element of courting behaviour that fell to a low point around 1900, when survey records began, and was merely rising back to a more usual rate. However, during the 1960s, and in conjunction with the pill, premarital sexual intercourse became radical sexual behaviour regardless of the intentions of those participating in it.

Very high effectiveness was one of the innovations offered by the pill; another was female control. As has been shown, comparatively few English women ever used female-controlled methods such as the diaphragm. Over two-thirds of white American women used female methods in the 1950s compared to a seventh of English women.[4] This comparison suggests that the introduction of a female-controlled method into English society had the potential to produce a greater change in contraceptive use and in turn sexual behaviour than was the case in the USA. There were restrictions on the availability of female methods of contraception. In 1960, there were only 340 of the volunteer-operated Family Planning Association clinics and these supplied contraception only to married women or engaged women who could supply evidence of an impending marriage.[5] The 118 government-funded local authority clinics were restricted to married women who required contraception on 'medical grounds'.[6] This limit was the result of strong resistance to the spending of public money in support of sexual activity, even within marriage. A large percentage of GPs believed providing contraception was not part of medical practice and would be demeaning to their status.[7] Distaste for preventive and sexual medicine reinforced each other, as in this 1962 letter in the *British Medical Journal*:

---

[4]   See ch. 12.

[5]   FPA Archives, *Family Planning Association 30th Annual Report*, 1960/1, 7. Lafitte, *Family Planning*, ch. 1.2.

[6]   Lafitte, *Family Planning*, chs. 3.1, 4.5.

[7]   A. Leathard, *The Fight for Family Planning: The Development of Family Planning Services in Britain, 1921–74* (1980), 80, 86, 99.

Sir...I write to protest against the giving of hormones to normal healthy women with the sole object of preventing conception. Our calling is to guard against illness...It is no business of a doctor to interfere with normal physiology. Use of drugs in this way is a debasement of our profession, a misapplication of our knowledge and totally unworthy of a great profession.[8]

Even those GPS who did provide contraception usually accepted, along with the rest of society, that single women should not have access to contraception. In 1963, an article in the *Observer* described the options open to unmarried (middle-class) women:

If she knows the right man in Harley Street she can get fitted for five guineas. If she is able to lie convincingly and stick to her story through often ruthless cross questioning, she can go to the family planning clinics and tell them she is about to get married. If she is confident enough she will go to her G.P. who may or may not be ready to help her. But he is probably a friend of her parents. The end result is that most girls give up, or hope that if they 'fall', the man will make an honest woman of them.[9]

The word 'girl' is used, but these restrictions applied to unmarried women of any age, and the options for working-class women and girls and those outside major cities were even more limited.[10] The small numbers of clinics and doctors' unwillingness to provide services meant that even for married women the regional availability of female methods varied considerably. Few doctors had or wanted the training needed to fit diaphragms. This also reflected an underlying attitude to physical contact with the body of the patient. The Australian author of a study of general practice carried out in 1948–9 was surprised that the GPs he observed were reluctant to conduct 'proper physical examinations'. He also found that most consultations ended with the prescription of 'the almost mandatory bottle of medicine'.[11] The pill was to fit perfectly into this approach to medical practice. In 1967–8, by which time the pill was well established as a

---

[8] A. R. Hill, letter, *BMJ* (7 July 1962).

[9] *Observer* (5 May 1963).

[10] See Brook Advisory Service Archive, Brook Annual Report 1965/6.

[11] J. Collings, an Australian academic based at the Harvard School of Public Health in the USA, was awarded Nuffield Trust Fund money in 1948 to study general practice in England. He looked at 55 practices, run by 104 GPs. J. Collings, *Lancet* (1950). See also P. Vaughan, *The Pill on Trial* (1972), 172.

method, a survey of family planning services found that if asked for contraceptive advice, 83 per cent of doctors discussed the pill, 60 per cent prescribed no other methods, and 64 per cent gave no physical examination.[12] One-sixth of the medical profession was also Catholic and these doctors were therefore (largely) opposed to the use of artificial birth control methods.[13] Aside from use of withdrawal, the primary source of contraception was the supply of condoms through some 6,000 barbers and chemists.[14] As these distribution methods imply, there were no restrictions on access to male methods, aside from youthful shyness. The arrival of the pill and the willingness of doctors to prescribe a contraceptive drug transformed these methods of distribution. During the 1960s, the number of outlets where a female method of contraception could be obtained increased from under a thousand clinics to an estimated 19,000 non-Catholic family doctors, and pill sales shot up accordingly.[15] The multinational drug companies involved in manufacturing the pill had large budgets to spend on promoting their individual brands to doctors. Thus, the pill involved three innovations: almost total reliability, widespread publicity, and large-scale modern distribution of a female contraceptive method.

THE FAMILY PLANNING ASSOCIATION

The birth control clinic movement was started, largely by women, in the inter-war period.[16] A number of small groups joined to form the national Birth Control Association, which, following the emergence of population decline fears in the late 1930s, became the Family Planning Association (FPA) in 1939. The FPA played a pivotal role in the introduction of the pill

[12] A. Cartwright, *Parents and Family Planning Services* (1970), 239.

[13] J. Peel, 'Contraception and the Medical Profession', *Population Studies*, 18 (1964), 145.

[14] Ibid. 123. Clinics and surgical stores are not included. There were also mail order firms which sent advertising to those who put engagement announcements in the press and to new mothers in hospitals.

[15] P. Bartrip, *Themselves Writ Large: The British Medical Association, 1832–1966* (1996), 333. There were around 22,000–23,000 GPs in total.

[16] Leathard, *Fight*, 67–8.

to Britain, and the changes taking place in the organization during the late 1950s and early 1960s reveal how women's contraceptive behaviour was being interpreted in this period. During the 1950s, the organization's leadership was still strongly dominated by the founding generation of women.[17] They had created a substantial organization with a central office in London that controlled national public relations and medical practice by the doctors in the clinics, while the branches that ran the clinics were started up and funded by local lay voluntary workers. During the 1950s the FPA grew quickly and in 1959 a working party was set up under the leadership of Professor François Lafitte to consider the future and the structure of the FPA. The working party's report, written by Lafitte, commented disapprovingly that the FPA was a female-dominated organization and recommended that it abandon its Women's Institute type of decentralized organization and adopt a more professional (medical) approach.[18] The one-sex, one-method (the diaphragm) clinics should be abandoned along with the concept of rescuing the 'worn out downtrodden housewife who must be protected against the consequences of her husband's demands'.[19] In this period organizations primarily for women were on the defensive, and the FPA hierarchy agreed that all these things were problems.[20] The recommendations were used as a basis for restructuring the entire organization, a process that continued to absorb much of the FPA's attention throughout the 1960s.

[17] Lafitte, *Family Planning*, ch. 6.18–21. For example, M. Pyke, who was then chairman of the Executive Committee, had been the first general secretary 1930–8. Although Lafitte's Report was concerned with the headquarters, this appears to have been true outside London also. All the women covered in this study who were associated with the FPA had long histories of involvement, e.g. M. Macaulay had been medical officer to the Liverpool FPA Branch 1930–56. L. Secor Florence had set up the Cambridge birth control clinic in the 1920s. She became chairman of the Birmingham FPA and remained involved until the 1960s. J. Malleson served for nine years on the National Executive Committee prior to her death in 1956.

[18] Leathard, *Fight*, 122. Lafitte (1913–2003) was Professor of Social Policy and Administration at Birmingham University and the adopted son of Havelock Ellis. The FPA was female dominated. Of the 95 persons who had served on the National Executive Committee since the war, only 16 were men, *Family Planning*, ch. 6.18–19. Only 530 of the 5,330 active branch members were men, ch. 5. Almost all the doctors were women and in the month surveyed less than 0.5% of new clients were men, ch. 3.2.

[19] Lafitte, *Family Planning*, ch. 7.14–15.

[20] *Guardian* (8 Mar. 1973).

A survey done for the working party found that FPA clinics recommended the diaphragm to over 97.5 per cent of clients, although a national survey done in 1960 revealed that the majority of couples used male-controlled methods—withdrawal or the sheath.[21] The Report's comments on methods reveal the background that Lafitte saw as relevant to discussions about method choice:

[T]he British family planning scene is one of strong preference for masculine birth control methods partly perhaps because most British wives trust their husbands, mainly no doubt for deeper and not easily altered psychological reasons. This is the context in which the family planning movement operates and to which, in our view, it should adjust itself. *FPA is not in business to advocate the moral or technological superiority of feminine over masculine birth control methods.* It could not indeed assert the latter with scientific honesty in view of what is known of the effectiveness in use of different methods, or the former without reviving a misplaced feminism. (italics in original)[22]

There was a preference for male birth control methods but research suggested that although some women did trust their husbands to withdraw in time, frequently women did not do so. There was no evidence offered to support the suggestion that where women did trust their husbands they chose their contraceptive method on this basis. Evidence of deep-seated resistance to the diaphragm did exist and this played an important role in the preference for male methods. A footnote to the previous quotation read:

the evidence...shows that the condom and cap are equally effective birth prevention techniques among urban Americans, with withdrawal not far behind. Marie Stopes' view of the male contraceptive method preferred by the majority of her fellow citizens is exemplified by her reference, in a scientific paper in 1931, to '*the condom...which...is generally to be condemned*'...How much influence did such attitudes exert on the then developing clinic movement?[23]

The substantial problems with inadequate condom manufacture during the inter-war period had been forgotten by the 1960s, enabling the preference of most of the early birth control clinics for caps to be ascribed

---

[21] Lafitte, *Family Planning*, ch. 3.2, 4. The Population Investigation Committee survey done by Rowntree and Pierce in 1959–60 produced a series of tabulations for the Report.

[22] Ibid., ch. 7.13.   [23] Ibid.

solely to feminism. In a section entitled 'Emotional barriers to birth control', the report comments on the 'primary desire in both women as well as men to have husbands in a dominant role and wives in a sexually submissive one'.[24] The reference to Marie Stopes (who was not involved in founding the FPA) comes from a biography by Keith Briant. He wrote that the 'success of her teaching was due to the fact that she was a woman writing with a male personality and a male approach to the sex act'.[25] The Report was arguing that resistance to condoms was ideological and originated with a woman whose sexual desires were masculine. It ran counter to wives' need to depend on their husbands. The Report discussed the possible influence of the pill but concluded that for the above reasons a contraceptive service for women will 'probably reach only a large minority of couples'.[26]

Instead, the direction proposed for the FPA was the involvement of men in clinics: 'there cannot be much doubt about the shape of the future ... *Growing partnership between husband and wife*' (italics in original).[27] The Report acknowledged that problems might exist for some women but the solution suggested was influencing husbands.[28] The men who did not co-operate were said to come from dysfunctional groups: 'family case-workers tell us continually of methods learnt at clinics never used because of ignorance or opposition of husbands.'[29] It was believed that male co-operation would be obtained if the FPA encouraged more male involvement at every level in the organization. Attempts were already being made to do this. In 1961, the FPA issued a revised version of its *Clinic Handbook*. For the first time clinic doctors were unequivocally advised, when consulted by intending brides, that 'it is a help to see both partners and, in any case, the agreement of the fiancé must be obtained before the patient is examined ... The wishes of the couple as regards stretching the hymen and choice of contraceptive method must be respected.'[30] Thus,

---

[24] Ibid., appendix 5.13. This section was written by E. Draper, the secretary and investigator to the working party.

[25] K. R. Briant, *Marie Stopes: A Biography* (1962). Quoted in L. Taylor, 'The Unfinished Sexual Revolution: The First Marie Stopes Memorial Lecture', *Journal of Biosocial Science*, 3 (1972), 474.

[26] Lafitte, *Family Planning*, ch. 7.13.   [27] Ibid., ch. 7.14.   [28] Ibid., ch. 7.14–15.

[29] Ibid., ch. 7.21.   [30] Ibid., ch. 3.3 n.1.

the FPA were heading towards even less concern with female autonomy when the pill was introduced to clinics.

By the late 1950s, there was already an expectation, created by news reports, and given credibility by other medical advances, that better, or even perfect, contraception was on its way. Terms such as 'facts' and 'experiments' were used, but the first newspaper articles on the pill described scientists as people who had dreams and visions.[31] Newspapers responded to reports from the USA where the pill was developed, and during this early period a wide variety of terms were used to identify the new 'wonder drug'. A phrase coined in 1957, 'Scientists are on the brink of perfecting the tablet which will control life', led to 'life tablet', 'life pill', and, from a Catholic source, 'death pill'.[32] The *Sunday Pictorial*, a popular newspaper, used 'X-pills', 'no-baby-drug', 'sex pills', and 'The free-love-formula' all in the same 1958 article.[33] The inventive light-heartedness of this plethora of names gives a sense of the intense optimism about the possibilities of change in the late 1950s and early 1960s. There were few doubts about the capacity of science to transform people's lives for the better. In 1963, Harold Wilson, then leader of the Labour Party, proclaimed the intent to forge a new Britain in the 'white heat' of scientific revolution. Science and technology was no longer the black and grimy stuff of satanic mills and belching chimneystacks. In an analogous fashion the oral contraceptive pill shifted the associations of contraception away from the red and pink, slime and rubber, of condoms and caps, sex and genitals. The new association of sex with secularized, scientific knowledge, the sterilized laboratory, and the hygienic white-coated scientist was a total break with previous representations. This meant that for the first time it was possible to report on an actual method in the national media and for individuals to discuss a contraceptive method in mixed company.[34] This greatly increased the impact of the pill.

In the early 1960s, much of the pressure to prescribe the pill in Britain came from women. The first indication of English women's attitude to the pill came with the enthusiastic response to the call for volunteers to join

[31]   *Daily Mirror* (7 Sept. 1962). *Women's Mirror* (22 Aug. 1958).
[32]   *Women's Sunday Mirror* (28 Apr. 1957). *Universe* (31 Oct. 1958).
[33]   *Sunday Pictorial* (19 Oct. 1958).
[34]   Cartwright, *Parents*, 245.

in clinical trials of the pill being run in conjunction with various Family Planning Association branches. Other examples include the 'flood of inquiries' following a TV programme on the pill in July 1961.[35] *Nursery World* magazine had many women writing in and enquiring about the pill.[36] By 1961, the birth rate was rising sharply and it is clear that, as soon as they heard about it, large numbers of women wanted this female-controlled contraceptive often far more than their doctors wanted to give it to them. By July 1962, less than eighteen months after the drug had been made available to family doctors (GPs) and only six months after the FPA clinics started to offer it to their patients, there were around 150,000 women on the pill.[37] The pill was available through FPA clinics only to married women and providing they obtained the permission of their doctor. This combination of medical and social criteria set by the FPA head office implicitly accepted substantial reductions in women's autonomy and there were complaints from some branches. But the pill was the first drug affecting the whole system or body ever to be given to a healthy population on a large scale. For this reason, there was no possibility of it being distributed except by clinicians, and that meant in the context of the existing societal constraints on female sexual behaviour. Mail order and other semi-covert or unsupervised outlets such as those where condoms could be purchased were never a possibility.

In 1961, an NHS prescription cost the patient two shillings whereas the full price of the drug without one was seventeen shillings.[38] Women's pressure on their doctors to provide the pill on the NHS resulted in the first extension of contraceptive provision since the 1930 Memo, which had also been the result of pressure from women.[39] In December 1961, it was

---

[35] *Slough Observer* (7 July 1961).

[36] *Nursery World* (26 July 1962). Vaughan, *Pill*, 61. *Sunday Times* (25 Mar. 1962). *Nursery World* (30 Sept. 1965).

[37] *Daily Mirror* (3 July 1962).

[38] The cost of the pill fell throughout the 1960s. In 1960, one month's supply of Conovid was 23s. *shillings*, by 1961 it was 17s. In 1962, clinics were selling them for 15s. for a month's supply and it was reported that there was a new pill costing only 10s. By 1965 this had come down to 5s. 9d. from the FPA, 10s. on private prescription. *Slough Observer* (26 Feb. 1962). *Financial Times* (4 Mar. 1965).

[39] Report on General Medical Service Committee meeting. *BMJ* (9 Sept. 1961). See L. Hoggart, 'The Campaign for Birth Control in Britain in the 1920s', in A. Digby and J. Stewart (eds.), *Gender, Health and Welfare* (1996).

announced that the pill would be available through the NHS, but only to married women whose health would be endangered by further pregnancies. This was the ground for provision of contraception laid down in the previous government statements on the subject, beginning with a Memorandum on local authority clinics dating from 1930.[40] There was one change. The Minister of Health, Enoch Powell, did not specify that the drug could be made available on prescription only to married women, as had been the case in local authority clinics since 1930, because to do so would have been to impinge upon doctors' fiercely guarded medical autonomy, a sensitive issue in relation to the creation of the NHS.

The advent of oral contraceptives forced many doctors who were previously unwilling to become involved with contraceptive work. Their attitude to this varied. Some doctors welcomed the possibility of prescribing an effective contraceptive method. But those for whom 'contraceptive work [was] still often regarded if not as a quack activity, at least as a chore or a joke' appear to have been in the majority.[41] According to the *News of the World*, a Ministry spokesmen said, with regard to the decision not to allow prescriptions for social rather than medical reasons, that 'We have decided that the Health Service cannot be used to satisfy a patient's social needs. It would be the same as if a heavy smoker asked for a drug to put him off tobacco.'[42] That is, in both cases, the drug would replace the need for self-control. One doctor wrote to the *Lancet*, 'Of course we can prescribe [the pill], we can prescribe bottles of brandy, but, how could we justify it?'[43] From the perspective of these men, contraception enabled indulgence in sex, just as brandy and tobacco enabled other forms of self-indulgence. It is difficult to assess the prevalence of such views amongst doctors. However, money was the major theme in the British Medical Association's response to the pill and contraception. In 1966, BMA negotiators were able to force the Ministry of Health to agree that general

[40] Memo 153/MCW, Ministry of Health, London, July 1930; repr. officially Mar. 1931. Ministry of Health, 'Family Planning' Circular 5/66, London, 17 Feb. 1966. repr. in *Family Planning*, 15/1 (1966).

[41] E. Draper, 'The Social Background', in M. D. Pollock, (ed.), *Family Planning: A Handbook for the Doctor* (1966), 161.

[42] *News of the World* (10 Sept. 1961).

[43] G. A. Stanton, letter to *Lancet* (2 June 1962), 1183.

practitioners could charge for family planning purposes where these prescriptions were not given for medical reasons. This made the pill the only drug for which doctors were permitted to charge their National Health Service patients a fee. Pill sales rose sharply from then on, and most British doctors' strong concerns about side effects in the early 1960s appeared to be forgotten, in spite of the increasingly convincing reports linking serious illnesses to pill use, and the setting up of major research projects to investigate the reports. By the 1970s some women were starting to feel that doctors were pressuring them to take the pill, dismissing the side effects and ignoring the alternative methods.[44] In 1972, one female medical researcher wrote: 'many doctors...seem to lose interest in a woman who does not wish for or who stops taking the pill. Some doctors seem to feel angry that their treatment has been rejected.'[45] Unfortunately there were no desirable alternatives. Many women tried a variety of methods. In the 1980s, in her critique of any and all technological and medical approaches to women's fertility, Germaine Greer was reduced to ill-informed praise of withdrawal. So-called natural methods offer women more control but these were still in development and associated with the Catholic Church.[46] It is also unlikely that women who had rejected the cap and diaphragm would have taken to observing their cervical mucus despite the huge benefits of this approach.

By 1964, there were around half a million women taking the pill. By 1989, the pill had been used at some time as a contraceptive method by over 75 per cent of all women born from 1945 to 1959.[47] Historians generally see contraception as a minor component of sexual change. However, the dominant sexual culture in Britain is heterosexual, and use of the pill enabled immense change to take place in this culture.

[44] *Chichester Observer* (19 Oct. 1973). P. D. Cauthery, 'The Unwanted Pregnancy', *Forum* (1974). *Guardian* (6 Nov. 1974). For women's feelings see M. Benn and R. Richardson, 'Uneasy Freedom: Women's Experiences of Contraception', *Women's Studies International Forum*, 7/4 (1984), 219–25.

[45] *Pulse* (23 Sept. 1972).

[46] G. Greer, *Sex and Destiny: The Politics of Human Fertility* (1984), 108–21. E. Billings and A. Westmore, *The Billings Method: Controlling Fertility without Drugs or Devices* (1980).

[47] See Ch. 12 for the impact of the pill on fertility decline. M. Thorogood and M. P. Vessey, 'Trends in Use of Oral Contraceptives in Britain', *British Journal of Family Planning*, 16 (1990), 48.

Women's role within this culture has been described as that of gatekeepers. This label does not tell us why women should perform such a role. It is better understood in terms of risk. The fundamental risk attached to heterosexual sex has been the risk of pregnancy, which is borne primarily by women, and it is this that has shaped women's attitude to sexual activity both in and out of marriage. Although women are only half of the population, 100 per cent of heterosexual sexual activity involves women. Therefore, it is probable that substantial changes in women's sexual risk would affect societal sexual mores, and it has done.

PREMARITAL SEX AND THE MASS MEDIA

Even before the arrival of the pill, increasing use of contraception and new attitudes to sexuality were combining with anxiety about rising illegitimacy figures to create comment on the existence of premarital sex and the denial of contraception to unmarried women.[48] We can place premarital sexual intercourse in the context of attitudes to other sexual activity occurring outside marriage in the late 1950s. The 1957 Report of the Wolfenden Committee on Homosexual Offences and Prostitution recommended that behaviour which took place in private between consenting adults should be decriminalized but that the legal penalties for public displays of sexual behaviour should be strengthened. Essentially, although it was not illegal, that was the already existing position as regards women and premarital sexual intercourse. Premarital sex, an activity in which both men and women participated, was carried out in private between consenting adults. Societal sanctions were severe enough to ensure it had to be concealed, but it was not illegal. If the woman became pregnant and could not marry, her sexual activity became public and society punished her for this. Having an abortion was illegal. Having an illegitimate baby was highly stigmatized and women concealed the fact as desperately as people did a criminal record. There were nearly 50,000 illegitimate births in 1961. The combination of these babies and the pill was able to force a new openness on many people and by the end of the 1960s this had

---

[48]   E. Chesser, *The Sexual, Marital and Family Relationships of the English Woman* (1956), 313.

resulted in public acceptance of a hitherto hidden and stigmatized private sexual activity.

The emphasis on public restraint and self-control in the Wolfenden Report reflected important values of the 1950s and, ironically, given the wide publicity the Report received, any public discussion of sexual activity was seen as a lack of appropriate restraint by many people. By the late 1950s there was, nonetheless, an increasing amount of such discussion. Aspects of the debates described here have been covered by a number of historians.[49] What these existing accounts lack is a sense of the development of the argument during the 1960s and the extent to which what it was possible to say in public altered. Each year *Family Doctor*, a magazine published by the British Medical Association (BMA), produced an annual supplement entitled *Getting Married*. In 1959, two articles caused offence. Dr Roger Pilkington's article contained a light-hearted question: 'so you are a bride and are you pregnant too?', a reference to the rising rate of births conceived before marriage. An article by psychologist Eustace Chesser suggested that contraception was removing the problems that arose from sexual activity outside marriage and 'people should have the right to choose between being chaste and unchaste as long as society doesn't suffer'.[50] This was reported disapprovingly in, for example, the *Daily Express*, the *Daily Mail*, *People*, the *Woman's Mirror*, and the *Sunday Graphic*.[51] The *Daily Express* alone had a circulation of over four million.[52] The provincial press also commented, as did the religious papers.[53] The BMA withdrew the issue two days after publication.[54] The *New Statesman* then reprinted Chesser's article in full and Chesser wrote a book called *Is Chastity Outmoded?* This was published in 1960 and then put out in a paperback edition that sold for two shillings and sixpence in 1961. Even in this book, Chesser felt obliged to state he was not defending

[49] J. Lewis, D. Clark, and D. Morgan, *Whom God hath Joined: The Work of Marriage Guidance* (1992). Weeks, *Sex* P. Ferris, *Sex and the British: A Twentieth Century History* (1994).

[50] E. Chesser, *Is Chastity Outmoded?* (1960; 1961), 15.

[51] Ibid. 15. This list of press coverage is given in the introduction to the 1961 paperback reprint.

[52] Circulation is from C. Bertrand, *The British Press: An Historical Survey* (1969).

[53] *Lancet* (29 Apr. 1961).

[54] Chesser, *Chastity. Women's Sunday Mirror* (6 Mar. 1959). This incident is also discussed in Bartrip, *Themselves*, 319–20.

promiscuity or even premarital sex.[55] In 1960, a medical expert could not publicly hold such a position.

In 1960, Penguin Books was unsuccessfully prosecuted under the Obscene Publications Act for the first full British publication of *Lady Chatterley's Lover* by D. H. Lawrence, originally published in 1928. C. H. Rolph was present in court and then edited a transcript of the Old Bailey trial. He wrote that the focus of the prosecution became the promiscuous and adulterous behaviour of Lady Chatterley, who had sexual intercourse before marriage as a young woman in Germany, and later had two affairs, one with her impotent husband's gamekeeper. Thirteen episodes of physical sexual activity were described in detail using 'four letter words' in the book.[56] The defence successfully defended the book on the basis of Lawrence's presentation of the sex as pure and holy, although outside the bonds of legal wedlock. To quote the defence lawyer, Mr Gerald Gardiner QC:

[B]roadly speaking . . . there are two views about this. One is that sex is disgusting and sinful and unclean; that it is very unfortunate children cannot be born without it; that really the least thing said about the whole thing the better. The view of [D. H. Lawrence], as is made clear from the book, is that as a puritan moralist he plainly disapproves of casual sex, of sex without love, of promiscuous sex; but he strongly approved and thought society as a whole paid too little attention to, the physical love of a man and woman in love and in a permanent relationship with one another.[57]

Evidence, such as novels and marriage manuals, shows that, by 1960, the sexually progressive accepted Lawrence's presentation of sex as justified by love.[58] The trial received extensive coverage and the Penguin edition of the novel itself sold extremely well. In 1960, the *Sunday Pictorial*, a popular newspaper with a circulation of five million, serialized a sequel to the novel called *Lady Chatterley's Daughter*, written by Patricia Robins, a romance writer. This clearly touched a chord with readers, as it was then published as a novel.

[55] Chesser, *Chastity*, preface, 12–16.

[56] C. H. Rolph, *The Trial of Lady Chatterley: Regina v. Penguin Books Limited* (1961), 6, 17.

[57] Ibid. 30.

[58] See Ch. 10. For novels, see H. Cook, 'The Long Sexual Revolution: British Women, Sex and Contraception in the Twentieth Century' (Ph.D. Thesis 1999), ch. 16.

The idea that sexual intercourse was validated by love and not by legal wedlock was not new. Presentation of the suggestion that different approaches to sex existed and need not be vilified in the national press, and in particular on national television, was very new. In his history of the BBC, Asa Briggs comments that 'what distinguished [the early 1960s]... from others in the history of broadcasting was that the BBC as an institution—with [Hugh] Greene [appointed in 1960] as its Director General—considered it necessary to align itself with change'.[59] For example, in 1962, Professor G. M. Carstairs, a psychiatrist and academic, was asked to give the annual BBC Reith Lectures. The subject was 'the state of the nation, in the light of changes, which have come about in the community and private life since the beginning of the century'.[60] In his third lecture, he suggested that 'pre-marital licence has been found to be quite compatible with stable married life'.[61] Although the BBC had a largely middle-class audience, the press relayed such controversial statements to a wider audience. Mary Whitehouse initially began her campaign opposing changes in sexual morality in 1964 in response to Hugh Greene's new approach at the BBC.[62]

Controversial Anglican theologians, such as the Bishop of Woolwich, revealed that new sexual standards and beliefs were being seriously debated within the Church of England. In *Honest to God* (1963) he wrote: 'nothing can of itself always be labelled as "wrong". One cannot, for instance, start from the position "sex relations before marriage" or "divorce" are wrong or sinful in themselves. They may be in 99 cases or even in 100 cases out of 100, but they are not intrinsically so, for the only intrinsic evil is lack of love.'[63] The Church of England appears to have had little relevance to personal sexual change by the 1960s. However, the Mass-Observation surveys on the birth rate and sexuality carried out during the 1940s found that even a nominal adherence to Christianity correlated with larger families and a more restrictive approach to sexual behaviour.[64]

[59] A. Briggs, *The History of Broadcasting in the United Kingdom: Competition, 1955–1974* (1995), 338–9.

[60] G. M. Carstairs, *This Island Now: The B.B.C. Reith lectures 1962* (1963), 7.

[61] Ibid. 50.   [62] Briggs, *Broadcasting*, 332–4.

[63] J. A. T. Robinson, *Honest to God* (1963), 118.

[64] Mass-Observation, *Britain and her Birth Rate* (1945), 184–6. L. Stanley, *Sex Surveyed 1949–1994: From Mass Observation's 'Little Kinsey' to the National Survey and the Hite Reports* (1995), 73, 155.

Statements from within the Church probably affected a larger percentage of the population than is usually thought to be the case. *A Quaker View of Sex* (1963) was an attempt by a group of Quakers to formulate a new liberal Christian morality. The group commented on premarital sexual behaviour as follows:

When [teenagers]...meet the taboo against premarital intercourse they will often be given as the reason for this that the girl may have a baby, that they are in danger of venereal disease and that it is contrary to Christian morals. It does not take them long to discover that intelligent use of contraceptives, with which most adolescents are familiar anyway, usually (but certainly not always) avoids the first result, and minimises the second. On the third point [they]...do not accept that Christian morality has claims upon them.[65]

Although this quotation exaggerated adolescent familiarity with contraception, it is an example of a new acknowledgement that people were not behaving as it claimed they should. Statements, debates, and publications of this kind were important, not just because of what was said but because they exposed the lack of consensus amongst authorities. There was an erosion of moral authority, not just of Christian morality but of a consensus-based morality, seen as correct and upheld by society as a whole, the morality that ensured single women should not obtain contraception without any need to legislate that this should be so. In 1963, it was revealed that John Profumo, the Minister for War in the Conservative government, had lied in a statement to Parliament about his affair with a 19-year-old call girl who it was claimed was also sleeping with a Russian naval attaché. The ensuing scandal gave a huge push to the growing emphasis on the hypocrisy of the establishment and the need for a new, more open and honest morality.

The first substantial alteration in the theoretical construction of sexuality came with Alex Comfort's *Sex in Society*. This book had attracted little attention when it was first published in 1950. In 1963, when a revised edition was published, it had a considerable impact, caused in part by Comfort's appearance on a BBC television discussion programme defending premarital sex.[66] Canon Bentley was one of several prominent

---

[65] A. Heron, *Towards a Quaker View of Sex: An Essay by a Group of Friends* (1964), 17.
[66] A. Comfort, *The Joy of Sex* (1964; 1972). BBC TV discussion, 14 July 1963.

and traditionally conservative Anglicans who responded to what was then being called the 'new morality'. In 1965, he described Alex Comfort's ideas as follows:

When your son brings a girlfriend on a visit, will you say to your mother in law, 'Do take a tray of lemonade into the garden for Charles and Mary; they've been playing tennis all day,' and next morning in exactly the same tones, 'Do leave a tray down the passage for Charles and Mary; they've been playing sex all night'? This looks like Dr Comfort's hope because he tells us we ought to know that sex is the healthiest and most important human sport.[67]

Comfort made a greater contribution to the creation of a new discourse on heterosexual sexual mores than anyone else had done since Lawrence. The crucial difference was that Comfort did not believe, as Lawrence had done, that enduring love in the form of a monogamous heterosexual union legitimized sex. Rather, Comfort argued, sex was a physical pleasure like eating. People should indulge as much as they wished providing only that they were considerate of the feelings of other people and that they ensured no unwanted children were born. Canon Bentley went on to ask, 'can we actualise these hopes in the 1960s? Alas no; for the key to realising this ideal is a wholly foolproof form of contraception.'[68] Bentley evidently did not see the pill in this light, but many others, including Comfort himself, did.[69] Thus by 1965 there were debates on sexual mores occurring that, while theoretical, presented alternative ways of responding to actual choices and possibilities in the lives of young people.

One major effect of these debates when combined with extensive media coverage of the pill was that, for many girls during the 1960s, the idea of the pill was as important as the reality. Mary Ingham, a journalist, went back in the late 1970s and asked her entire class year of 11-plus grammar school girls, who were aged 20 by 1966, about growing up in the 1960s. She described the effect of the publicity given to the pill: 'Our generation was growing up with the knowledge that somewhere out there existed a contraceptive which promised you would be able to get away with it, in

---

[67] R. Sadler, R. S. Acland, and G. B. Bentley, *Sexual Morality: Three Views*, ed. C. L. Gough (1965), 21. See also A. Lunn and G. Lean, *The New Morality* (1964), 40–5.

[68] Sadler et al., *Morality*, 21.

[69] Comfort, *Joy*, 54.

the way only men had before.'[70] So there were alternative attitudes to that of sexual restraint and young women were aware of these choices. These grammar school girls were, of course, not typical of the population as a whole. But as more-educated, non-manual-class young women they were typical of the first unmarried pill takers. The refusal to give the pill to these young single women created a concrete issue on which the debates about sexual morality could be brought to bear. In the early 1960s there was increasing coverage in the press, in novels and plays, and on television of the distress and desperation an unwanted pregnancy created for single women. Unmarried mothers were believed to have personality problems or character disorders and treated accordingly.[71] Adoption caused many women lasting grief. In the three-year period 1958–60 there were eighty-two recorded deaths from illegal abortion and many more women were hospitalized or left with permanent damage.[72] Women were often willing to try anything once pregnant and were frequently terrified rather than unaware of the risks. The only acceptable outcome was that the woman should marry before the baby was born, but even in that case research had revealed that such marriages were more likely to break down.[73] This coverage made it obvious that unmarried women were having sexual intercourse and created a case for providing them with contraception.

The first birth control clinic in Britain openly and publicly set up for unmarried women was started in London in 1964 by Helen Brook, a banker's wife, who had been involved in family planning work since 1951.[74] No historical precedent existed for openly providing young unmarried women with the means to have sexual intercourse outside of marriage. In 1966, Brook said: 'Four years ago my hair would have stood on end if someone had said to me: "Give contraceptives to the young."

[70] M. Ingham, *Now we are Thirty: Women of the Breakthrough Generation* (1981), 89. See also C. Dix, *Say I'm Sorry to Mother* (1978), 86–7.

[71] e.g. V. Wimperis, *The Unmarried Mother and her Child* (1960), 93. See J. Lewis, H. Land, and K. E. Kiernan. *Lone Motherhood in Twentieth-Century Britain* (1998), 104.

[72] H. Arthure et al., *Report on Confidential Enquiries into Maternal Deaths in England and Wales 1967–1969*, Department of Health and Social Security Reports on Health and Social Subjects No. 1 (1972), 39.

[73] P. Ferris, *The Nameless* (1967), 42–3.

[74] Leathard, *Fight*, 139–41. *Birmingham Sunday Mercury* (18 Sept. 1966), *Daily Telegraph* (17 Dec. 1964).

Today I still wake up in a sweat sometimes at night and wonder how I came to take this responsibility.'[75] The clinics were constantly accused of encouraging promiscuity.[76] Helen Brook's response to this accusation was as follows:

I think that is a lot of nonsense. If you are promiscuous this is the sort of clinic you need. You are the one who most needs to be helped and guarded. If a girl is promiscuous, you have got to ask why. Promiscuity is a sign of some sort of disturbance. They are the ones who need the most love and the most help.[77]

All young women who came to the clinic received what Brook and the clinic doctors repeatedly referred to as psychiatric counselling. This was taken very seriously.[78] This first Brook clinic was a tiny operation. Only 564 cases were seen in that first year during which over 63,000 illegitimate births occurred.[79] Thus, the historical significance of the Brook clinics lies in the role they played in legitimizing the open public provision of contraception to young women and in shaping the developing public discourse on the issue. In mid-1965, a committee was set up to open a clinic in Birmingham. The spokesman, Martin Cole, a geneticist and member of Abortion Law Reform Campaign, explained his reasons for setting up clinics for the unmarried:

There are two chief reasons. Firstly, the need to stem the appalling tide of illegitimate births. Secondly, to produce a society which will allow young people to enjoy sexual experience free of feelings of guilt and disease. Most people start with the idea that sex is basically undesirable and is only allowable within certain circumstances—for example—within marriage. I start with the opposite idea—that sex is desirable and should only be discouraged where there is lack of sex education, where there is disease or a likelihood of someone being hurt or exploited.[80]

In the context of the existing discourse on birth control, these statements were shocking. Martin Cole did not regard female promiscuity as evidence of neurosis in the way that society, including the Brook clinic and the majority of FPA workers, did. The transition can be understood as that

---

[75] *Birmingham Sunday Mercury* (18 Sept. 1966). [76] e.g. *Birmingham Post* (29 Nov. 1965).
[77] *Birmingham Sunday Mercury* (18 Sept. 1966).
[78] *Observer* (6 Feb. 1967). *New Society* (2 Mar. 1967).
[79] Brook Annual Report 1964/5. [80] *Birmingham Post* (30 Nov. 1965).

from a Lawrentian view of sexual intercourse as legitimized by love between two people and only by that, to Alex Comfort's idea of sex as sport. To Cole sex was merely a desirable activity, which, like sport, did not need the sanction of the law, religion, or love. The new approach taken by Cole certainly did not dampen down controversy. The Birmingham clinic met considerable resistance and, although they proved to be unneeded, there were police in attendance at the first session in 1966. This apparently general debate about access to contraception was increasingly about access to the pill. Young women preferred the pill and, as their confidence grew, they rejected the advice given by the Brook and FPA doctors who wanted them to use diaphragms. The vast majority of GPs preferred to prescribe the pill, in any event.[81] The word pill was frequently used in the press as a synonym for contraception and vice versa by the early 1970s.

From 1966, there was an expansion of government provision of contraception. This is discussed in detail in the following two chapters; however, at this point it is relevant that there was no discrimination on grounds of marital status. In 1968, the FPA finally gave their branches permission to provide contraception for unmarried women, and from 1970 they were required to make provision. In this five-year period, the Labour government passed a wave of liberalizing social legislation that affected the lives of individuals. This included the Sexual Offences Act 1966, which made male homosexual acts between consenting adults legal; the Equal Pay Act; two Race Relations Acts in 1965 and 1968; the removal of theatre censorship; and divorce law reform in 1969. These reforms enabled a wide range of people to take actions they saw as improving their quality of life, or dissuaded others from preventing them from doing so. Abortion law reform also took place in this period. The 1967 Act was greatly influenced by the BMA, and the Royal College of Obstetricians and Gynaecologists, who believed that it would not result in a greater number of abortions being performed and explicitly rejected any extension of female sexual

---

[81] There were concerns about the impact of the pill on young women, and their experience with earlier generations of women led clinic doctors to believe that diaphragms helped women accept their genitals; see Lay workers' leaflet on oral contraception 1961, SA/FPA/A5/124 Wellcome Trust Medical Archives. Brook Annual Report 1966, 49. Brook Annual Report 1969, 18. Cartwright, *Parents*, 239. Vaughan, *Pill*, 88.

autonomy.[82] In practice, the Act has been crucial in enabling women to prevent unwanted births, but reliance on a combination of abortion and male-controlled methods would still have meant women were subject to very different sexual constraints from men, as revealed in the sexual cultures of Japan and Eastern Europe, where this remained true until the 1990s.[83] In the late 1960s, it appeared to many people that the pill meant men and women were now on equal terms. Many women's comments on their experience at this time still reflect the intense optimism with which people greeted news of the pill in the late 1950s.

In reports towards the end of the 1960s, comments from young women reveal a growing sense of confidence. A 1969 article on middle-class 'flat sharers' described a young woman who shared 'a £15-a-week flat in Fulham with two other girls and, more often than not, her boyfriend' whom she had met at a party two years earlier and had been sleeping with ever since. The journalist quoted her as follows: ' "It was the first time", she says. "I suddenly got scared that I would end up putting too much value on my virginity. . . . It would break my mother's heart if she knew I was on the pill." She added, "I suppose I'm happier today than I've ever been." '[84] There were also reports which showed some women gaining a much needed control over their own fertility. A 19-year-old girl wrote: 'My boyfriend would not use contraceptives, so I lived in constant fear of becoming pregnant. Our engagement did not work out . . . I often thank God I took the pill or I could be either an unmarried mother or the victim of a shotgun wedding.'[85] Even in these brief comments women reveal the direct role that effective contraception and consequent protection from pregnancy played in diminishing the extent of control that men or parents could exercise over young women. Continued limits on access to contraception and abortion, the difficulties of resisting male pressure and knowing one's own desires, have all been emphasized by previous

---

[82] V Greenwood and J. Young, *Abortion in Demand* (1976), 31.

[83] S. Coleman, *Family Planning in Japanese Society: Traditional Birth Control in a Modern Urban Culture* (1983), 5, 162.

[84] *Sunday Express* (27 Apr. 1969).

[85] *Sun* (20 Jan. 1969). See also *People* (28 Sept. 1969). Carter, 'Truly' 209–16. Dix, *Say*, 84–103. Ingham, *Now*. J. (pseud.). 'Unwomanly and Unnatural', in Maitland (ed.), *Heaven*, 149–52. S. Rowbotham, ' "Diary in the Life of Sheila Rowbotham," From *Red Rag* 1968', in *Dreams and Dilemmas: Collected Writings* (1983). L. Segal, *Straight Sex: The Politics of Pleasure* (1994), ch. 1.

historians.[86] Yet, though the euphoria did not last long, there were very substantial improvements for women in all these aspects of their lives in this period.

These quotations were published only a few months before the first substantial health warning about the pill in December of 1969. This occurred as a result of research which showed that there was a substantially increased risk of thrombosis or blood clots in women taking oral contraceptive formulations containing high doses of the hormone oestrogen. The Ministry of Health withdrew eleven of the twenty-nine brands available from the market and the national press responded with extensive coverage. The resulting short-term drop in use merely slowed sales which continued rising until 1976. After the initial fright the response of many women to the major and life-threatening side effects seems to have been that the risk was worth it in exchange for freedom from the nagging anxiety that fear of pregnancy produced. Many were already enduring the range of minor side effects, including nausea, headaches, and loss of sexual desire, which were a common response to pills containing high doses of oestrogen. Two-thirds of all pills prescribed in 1963 contained over 70 μg of oestrogen. By 1973, less than 2.5 per cent did, and dosages continued to fall.[87]

THE PACE OF CHANGE

The pace of change in the second half of the 1960s was astonishing. By the late 1960s, many of those who wanted a new sexual morality felt able to talk openly about wanting sex before (and a different approach after) marriage, instead of claiming they were being forced into providing a solution to a difficult social problem. In 1969, Dr R. W. Kind, the school medical officer for Leicestershire, who was writing a series of books on sex education, told the *Sunday Telegraph* that he found himself 'continually

---

[86] Benn and Richardson, 'Uneasy Freedom'. A. Coote and B. Campbell, *Sweet Freedom: The Struggle for Women's Liberation* (1982), 223–7. Lewis, *Women*, 55. E. Wilson, *Only Halfway to Paradise: Women in Post-War Britain, 1945–1968* (1980), 98.

[87] M. Thorogood and M. P. Vessey, 'Trends in Use of Oral Contraceptives in Britain', *British Journal of Family Planning*, 16 (1990).

overtaken by the speed of change'. 'If you'd come out two years ago with a statement that there may be perfectly good grounds for pre-marital or extra-marital sexual experience, it would have been fairly dramatic,... A year ago it wouldn't have mattered. Today it wouldn't be noticed.'[88] Sex became more visible in a variety of ways. In 1960, pubic hair could not be legally shown in magazines. By 1970, naked actors were simulating sex on stage in *Oh! Calcutta!*, an erotic revue by theatre critic Kenneth Tynan, and, while the vast majority of the population did not see either pornographic magazines or theatre shows, this was reported extensively by the press. The explicit physical sexual content of films, television plays, and popular music greatly increased from the mid-1960s.[89] In 1960, the Top Twenty song charts were dominated by anodyne pop songs such as 'Itsy Bitsy Teeny Weeny Yellow Polka Dot Bikini'. By 1965, songs such as 'It's my Life' by the Animals were telling the older generation where to go, while 'Satisfaction' by the Rolling Stones mixed sexual desire with anti-commercialism.[90] By the early 1970s, it was said that real and substantial change had occurred. In mid-1971, a leader in *The Times* said, '[t]here has undoubtedly been a revolution in sexual attitudes over recent years, and there is a good deal of evidence to suggest a corresponding revolution in sexual behaviour'.[91] This was not what Helen Brook and her generation of family planners had intended to have happen. Many of these people were defending changes about which they were feeling increasingly ambivalent.[92] By 1971, it was becoming obvious that providing contraception for the unmarried was not having the intended effect. Well-publicized government statistics showed that although the actual number of illegitimate births was falling from 1967, the overall number of births was falling even faster, so the rate of illegitimacy remained almost stable, while the number of now legal abortions performed on single women increased rapidly.[93] Promiscuity also appeared to be rising as young women's sexual

---

[88] *Sunday Telegraph* (30 Dec. 1969).

[89] See Lord Longford, *Pornography: The Longford Report* (1972). M. Tomkinson, *The Pornbrokers: The Rise of the Soho Sex Barons* (1982).

[90] T. Jasper, *The Top Twenty Book: The Official British Record Charts, 1955–1983* (1983), 53, 112–13.

[91] *The Times* (16 June 1971).

[92] *Observer* (18 July 1971).

[93] e.g. *Bristol Evening Post* (19 Jan. 1967). *Daily Record (Glasgow)* (30 Jan. 1968).

behaviour became less covert and more visible. The development of new arguments revealed the major shifts that had taken place.

Those defending use of the pill shifted their ground. Promiscuity, hitherto undefined, was examined in more detail. In 1972, the *Sunday Times* reported on a study in which 3,000 women who suffered unwanted pregnancies were interviewed and then divided into four classes: permanent cohabitees; people in stable liaisons (anything over three months); temporary relationships (under three months or undefined), and lastly 'those who had disordered casual sex with a variety of partners'.[94] Only the last group, women who tended not to use contraception, was identified as promiscuous. This enabled Joan Lambert, the author of the study, to assert that 'the facts of contraception at the moment are that *the more promiscuous you are, the less likely you are to be on the pill*' (italics in original).[95] In the 1950s, all of these women would have been considered immoral and all of those not in permanent relationships would have been considered promiscuous. The fact that such an argument could be put forward in a major serious newspaper was an indication of the degree of change that had taken place by the early 1970s. Those arguing against contraception and the liberalization of sexual mores ceased referring to 'the unmarried' and 'pre-marital sex', they shifted to 'girls' or 'schoolgirls' and focused on the age at which sex took place. A 1974 headline in the *Times Educational Supplement* summed up the fears that were being expressed: 'Young teenagers and the pill, the assault on childhood.'[96] The use of non-gendered terms such as teenagers or schoolchildren is frequently revealed by the context to refer solely to girls, as was the case with use of the phrase 'the unmarried' ten years previously. Paul Ferris, a journalist and writer, commented in 1971 that the 'old argument for contraception, that "anything is better than unwanted pregnancies," has moved down the age-scale until now it can be respectably applied to any woman of about 19 and above. With single girls who are younger than this, it begins to meet the controversy about "teenage immorality." '[97] By the mid-1970s, this was the only remaining issue on the basis of which pressure could be applied. The percentage of girls who were having sex under 16, the legal

---

[94] *Sunday Times* (27 Feb. 1972).   [95] Ibid.

[96] *Times Educational Supplement* (1 Nov. 1974). See also *Daily Express* (12 Oct. 1971).

[97] *Observer* (18 July 1971).

age of consent, was small but growing.[98] The debate regarding 'young' girls, contraception, and sexual activity has continued into the twenty-first century.

To sum up the process: for the best part of a century, contraception had been a matter of self-help. After nearly half a century of pressure the government and the market were still being dragged slowly and reluctantly into the supply of advice and devices. By the end of the 1950s, sexual liberalization was producing rising fertility, and young married and unmarried people were looking for a way out of the dilemma this created. The methods the English had chosen, withdrawal and condoms, diminished sexual pleasure and left women dependent on male control of fertility. When the pill was introduced in 1961, illegitimacy was rising to new heights and the drug became an essential element in debates about changing sexual mores. A new generation, aided by a reformist Labour government, then ensured that when change came, it came with a bang. From 1965 to 1969, there was a transformation of sexual mores. This happened as a result of supplying contraception to women publicly and solely for the purpose of sexual pleasure, indeed explicitly to prevent reproduction. The next two chapters look first at political change and the erosion of female deference in this period, and then at the statistical evidence supporting this claim.

[98] See K. Wellings, J. Field, A. M. Johnson, J. Wadsworth, and S. Bradshaw, *Sexual Attitudes and Lifestyles* (1994), table 4.4, 74. The data is presented in the form of age at interview cohorts, but approximately 10% of those aged 16 1971–5 had intercourse before 16 years, increased from 8.6% aged 16 from 1966–70, and 5.8% in the early 1960s.

14

Population Control or 'Sex on the Rates'?
Political Change 1955–1975

Between 1955 and 1975, the British government moved from being almost wholly uninvolved in the provision of contraception to free provision of contraception to all women and men regardless of age or marital status. In 1977, Audrey Leathard described the campaigns and the expansion in services, and in 1976 Gillian Walt examined family planning policy-making at local and government level.[1] These two writers accepted unquestioningly the value of what had been and was being achieved by the Family Planning Association (FPA) and other similar groups. They tell a tale of well-intentioned progress towards the light. However, Jeffrey Weeks asserted in 1981 that it was right-wing fears of population growth and support for eugenics that led to the provision of birth control on the NHS. Elizabeth Wilson suggested in 1977 that a 'view of the Pill as a method of controlling young women has indeed gained ground'.[2] These Marxist historians present a grim narrative of shifting control. This interpretation is not grounded in an accurate representation of the events or the changes in women's lives yet it is this interpretation which has largely been followed. For example, Jane Lewis commented in 1992 that '[i]n regard to sexual autonomy it may be argued that there has been no slackening in government's determination to regulate women's sexual behaviour'.[3] In

[1] A. Leathard, *The Fight for Family Planning: The Development of Family Planning Services in Britain, 1921–74* (1980). G. Walt, 'Policy Making in Britain: A Comparative Study of Fluoridation and Family Planning, 1960–1974' (D.Phil. thesis, 1976).

[2] J. Weeks, *Sex, Politics and Society: The Regulation of Sexuality since 1800* (1981; 1989), 259. E. Wilson, *Women and the Welfare State* (1977), 69.

[3] J. Lewis, *Women in Britain since 1945* (1992), 95.

fact exactly the opposite took place: there was an unprecedented retreat from government and community attempts to control women's behaviour and an erosion of female deference.

POPULATION CONTROL

Interpretations of the role played by the growing debate on population control are central to the difference between these two versions of change. From the late 1950s the popular press relayed the increasing knowledge of world population growth in the most graphic form: 'THE GREATEST MENACE OF ALL . . . A NEW "BOMB"—more dangerous than an H-bomb —is threatening the world. It is the "POPULATION BOMB"' (capitals in original).[4] The concept of the population explosion gave birth control huge importance, while placing it in a sphere of scientific, depersonalized concerns separate from sex and morality.[5] Proponents argued that improvements in modern Western medicine had led to a massive increase in the human population, with which food production could not keep up—as Thomas Malthus had predicted—and famine, for which the West was responsible, would result. It was now selfish to resist the use of birth control rather than selfish to wish to limit one's family. This gave private behaviour a public dimension and provided opportunities to speculate about the pill, a daringly sexual topic in the late 1950s, in the press.[6] There are two questions it would be useful to answer before looking specifically at Britain and the relationship of support for population control to improvements in birth control provision. First, was international population growth a problem as was claimed? Secondly, what did those in developing countries feel about the birth control programmes they

[4] *Sunday Pictorial* (24 July 1960).

[5] *Women's Sunday Mirror* (14 Apr. 1957). Other examples of the concept of death control: *New Statesman* (6 Nov. 1965). *Sunday Pictorial* (7 Oct. 1959). *Sunday Pictorial* (18 Nov. 1959). Letter from J. Yudkin, *The Times* (1 Oct. 1963). E. Brooks, MP, PP *Hansard*, National Health Service (Family Planning) Bill 1967, 6th series, House of Commons, vol. 741, cols. 936–7.

[6] e.g. Review of BBC Brains Trust, J. Huxley supporting Dr W. G. Walter, 'the hope of the world lies in a pill', *Birmingham Sunday Mercury* (10 Dec. 1961). *Universe* (31 Oct. 1958). *Women's Sunday Mirror* (22 Aug. 1958). *Women's Sunday Mirror* (28 Apr. 1957). *Women's Mirror* (22 Aug. 1958).

received? The results of international population conferences provide one way to briefly chart the answers to these questions.

Prior to the 1940s, the recent and dramatic changes in areas like fertility, mortality, and immigration in the West had absorbed the attention of the small number of researchers with interests and skills in demography.[7] The first international meeting on population in Rome in 1954 focused on Western countries and demographic techniques. By 1965, at the second conference in Belgrade, the focus had shifted to the underdeveloped countries.[8] Both meetings warned of an upcoming surge of world population, which has since occurred. In the 1960s, the USA and other nations launched a multilateral effort to provide family planning services or population programmes in developing countries. Following the failure of voluntary measures there was increasing use of programmes employing rewards to persuade supposedly ill-informed local people to accept sterilization or IUDs and discussion of possible coercive measures.[9] Strong criticism of these population programmes emerged at the first United Nations World Population Conference, in 1974. The industrialized nations called for measures to control population growth, but the developing nations urged greater attention to economic problems, arguing that 'development is the best contraceptive'. In the USA, the discovery of the life-threatening side effects of the pill and medical arrogance had radicalized the emerging women's health organizations in the early 1970s, encouraging strong feminist opposition to birth control programmes.[10] This was reinforced by the increasing awareness of the use of sterilization without consent on vulnerable groups throughout much of the twentieth century.

However, by 1984 most developing countries at the Mexico City Conference had concluded that population growth did create problems that could not be solved simply by economic growth and that access to birth control was necessary. By the 1994 International Conference on Population and Development in Cairo, research, much of it feminist inspired,

[7] D. V. Glass, introd., in D. V. Glass and D. E. Eversley (eds.), *Population in History* (1965).
[8] *World Population Conference, Second, Belgrade, 1965* (1966).
[9] L. Gordon, *Woman's Body, Woman's Right: A Social History of Birth Control in America* (1976), 398, 401, 461.
[10] L. Grant, *Sexing the Millennium* (1993), 185. Gordon, *Woman's Body*, 401–2. B. Seaman, *The Doctors' Case against the Pill* (1970). E. R. Watkins, *On the Pill: A Social History of Oral Contraceptives in America, 1950–1970* (1998), ch. 5.

into the experience of women in developing countries had revealed that improving female access to education, resources, and opportunity is vital to achieving low fertility rates.[11] There was strong criticism of quantitative programme targets and the final conference document emphasized that these were unnecessary. Research showed that if birth control was made available to women and men who wanted it but were currently unable to obtain it this would bring down population growth to sustainable levels. The key issue in making judgements about the provision of birth control is whether people, especially women, can make voluntary and individual decisions or if coercion is being used, in however subtle a fashion. From this brief overview, it can be seen that concerns about the issue of population growth did not merely reflect an ideological debate occurring within wealthy societies. Criticism has contributed towards creating programmes that are sensitive to local needs and are not coercive. Voluntary access to contraception for women in the developing world was, and is, as important in improving their lives as had been the case for women in Western nations earlier in the twentieth century.

The approach of British historians to population control has followed the lead taken by historians such as the American feminist Linda Gordon, reflecting the negative opinions expressed by developing countries in 1974 and the international history of the pre-Second World War eugenics movement.[12] This is a distorting lens through which to view the relationship between the British birth control movement and population control in 1950s and 1960s Britain, or indeed eugenics in Britain full stop, as the movement had little or no success in this country. Attempts to introduce a law providing for sterilization on grounds of mental deficiency in 1913 failed.[13] Many of the doctors and scientists involved in the birth control movement supported eugenics[14] but, for example, Marie Stopes's eugenic

[11] *Population and Women: Proceedings of the United Nations Expert Group Meeting on Population and Women, Gaborone, Botswana, 22–26 June 1992* (1996). See also S. Jejeebhoy, *Women's Education, Autonomy, and Reproductive Behaviour: Experience from Developing Countries* (1995).

[12] e.g. L. V. Marks, *Sexual Chemistry: A History of the Contraceptive Pill* (2001), ch. 1.

[13] J. Macnicol, 'The Voluntary Sterilisation Campaign in Britain, 1918–1939', *Journal of the History of Sexuality*, 2/3 (1992), 422–38.

[14] e.g. Female Eugenics Society Fellows included; Dr J. Malleson, Dr E. Mears, M. Pyke, Dr Helena Wright. Jean Medawar's husband Peter Medawar was a member. Opposed to eugenics were Lella Secor Florence and Enid Charles.

beliefs did not result in differential treatment of women in her mothers' clinics for birth control.[15] Furthermore, although eugenics was a major strand within late nineteenth- and twentieth-century middle- and upper-class thought, these ideas had no discernible impact upon birth rates or other aspects of sexual behaviour.[16] Although, the tiny number of clinics played an important role in legitimizing use of birth control, the actual lowering of fertility was achieved through working-class self-help. With-drawal, which was rejected by the birth control movement, remained the method used by the majority until the 1950s. Rising birth rates in the 1950s did briefly coincide with desires for an increase in population but this is not evidence of a causal link.[17] There is no evidence that, at any point in nineteenth- and twentieth-century England, birth rates responded to the desires of eugenicists or population controllers.

The FPA did accept financial support from the British Eugenics Society, but they successfully held the organization at arm's length. The historian of eugenics, Richard Soloway, has commented that by the 1970s heredi-tarian class-oriented eugenicists must have wondered why the Eugenics Society had invested so much in the birth control movement.[18] In 1963, they specifically stated in a letter to the *Observer* that the 'FPA has never advocated limitation of family size in the *national* interest' (italics in original).[19] The FPA also rejected use of coercive measures. From the 1950s, birth control supporters, including the FPA, did employ arguments for population control to further their interest in ensuring birth control was widely available to individual women internationally as well as in Britain.[20] Population control enabled them to talk about birth control without raising moral, sexual, or women's rights issues. By the late 1960s,

[15] D. A. Cohen, 'Private Lives in Public Spaces: Marie Stopes, The Mother's Clinics and the Practice of Contraception', *History Workshop*, 35 (1993).

[16] For an analysis of the impact of pro-natal policies, see D. V. Glass, *Population Policies and Movements in Europe* (1940). P. McDonald, 'Gender Equity, Social Institutions and the Future of Fertility', *Journal of Population Research* (Australia), 17/1 (2000).

[17] See P. M. Thane, 'The Debate on the Declining Birth Rate in Britain; The "Menace" of an Ageing Population, 1920s–1950s', *Continuity and Change* (1990).

[18] R. A. Soloway, *Demography and Degeneration: Eugenics and the Declining Birth Rate in Twentieth-Century Britain* (1990), 360.

[19] *Observer* (5 Dec. 1963). Also see *Guardian* (10 Aug. 1972).

[20] For an Indian perspective on family planning in this era, see D. Rama Rau, *An Inheritance: The Memoirs of Dhanvanthi Rama Rau* (1978).

birth control had been transformed from an issue concerning individuals and sexuality into the solution for an international problem. This helped create a climate in which it was seen as appropriate for birth control to be supplied by local authorities or the NHS, rather than paid for by individuals. For example, a group of individuals who had been involved in abortion law reform formed the Birth Control Campaign in 1971 especially to push for free NHS services. They saw themselves as 'women's rights campaigners' but they realized that concern for population could be used to further the development of services, while concern for women would not be effective.[21] In the press by the 1970s the label of population control was sometimes used even when referring to the use of birth control by individual women to fulfil their own needs: '[T]o be really effective our thinking on population control must go deeper... With Women's Lib we have seen the beginnings of a social revolution in Western Society. Complete equality in a career or profession coupled with the Pill can develop an independent woman who does not need an early marriage, or more than one or two babies to bring interest into her life.'[22]

There were many people whose concern about international overpopulation was part of a commitment to social justice and equity. They espoused the notion that wealthier nations have a duty to poorer countries and addressed the issue of racism within the UK: '[Family planning] is a vital part of any sensible policy of development... There is a simple moral duty to help those so much poorer than ourselves... How can we, a multi-racial society, expect to solve our domestic problems, unless we play a constructive part in a multi-racial world?'[23] It was unusual to find writers acknowledging Britain's responsibility for any problems abroad and the attitudes expressed were paternalistic, but, from this perspective, support for international population control did imply a financial contribution from Britain. Many Conservatives rejected the suggestion that Britain should contribute financially, or indeed in any other way, to less developed nations. The *Daily Telegraph* suggested that, although the underdeveloped world had to worry about overpopulation, that was not Britain's problem.[24] Mrs Jill Knight, a Conservative MP, simply ignored the international

[21] Leathard, *Fight*, 186.   [22] *Cambridge Evening News*, 27 June 1974.
[23] *Observer* (19 Oct. 1969). *Financial Times* (9 May 1973).   [24] *Daily Telegraph* (7 Jan. 1972).

dimension in favour of encouraging racism at home: 'People are looking at the problem of over population far too simply . . . There is also the problem of immigration. I am in favour of stopping all immigration to this country.'[25] Anxiety about the growth of the black population in Britain strongly reinforced racist support for population control in the late 1960s and 1970s. Some supporters of population control believed that the state should use coercive measures to enforce population targets. Examples that appeared in the press include a statement from the Greater London Young Conservatives: 'Steps should be taken to encourage voluntary limitation of family size, [if not] . . . it is our belief that in ten years time it will be necessary to introduce compulsory control.'[26] As this survey of the press coverage reveals, supporters of population control were motivated by a variety of concerns in this period. The range of conflicting reasons for supporting population control across the political spectrum was what made the provision of birth control by the NHS politically conceivable.

LEGISLATIVE CHANGE: 'SEX ON THE RATES'

In February 1966, Kenneth Robinson, the Labour Minister of Health, who was a long-time supporter of birth control and the legalization of abortion, sent out a circular to all local authorities (LAs) encouraging them to use their existing limited powers to support family planning. Circular 5/66 requested that local health authorities should make provision for free treatment for 'the benefit of women to whom pregnancy would be detrimental to health', and undertake full responsibility for publicizing the places and times of voluntary clinics.[27] The National Health Service Amendment (Family Planning) Act, which followed in 1967, gave permis-

---

[25] *Guardian* (10 Aug. 1972). See also *Sunday Pictorial* (18 Nov. 1959).

[26] *Evening Standard* (18 Oct. 1971).

[27] Ministry of Health, 'Family Planning' Circular 5/66, London, 17 Feb. 1966. reprinted in *Family Planning*,15/1(1966). The 118 local authority clinics and a small number of existing hospital clinics were still operating on the basis of a Ministry of Health Memo of 1930, which allowed birth control advice only to married women where further pregnancy would be detrimental to health. Memo 153/MCW, Ministry of Health, London, July 1930. Reprinted officially, Mar. 1931. For clinic numbers see F. Lafitte, *Family Planning in the Sixties: The Report of the Family Planning Association Working Party* (1963), chs. 3.1, 4.5.

sion for LA contraceptive provision to be expanded from medical grounds only to social criteria and placed no restrictions such as age or marital status upon eligibility. This meant that LAs could provide contraceptive services for unmarried women and for married women who simply did not want a child, not just for those married women whose health would be endangered by further pregnancies. The 1949 Royal Commission on Population had recommended that contraception be included in the NHS and suggestions were made during the debates on the 1967 bill that supplies should be free of charge, as advice was to be. This was rejected, as it was felt that the mandatory provision of 'sex on the rates' would arouse strong opposition. However, once the 1967 bill received royal assent, LAs could legally provide contraception free if they chose to do so, and a series of battles between the supporters of free contraception and their opponents commenced in council chambers throughout Britain.

Supporters saw the opposition to local authority provision of birth control advice and appliances as a conservative fear of sex, and treated it as a Freudian subconscious resistance. The opponents of free contraception were seen as responding 'emotionally' as opposed to the rationality of those arguing the case for birth control. For example, the *Report on the Family Planning Association* (1963) gave a list of conflicts 'which produce in the individual emotional barriers of great and often unsuspected strength, to the reasoned adoption of birth control'.[28] More polemically, the controversial sex educator Martin Cole suspected 'that with some persons more vociferous it would be a matter of sour grapes. "I didn't have sex when I was young, so why should the younger generation have it?" They don't realise it because it is deep down in the subconscious.'[29] Yet, in fact, 'sex on the rates' (or on the taxes) *was* what was being demanded when free contraception was called for. In the 1972–3 parliamentary debates which are described below, the Conservative MP Elaine Kellet Bowman said that the 'best form of oral contraceptive is, as it has always been, the perfectly simple word "No" ' and this was repeated by Conservative MP Dame Joan Vickers.[30] Rejection of the underlying beliefs expressed by this statement

[28] Lafitte, *Family Planning*, appendix 5.13–14.

[29] *Birmingham Post* (30 Nov. 1965).

[30] *Hansard*, Parliamentary Debates, National Health Service Reorganization Bill, 6th series, House of Commons (1973), vol. 853, cols. 1018, 1188.

diverts attention from the fact that it was, and is, correct. While birth control enables women to engage more fully in a wide range of other activities, as well as heterosexual sexual intercourse, saying no to sexual intercourse is a totally effective method of achieving this end. Many of the people arguing against LAs paying for contraception had themselves lived lives in which values such as self-control and restraint were paramount and they did not see why others, particularly the unmarried, should not do the same. The results of widespread provision of contraception have been what those opposed to it claimed would be the case: greater promiscuity and the breakdown of the family, as they understood it. These people were seeing a way of living, or, as they described it, a society, which they believed in, being irreversibly altered by the new technology of contraception. We should not condescend to them by continuing to deny that their fears were accurate: as E. P. Thompson wrote, 'Their aspirations were valid in terms of their own experience; and if they were casualties of history, they remain, condemned in their own lives, as casualties.'[31]

In 1958 the Lambeth Conference of Anglican Bishops had given firm approval to birth control, leaving the Catholic Church as the only major denomination which specifically opposed the use of so-called artificial birth control (Pope Pius IX had given approval to the use of abstinence and the rhythm method in 1930).[32] Catholics influenced the public approach to birth control in the post-Second World War period in part because many Catholics felt a duty to act against the spread of contraception.[33] Resistance to the 1967 Amendment had been muted because the Catholic opposition was divided internationally by the pill, and distracted nationally by the Abortion Law Reform Act passed the same year. Until the Papal Encyclical *Humanae Vitae* on 25 July 1968, there appeared a strong possibility that papal approval might be given to the pill. Only 8 per cent of the population were Catholic in 1960, but 22 per cent of the BMA were, and, although actual percentages are not available, there was also a sizeable and vocal Catholic

---

[31]   E. P. Thompson, *The Making of the English Working-Class* (1980), 12.

[32]   *Family Planning*, 7/3 (1958). The Anglican position was shared by the other main religious groupings. See Leathard, *Fight*, 96. *Daily Mail* (7 Sept. 1962). *Newcastle Evening Chronicle* (16 June 1962). *Peterborough Citizen* (19 Jan. 1973). Pope Pius XI, Papal Encyclical *Casti Connubii*, 1930.

[33]   e.g. Catholic MP for Brighton Pavilion, Mr Teeling, in *Family Planning*, 8/3 (1959) 5.

presence on local councils and in Parliament.[34] It was widely felt that it was improper to discuss contraception or other sexual issues in public and that to do so would encourage sexual immorality. Frequently criticism of the FPA or of the pill made by Catholics was not identified as such because criticism of the religious beliefs of others was seen as discourteous. A 1963 column by Katherine Whitehorn in the *Observer* objected to Catholic pressure against FPA activities. She commented on the response to the column, 'that an article so tame, so careful, so measured should have caused such a furore just shows how silent everyone usually is on the subject'.[35] That the furore occurred was itself a sign of change.

The Irish distributor of the newspaper refused to print the column and also demanded that the *Observer* not report this in the English editions, although the editor refused to accept the latter demand.[36] Such censorship was an important source of indirect Catholic influence. British newspapers and magazines were sold in Ireland and were subject to the strict Irish censorship of birth control coverage, including mention of the FPA. In 1956, the four British women's papers with a large circulation were said to be 'afraid to print anything which would affect their Irish circulation although this was tiny compared to the general circulation'.[37] Many dailies started to print special Irish editions but the contraceptive researcher John Peel was told in 1963 that 'newspapers charge more for contraceptive ads because of the cost of removing the ads "from our Eire edition" '.[38] It is probable that editorial content that would cause problems in Ireland was considered not worth the trouble by most newspapers unless particularly newsworthy. By the second half of the 1960s, as discussion of contraception became a public matter, religious influence was acknowledged and challenged. The following exchange took place during the debate on the 1967 National Health Service (Family Planning) Bill:

[34] J. Peel, 'Contraception and the Medical Profession', *Population Studies*, 18 (1964), 145.

[35] K. Whitehorn, 'Catholics and Birth Control', *Family Planning*, 13/1 (1964), 7.

[36] Ibid. 6.

[37] Internal FPA Memo, notes from lunch with the *Women's Sunday Mirror* production manager, 31 Jan. 1956. The four 'papers' were the *Woman*, *Woman's Own*, *Woman's Weekly*, *Women's Illustrated*. SA/FPA/A17/94 Wellcome Trust Medical Archive. See also P. Makin, *The Evelyn Home Story* (1975), 142–3.

[38] J. Peel, 'The Manufacture and Retailing of Contraceptives in England', *Population Studies*, 17 (1963), 124.

Mr Bernard Braine: . . . I know from my own constituency experience that this is a subject which arouses intense feeling in certain quarters. The idea that free contraceptives might be supplied on the rates to unmarried as well as to married people for social reasons. Mr Houghton: What about religious education on the rates? Mr Braine: I am not arguing about that. Mr Houghton: Let us have it out. These certain quarters are religious quarters. Mr Braine: . . . I agree with the hon. Gentleman that here we are in the realm of prejudice as well as deeply-held feelings.[39]

Mr Houghton's 'Let us have it out' reflected a new openness that was rapidly becoming less tame, careful, and measured. This new attitude was of major importance in the changes taking place by the late 1960s.[40] This openness reflected the gulf that had opened up between what could be said about birth control in public and its increasingly routine use in private. Twenty years previously the level within the population of private discomfort and unease about sexuality and uncertainty as to the morality of birth control was too high for supporters to be so confident.[41]

Over the five years following the 1967 legislation, those opposing local body provision of contraception on moral grounds were rapidly left behind. Such people ceased to be a serious opposition and became the stuff of which the comedy series *Monty Python's Flying Circus* was made. The argument about population growth and the attendant need for action was one rhetorical strategy used to shift the debate in such a way that concerns about self-restraint and chastity appeared trivial. For example, in a debate on contraceptive provision, Cheshire County Councillor Bryan Leck said, 'I am also conscious of the terrible consequences that failure to make use of knowledge available to medical science will entail to future generations if attempts are not made to control the rising popula-

[39] *Hansard*, Parliamentary Debates, Official Report, Standing Committee H, National Health Service (Family Planning) Bill. vol. xi (26 Apr. 1967) cols. 117–18. Other examples: MP P. Jackson said, 'Theology won in Bootle.' The Labour-dominated LA rejected a grant for the FPA because of religious influence. *Hansard*, Parliamentary Debates, 6th series, House of Commons, vol. 741, (17 Feb. 1967), col. 1010. K. Robinson asked E. Powell, 'Is it not time that the Minister ceased to be intimidated by a religious minority', *Hansard*, Parliamentary Debates, 6th Series, House of Commons, vol. 659 (14 May 1962), cols. 910–11.

[40] e.g. *The Times* (3 July 1959). *Birmingham Sunday Mercury* (10 Dec. 1961). *Daily Mail* (9 July 1962).

[41] G. Rowntree and R. M. Pierce, 'Birth Control in Britain: Part One' *Population Studies*, 15/1 (1961), 10.

tion that threatens to engulf the world's capacity to sustain it.'[42] The county council agreed unanimously to adopt a free birth control service for all, at an annual cost of £66,000. The other main strategy was to claim that free contraception would save money for the local authority. This financial argument was of considerable importance in persuading authorities to fund family planning programmes. Gillian Walt undertook a case study of LA family planning policy in Birmingham in the early 1970s. The multifaceted nature of the support for population control was evident. The Conservative chairman of the Birmingham Health Committee was very happy to explain to Walt that he had been alarmed by the arrival of Kenyan Asians in 1968, and that it was concern about high immigrant birth rates that led to his support for free birth control services.[43] In spite of the varying motives, Walt argued that the move towards a free service introduced party political ideology into the issue of birth control because the Labour-controlled LAs, which had started giving a free service following the 1967 Act, took on the role of pressure groups.[44]

LEGISLATING FOR BIRTH CONTROL PROVISION

By 1972, these LA initiatives were an important element in the pressure that led to the provision of contraceptive advice and supplies by the NHS. This was achieved by inclusion of a clause in the 1972 National Health Services Reorganization Bill. The three sections of the NHS were family doctors, community care run by the local authorities, and the hospitals. The reorganization was to centralize the NHS further, and this meant that existing local authority schemes would be transferred to the new district health authorities being created by the bill. Initially the author of the bill, the Conservative Secretary of State for Social Services Sir Keith Joseph, intended advice but not supplies to be free, which was going to result in a cutting back of services in some local authorities. The Lords, where there was a large contingent of members committed to free services, passed an amendment that made contraception entirely free of charges. Members

---

[42] *Liverpool Echo* (27 Oct. 1972). Also see *Peterborough Citizen* (19 Jan. 1973). *Wisbech Standard* (11 Feb. 1972). *Cambridge Evening News* (8 Feb. 1972).
[43] Walt, 'Policy Making', 127–8.   [44] See also Leathard, *Fight*, 60–8.

then supported this on both sides in the Commons.[45] Supporters of free contraception argued that any cost would dissuade those most in need, whereas Joseph, having retreated to a twenty pence prescription charge only, insisted that this was an acceptable compromise. Over the previous five years both Labour and Conservative governments had greatly increased the amount of money made available for birth control. The Labour Minister of Health, Kenneth Robinson, had introduced spending of £750,000 a year in 1968. Joseph had already increased this to £3,000,000 and the provisions in his bill were further to increase spending to thirty millions each year.[46]

Resistance to free contraception did arise in part on the moral issue of chastity and the unmarried. In both houses those members who believed that the measure was immoral put up strenuous opposition and took up a fair amount of time, but these people had lost the war by 1972. They often argued on the basis of other factors, such as the spread of venereal disease or the medical side effects of the pill, rather than for the importance of chastity. The cross-party opposition to this moral case was also put indirectly. Members in favour did not argue for the creation of choice, but for the prevention of the suffering that uncontrolled fertility caused to women and their unwanted children. In a period in which birth control had only recently been publicly accepted such sentiments were not always the clichés they appear today. Conservative government support for making contraception a part of NHS services also sprang from the clarity with which increasingly detailed research exposed the financial calls made on government by unmarried mothers and large families living in poverty.[47] However, it is evident that the Conservatives had conceded that control of the sexual behaviour of women, married or unmarried, was not possible and they must instead provide contraception.[48] This was an extraordinary expansion of government support for women's control over their own lives. It marks the overturning of the right that had been taken for granted by those in moral or medical authority to determine the context in which women's reproductive,

[45] See also Leathard, *Fight*, 89.

[46] *Hansard*, Parliamentary Debates, House of Commons Official Report, Standing Committee G, National Health Service Reorganization Bill, (5 Apr. 1973), col. 236.

[47] Ibid., col. 961.   [48] Ibid., col. 238.

and thus sexual, activity could take place. From this point on, moralists were reduced to opposing the legal provision of contraception to girls under 16 and even in this they were to be unsuccessful.

Jeffrey Weeks saw the passing of this clause as a success not for the left wing but for the old-fashioned right in disguise. According to him:

[T]wo traditional concerns of the right had to battle: the fear of encouraging promiscuity against the fear of a disproportionate birthrate among the lower orders, and in the new context it was likely that birth control would win (it was an anxiety over the birth rate that prompted the House of Lords to revolt against the government... in 1974).[49]

In the opinion of the historian of eugenics Richard Soloway, there is little evidence of concern for a differential birth rate in British society by this stage.[50] The debates support this. Such concerns attracted considerably less attention even than the moral issues. Moreover, the Tory government of the 1980s did not try to alter the 'moral', that is, sexual, behaviour of working-class women, particularly of young single mothers. With rising unemployment, this could have been attempted relatively easily by manipulating the benefit system (whether it would have been successful is a different issue). That such efforts did not occur suggests that the consensus that had been reached was of a different nature from that described by Weeks.

Sir Keith Joseph gave a speech following the election held on 10 October 1974, which the Conservatives lost. The speech, two years after the 1972–3 NHS Act, was taken as the first sign of the harsh new mood that was to dominate the Tory Party through the 1980s. Joseph attacked the expansion of tertiary education, moral chaos, welfare dependency, the unions, the decline of Britain, and so on. However, the speech, entitled 'Remoralizing Britain', was said to have destroyed his chance of gaining the Conservative Party leadership, because of a widely condemned passage:

The balance of our population, of our human stock is threatened. A recent article in *Poverty*, published by the Child Poverty Action Group showed that a rising proportion of children are being born to mothers least fitted to bring children into the world and to bring them up... They are producing problem

[49] Weeks, *Sex*, 259.   [50] Soloway, *Demography*, 351, 359.

children, the future unmarried mothers, delinquents...subnormal...prisons...these mothers, the under-20s in many cases, single parents, from classes four and five, are now producing a third of all births...If we do nothing, the nation moves towards degeneration...Yet proposals to extend birth control to these classes of people, particularly the young unmarried ones, evoke entirely understandable moral opposition.[51]

The response focused almost exclusively on the remarks about mothers in social classes IV and V.[52] *The Times* revealed the extent to which public comment suggesting that working-class people were inadequate human stock had become politically unacceptable. The first leading article on the topic in *The Times* said: 'Sir Keith's brief excursus into eugenics was bound to raise the roof since he introduced into it distinctions of social class.'[53] A distinction was being made between eugenics *per se* and a eugenics that related to class. A second leader in *The Times* suggested, more in sorrow than in anger, that he had simply been careless: 'If Sir Keith had not been unwary enough to use a phrase or two from the suspect terminology of eugenics...'[54] These leader writers were not disagreeing with Joseph's swingeing attack on modern egalitarian Britain and on lone mothers in classes IV and V, but eugenics was no longer a rallying call.

There was comment on the moral issues. An article in *The Times*, by Ronald Butt, who was well to the right of Joseph on birth control and sex education, declared:

I suspect the truth was that, making a speech about influences that undermine moral values, it struck him that at the end of it some people might say that he himself had actually assisted this process as a minister by providing the basis of a free birth control service for all, which is now to operate without regard to age or moral status.[55]

It seems possible that Butt was right about Joseph's motivation. The expansion of the welfare state was increasing the financial calls made on government by lone mothers, but the shift to the left in post-war Britain had led to widespread acceptance that the sins of the parents should not be visited upon their children, and it was politically inexpedient to deprive mothers

---

[51] *The Times* (21 Oct. 1974).
[52] Based on the coverage in the *Sun, Daily Mail, Daily Mirror, Observer, The Times* and *Spectator*:
[53] *The Times* (21 Oct. 1974).   [54] Ibid. (26 Oct. 1974).   [55] Ibid. (24 Oct. 1974).

of support.[56] Although his previous record indicated a genuine concern for the disadvantaged, Joseph's primary motive probably had been to prevent births and thus save money.[57] In any event, neither compassion nor corporatism would have been likely to sound well in his clarion call to a resurgent Tory right. It was still unclear at an ideological level that sexual morality had now changed forever, though the switch away from repressing female sexuality to financial concerns reveals that the new reality had become apparent to those in charge of the accounts.

So, were socialist historians such as Weeks and Wilson, who were present at the time, completely wrong in their estimate of what was taking place? In his evidence to the population panel of the Select Committee on Science and Technology in 1972, Joseph insisted, to the irritation of the panel, that as Secretary of State for the Department of Social Security, his job had no relation to population issues. He stated that groups with higher fertility should have access to birth control information to make use of 'if they wish to do so', and it was 'not my task to interfere at all with pregnancies that are not regretted'.[58] There is no evidence that he would ever have intended forcing birth control onto the young women of socio-economic classes IV and V. However, he did believe that such people should be encouraged to make 'rational' choices. Dr Tom Stuttaford (Con.) asked Joseph:

So you get big families at the top end, those with university degrees, and big families again among people who have abandoned all hope and are living on supplementary. Do you agree that there is a sort of a "U" shape with big families at both ends? . . . [Keith Joseph] — . . . my concern is with the degree to which the parents concerned make rational decisions in the light of their own family circumstances about the number of pregnancies they will seek. There is all the difference in the world between rational decisions made at one end . . . and the rational decisions which may or may not be made at the other end.[59]

[56] See J. Lewis, H. Land, and K. E. Kiernan, *Lone Motherhood in Twentieth-Century Britain* (1998), ch. 6.

[57] Joseph had belonged to the Child Poverty Action Group and his 1972 NHS Reorganization Bill aimed to divert resources into the 'Cinderella sector', mental health and long-stay patients. See also Leathard, *Fight*, 163.

[58] Fifth Report from the Select Committee on Science and Technology: *Population Policy*, vol. xxxv, Reports, Accounts and Papers, 1971/2. para. 31.

[59] Ibid. 33–4.

The obvious implication of Joseph's evidence is that the rational decision for those on the poverty-stricken side of the 'U' curve to make is to have fewer children than those at the 'top end'. Stuttaford reveals the immensity of the gap between such people and these upper-class, public-school-educated parliamentarians in his allusion to the inscription above the entrance to hell in Dante's *Divine Comedy*, 'abandon all hope, you who enter!'[60] They could not comprehend why people on low incomes might choose to ignore the 'rational' decision and have more children.

THE EROSION OF DEFERENCE

There has been an emphasis on the failure of the 1960s and 1970s to deliver on expectations of radical transformation but these decades saw growing egalitarianism and rising expectations of participation within the existing social structures. The rate and form of the expansion in some areas of women's lives enables a beginning to be made in charting these broader changes. In the early 1960s, health service users were starting to form groups and the decade saw a huge expansion in voluntary activity and groups of service users. The kind of experiences that led to the formation of the National Association for the Welfare of Children in Hospital illustrate the approach of professionals and those in authority to the public in the post-Second World War period. The Platt Committee and the Minister of Health had proposed that unrestricted visiting by parents to their young children in hospital should be permitted.[61] But mothers found:

[W]hereas a hospital administration may in good faith give official sanction to this principle and publish official statements to this effect, it is found not once but repeatedly that when a mother brings her baby or small child in as a patient she is told there is no such opportunity. A typical incident occurred only a week ago when the mother was told 'Yes, we have unrestricted visiting here, but I want you to co-operate by coming only between twelve and one, and from two or three in the afternoon'.[62]

---

[60] Dante Alighieri, *Inferno*, canto 3, 1. 1.
[61] R. Klein, *The Politics of the NHS* (1989), 77. *Guardian* (9 July 1965).
[62] *Guardian* (9 July 1965).

The Association, composed largely of middle-class women, was seeking only to co-operate with nurses and doctors, but they found that 'organisations like [the association] and the Pre-school Playgroups must inevitably seem, like the suffragettes, both revolutionary and challenging to some of the older professionals who in earlier days made many sacrifices to attain the positions they have achieved today'.[63] It took very little for service users to be seen as extremely challenging to authority in the early 1960s. The mention of the suffragettes is typical of the almost subliminal introduction of women's rights as an issue in any number of contexts from the mid-1950s.

The upholding of routine, of rigid hierarchies, and the maintenance of a suitable distance between themselves and the untrained person were seen to be of great importance by professionals. This generation of professionals came of age before or during the Second World War. Schools and workplaces followed by the wartime experience, and, for young men in the following years, national service, habituated most of society to rigid systems based on innumerable petty rules. Demands that people should accept systems that caused emotional distress without question were a part of this, and the erosion of public compliance with such rules was a major feature of social change in the 1960s and 1970s. From insisting that they were not 'competing in any way . . . with those trained in the science of medicine, but [merely wanted] . . . to co-operate with the hard-pressed doctors and nurses', the National Association for the Welfare of Children in Hospital became far more assertive.[64] This was symptomatic of a wider trend in welfare rights groups and patients' rights groups. In a 1977 article on the potential effectiveness of patients' rights groups, C. J. Ham showed that in two of his case studies, the established groups Age Concern and MIND, the mental health group, this growth in assertiveness occurred in the early 1970s. The third, the Patients' Association, was founded later than these, in 1963, and was more assertive from the start.[65] There was a

---

[63] Ibid.

[64] Ibid.

[65] C. J. Ham, 'Power, Patients and Pluralism', in K. Barnard and K. Lee (eds.), *Conflicts in the National Health Service* (1977), 102–6. For an example of this change, see R. Lowe and P. Nicholson, 'The Formation of the Child Poverty Action Group (Witness Seminar)', *Contemporary Record*, 9/3 (1995).

sharp rise in the numbers of such groups in the 1960s and 1970s, with 230 patients' groups listed in a directory by 1979.[66]

By the early 1970s, there was, for the first time, considerable discussion of patients' rights in the medical press. The introduction of the NHS had enabled access to medical care by working-class women, and the visits necessary to obtain the pill hugely increased women's contact with doctors. The doctor–patient relationship was an archetypal example of deference, and the coverage of these issues in the medical press during the early 1970s lurched from self-serving apologias to a tentative willingness to entertain criticism. For example, the December 1972 number of the *Journal of the Royal College of Practitioners* was devoted to the patient's viewpoint, but the editorial was both patronizing and critical of the patients' associations. The regular columnists of *Pulse*, a magazine for GPs, believed criticism of doctors should not be voiced publicly at all: 'There is a tradition that clinical competence is not decently a topic for discussion . . . Such a state of affairs has much to recommend it. The stimulus it offers to a diffused respect harms neither the patient nor the doctor.'[67] But in the same year, 1974, the magazine carried an article written by Jean Robinson, who went on to become the chair of the Patients' Association, in which she suggested that many problems were due to 'male domination of medicine'.[68] The pressure for change was beginning to make an impact.

This evolution in attitudes can be charted amongst younger women. From 1957 to 1972 Mary Stott, who eagerly reported activity promoting the equality of women, edited the 'Women's Page' of the *Guardian*. I examined the page from 1960 through to 1974. In this context the links between public and personal life are evident. In the 1960s, women were presented as contributing to society and/or to other women. Achievement was described in terms of participating or being given opportunities to contribute.[69] The 'Women's Page' ran articles on women obtaining jobs and positions previously not held by them. Prior to 1970, and frequently

---

[66]   Klein, *Politics*, 116.

[67]   *Pulse* (26 Jan. 1974). For an extended discussion of doctors' response to the pill, see H. Cook, 'The Long Sexual Revolution: British Women, Sex and Contraception in the Twentieth Century' (D.Phil. thesis, 1999), ch. 13.

[68]   *Pulse* (7 May 1974). See also *Pulse* (20 Jan. 1973).

[69]   e.g. *Guardian* (17 Feb. 1967).

even after that date, humour or a conciliatory comment appeared in every article of this type; even when research into women's role on local and regional policy-making bodies uncovered an 'influential core of masculine prejudice', women were 'to blame in part'.[70] There was a similar approach taken to the private sphere. For example, in 1973 Mrs Blooman was interviewed because she was the first woman to become a principal probation officer:

> After marriage in 1952, she . . . felt her mind was idling away, and Charlie Blooman's answer was, 'Go to university' . . . Mr Blooman proudly claims that he can now eat home-cooked meals 10 nights on the trot, minus the presence of his wife, by eating casseroles from the freezer which she prepares when time permits, plus a little modest cooking of his own. It is clear that Mr Blooman is content in his supportive role to a busy woman. Women's Lib could do worse than pin a medal on him.[71]

Charlie's encouragement and willingness to allow his wife to inconvenience him was unusual and worthy of mention.[72] Many examples were available of men who did not encourage their wives and the gratitude women felt toward men who were 'supportive' was an appropriate response within the social context of their time. However, by the 1970s the younger women appearing on the 'Women's Page' would not give Charlie a medal because their expectations had risen. They decided that women should not be grateful for not having to act as servants and some had returned to political activism.[73] This was a sharp change according to the delighted Stott, who remarked in 1973 about the resurgence of women's groups:

> Only five years ago . . . Cambridge graduates [were saying] . . . that they were uninterested in political activity and . . . explaining winningly on television 'You see, I think men want women to be feminine.' Less than five years ago I suggested in a Guardian Column that it was time that the women's organisations began to think about winding themselves up . . . I said then that as young

---

[70]   Ibid. (25 Jan. 1967).   [71]   Ibid. (7 Feb. 1973).

[72]   Other examples: Makin, *Evelyn Home V. Brittain, Testament of Experience* (1957), M. Stott, *Forgetting's No Excuse* (1975). V. Grove, *The Compleat Woman: Marriage, Motherhood, Career: Can she Have it All?* (1987; 1988).

[73]   *Guardian* (10 Aug. 1972). *Guardian* (17 Feb. 1967). This was a radical stance even for those in paid employment: see D. Beyfus, *The English Marriage: What it is Like to be Married Now* (1968).

women were enjoying a new togetherness with young men, it was likely that in the future women would prefer to work in integrated organisations.[74]

Instead, there was the emergence of second-wave feminism and a new agenda for change. This is largely beyond the scope of this book (except in the guise of historiography), but the availability of effective female-controlled contraception (and safe legal abortion as a back-up) was a major contributor to this new confidence.

The changes charted here were important; the growing confidence of women and non-professionals as well as that of working-class people, and the breaking down of a rigid, rule-bound consensus that imposed deferential behaviour upon people while insisting that they were co-operating freely. Much of this was occurring in areas of personal life and behaviour, but these shifts cannot be confined within that category. This evolution can be charted in the existing work that covers birth control in this period. The work of Walt and Leathard tells us little of the power relations between the various groups they discuss. The social legislation of the 1960s was passed as a result of agitation by groups that had, in the main, been established in the inter-war period and were rapidly becoming as much a part of upper-middle-class society as were MPs. *The Times* commented on the FPA that 'local notables certainly loom impressively large in the branches'.[75] While they unequivocally rejected coercion, the FPA nonetheless accepted the assumption that the values of the middle class were those to which the whole society should aspire. They accepted 'the need for classes four and five to effectively control their own fertility when they could not afford children'.[76] A 'rational' decision in this period was not one which was made according to the felt desires, aspirations, and needs of the individual. Rather the word rational was used to refer to a sensible, financially responsible, mature decision, that is, one consistent with the values of society as conceived of by respectable men and women of the class and type of Stuttaford, Joseph, and the FPA. In his speech,

[74] *Guardian* (8 Mar. 1973).

[75] *The Times* (30 May 1962). See also Lafitte, *Family Planning*, ch. 5.13.

[76] Reponse to K. Joseph's speech. *The Times* (21 Oct. 1974). For working-class responses to the FPA, see M. Lassell, *Wellington Road* (1962; 1966), 132, 135–7. D. Sanders, *The Woman Book of Love and Sex* (1985), 98. *Sun* (24 Oct. 1974).

Joseph had declared that '[t]he worship of the instinct, of spontaneity, the rejection of self discipline is not progress; it is degeneration'.[77] One of the things that was occurring in the work of young politically radical historians such as Elizabeth Wilson and Jeffrey Weeks was a rejection of this class-bound rationalism in favour of an awareness of relations of power. In the absolutism of their insistence that improvement in birth control provision was right-wing change, there are also traces of the millenarian optimism about the possibility of transformation and the rejection of anything less that was felt in the early 1970s.[78] These are the interpretations that were accepted and repeated and these writers were attempting to integrate new ideas about class and power which reflected, albeit obliquely, the importance of the erosion of deference in the 1960s and 1970s. However, it is quite untrue to suggest that the pill functioned as a method of controlling young women.[79] Rather there has been a huge increase in women's autonomy and, as Walt and Leathard believed, this is a story of progress towards the light.

[77] *The Times* (21 Oct. 1974) (full text of the speech).

[78] See E. Wilson, *Only Halfway to Paradise: Women in Postwar Britain 1945–1968* (1980), 98. S. Rowbotham, *Women's Conciousness, Man's World* (1973), 41. Gordon, *Woman's Body*, 403.

[79] Lewis, *Women*, 95. Wilson, *Women and the Welfare State*, 69.

15

'A Car or a Wife?' The Northern European Marriage System and the Sexual Revolution

The introduction of the pill and the transformation in social and political attitudes to the sexual activity of unmarried women during the 1960s have been described in the previous chapters. This chapter looks in detail at the quantitative evidence showing changes in the events which make up women's reproductive and sexual lives, and in the timing of these events. The role played by premarital intercourse in the post-Second World War fertility regime of almost all working-class women, and many middle-class women, is explained. It is shown that young women's reproductive careers continued to be governed by the constraints that made up the north-west European marriage system right up until the late 1960s. The link between economics, sexual intercourse, childbearing, and marriage (a permanent relationship in a shared household) had been central to the management of sexuality in England for centuries. This world has been turned upside down. Sexual intercourse is no longer directly linked to family formation and marriage is now optional. Changes in levels of premarital sexual intercourse have been dismissed as irrelevant by most researchers since the 1970s, but the small proportion of unmarried middle-class women who had begun having sexual affairs with men whom they did not intend to marry, using contraception and abortion to control the consequences, were the harbingers of change. In this chapter, it is shown how these changes before marriage led on to the substantial changes in families and sexuality with which we are all living today.

AGE AT FIRST INTERCOURSE

However, in *Sexual Attitudes and Lifestyles*, the report of a large-scale national survey of sexual behaviour in Britain, published in 1994, Kaye Wellings and Sally Bradshaw reject both the notion that the sexual revolution took place in the 1960s and that oral contraception produced sexual change.[1] Instead, they suggest that sexual change in the 1950s (somehow) produced technological advance. This conclusion has been widely accepted.[2] An examination of their argument helps to establish the relevant issues. The authors explained that they had found a steep decline in the average age at first heterosexual penetrative intercourse between the 1950s and the 1960s. The pill was not introduced until 1961 and, they suggest, not widely available until the end of the 1960s, and they conclude from this that it 'seems as likely that legal and technological advance has occurred in response to changing sexual mores as vice versa. These data give no evidence of a sexual revolution co-terminous with the 1960s; rather the major changes seem to have occurred in the previous decade.'[3] There is a slippage in the analysis between 'major change in age at first intercourse' and the 'sexual revolution' which leads to the conflation of these events. A fall in the age at first intercourse is a sexual revolution to the survey authors. The meanings that are attached to physical sexual acts are seen to be self-evident and thus incontestable. More or less sex, earlier or later sex, means more or less revolutionary sex. It should be noted that other writers could not even be pinned down to clear definitions. For example, Jane Lewis and Jeffrey Weeks state that sexual behaviour remained conservative in the 1960s yet at no point do they offer a definition of non-conservative sexual behaviour.[4] Wellings and Bradshaw's assumption that the meaning of physical sexual events is self-evident arises from their disciplinary context as academic researchers in medicine and public health.

---

[1] K. Wellings and S. Bradshaw, 'First Intercourse between Men and Women', ch. 4 in K. Wellings, J. Field, A. M. Johnson, J. Wadsworth, and S. Bradshaw, *Sexual Attitudes and Lifestyles* (1994).

[2] e.g. D. E. Massey, *Sex Education Source Book: Current Issues and Debates* (1995), 8. L. Hudson and B. Jacot, *Intimate Relations: The Natural History of Desire* (1995), 37.

[3] Wellings et al., *Sexual Attitudes*, 80.

[4] J. Weeks, *Sex, Politics and Society: The Regulation of Sexuality since 1800* (1981; 1989), 254. J. Lewis, *Women in Britain since 1945* (1992), 48.

Table 15.1. *Female age at first intercourse*

Estimated year aged 20	Quartiles			Born	Age at Interview
	1st	Median	3rd		
1951–5	19	21	23	1931–5	55–9
1956–60	18	20	22	1936–40	50–4
1961–5	18	19	21	1941–5	45–9
1966–70	17	19	21	1946–50	40–4
1971–5	17	18	20	1951–5	35–9
1976–80	16	18	19	1956–60	30–4

Note: Approximate birth cohort and five-year period in which cohort aged 20 added by this author.

Source: K. Wellings, J. Field, A. M. Johnson, J. Wadsworth, and S. Bradshaw, *Sexual Attitudes and Lifestyles* (1994), table 4.1, 70.

For the survey, nearly 19,000 British men and women, aged from 16 to 59, were randomly selected, and those who agreed to participate in the survey were interviewed and given a questionnaire. Age at first heterosexual penetrative sexual intercourse was an event which was both clearly defined and subject to reliable recall. Most sexual events taking place in the distant past do not come into this category and the importance accorded to age at first intercourse results in part from this fact.[5] The survey authors ordered the responses in the form of birth cohorts, labelled according to age at the time of the interview in 1990–1. The approximate dates of birth and the five-year period in which the interview cohorts were aged 20 have been added to Table 15.1. This allows the age at which the respondents first had intercourse to be related to the period in which this event took place. The results of the survey showed that from the 1950s until the 1980s, the median age at which people first had sexual intercourse fell by four years. The steepest decline in the age at first intercourse occurred between 1956 and 1960.[6] The median age at first intercourse was two years higher, at age 21, for those born in the first half of the 1950s, than it was for those born in the first half of the 1960s, who first had intercourse at the median age of 19. Based on this finding the authors claimed that the major changes in sexual behaviour seem to have taken place in the 1950s.

[5] Wellings et al., *Sexual Attitudes*, 69.
[6] Ibid. 79.

For what reasons might age at first intercourse have fallen during the 1950s? What meanings did young people's heterosexual, embodied, sexual activity have? 'Petting' was discussed in all surveys of sexual behaviour. This term defined sexual activity stopping short of heterosexual inter-course, and was, according to adult commentators, a heavily self-regulated activity.[7] In 1956, Eustace Chesser found that there was a steady upward trend in the incidence of petting from his oldest informants, those born before 1904, and a similar trend to a greater prevalence of premarital intercourse. Middle-class women were more likely to have engaged in petting.[8] Thus, the trend towards sex outside marriage found by the 1994 survey was not new in the 1950s. Until the mid-1970s, 'premarital inter-course' and 'sex between unmarried people' were seen as very different. Before the mid-1960s, most people disapproved strongly of sex between the unmarried, but premarital intercourse was a term used to describe sexual intercourse between a couple that were intending to marry in the relatively near future. The Mass-Observation sex survey carried out in 1949 found that the level of disapproval was greatly lessened where this was the case, as did later surveys.[9] This was reflected in experience. Even in 1971, in Geoffrey Gorer's survey, over 90 per cent of married women and just under half of men under the age of 45 who had had premarital sex claimed to have done so only with their intended spouse.[10] Having intercourse marked a point in courtship, a staging post en route to marriage and household formation.

In the 1950s, there was a high rate of marriage, a low divorce rate, and a reduced possibility of death on the part of one of the partners. This produced what the demographer Michael Anderson has described as a moment of marital stability without known historical precedent.[11] Petting

[7] For a description of progression to intercourse in the mid-1960s, see C. Dix, *Say I'm Sorry to Mother* (1978), ch. 4, 75–80.

[8] Eustace Chesser, *The Sexual, Marital and Family Relationships of the English Woman* (1956), 329–31, 313–14. Amongst single women, only one-fifth of those who had not had intercourse had petted, while two-fifths of those who had had intercourse had petted.

[9] L. England, 'A British Sex Survey', *International Journal of Sexology*, 3/3 (1950).

[10] G. Gorer, *Sex & Marriage in England Today: A Study of the Views and Experience of the under-45s* (1971), 30–1; attitudes, 34–5.

[11] M. Anderson, 'The Social Significance of Demographic Change in Britain, 1750–1950', in F. M. Thompson (ed.), *Cambridge Social History of Britain 1750–1950* (1990), 29–30.

followed by premarital sex during this period of stability in the 1950s was another form of the varied culturally determined approaches to regulating young working-class people's sexual contact in pre-twentieth century Europe. This involved parental and community controls over courtship. For example, Barry Reay has found that in Hernhill, a parish in Kent, from 1780 to 1851, women conceived over two-fifths of first births before marriage, over 10 per cent were illegitimate and under half were conceived in wedlock. The court records of maintenance cases for illegitimate babies revealed that there was a community 'framework of moral vigilance and comment'.[12] Premarital sex was usual, not exceptional, and vigilance ensured that males could not deny paternity and leave the community or family financially responsible for an unwed mother and her illegitimate child.[13] These earlier practices are very evocative of the ritualized dating, petting, and premarital sex of the 1950s, which gave opportunities for sexual activity, while simultaneously insisting that it must not take place. There were well-established routines for dealing with the pregnancies that did happen. These ranged from male acceptance of responsibility and marriage to shotgun weddings, illegal abortions, and sending the girl away until the baby was born and then adopted. So, if many people conceived of, and accepted, first intercourse solely as sex with an intended marriage partner, why did the age at which it began to occur fall?

Over centuries, there was a link between economic performance and fertility created by marriage. Individual caution and community attitudes stopped most couples from marrying until they had sufficient savings and income to support a new separate household. The low level of average wages in Britain meant that there was a relatively high average age at marriage and a high proportion of people, from 10 to 20 per cent of each cohort, who never married at all right up until the post-Second World War period. In 1965, John Hajnal described this pattern of late and infrequent marriage as the European marriage system because it has occurred only in that area, and even more specifically only in north-

[12] B. Reay, 'Before the Transition: Fertility in English Villages, 1800–1880', *Continuity and Change*, 9 (1994), 235, 242.

[13] See Ch. 3 for a discussion of the breakdown of this system in much of 19th-century England.

west Europe.[14] In most societies, newly-wed couples are not expected to set up a separate household and so nearly 100 per cent of women and men are able to marry, and women, especially, tend to do so at a younger age. This marriage system also regulated premarital sex. Unmarried women would usually not agree to sexual intercourse until the man promised marriage and, while community control prevented them from abandoning financial responsibility for women if they became pregnant, men did not make such promises lightly.

Demographers had suggested that this system of prudential marriage had broken down as a result of industrial and social change prior to 1870, and that by then fertility was managed by the use of contraception or not at all. However, Simon Szreter recently commented that '[D]elayed marriage apparently existed as a practice . . . *throughout* the protracted period during which the planned control of fertility within marriage became established as a behavioural norm.'[15] Szreter was referring to the period from the 1860s to the 1940s, the cut-off date originally proposed by John Hajnal in 1965. However, Hajnal identified the marriage system by a high proportion never marrying at all and relatively high age at marriage. The proportion of women who remained unmarried in the age group 45–9 did not fall below 10 per cent until the 1971 census. The median age at marriage fell sharply, in line with rising real wages, but it did not reach its lowest point of 21.29 until 1966–70. Two reasons exist for continued adherence to the cut-off point of the 1940s. First, from the 1940s, the percentage of women who were marrying rose sharply, and the age at which they married fell sharply. However, average real wages were rising to historic heights, and it is consistent with the marriage system that marriage should also change as it did. Secondly, contraceptive methods were apparently widely used throughout the community. However, as explained, the marriage system worked to lower fertility because the cost of household formation, one component of which was the cost of children, prevented couples marrying. Until the 1960s, people still expected marriage to be the occasion for separate household formation. Where the housing shortage following the war made it necessary for a new

---

[14] J. Hajnal, 'European Marriage Patterns in Perspective', in D. V. Glass and D. E. Eversley (eds.), *Population in History* (1965), 101, 134.

[15] S. Szreter, *Fertility, Class and Gender in Britain, 1860–1940* (1996), 391.

couple to share the home of one or other's parents, they, and often their parents, felt this to be a great hardship. People were attempting to defer having children while they saved for a home, but, in practice, contraception was so inefficient that many failed. The cost of supporting a separate household remained a major deciding factor in whether young men were willing to marry at all. For example, in 1961, the researcher Ferdynand Zweig wrote:

What is better, a car or a wife? 'I was courting,' confided one, 'and should have been married by now, but instead I bought a car.' At first I treated this as a joke, but I heard it so many times in so many versions ('I can't afford a car and a wife, so I drifted away from my girl') that I had to regard it as a major issue for youth at present.[16]

Women were increasingly working for wages, both before and after marriage, but it was still expected that a new wife would get pregnant fairly fast, if she was not so already, and stop earning (Table 15.10). Rising wages led to higher expectations of consumer goods amongst the unmarried of both sexes, not to a shift in fundamental determinants. The transition away from the north-west marriage system in England was not fully completed until the mid-1970s, a quarter of a century later.

By the mid-1950s, working-class manual employees and managers were already earning over three times more than had been the case in the mid-1930s, and most other occupational groups were earning over two and half times as much. Real wages for both males and females then doubled between 1951 and 1973.[17] Thus, we would expect to see fertility increasing throughout the period as more people could afford marriage and the accompanying household formation; initially this was so. Marriage became more popular. From 1951 to 1971, the proportion of women aged from 16 to 44 who were married rose from just under two-thirds (65 per cent) to nearly three-quarters (73 per cent). Alongside this, a fall in the age at marriage from 22.96 years to 22.01 years also occurred.[18] The majority of first sexual intercourse was premarital sex and a feature of

---

[16] F. Zweig, *The Worker in an Affluent Society* (1961), 155.

[17] G. Routh, *Occupation and Pay in Great Britain, 1906–79* (1980), table 1.1, 6; table 2.27, 120; 119.

[18] *Marriage and Divorce Statistics: Review of the Registrar General on Marriages and Divorces in England and Wales, 1980*, OPCS Series FM2 no. 7 (1983), derived from table. 1.1(b), 11; table.3.5. (a), 23.

courtship, or intended as such. Thus the average age at first intercourse fell, because sexual activity increased in line with the improved economic conditions that also led to a fall in the age at marriage. There is a discrepancy of over a half a year between the fall in age at first intercourse as presented for publication and the fall in age at marriage, so this discussion is not conclusive.[19] Nonetheless, there is sufficient evidence to argue that the fall in the age at which first sexual intercourse occurred in the 1950s was not a sexual revolution as Wellings et al. have claimed. It was a response to the rising real wages, which were causing a fall in the age at marriage and enabling increasing numbers of women and men to marry at all. However, in the following decade a sexual revolution did take place. What follows describes the changes that women made in their own lives and reveals the magnitude of the shift that has occurred.

THE SEXUAL REVOLUTION

In the quarter of a century between the 1940s and the mid-1970s there were two main trends in female sexual activity, both of which were moves away from the tight sexual control of the first half of the century. Sexual knowledge, including knowledge of contraception, remained very unevenly distributed in society and the first trend was a shift back to the pre-fertility decline package of premarital sexual intercourse followed

---

[19] The median 'age at first marriage' for women fell by exactly a year from the 1951–5 marriage cohort to the 1961–5 marriage cohort. (Median average age at spinsters' first marriage—1951–5: 22.39; 1961–5: 21.39 = 1.00.) *Marriage, Divorce and Adoption Statistics, 1995*, OPCS Series FM2 no. 23 (1998). According to the *Sexual Attitudes and Lifestyles* survey, the 'age at first intercourse' fell 1.7 years in the same period; 79. (Averaging the quartiles gives aged 21 in 1951/5, aged 20 in 1956/60, aged 19.3 in 1961/5; table.15.1.) The fall in the age of marriage of one year would account for one year of the fall in the age at first intercourse. There appears to be a year to account for in rates of first intercourse but the first intercourse figures are rounded up or down to make whole years whereas the marriage figures are percentages. The decline in age shown in the first quartile of the 1945–9 age cohort was not as great as in the previous cohorts. This suggests that the overall fall was less than a full year. It is not possible to go further with these figures. Another possibility exists: Chesser found that the younger the age at first intercourse the greater the time period before marriage. (An average age of 16 at first intercourse led to marriage 4.5 years later at an average of 20.6 years. Age 19 resulted in a three-year gap. Age 23, a two-year gap. Age over 25, average 27.5, a one-year gap. Chesser, *English Woman*, table 320, 354.) If this continued to be the case then a fall in age at marriage would correlate with a greater fall in age at first intercourse.

by marriage to a partner for life when pregnancy occurred. This trend peaked in the late 1960s. The second trend depended upon the growing availability of contraception and consisted of a move to sexual intercourse outside marriage between partners who might or might not intend to marry. This trend continued into the 1980s, and remains central to the ongoing reshaping of societal sexual mores. Initially, these two trends varied strongly by class. The first trend was followed mainly by working-class women who did not have access to contraceptive knowledge, and the second trend by those middle-class women who did. The following section describes a number of small shifts that differed according to age and class amongst women who married. Cumulatively these added up to considerable differences in the lives of women.

The authors of the *Sexual Attitudes and Lifestyles* survey mentioned in passing that there was a shift from 38 per cent of female first intercourse occurring within marriage 1950–65 to only 15 per cent of first inter-course occurring within marriage 1965–75.[20] Unfortunately, they pre-sented the data in two cohorts of different time lengths and it is not

Table 15.2. *Married women and single women who reported coitus before marriage*

Period of birth	Estimated year aged 20	% reporting coitus		No coitus over the lifetime[a]
		Married	Single	
Chesser, 1956				
Pre-1904	Pre-1924	19	18	
1904–14	1924–34	36	32	
1914–24	1934–44	39	30	
1924–34	1944–54	43	30	
Wellings et al.				
1931–45	1951–65	61.5		1.5
1946–55	1966–75	86.2		0.7
1956–65	1976–85	94.7		2.1

Note: Estimated year aged 20 added.

[a]Does not include homosexuals.

Source: E. Chesser, *The Sexual Marital and Family Relationships of the English Woman* (1956), T. 276, 311. Wellings et al., *Sexual Attitudes*, table 5.1, 115.

[20] Wellings et al., *Sexual Altitudes*, table 4.14, 97.

Table 15.3. *Women who reported premarital coitus with their husbands before first marriage, by year of marriage*

Year of first marriage	% reporting premarital coitus			
	Under 20	20–4	25 and over	Total
1956–60	52	31	33	35
1961–5	64	41	36	47
1966–70	74	55	55	61
1971–5	82	72	64	74

Source: K. Dunnell, *Family Formation 1976* (1979), table 2.4, 7.

Table 15.4. *Use of contraception before marriage by married women in different social class and age at interview cohorts who reported premarital sexual relations with their husbands*

Estimated year aged 20	Age at interview	Method choice	Social class			
			I and II	III NM	III M	IV and V
1947–56	40–9	Pill	5	—	—	—
1957–66	30–9		18	12	3	2
1967–76	20–9		51	43	34	27
1947–56	40–9	Always used	45	67	41	28
1957–66	30–9	method	64	59	47	33
1967–76	20–9		65	61	55	45
1947–56	40–9	Sometimes took	14	10	19	16
1957–66	30–9	chances	19	24	19	26
1967–76	20–9		25	22	25	25
1947–56	40–9	Not used a method	41	23	40	56
1957–66	30–9		17	17	34	41
1967–76	20–9		10	17	20	30

Note: Estimated year aged 20 added.

Source: Dunnell, *Family Formation*, table 9.6, 54.

possible to relate it directly to social trends or to the age-at-first-intercourse data. *Family Formation 1976* (1979) by Karen Dunnell provided more detailed data. For this survey a random sample of 6,500 married and single women between the ages of 16 and 49 were interviewed in 1976 about their fertility and their use of contraception. This was the first government-funded survey to ask women about sexual experience outside marriage. Concerns about the social acceptability of such enquiries limited the questions to asking married women only if and when they had had sexual intercourse with their husband before marriage. Single women were asked only when they first had intercourse with their current partner, if they had one.[21] The stigma attached to female promiscuity is evident in these decisions and the result of them is that the reported levels of sexual activity outside marriage are the minimum that was occurring. Wellings et al. for the whole period, and Chesser in the brief period of overlap, both found higher levels of sexual experience outside marriage. Dunnell suggested that because older women were reluctant to admit to premarital intercourse the rate of increase may have been exaggerated, but the other research suggests the later cohorts were also under-reporting. The conclusion to be drawn is that the overall level of premarital sexual intercourse reported to Dunnell was probably an underestimate but the rate of increase is probably reasonably accurate. The discussion below of Dunnell's data closely follows her elegant and perceptive analysis.

MANUAL WORKING-CLASS WOMEN

The proportion of all married women who reported having had premarital intercourse with their husbands-to-be more than doubled between the 1956–60 marriage cohort and the 1971–5 marriage cohort. The largest increase was between the cohorts married in 1961–5 and in 1966–70. However, there was a higher rate of premarital intercourse in women aged under 20 compared to those aged over 20, with an increase in the difference from 1961–5 and a decreasing rate of difference thereafter (Table 15.3). More of those who had intercourse under 20 were working-class women and this means that working-class women's risk of pregnancy was increased to a greater extent than that of middle-class women.[22] This risk was further increased because the percentage of

---

[21] K. Dunnell, *Family Formation 1976* (1979), 2.

[22] Ibid., table 10.4, 59. Women's social class was based on the husband's occupation at time of first marriage for ever married women, or for single women, on their father's occupation.

women under the age of 20 who did not use a method of contraception when having intercourse or who 'sometimes took a chance' was double that amongst women aged 20 and over. The overall percentage of brides who were pregnant at marriage increased through the 1950s, reached a peak in the late 1960s, and only began to decrease among women married in the 1970s. Dunnell suggested this was occurring because the increase in sexual relations during the 1960s was greater than the increase in the use of contraception. Amongst those who had premarital sex with their husbands, the proportion of women who 'always used' contraception went up and the proportion who never used a method fell, but the proportion of women who 'sometimes took chances' rose and the methods used were often not very effective. As the proportion of women who were having sex more than doubled, this led to an increase in the number of women at risk of pregnancy (Table 15.4).

The level of premarital conceptions ending in marriage differed by class. Working-class women, especially those in classes IV and V, continued to marry before the birth in greater numbers. Over twice the number of working-class women aged 20 from 1947–56 were married. By the late 1960s this difference had risen, with over four times as many working-class women aged 20 married as women in social class I and II and twice as many as in social class III Non Manual (Table 15.5). Thus, the small differences in the behaviour of young working-class women added up to considerable differences between their lives and those of middle-class women. To sum up Dunnell's findings, working-class women were more likely to start

Table 15.5. *Women in age at interview cohorts, by social class, who were first married by age 20*

Estimated year aged 20	Age at interview	Social class				
		I and II	III NM	III M	IV and V	Total
1947–56	40–9	8	8	22	20	18
1957–66	30–9	9	22	36	32	28
1967–71	25–9	10	21	33	41	28
1972–6	20–4	11	25	38	42	31

Note: Estimated year aged 20 added.

Source: Dunnell, *Family Formation*, table 4.1, 14.

having premarital intercourse at a younger age, then more likely to take a chance with contraception. Because of this they were more likely to become pregnant and then more likely to marry when they did so. The result was they married younger and they started having children younger in large numbers.

NON-MANUAL WORKING-CLASS AND MIDDLE-CLASS WOMEN

Dunnell grouped women in social classes I, II, and III NM as non-manual-class women. This group includes the young middle-class women who feature very prominently in the qualitative evidence for sexual change in the 1960s. The proportion of these women who had premarital intercourse was 10 per cent less at most than that of manual working-class women (Table 15.6). But their higher age at first intercourse, greater use of contraception, and lesser willingness to marry when pregnancy occurred produced a very different outcome. Initially, from 1956 to 1965, there was a switch in the choice of male methods away from withdrawal (30 to 25 per cent) to more effective condoms (35 to 44 per cent).[23] Use of the pill amongst those women having premarital sex increased most from the 1966–70 cohort to the 1971–5 cohort. Pill use by women having premarital sex differed by class to a far greater extent than was the case with pill

Table 15.6. *Women in age at interview cohorts, by social class, who reported premarital sexual relations*

Estimated year aged 20	Age at interview	Social class			
		I and II	III NM	III M	IV and V
1947–56	40–9	27	21	28	31
1957–66	30–9	47	42	49	52
1967–71	25–9	70	68	73	76
1972–6	20–4	48	44	48	52

Note: Estimated year aged 20 added.

Source: Dunnell, *Family Formation*, table 9.5, 53.

[23] K. Dunnell, *Family Formation 1976* (1979), table 8.9 (b), 46; table 8.8, 45; table 8.7, 44.

use by married women. This produced a widening of the differences in behaviour between social classes during the premarital period.

Non-manual and middle-class women were more likely to use the pill and more likely to use it before marriage (Table 15.4). These women were already marrying later and less often, and from the late 1960s, they were increasingly more likely to have an abortion rather than to marry if they became pregnant. Even before the Abortion Act 1967 came into operation, a higher proportion of non-manual-class women's pregnancies ended in abortion, and this remained true through the early 1970s. Dunnell found that, contrary to expectations, before the passing of the Abortion Act of 1967, the increased number of abortions to single women reduced the number who might otherwise have married before the birth of the child. There was no evidence from the survey that it reduced the proportions of premarital pregnancies ending in an illegitimate live birth.[24] So the increasing availability of effective birth control made it possible for these young non-manual and middle-class women to have sexual relations without becoming pregnant and/or marrying, thus moving towards autonomous sexual activity. This was the new trend made possible by effective birth control. It was very different from the working-class trend towards rising rates of premarital intercourse as a result of a falling age at marriage and increasing numbers marrying. The behaviour of young working-class women before marriage was based on pre-fertility decline approaches to the management of sexuality and reproduction. Their low age at marriage was made possible by rising real wages and did not reflect a full break away from the northern European marriage system. The trends that resulted from their behaviour peaked in the late 1960s, whereas the trends resulting from the behaviour of young non-manual and middle-class women who had earlier access to contraceptive knowledge continued into the 1970s and beyond. This becomes more evident when we examine the behaviour of single women.

---

[24] Ibid. 61–2. Women under-reported legal abortions (that is, after 1967) and premarital births by up to about 50% compared to registration data. Premarital conceptions resulting in births in marriage were misreported as conceptions within marriage; however, the pattern of these births was consistent with national data. As with premarital sex the trends were probably accurate; 10–13.

SINGLE WOMEN

The proportion of women who had sexual intercourse completely outside marriage rather than having premarital sex before marriage had increased after the First World War. In Chesser's sample 32 to 30 per cent of single women born 1904–34 had had sexual intercourse.[25] Chesser referred to this as premarital sex although the older single women may have been referring to events well in the past and many would never have married. The lack of any other term highlights how unacceptable it then was for women to have sex outside marriage. In the 1994 survey less than 2 per cent of all women admitted to no coitus in their lifetime. (Table 15.2). In Dunnell's sample of never married, i.e. single, women, 28 per cent of those aged 40–9 at the time of interview in 1976 (born approximately 1927–36), and thus unlikely to marry, had had sexual intercourse.[26] Before the late 1950s, the sexual activity of single women was unacceptable to the majority of the population and likely to result in severe social sanctions if they revealed it. However, the use of increasingly effective contraception resulted in the boundary between married and single women becoming blurred. From the 1950s, the duration of premarital sex increased as well as the incidence. The percentage of women having premarital sex for between six and eleven months remained fairly stable (Table 15.7). But in the earliest marriage cohort shown, 1956–60, twice as many women had

Table 15.7. *Length of time before first marriage sexual relations with husband started, for women first married in different years*

Year of first marriage	Length of time before first marriage that sexual relations with husband started				
	Under 3 months	3–5 months	6–11 months	12–23 months	2 years and over
1956–60	20	24	30	17	9
1961–5	13	23	29	25	10
1966–70	14	20	30	20	16
1971–5	14	16	27	23	20

Source: Dunnell, *Family Formation*, table 2.5, 7.

[25] Chesser, *English Woman*, 311.
[26] Dunnell, *Family Formation*, 52. Only 5% of those aged 30–49 were single; 5.

premarital sex for only three months as did so for over two years, whereas in the 1971–5 cohort only 14 per cent had premarital sex for up to three months and 20 per cent did so for over two years. Thus for increasing numbers of women, marriage ceased to signal a substantial change in the nature of their sexual activity. Increasing numbers of women began to cohabit with their husbands before marriage. Dunnell found that the percentage of those who admitted cohabiting before their first marriage increased from 1 per cent in the 1956–60 cohort to 9 per cent in the 1971–5 cohort.[27] For these women household formation was no longer directly connected to marriage.

Direct information is not available about levels of premarital sex in the Medical Research Council 1946 cohort.[28] However, the women were asked to give the year in which they first used the pill and the year in which they married. This means that the percentage of women who first used the pill before the year that they married is available (Table 15.8). Thirty per cent of the women who first used the pill before marriage began doing so more than two years prior to the marriage. These women were moving away from the socially acceptable pattern of sexual intercourse during court-ship toward a pattern of routine sexual expression outside of marriage. Fig. 15.1 shows only first use of the pill and does not indicate the duration of

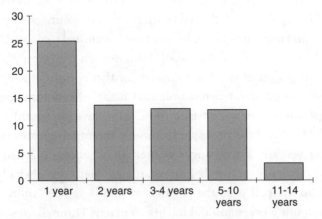

Fig. 15.1 Period by which first use of the pill pre-dates the year of marriage, as a percentage of the total pill use before marriage

[27] Ibid. 8.   [28] See Ch. 13 for a description of the cohort.

Table 15.8. *Ever married women who first used the pill before the year of marriage,
in the same year as marriage, and following the year of marriage*

Age at first use	Base	% before marriage	% same year	% after marriage
15–19	109	24	39	38
20–1	277	33	40	27
22–3	354	49	33	18
24–5	212	60	22	17
26–9	174	76	10	14
30+	74	85	9	5
Total	1,200	20	28	51

Source: MRC 1946 cohort.

time for which the pill was used. Some women who used the pill did
so for only a short period and it may have been an isolated episode of
sexual activity in their lives. However, when they first started having
sexual intercourse women rarely used the pill, and only once they were
in an ongoing sexual relationship did they begin using the pill.[29] A further
6 per cent of the total pill users in the 1946 cohort never married. Adding
the pill users who started use of the pill more than two years before
marriage and the single pill users together shows that 14 per cent of the
total pill users were engaging in sexual lifestyles that did not fit into a
pattern of premarital sex followed by marriage. The younger women were
when they first used the pill the longer they continued to do so. Use of the
pill would have ensured that most of those women who would otherwise
have become pregnant and had to marry for that reason remained single.
Dunnell suggested about her sample that it 'is . . . likely that considering
only single women is to consider those who have successfully avoided
pregnancy'.[30] This is the probable reason for the much greater use of the
pill among sexually active single women than among married women
who were sexually active before marriage. Had the sexually active
women who married used the pill they would have been more likely to
'escape' becoming pregnant and having to marry. Dunnell goes on to say
that single women in different social classes have very similar contracep-

[29] Wellings et al., *Sexual Attitudes*, 87. Dunnell, *Family Formation*, 52.
[30] Dunnell, *Family Formation*, 55.

tive behaviour and this is probably because these are the contraceptive choices which enable women to stay single.[31] In the second half of the 1960s, the pill became widely available to young single women. Contraception became free to all women regardless of marital status from 1975. By the late 1980s, less than 1 per cent of first intercourse occurred within marriage and there was a gap of several years between the median age at first intercourse and the median age at marriage.[32]

WOMEN AND PAID EMPLOYMENT

During the post-Second World War decades women were entering paid employment in greater numbers. According to the census, from 1901 to 1951 the proportion of women in paid employment was stable around 38 per cent. There was a shift in the 1950s from women giving up paid work on marriage to giving up at first pregnancy. From 1955 to 1965, the demand for female labour grew because of the tight male labour supply, hence women were more easily able to continue in paid employment should they decide to defer childbirth.[33] The greatest increase in the percentage of married women working was from 1961 to 1971 (Table 15.10). Historically marriage had marked the start of childbearing for

Table 15.9. *Use of the pill between first marriage or 'going steady with your husband' and first birth and following birth intervals by women married in different years*

Year of marriage	Use of the pill before and between births		
	Before 1st birth	Between 1st and 2nd	Between 2nd and 3rd
1956–60	1	4	7
1961–5	4	15	29
1966–70	29	38	36
1971–5	43	51	—

Source: Dunnell, *Family Formation*, table 8.11, 47.

[31] Ibid.   [32] Wellings et al., *Sexual Attitudes*, 235.
[33] A. T. Mallier and M. J. Rosser, *Women and the Economy: A Comparative Study of Britain and the USA* (1987), 96–101.

Table 15.10. *Married and single women aged 15–64 in paid employment*

	1951	1961	1971	1981	% change 1951–81
Married	23.4	32.1	46.5	53.9	+130.3
Single	79.8	77.7	68.9	62.3[1]	−21.5

[1]Single women's participation drops due to the rise in the school-leaving age and because more women were marrying.

Source: A. T. Mallier and M. J. Rosser, *Women and the Economy* (1987), table 4.1, 60.

women but increasingly many women used contraception to extend this childless but sexually active period into marriage, further blurring the boundaries between sexual activity within marriage and outside it. Women marrying between the ages of 20 and 24 in 1961–5 had their first baby even faster than those who married 1956–60. This was then followed by a sharp fall in the pace at which those married 1966–70, whose pill use had shot up, produced their first child.[34] After two years of marriage 48 per cent of the 1961–5 marriage cohort had a baby compared with only 40 per cent of women married between 1966 and 1970. This lengthening of the interval between marriage and the first birth continued in the 1970s. Thus, the boundary between married and single women was further blurred. Single women could continue to be sexually active and married women could remain voluntarily childless. The availability of adequate paid employment enabled them to be financially independent. Economic self-sufficiency becomes immensely more difficult for women once they have children. These changes in marriage have resulted in a shift in concern to women with children and a gradual return to the pre-nineteenth-century interest in pressuring men into taking financial responsibility for their children.[35]

This examination of the fertility surveys and the 1946 cohort data on pill use helps to explain why beliefs about sexual change during the late 1960s and 1970s and the quantitative evidence gathered in the mid-1970s were so at variance. The quantitative evidence contributed considerably to the conclusion that the changes brought about by the pill and the sexual

[34] Dunnell, *Family Formation*, 12.

[35] A. Garnham and E. Knights, *Putting the Treasury First: The Truth about Child Support* (1994). J. Lewis and K. E. Kiernan, 'The Boundaries between Marriage, Nonmarriage, and Parenthood: Changes in Behaviour and Policy in Postwar Britain', *Journal of Family History*, 21/3 (1996).

revolution had been greatly overestimated. The percentage of non-manual women aged 20–4 as a proportion of the population is fairly small. As it was the behaviour of these women that was changing first and fastest, the shift did not appear very substantial when viewed statistically. The different trends in women's behaviour were also confusingly close. Rates of premarital sexual intercourse were rising among all classes of young women, but young working-class women were still courting with men whom they intended to marry, then marrying young and having families larger than those achieved using the self-control of the inter-war period. Change was led by the tiny proportion of young, mainly middle-class women who began in the late 1950s to have open sexual affairs with men whom they did not intend to marry, using contraception and abortion to control the consequences. The advent of the pill dramatically increased their numbers, severing the chain that had led women from the start of sexual activity to marriage and from there to childbearing. As soon as it was possible, women had begun to defer childbirth even when married, but now they did so in large numbers, producing a sexual lifestyle in which reproduction was separate from sexual activity and marriage was no longer a marker of either. By the 1970s, young working-class women were also starting to follow a similar path as a growing proportion of them began using the pill. It became possible for women to lead lives in which they could engage in sexual activity without lifelong economic and social consequences, as only men had previously done. Women who began sexual careers that had previously led almost inexorably to marriage because they got pregnant, did not become pregnant. They were faced with making decisions about their lives in a way that had never been possible before. Cumulatively, from the 1970s on, these small shifts enabled many young women to start leading a life that was without historical precedent.

Conclusion

In 1967, after the reform of homosexual law on the basis of the principles laid down in the Wolfenden Report, Lord Arran, who piloted that bill through the House of Lords, said, 'I ask those who have, as it were, been in bondage and for whom the prison doors are now open to show their thanks by comporting themselves quietly and with dignity.'[1] Unmarried women who were provided with contraception had also been expected to continue being discreet and keeping their private lives private but it was not considered necessary to make this kind of comment in relation to women. It was believed women had a natural modesty. Those who opposed contraception in the nineteenth century as well as the twentieth believed that it would lead women to become promiscuous and adulterous, that the institution of marriage would collapse.[2] To a remarkable extent, it appears they were correct. Since the fear of pregnancy was removed women's behaviour has become closer to that long considered acceptable for men and a sexual morality based on a double standard and central to the social construction of male and female sexuality has increasingly faltered and lost all certainty.

There has been a supposed crisis in the family since the 1970s. The revolution in sexual attitudes during the second half of the 1960s was followed by a sexual revolution in behaviour in the 1970s, which accelerated in the 1980s and 1990s.[3] This has resulted in the transformation of the wider family into an extended grouping that is fluid and shifting over

[1] J. Weeks, *Sex, Politics and Society* (1981; 1989), 274.

[2] e.g. C. H. F. Routh, *The Moral and Physical Evils* (1878; 1879), 21.

[3] For example, 8% of births occurred outside marriage in 1971, 32% did so in 1994. In 1971 45% were jointly registered. In 1991 75% were. Separated, divorced, widowed, and never married mothers made up 7.5% of all families with dependent children in 1971, 17.5% in 1991. J. Lewis and K. E. Kiernan, 'The Boundaries between Marriage, Nonmarriage, and Parenthood: Changes in Behaviour and Policy in Postwar Britain', *Journal of Family History*, 21/3 (1996), 380.

time. It is primarily defined by the individuals involved rather than by legal forms such as marriage or legitimate birth. An individual may now include in their wider family grouping unmarried couples, several ex-partners to whom they may or may not have been legally married, stepchildren, divorced parents with new partners, or sexually active teenagers. They may be gay parents, choose not to have children at all, or, within a family unit, there may be children with differing legal statuses and parents. Although there may still be strong objections raised on occasion, these social outcomes of sexual behaviour are now accepted. Nonetheless, the change occurring in the 1970s was not primarily cultural. The force which propelled the cultural transformation of attitudes to sexual behaviour forwards was the transformation of conception and pregnancy from an uncontrollable risk to a freely chosen outcome of sexual intercourse. It might be suggested that these shifts in family structure are not the same as changes in physical sexual activity. However, these new family forms are created by and allow different physical sexual behaviour to take place. They result from the open exercise of sexual choice in order to create lifestyles which were unacceptable before the late 1960s and resulted in severe societal sanctions unless they were concealed.

These changes have made sexual acts less important in people's lives. They may well engage in more sexual activity more often, or with more partners, than was the case fifty or even thirty years ago. Nevertheless, it has become less important. When having sexual intercourse with a person of the opposite sex was tantamount to choosing them as a lifetime partner the act had immense emotional, economic, and symbolic weight attached to it. Lifelong monogamous marriage is now only one option among several. A period of relatively casual sexual activity followed by 'settling down' to serial monogamy results from and in turn creates different sexual expectations from those entailed in the lifelong responsibility preached by marriage manual writers and others in the 1950s. The relaxation of anxiety about sexuality among heterosexuals led to a relaxation of legal and social penalties on homosexuals, making same-sex physical sexual expression carry less weight also. It is because of the changes in lived experience, which altered the consequences of sexuality, that sexual desires could be commercialized, not because of the operations of the free market that sexuality has altered, as Jeffrey Weeks suggested.[4]

In the early 1970s, there were almost millenarian hopes on the part of some groups of people for a sexual revolution which would involve greater honesty and the rejection of fixed sexual identities, the sexual double standard, and monogamy. It was believed that this revolution would transform human relationships. This did not occur. However, as has been shown, the current chaos in family forms is part of a long-drawn-out process of change. There has been a slow movement, generation by generation, towards a society in which the lives of men are enhanced by involvement with their children and greater emotional expression, while the lives of women are enhanced by greater educational opportunities, by paid employment, and by sexual pleasure. People's expectations of their partners have risen and so too have the possibilities for more open, more emotionally close and relaxed relationships. More and more every child is a wanted child. The repeated recessions of the last twenty years (and the advent of AIDS) have overshadowed these positive shifts. This, and the lack of historical memory of the emotional and sexual life of previous generations, conceals the extent to which the changes described in this book have improved the lives of women in this society. However there are still many women throughout the globe who continue to have minimal access to medical care in childbirth and afterwards, and to safe, affordable contraception and abortion should they choose not to have children. Even in Western cultures the improvements in people's lives made possible by the political and social agitation of previous generations have been eroded by neo-liberal economic measures resulting in casualization and long hours for those in employment and increasing poverty for those who are dependent on social welfare. Contraception is now part of the technological armoury of a society in which many feel they cannot afford children, not a choice for those who do not want them. Many men still feel they have the right to dominate women. Acknowledging the immense positive change that has taken place does not imply blindness to existing problems. Instead it should give confidence and hope to those who seek such change in the future.

[4] J. Weeks, 'Sexual Values Revisited', in L. Segal (ed.), *New Sexual Agendas* (1997; 1998), 50.

Analysis of the Sex Manual Authors

The following discussion is based upon a total of 104 authors of sex manuals published between 1918 and 1972. In Chapter 8, the definition was provided of sex manuals as legally available books intended for women and men to read in order to obtain knowledge about their own physical sexual body, and that of the opposite sex, and about physical sexual practice, primarily coitus. As this suggests, the genre is almost exclusively concerned with heterosexual sexual practice. Some of the texts contain only a few pages describing the body or discussing physical sexual practice. The start date of 1918 is the year in which *Married Love* by Marie Stopes was published. The immensely successful manual *The Joy of Sex* by Alex Comfort published in 1972 is the last manual to be included. The period has been divided into two parts, the first period 1918–45, and the later period from 1946 to 1972. These two periods correspond to the inter-war period, and the post-Second World War era. Few manuals were published in the 1940s and the division reflects the different sensibility of the new generation of adults born after the First World War, as much as, or more than, the impact of the Second World War.

The basis for inclusion of texts in this list is contemporary availability, usually publication, in England. The manuals were found by going through the catalogues of the British Library and the Wellcome Trust Library for the History of Medicine, in second-hand bookshops, in contemporary sex research and bibliographies by these researchers, and in the existing secondary literature. This is not a sample of the manuals, as I have attempted to include all that were available. Some books and their authors have undoubtedly been missed. These are most likely to be reprints of pre-First World War manuals, American manuals imported into inter-war Britain, most of which sold in small numbers, and manuals imported or published in paperback after 1960, some of which were not deposited in the British Library. However, the content and approach of the manuals falls into loose categories and it is unlikely that whole categories have been omitted. Where pre-First World War manuals were reprinted and sold during the later period these have been included (Guyot, Howard, Robie,

Stephens, Trall). Only a small number of health guides and encyclopedias is included and complete coverage of these was not attempted.

A combination of the author's nationality in the case of manuals published in Britain, and either nationality, or place of publication where this is unknown, in the remainder, has been analysed to give some indication of the influence of other sexual cultures on the genre. The percentage of British-authored manuals falls from 44 to 38 per cent of the total between the inter-war period and the post-war period. A quarter of the manuals were first published in countries other than Britain or America in the early period but this fell to a fifth in the later period. The deficit is made up by a rise in the number of American manuals sold in Britain from 30 per cent to 43 per cent or over two-fifths of the total. The foreign category consists mainly of Germans in the first period but in the second period there are authors from Denmark, India, Japan, New Zealand, and Sweden.

Publishers and authors were justifiably concerned about the prospect of having their books seized and destroyed by the police. The majority of the sex manual authors were ethically concerned, progressive, and relatively socially conventional people, whose concern was with the sexual activity of the hetero-sexual majority of the population. Many of these authors did believe that sexual activity should take place only within marriage or that homosexuality was an illness, but even those who did not believe this could not say so openly. Books including discussion of physical sexual practice might well be banned if they included, for example, expressions of support for female premarital inter-course. The following three texts presented a less conventional approach to sexual practice. *The Sexual Impulse* (1935) by E. Charles was ordered to be destroyed by the court that same year. In 1942 the publishers and E. Chesser, the author of *Love without Fear* (1940), defended their case before a jury and were acquitted. A man who ran a postal lending library was imprisoned for lending out *The Encyclopedia of Sexual Knowledge*, ed. N. Haire (1934), in the 1930s, and the book was condemned to be destroyed in a case in 1950. Even after 1959 when censorship law was greatly eased there were still restrictions on illustrations and limits on content.

The available information gives a minimum level of involvement in marriage guidance, religion, eugenics, and birth control. Further research would probably raise these percentages. The marriage guidance movement emerged during this period and the concept of a marriage guidance counsellor was created.[1] The number of marriage counsellors who write manuals increases as the movement expands from 7 per cent in the early period to 15 per cent in the late period. The

[1] Jane Lewis, D. Clark, and D. Morgan, *Whom God hath Joined: The Work of Marriage Guidance* (1992). J. H. Wallis and H. S. Booker, *Marriage Counselling: A Description and Analysis of the Remedial Work of the National Marriage Guidance Council* (1958).

movement's goal was preserving marriages and so they emphasize the relationship, not increasing the sexual satisfaction of the individual. Usually this meant that women were advised to accommodate themselves to their husband's sexual needs and resulted in a more socially conservative approach when compared to other manuals from the same period (Boulton, Bovet, Butterfield, Geldenhuys, Gray, Griffith, Kelly, Macaulay, Mears, Miles, Popenoe, Tizard, Tyrer, Wallis, Wrage).

Many of the authors had a substantial religious commitment. Nearly a third, 28 per cent, were active Christians. Wright went as a medical missionary to China. Cochran belonged to the Society of Friends. Eyles searched for a religious faith. The nature of this commitment differed widely and it has no consistent impact on the manuals (Barnes, Boulton, Bovet, Bross, Butterfield, Calderone, Clark, E. Cole, M. Davis, Eichenlaub, Eyles, Gedenhuys, Gray, Griffith, Hutton, Johnson, G. A. Kelly, Long, Macandrew, Macaulay, Mears, Miles, Olsen, Rayner, Tenenbaum, Tizard, Tyrer, Walker, Wallis, Weatherhead, Witt, Wright). Nearly a tenth of the total were actually ministers.

Over a fifth of those who wrote manuals in the early period had a substantial involvement in the birth control movement (Calderone, Cole, Cox, Griffith, Haire, Himes, Macaulay, Malleson, Mears, Pillay, Popenoe, Sanger, Smyth, A. and H. Stone, Stopes, Wright). This fell to only 11 per cent in the later period. Malleson, Chesser, Cole, Griffith, and Wright were involved in British abortion law reform or provision of abortion.

There are a number of manuals specifically written for unmarried adults. With the exception of those by the Barneses and M. Cole and Cauthery, these are conservative and frequently prescriptive (Bevan, Bross, E. Cole, Hacker, Johnson, Macaulay, Mears, Rayner, Tizard). Weatherhead, and Costler and Haire, also address themselves to homosexuals in the inter-war period.

The majority of authors did not belong to either the American or the British Eugenics Society (members: Chesser, M. Cole, Cox, Griffith, Haire, Himes, Hoff and Whitehead, Hutton, Levine, Malleson, Mears, Pillay, Popenoe, Sanger, Stone, Stopes). Popenoe was a major figure in both the American eugenics movement and marriage guidance. None of the professional writers belonged. The overtly racist Charles, who was a writer, did not belong to the Society but Pillay, an Indian doctor, did. Further research is needed to understand what membership represented to contemporary individuals.

There were two bases for a positive approach to variation in physical sexual practice. Within the context of each period, there was a libertine approach, which might involve support for prostitution, extramarital sex for men, and male domination, and rejection of homosexuality (Charles, Chartham, Ellis, Hastings,

Havil, Hendrickson, Macandrew, Scott, Toft Tufill,). The most inaccurate and bigoted of the top-selling manuals, *Everything you Always Wanted to Know about Sex but were Afraid to Ask* by David Reuben, falls into this category. Sexual radicalism could include support for feminism, homosexuality, open marriage, premarital sex for women, and, sometimes, opposition to prostitution. The following authors are the closest to this position (Chesser, Comfort, Costler, Eyles, Haire, Wright). Norman Haire is the only known homosexual and there were no known lesbians. Chesser and Walker both supported homosexual law reform and attempted to promote tolerance. In the 1950s some of the psychotherapists were involved in attempting to convert homosexuals to heterosexuality (Caprio, Ellis). There were authors who emphasized male control of sexuality (Andrews, Berg and Street, Borgeson and Kaufman, Buschke and Jacobsohn, Charles, Chartham, Lowen, Eichenlaub Scott, Tenenbaum).

Women made up just under a fifth, or 18 per cent, of the total number of manual authors. Manuals by women were just as likely, and just as unlikely, to be remote and authoritarian as those by males.[2] The extent to which the manuals were prescriptive or promoted a submissive role for women cannot be correlated to the gender of the writer. It can be correlated with the period, and the high point of this approach was the 1950s, especially manuals by psychoanalysts. There are no women in the second period of the stature and impact of Stopes and Wright. The main association between the sex of the author and the attitudes expressed in the manuals is quite different. As a group the women appear to be considerably more sexually conservative than the men in the second period. The average age of the female manual authors at publication of their first manual rose from 41 years in the first period to 46 in the second period. They were all well-established professional journalists or doctors, with one exception, 'J.', or Garrity, the author of *The Sensuous Woman*. Women were vulnerable to having their professional identity diminished and belittled if they revealed sexual experience. Calderone was castigated for political *naïveté* as late as 1971 for having admitted to pregnancy before her first marriage in 1926. Malleson concealed having had her first child before she and the father married. Couples wrote 13 per cent of the manuals. Where there is information available the career and age details suggest that the woman played a major role (Baruch and Miller, Cochranes, Stones, Rainers). This was not so in the well-known case of the scientific sexologists William Masters and Virginia Johnson, but they may be exceptional.

[2] See B. Ehrenreich, E. Hess, and G. Jacobs, *Re-making Love: The Feminisation of Sex* (1987), 3.

In the early period over half (54 per cent) of the manual authors were medical doctors, but by the later period this had fallen to 41 per cent. Instead the number of psychologists more than doubled from only 7 per cent to 20 per cent of the total, and writers rose from 11 per cent to 20 per cent. In the early period 16 per cent of manuals are by urologists but that falls to under 2 per cent while those by gynaecologists rise from 7 per cent to 16 per cent. This is possibly because male physical sexuality ceased to be perceived as a problem and urologists had less contact with sexual problems as venereal disease declined in importance. The occupations of manual authors ranged from doctors, whose work entailed considerable physical contact with the body and knowledge of its physiology, to writers who had no contact with the person, let alone the body. Comfort and Stopes were scientists, but aside from these two, authors with medical training were more likely to write less confusing, more innovative, and more physiologically helpful sex manuals. This is probably because of their initial concentration on the physical body. Initially outrage, compassion, and a desire to help others escape problems they themselves had experienced often motivated these authors (Eyles, Griffith, Stopes, Tyrer, Walker, Wright). Writers and psychotherapists tended to produce more prescriptive manuals, which imposed rigid theoretical constructs upon the body. Once it became apparent that the manuals had the potential for huge sales, new authors often appear to be motivated only by financial gain. There is a definite shift, beginning with Scott in the 1930s, toward jobbing writers who obtain the required medical knowledge from their co-authors or from manuals by doctors (Andrews, Chartham, Davis, Loth, Macandrew, Oakley, Rainer and Rainer, Street).

The information on author's lives and careers comes from a variety of sources and is not comprehensive. The book jackets have provided the only information on a number of authors. Where it has been possible to check book jacket information from other sources it has been correct. There are five pseudonymous authors about whom I have no information (Beale, P. Davis, Howarth, James, Parkinson-Smith). Their books do not differ in any consistent fashion from the other texts. Nationality is noted for non-British authors. Where known, place of birth is noted for individuals who later became British or American. Medical degrees have been confirmed in the *British Medical Directory* and the *American Medical Directory*. Other sources include *Contemporary Authors*; *Who's Who*; *Who's Who among English and European Authors, 1931–1949* (1978); 'Notes on Contributors', in Albert Ellis and A. P. Pillay, *Sex, Society and the Individual* (1953); and British Library and Library of Congress catalogues. It has not been possible to confirm non-English-language qualifications or those of psychotherapists.

Unless otherwise stated the authors were British and the manuals were published in London. The manuals were placed in periods according to the date they were first published in Britain or, if a British edition was not published, according to the date of first publication elsewhere. The date of first publication has been chosen in order that the texts can be analysed as a reflection of the existing sexual culture. The author's first manual is listed. Further manuals and other writing can be found in the Bibliography. Many of the authors were prolific, several publishing over forty books (Chesser, Comfort, A. Ellis, Walker), but they usually establish their basic perspective on sexuality in their first book on the topic. Some of the sales figures that are given come from the book cover and they could be exaggerated. However, those books that claim to have large sales are more likely to be mentioned in other sources and second-hand copies are more easily obtained, suggesting that they did sell in large numbers as claimed. Repeated editions also provide information of sales, albeit limited, as there is no indication of edition size. Other sources of sales information include biographies, and articles.[3]

[3] L. S. Lewis and D. Brissett, 'Sex as Work', *Social Problems*, 15/8 (1967). *Newsweek* (18 Oct. 1965, 24 Aug. 1970).

List of Sex Manual Authors

Andrews, A., writer (b. 1911). Rejects female emancipation. *Sex and Marriage*, introd. E. Chesser (Newnes, 1964).

Barnes, Frances (1927–25 May 1969). Barnes, Kenneth Charles, teacher (b. 1903). *Sex, Friendship and Marriage* (Allen & Unwin, 1938). Sex education. More explicit than K. Barnes's second sex education manual, *He and She* (Darwen Finlayson, 1958).

Baruch, Dorothy W., USA, child psychologist, MD (b. 1899). Miller, Hyman, USA, MD (b. 1918). *Sex in Marriage: New Understandings* (George Allen & Unwin, 1962).

Beale, G. Courtenay [pseud.]. There is no information about Beale, though the type of information given suggests he was a doctor as claimed. Stopes was convinced he had plagiarized *Married Love* (1918). Comparison of the text does not support her. Beale disagrees with Stopes on several points, has a different range of references, and his own style. *Wise Wedlock: The Whole Truth* (Health Promotion, 1922 [1st pub. date not in book, taken from British Library catalogue]). *Sales*: by 1939 100,000, from book jacket of Macandrew, 1939.

Berg, L. M., USA, psychologist (1901–72). Street, Robert, USA, author. *The Basis of Happy Marriage: The Art of Sexual Relationship* (W. H. Allen, 1955).

Bevan, James Stuart, doctor (b. 1930). *Sex: The Plain Facts* (Faber & Faber, 1966).

Borgeson, Griffith, USA, psychologist. Kaufman, Joseph J., USA, urologist (b. 1931). *Man and Sex* (Victor Gollancz, 1961).

Boulton, W., minister, Provost of Guildford (b. 1899). *Marriage* (SPCK, 1963), originally pub. Mothers' Union, London, 1960.

Bovet, Theodor, Swiss, doctor, (b. 1900). Marriage counsellor *Love, Skill and Mystery* (New York, Doubleday, 1958). *Sales*: from book jacket of 1st USA edition: 'Over 100,000 copies sold in Europe'.

Bross, Barbara, USA, gynaecologist. *The Pleasures of Love* (Rapp & Carroll, 1967). Sex education for women.

Buschke, Abraham, German, MD, specialist in urology and dermatology (b. 1868). Jacobsohn, Friedrich, German, urologist (b. 1894). *Sex Habits: A Vital Factor in Well-Being*, trans. Eden and Cedar Paul (G. Routledge & Sons, 1932).

Butterfield, Oliver, McKinley. USA, revd, marriage counsellor (b. 1891). *Sex Life in Marriage* (Duckworth, 1937). *Sales*: L. S. Lewis and D. Brisset, 'Sex as Work', *Social Problems*, 15/8 (1967) include as having high sales. *Sexual Harmony in Marriage* (New York, Emerson, 1953).

Calderone, Mary Steichen (with Goldman, P. and Goldman, R. P.), USA, MD (b. 1 July 1904). *Release from Sexual Tensions: Toward an Understanding of their Causes and Effects in Marriage* (New York, Random House, 1960).

Caprio, Frank S., USA, Psychiatrist (b. 1906). *The Sexually Adequate Male* (New York, Citadel Press, 1952). *The Sexually Adequate Female* (New York, Citadel Press, 1953).

Cauthery, P. D., doctor (b. 1925). Cole, Martin D., plant geneticist (b. 1931). Sex therapist, co-founder abortion clinic in Birmingham. *The Fundamentals of Sex* (W. H. Allen, 1971). Sex education for unmarried adults.

Charles, Edward [according to BL Catalogue pseud. Charles Edward Hempstead], lecturer/writer (b. 1898, Ana Capri, Isola di Capri). *The Sexual Impulse: An Introduction to the Study of the Psychology, Physiology and Bio-chemistry of the Sexual Impulse among Adults in Mental and Bodily Health* (Boriswood, 1935).

Chartham, Robert [pseud. Ronald Seth], professional writer (1911–85). *Mainly for Women: A Practical Guide to Love-Making in Marriage* (MacDonald, 1964).

Chesser, Eustace, doctor, psychiatrist, abortionist (b. 1902). *Love without Fear (A Guide to Sex Techniques)* (Rich & Cowan, 1941). *Sales*: book jacket of 1951 UK printing of 1948 edn.: 62,000. *Newsweek* (18 Oct. 1965): 2,800,000.

Clark, LeMon [*sic*], USA, MD, obstetrician/gynaecologist (b. 1897). *Sex and You* (Indianapolis, Bobbs-Merrill, 1949).

Cochran, Joan (née Feltham), NZ, teacher (1912–95) (main author). Cochran, Bruce, NZ, English professor (1903–70). *Meeting and Mating: A Treatment of the Mental and Physical Aspects of Love and Marriage* (Wellington, A. H. & A. W. Reed, 1944). Sex education for unmarried adults.

Cole, Estelle, medical psychologist (b. Ireland). *Education for Marriage* (Duckworth, 1938). Sex education for unmarried women.

Cole, Martin D. (With Cauthery above).

Comfort, Alex, scientist (1920–2000). Wrote ten books and had an entry in *Who's Who* by the time he was 24. *The Joy of Sex* (Modsets Securities, 1972).

Costler, A. [according to Library of Congress, pseud. Arthur Koestler, with A. Willy and others], novelist, journalist, and critic (b. 1905, Budapest, d. 1983). *Encyclopædia of Sexual Knowledge* (*Encyclopédie de la vie sexuelle*), general editor Norman Haire (Francis Aldor, 1934).

Cox, Gladys M., MB award 1923. *The Woman's Book of Health: A Complete Guide to Physical Well-Being* (The Lady's Companion, 1933).

Davis, Maxine, USA, journalist (1899–1978). *The Sexual Responsibility of Woman* (William Heinemann, 1957). *Sales:* numerous paperback reprints into the late 1970s.

Davis, Porter [BL Catalogue pseud. Gordon Schindler] (b. 1918). As Schindler wrote about Danish pornography and a novel. *Handbook for Husbands (and Wives)* (El Segundo, Calif.: Banner Books, 1949).

Eichenlaub, John Ellis, USA, MD (b. 1922). *Publications:* books on medical self-help, over 300 magazine articles. *The Marriage Art* (New York, Lyle Stuart, 1961). *Sales:* book jacket: sold 1,500,000 USA. Eleven UK reprints by 1966.

Ellis, Albert, USA, sexologist/psychologist/author (b. 1913). *Publications:* Over one hundred listed on PsycINFO database. Over 50 books pub., incl. self-help manuals, male and female sexuality. *The Art and Practice of Love* (Souvenir Press, 1961). Originally pub. as *The Art and Science of Love* (New York, Lyle Stuart, 1960). *Sales:* hardback: 140,000 in 3 years (*Newsweek,* 18 Oct. 1965).

Evans, Charles Benjamin Shaffer, USA, MD (b. 1901). *Man, Woman and Marriage,* preface N. Haire (John Lane, 1932).

Everett, Milliard Spencer (b. 1897). Also pub. on nursing ethics, and ethics. *Marital Hygiene: A Detailed Consideration of Sex and Marriage, etc.* (Rider & Co., 1933).

Exner, Max Joseph, USA, MD (b. 1871). Undertook early sex survey research in 1915. *The Sexual Side of Marriage* (George Allen & Unwin, 1932). Nine British reprints listed in 1951 Guild Books edition.

Eyles, Leonora, journalist/novelist (1889–1960). *Publications:* several novels, books of social comment, prolific journalist, e.g. contributed to *Labour Leader,* problem page *Modern Woman,* woman's page *Daily Herald. Commonsense about Sex* (Victor Gollancz, 1933).

Felstein, Ivor Leslie, USA, geriatrician (b. 1933). *Sex and the Longer Life* (Allen Lane, 1970).

Geldenhuys, Johannes Norval, USA, revd (b. 1918). *The Intimate Life: or, The Christian's Sex Life, a Practical, Up-to-Date Handbook Intended for Engaged and Newly Married Christians* (James Clarke, 1952).

Gray, A. Herbert. revd. (b. Edinburgh 1868). *Publications:* over ten books pub. contributed to *St Martin's Review. Men, Women and God: A Discussion of Sex Questions from the Christian Point of View* (SCM, 1923). *Sales:* book jacket, 17th edn. 1947: worldwide about 150,000.

Gregory, Stephan, USA. *How to Achieve Sexual Ecstasy* (USA, Running Man Press, 1968).

Griffith, Edward F., doctor, (b. 1895 California, d. 1988). Founder NMGC *Modern Marriage and Birth Control* (Victor Gollancz, 1935). *Sales:* Continued into 27th edn. 1973.

Guyot, Jules France (1807–72). The translator was the first president of the USA National Birth Control League and helped fund the Committee on Maternal Health. *A Ritual for Married Lovers*, trans. Gertrude Minturn Pinchot (Noel Douglas, 1933; Baltimore, Waverly Press, Inc., 1931). Privately circulated, 1859.

Hacker, Rose, (b. 1904). voluntary worker NMGC *The Opposite Sex* (André Deutsch, 1957). Sex education for young women.

Haire, Norman, Australia, gynaecologist/sexologist (1892–1952). Homosexual. *Everyday Sex Problems* (Frederick Muller, 1948).

Hastings, Donald W., USA, MD. *A Doctor Speaks on Sexual Expression in Marriage* (Little Brown, 1968).

Havil, Anthony [pseud. of Dr Elliot Elias Phillip] (b. 1915). *The Technique of Sex: Towards a Better Understanding of Sexual Relationship* (Wales, 1939). *Sales*: 29th revised edn. 1959.

Hegeler, Inge, Danish, psychologist/author (1927–96). Hegeler, Sten, Danish, psychologist/sexologist/author (b. 1923). *An ABZ of Love* (Neville Spearman, 1963). *Sales*: 1969 book jacket: 1,000,000 in hardback.

Hendrickson, T. See also Toft, below. *Variations on a Sexual Theme* (Julian Press Business Promotions, 1969).

Himes, Norman E., USA, sociologist (1899–1949). *Publications: The Medical History of Contraception* (New York, Wilkin & Wilkin, 1936). *Happy Marriage*, ed. F. L. Secor (George Allen & Unwin, 1941). Orig. pub. USA, 1940.

Hirsch, Edwin Walter, USA, Urologist (b. 1892). *The Power to Love: A Psychic and Physiologic Study of Regeneration* (Bodley Head, 1936).

Hoff, Charles A., USA, MD, 'Eminent authority and formerly Physician to the Southern Ohio Hospital Author of Treatise on "The Use of Sedatives," "General Paralysis," etc, etc.' Whitehead, Clayton S., USA, MD (b. 1879). *Ethical Sex Relations: or, The New Eugenics. A Safe Guide for Young Men-Young Women . . . Part II. Parents' Medical Counselor* (J. A. Hertel Co., Chicago, Toronto, 1928).

Howard, William Lee, USA, MD (1860–1918). Strongly anti-birth control. *Facts for the Married* (London and Rahway, NJ, Grant Richards, 1913).

Howarth, Vyvyan, doctor, 'International consultant sexologist and clinician', according to the book. No listing for Howarth in *AMD* or *MD*. *Secret Techniques of Erotic Delight* (New York, Lyle Stuart, 1966).

Hutton, Isabel E., psychiatrist (1887–1960). *The Hygiene of Marriage* (William Heinemann, 1923). Poor sales, according to the author's memoirs.

J. [pseud. J. T. Garrity], USA (b. late 1930s, Minnesota). *The Sensuous Woman: The First How-to Book for the Female who Yearns to be All Woman* (Herts., Lyle Stuart, 1969). *Sales*: six months 250,000 (*Newsweek*, 24 Aug. 1970).

Jacobsohn, Friedrich (with Buschke, above).

James, John [pseud.], doctor? *The Facts of Sex* (MacGibbon & Kee, 1969).

Johnson, Eric Warner, USA, teacher/relief worker, (b. 1918). *Love and Sex in Plain Language* (Philadelphia, Lippincott, 1965).

Kaufman, Joseph J. [with/Borgeson, above].

Kelly, George Anthony, USA, priest (b. 1916). Member of Papal Birth Control Commission, 1965. *The Catholic Marriage Manual* (New York, Random House, 1958).

Kelly, George Lombard, USA, MD (b. 1890). *Sexual Feeling in Married Men and Women* (New York, 1938).

Kokken, Sha [pseud. of Hsieh Kuochuan], Japan, gynaecologist. *A Happier Sex Life* (1964). *Sales:* Japanese edition pub. 1960, by August 1966, sales of over 1,600,000 (New English Library edn. 1972).

Lamare, Noel, France. *Love and Fulfilment in Woman*, trans. R. and A. Case (George Allen & Unwin, 1955).

Lazarsfeld, Sofie, Austria, Adlerian psychologist (b. 1882). *Rhythm of Life: A Guide to Sexual Harmony for Women*, trans. E. P. and K. Stapelfeldt (G. Routledge & Sons, 1934).

Levine, Lena, USA, MD, psychiatry (b. 1903). Sex counselling with H. and A. Stone Loth, David. *The Frigid Wife: Her Way to Sexual Fulfilment* (Arthur Barker, 1963).

Long, Harland W., USA, MD (b. 1869). *Sane Sex and Sane Sex Living* (Boston, Richard G. Badger, 1919). Eugenic Publishing, 1919, 1932, 1937.

Lowen, Alexander M., USA, psychoanalyst (b. 1910). Freudian, acknowledged a debt to Wilhelm Reich, his analyst, but insisted that his bioenergetic therapy was a new concept. *Love and Orgasm: A Revolutionary Guide to Sexual Fulfillment* (Macmillan, 1965).

Macandrew, Rennie [pseud of Elliot, Andrew George] (b. 1907). No information under either name. As Elliot, wrote e.g. *Gun Fun and Hints* . . . (Kingswood, 1956), *Hell! I'm British. A Plain Man Looks at America, Americans and Englishmen* (Herbert Joseph, 1939). *Life Long Love: Healthy Sex and Marriage* (Wales, 1938). *Encyclopedia of Sex and Love Technique* (Wales, 1941). *Sales:* book jacket claims over 60,000 sold by 13th rev. imp. 1951.

Macaulay, Mary, gynaecologist (b. 1902 India). FPA, Marriage guidance. *The Art of Marriage* (Delisle, 1952). Sold by FPA clinics. Sex education for unmarried women.

Malleson, Joan [pub. as 'Medica'], gynaecologist (1900–56). Founder member Abortion Law Reform Association. Referred girl to Aleck Bourne in Bourne case 1938–9. FPA. *Any Wife or Any Husband* (Heinemann, 1951).

Mears, Eleanor, gynaecologist (1917–92). FPA, Marriage guidance *Marriage: A Continuing Relationship* (W. & G. Foyle, 1960).

Miles, Herbert Jackson, USA, revd (b. 1907). *Sexual Happiness in Marriage: A Christian Interpretation of Adjustment in Marriage* (London and USA, Zondervan, 1967).

Miller, Hyman (with Baruch, above).

Oakley, Eric Gilbert [also wrote as Peter Capon, Paul Gregson, Grapho], journalist/editor (b. 1916). *Sane and Sensual Sex* (Walton Press, [original date of publication unknown] repr. 1963). Listed in *CA* as first pub. 1964.

Olsen, Henry, Danish, MD. *Sexual Adjustment in Marriage* (New York, Henry Holt & Co., 1952).

Parkinson-Smith, Ernest, doctor (b. 1884). Not in *MD*, probably a pseudonym. *The Physical Content of Marriage* (Wales, 1952).

Pillay, A. P., India, doctor, OBE (1890–1956). Founder and managing editor of *Marriage Hygiene* (1934–7) and of *International Journal of Sexology* from 1947. *The art of Love and Sane Sex Living, Based on Ancient Classics and Works of American and European Sexologists* (Bombay, D. B. Taraporevala Sons & Co., Private, 1964).

Popenoe, Paul B., USA, marriage guidance (b. 1888). *Modern Marriage: A Handbook* (New York, Macmillan, 1925).

Radl, Lucia, Romania/USA, MD (b. 1900). *Illustrated Guide to Sex Happiness in Marriage* (Heinemann, 1953).

Rainer, Jerome [pseud. of Gerald Goode], USA, press agent and author (b. 1899?–1983). *Publications:* 2 books on ballet. Rainer, Julia [pseud. Ruth Goode], journalist, USA (1905–97). From 1920s to 1960s, contributed to *Nation, New York Evening World, New York Evening Post, MD Medical News Magazine*, also wrote fiction and was a ghost writer for medical and child care books. *Sexual Pleasure in Marriage* (Souvenir Press, 1959).

Rayner, Claire Berenice, agony aunt/author/novelist [5 pseudonyms-see *CA*] (b. 1931). *People in Love: A Modern Guide to Sex in Marriage* (Paul Hamlyn, 1968). Sex education for unmarried people.

Reuben, David, USA, psychiatrist (b. 1933). Inaccurate, homophobic, slated by professional peers. *Everything you Always Wanted to Know about Sex* but were Afraid to Ask* (New York, W. H. Allen, 1970). *Sales:* eight million copies within two years. *CA*.

Robie, Walter Franklin, USA, MD (b. 1866). Written with wife. *Rational Sex Ethics: A Physiological and Psychological Study of the Sex lives of Normal Men and Women* (Boston, G. Badger, 1918).

Robinson, Marie Nyswander, USA, psychiatrist (b. 1919). Rigid populist Freudian. *The Power of Sexual Surrender* (W. H. Allen, 1960). *Sales:* often available second hand.

Sanger, Margaret, USA, nurse/birth control agitator (1879–1966). *Happiness in Marriage* (Jonathon Cape, 1927). Simple populist manual, little detail.

Scott, George Ryley, author (1886–1954). Unconcerned with respectability or ethics. Member Royal Anthropological Society. *The New Art of Love* (John Bale Sons & Danielsson, 1934). *Sales*: reached 4th edn. 1955.

Stephens, Margaret, writer/poet. *Women and Marriage: A Handbook*, introd. M. D. Scharlieb and S. A. Barnett (T. Fisher Unwin, 1910). *Sales*: 3rd edn. 1918.

Stone, Abraham, USA, MD, urologist (1890–1959). Stone, Hannah Mayer, USA, MD, gynaecologist (1894–1941). Marriage guidance/birth control. *A Marriage Manual: A Practical Guide to Sex and Marriage* (Victor Gollancz, 1936). *Sales*: USA 1965, 600,000, 48th printing (*Newsweek*, 18 Oct. 1965).

Stopes, Marie, scientist/birth control pioneer (1880–1958). *Married Love: A New Contribution to the Solution of Sex Difficulties* (A. C. Feild, 1918). *Sales*: Dec. 1923, 406,000 worldwide; end 1938, 810,000; 1955, 1,032,000.

Street, Robert (with Berg, above).

Tenenbaum, Joseph Leib, USA, urologist (b. 1887 Austria). *The Riddle of Sex: The Medical and Social Aspects of Sex, Love and Marriage*, introd. V. Brittain (George Routledge & Sons, 1930).

Tizard, Leslie J., revd, chairman Birmingham Marriage Guidance Council. *Guide to Marriage* (Allen & Unwin, 1948). Sex education for engaged adults.

Toft, Mogens, Denmark. Hendrickson (see above) was probably plaigarizing Toft. *Sexual Techniques: An Illustrated Guide* (London and Copenhagen, Souvenir Press, 1969).

Trall, Russell Thatcher, USA, MD (1812–1877). Founder of New York Hygieo-therapeutic College in 1854. Licensed to give medical degrees, promoted vegetarianism and water cures. *Sexual Physiology: A Scientific and Popular Exposition of the Fundamental Problems in Sociology* (Health Promotion Ltd., 1866). *Sales*: reprint edn. 1919.

Tuffill, S. G., FRCS. Based on letters to *Forum* and similar sources. *Sexual Stimulation in Marriage* (MacGibbon & Kee, 1971).

Tyrer, Alfred Henry, Canada, revd (1869–approx. 1940). Marriage guidance. *Sex, Marriage and Birth Control: A Guide-Book to Sex Health and a Satisfactory Sex Life in Marriage* (Toronto, Marriage Welfare Bureau, 1943). *Sales*: book jacket: 1943, 320,000 in Canada.

van de Velde, Theodore H., the Netherlands, gynaecologist (1873–1937). *Publications*: over 70 medical journal articles. *Ideal Marriage: Its Physiology and Technique*, trans. Stella Brown (William Heinemann, 1928). *Sales*: 1970, UK edn. 700,000; 1,000,000 USA and was still being reprinted (*Newsweek*, 24 Aug. 1970).

von Urban, Rudolf D., Vienna/USA, psychoanalyst (b. 1879, Vienna). Believed sexual feeling was 'bio-electrical potential'. *Sex Perfection* (Rider & Co., 1952).

Walker, Kenneth M., urologist/author (1882–1966). *Publications*: over 40 books, also incl. medical texts and popular philosophy. *Sex Difficulties in the Male* (Jonathan Cape, 1934).

Wallis, J. H, training officer of the NMGC (b. 1907). *Sexual Harmony in Marriage* (Routledge Kegan Paul, 1964).

Weatherhead, Leslie Dixon, minister, CBE (1893–1976). Was a pace setter in the reconciliation of religion with psychoanalysis, gained fame as a preacher. *The Mastery of Sex through Psychology and Religion* (SCM, 1931). *Sales*: 11th edn. 1942. Book jacket: by 1942 the book had sold 58,000.

Weider, Ben, USA. Content suggests this was self-published by a non-professional from the USA, not the Ben Weider (b. 1923) listed in *CA*. *Sexual Happiness* (A Weider Publication, 1963).

Whitehead, Clayton S. (with Hoff, above).

Witt, Elmer N., USA, revd. Also wrote three books on Christianity. *Life can be Sexual* (St Louis, Concordia, 1967).

Wrage, Karl Horst, German. *Man and Woman: The Basis of their Relationship*, trans. Stanley S. B. Gilder (Collins, 1966).

Wright, Helena, gynaecologist (1887–1982). FPA. *The Sex Factor in Marriage*, introd. A. Herbert Gray (Williams & Norgate Ltd., 1930). *Sales*: book jacket: by 1947, 147,000.

Bibliography

Place of publication is London unless otherwise stated

Government Publications

ARTHURE, HUMPHREY, et al., *Report on Confidential Enquiries into Maternal Deaths in England and Wales 1967–1969*, Department of Health and Social Security Reports on Health and Social Subjects No. 1 (1972).

Birth Statistics: Historical Series of Statistics from Registrations of Births in England and Wales, 1837–1983, OPCS Series FM1 no. 13 (1983).

Birth Statistics: Review of the Registrar General on Births and Patterns of Family Building in England and Wales, 1992, OPCS Series FM1 no. 21 (1994).

BONE, MARGARET, *Family Planning Services in England and Wales*, OPCS Social Survey Division (1973).

—— *Measures of Contraceptive Effectiveness and their Uses*, Studies on Medical and Population Subjects No. 28 (1975).

—— *The Family Planning Service: Changes and Effects (1970–1975)*, OPCS Social Survey Division (1978).

—— 'Trends in Contraceptive Practice among Married Couples', *Health Trends*, 12 (1980).

—— *Family Planning in Scotland in 1982* (1985).

CARTWRIGHT, ANN, *Recent Trends in Family Building and Contraception*, Studies in Medical and Population Subjects No. 34 (1978).

—— and WILKINS, W., *Changes in Family Building Plans: A Follow up Study to 'How Many Children?'*, Studies on Medical and Population Subjects No. 33 (1976).

DUNNELL, KAREN, *Family Formation 1976* (1979).

Legal Abortions Carried out under the 1967 Abortion Act in England and Wales, OPCS General and Demographic Series AB1 (1976).

Marriage and Divorce Statistics: Historical Series of Statistics on Marriages and Divorces in England and Wales, 1837–1983, OPCS Series FM2 no. 16 (1990).

Marriage and Divorce Statistics: Review of the Registrar General on Marriages and Divorces in England and Wales, 1980, OPCS Series FM2 no. 7 (1983).

Marriage, Divorce and Adoption Statistics, 1995, OPCS Series FM2 no. 23 (1998).

MURPHY, MIKE, and NI BHROLCHAIN, M. (eds.), *Time-Series Approaches to the Analysis of Fertility Change*, Studies on Medical and Population Subjects No. 55 (1993).

WOOLF, MYRA, *Family Intentions* (1971).

—— and PEGDEN, SUE, *Families Five Years on* (1976).

Parliamentary Papers

Fifth Report from the Select Committee on Science and Technology: Population Policy, vol. xxxv, Reports, Accounts and Papers, 1971/2.

GLASS, D. V., and GREBENIK, E. *The Trend and Pattern of Fertility: A Report on the Family Census of 1946*, Papers of the Royal Commission on Population 1944–1949 vol. vi, (1954).

HANSARD, Parliamentary Debates, 6th series, House of Commons, vol. 659 (14 May 1962), cols. 910–11; vol. 694 (4 May 1964), col. 880; vol. 702 (23 Nov. 1964), cols. 904–5.

HANSARD, Parliamentary Debates, Official Report, Standing Committee H, National Health Service (Family Planning) Bill, vol. xi (26 Apr. 1967).

HANSARD, Parliamentary Debates, 5th series, House of Lords, vol. 283 (5 June 1967), cols. 153–77.

HANSARD, Parliamentary Debates, 6th series, House of Commons, vol. 741 (17 Feb. 1967), cols. 935–1020.

HANSARD, Parliamentary Debates, 5th Series, House of Lords, vol. 337 (4 Dec. 1972), cols. 8–136; (18 Dec. 1972), cols. 823–914; (19 Dec. 1972), cols. 950–69, 987–1037; vol. 338 (12 Feb. 1973), cols. 1284–390.

HANSARD, Parliamentary Debates, 6th series, House of Commons, vol. 853 (26 Mar. 1973), cols. 923–1052; (27 Mar. 1973), cols. 1101–226; (12 June 1973), cols. 1223–438; vol. 858 (19 June 1973), cols. 378–414; vol. 859 (2 July 1973), cols. 173–210.

HANSARD, Parliamentary Debates, House of Commons Official Report, Standing Committee G, National Health Service Reorganization Bill (5 Apr. 1973), cols. 231–310.

LEWIS-FANING, E., *Report on an Enquiry into Family Limitation and its Influence on Human Fertility during the Past Fifty Years*, Papers of the Royal Commission on Population, vol. i (HMSO, 1949).

Report of the Royal Commission on Venereal Disease, PP 1916 (8190).

Report of the Committee Appointed to Enquire into the Pathology and Treatment of the Venereal Disease with the View to Diminish its Injurious Effects on the Men of the Army and Navy, PP 1868.

Report of the House of Commons Select Committee on the Contagious Diseases Act, PP 1868–9.

Archives

Wellcome Trust Library for the History of Medicine, London:
Family Planning Association Archives:
SA/FPA/AM 53–113
FPA Annual Reports 1960/1–1975/6.
Birth Control Campaign:
SA/BCC/e.8, 9, 11, 13, 19, 21, 24, 27, 30, 31.
Abortion Law Reform Association:
SA/ALRA/e.9, 31, 32, 40.
British Medical Association Archives, London:
E1/Misc 17/2, 4, 15.
Brook Advisory Service Archive, London:
Press clippings files.
Annual Reports 1966–75.

Other Reports

LAFITTE, FRANÇOIS, *Family Planning in the Sixties: The Report of the Family Planning Association Working Party* (1963).
Levels and Trends of Contraceptive Use as Assessed in 1994 (New York, United Nations, 1996).
Population and Women: Proceedings of the United Nations Expert Group Meeting on Population and Women, Gaborone, Botswana, 22–26 June 1992 (New York, United Nations, 1996).
Which Report on Contraception (Consumers' Association, 1963).
Which? Supplement on Contraception (Consumers' Association, 1971).
World Population Conference, Second, Belgrade, 1965 (New York, United Nations, 1966).

Local, Provincial, and National Newspapers and Magazines

Aberdeen Press and Journal.
Bath and Wilts Evening Chronicle.
Birmingham Evening Dispatch.
Birmingham Evening Post.
Birmingham Planet.
Birmingham Sunday Mercury.
Bookseller.

Acton Gazette.
Birmingham Daily Mail.
Birmingham Evening Mail.
Birmingham Mail.
Birmingham Post.
Bolton Evening News.
Bournemouth Times.

Brighton Argus.

Bristol Evening Post.

Cambridge Daily News.

Catholic Times.

Chemist and Druggist.

Chichester Observer (Portsmouth).

Coalville Times.

Coulsdon & Purley Advertiser.

Courier (Dundee).

Daily Express.

Daily Mail.

Daily Record (Glasgow).

Daily Telegraph.

Daily Worker.

Derbyshire Advertiser.

Doctor.

Dumfries Standard.

East Anglia Times.

Eastbourne Herald.

Eastern Daily Press (Norwich).

Epsom and Ewell Advertiser.

Evening Advertiser.

Evening Argus.

Evening Citizen.

Evening Courier (Halifax).

Evening Echo (Southend).

Evening Mail (Slough).

Evening News (Edinburgh).

Evening Post and Chronicle.

Evening Times.

Express & Star (Wolverhampton).

Financial Times.

General Practitioner.

Glasgow Daily Record.

Glasgow Sunday Mail.

Greenock Telegraph.

Guardian Journal (Nottingham).

Hampstead & Highgate Express.

Herald Tribune.

Brighton Evening Argus.

British Medical Journal.

Cambridge Evening News.

Cheltenham Chronicle.

Chester Chronicle.

Church Times.

Competition Journal.

County Express (Stourbridge).

Croydon Advertiser.

Daily Herald.

Daily Mirror.

Daily Sketch.

Daily Telegraph and Argus.

Derby Evening Telegraph.

Derbyshire Times.

Dublin Sunday Independent.

East Anglian Daily Times.

Eastbourne Gazette.

Eastern Daily Press.

Edinburgh Evening News.

Essex County Standard (Colchester).

Evening Advertiser (Swindon).

Evening Chronicle (Newcastle-upon-Tyne).

Evening Citizen (Glasgow).

Evening Dispatch.

Evening Echo (Watford).

Evening News.

Evening Post (Bristol).

Evening Standard (London).

Express.

Family Planning, (Subtitle varied).

Forum.

Glasgow Citizen.

Glasgow Herald.

Gloucestershire Echo.

Guardian.

Hampshire Chronicle.

Herald of Wales.

Hereford Evening News.

Honey.
Hull Daily Mail.
Ilford Recorder.
Ipswich Evening Star.
Jewish Chronicle.
Journal (Newcastle-upon-Tyne).
Kensington Post.
Lancashire Evening Telegraph.
Lancet.
Leicester Mercury.
Leytonstone Express.
Liverpool Daily Post.
Liverpool Post.
Manchester Evening News.
Manchester Evening Star.
Mddx Chronicle.
Medical News Tribune.
Middlesex Advertiser.
Morning Star (London).
Mother.
Newcastle Journal.
New Society.
New Statesman.
Northern Despatch.
Northern Mercury.
Nursery World.
Nursing Week.
Oldham Chronicle.
Paisley Daily Express.
Peterborough Citizen.
Press & Journal (Aberdeen).
Readers Digest.
Reading Standard.
Reveille.
Scotsman.
Scottish Daily Mail.
Scottish Sunday Express.
Sheffield Star.
Shields Gazette.

Hornsey Journal.
Ilford Pictorial.
Illustrated London News.
Islington Gazette.
Journal.
Keighley News.
Kent Messenger.
Lancaster Evening Post.
Leicester Mail.
Lewisham Borough News.
Lincolnshire Echo.
Liverpool Echo.
London Review of Books.
Manchester Evening News & Chronicle.
Manchester Guardian.
Medical News.
Medical Tribune.
Morning Advertiser.
Morning Telegraph (Sheffield).
Newcastle Evening Chronicle.
News (Portsmouth).
News of the World.
Newsweek.
Northern Echo (Darlington).
Nottingham Evening Post.
Nursing Mirror.
Observer.
Oxford Mail.
People.
Petticoat.
Pulse (a magazine for GPs).
Reading Evening Post.
Retail Chemist.
Runcorn Guardian.
Scottish Daily Express.
Scottish Daily Record (Glasgow).
SHE.
Sheffield Telegraph.
Slough Observer.

Social Worker.

Southampton Evening Echo.

Southland Standard.

South London Press.

South Wales Echo.

South Wales Post.

Star (Sheffield).

Stratford Express.

Sun.

Sunday Express.

Sunday Mirror.

Sunday Telegraph.

Surrey Comet.

Telegraph.

Telegraph and Argus (Bradford).

Time Magazine.

Times Educational Supplement.

Tit Bits.

Universe.

West Lancashire Gazette.

Western Mail (Cardiff).

West Lancashire Evening Gazette.

Willesden Chronicle.

Wolverhampton Express and Star.

Woman's Choice.

Woman's Own.

Women's Mirror.

Yorkshire Evening News.

Yorkshire Post.

Sound and T.V. Today.

Southern Weekly News.

South London Advertiser.

Southport Visitor.

South Wales Herald.

Spectator.

Stethoscope.

Streatham News.

Sun (London).

Sunday Mercury.

Sunday Pictorial.

Sunday Times.

Teeside Evening Gazette.

Telegraph and Argus.

Thames Valley Times.

The Times.

Times Literary Supplement.

T.V. Mail.

Vanity Fair.

Western Daily Press (Bristol).

Western Press.

Willesden and Brent Chronicle.

Wisbech Standard.

Woman.

Woman's Mirror.

Woman's Sunday Mirror.

Yarmouth Mercury.

Yorkshire Evening Post.

Yorkshire Post (Leeds).

Books, Theses, and Articles

ACKLAND, VALENTINE, *For Sylvia: An Honest Account* (1949; 1989).

ACTON, WILLIAM, *Prostitution*, ed. Peter Fryer (1857).

ADAIR, R., *Courtship, Illegitimacy and Marriage in Early Modern Engand* (Manchester, 1996).

ALBERTI, JOHANNA, *Beyond Suffrage: Feminists in War and Peace, 1914–28* (1989).

ALEXANDER, S., 'The Mysteries and Secrets of Women's Bodies: Sexual Knowledge in the First Half of the Twentieth Century', in M. Nava, and A. O'Shea, (eds.), *Modern Times: Reflections on a Century of English Modernity* (1996).

ALLBUTT, HENRY A., *The Wife's Handbook* (1886).

ALTER, G., 'Theories of Fertility Decline: A Nonspecialist's Guide to the Current Debate', in John R. Gillis, Louise A. Tilly, and David Levine (eds.), *The European Experience of Declining Fertility: A Quiet Revolution 1850–1970* (Oxford, 1992).

ANDERSON, MICHAEL, 'The Social Position of Spinsters in Mid-Victorian Britain', *Journal of Family History* (Winter 1984).

—— 'The Emergence of the Modern life Cycle in Britain', *Social History*, 10 (1985).

—— 'Households, Families and Individuals: Some Preliminary Results from the national sample of the 1851 census of Great Britain', *Continuity and Change*, 3 (1988).

—— 'The Social Significance of Demographic Change in Britain, 1750–1950', in F. M. Thompson (ed.), *Cambridge Social History of Britain 1750–1950* (Cambridge, 1990).

—— 'Highly Restricted Fertility: Very Small Families in the British Fertility Decline', *Population Studies*, 52 (1998).

Aristotle's Master-Piece Compleated. In Two Parts. The First Containing the Secrets of Generation . . . The Second . . . being, a Private Looking-Glass for the Female Sex. Treating of the Various Maladies . . . Incident to Women | [Aristotle] (Glasgow, 1782).

ASBELL, B., *The Pill: A Biography of the Drug that Changed the World* (New York, 1995).

AYRES, PAT, and LAMBERTZ, JAN, 'Marriage Relations: Money and Domestic Violence in Working Class Liverpool, 1919–1939', in Jane Lewis (ed.), *Labour and Love: Women's Experience of Home and Family 1850–1940* (Oxford, 1986).

BAILEY, PAUL, *An English Madam: The Life and Work of Cynthia Payne* (1982).

BAILEY, SHERWIN D., *The Mystery of Love* (1952).

—— *The Man–Woman Relation in Christian Thought* (1959).

—— *Common Sense about Sexual Ethics: A Christian View* (1962).

BAKER, J. R., *The Chemical Control of Conception* (1935).

BANKS, J. A., *Prosperity and Parenthood: A Study of Family Planning amongst the Victorian Middle-Classes* (1954).

—— *Victorian Values: Secularism and the Size of Families* (1981).

—— and BANKS, OLIVE, 'The Bradlaugh–Besant Trial and the English News-papers' *Population Studies*, 8 (1954).

—— —— *Feminism and Family Planning in Victorian England* (Liverpool, 1964).

BANKS, OLIVE, *Becoming a Feminist: The Social Origins of First Wave Feminism* (1986).

—— *Faces of Feminism* (1981; 1986).

BARNES, KENNETH C., *He and She* (1958; 1962).

BARRET-DUCROCQ, FRANÇOISE, *Love in the Time of Victoria* (1992).

BARTLEY, PAULA, *Prostitution: Prevention and Reform in England, 1860–1914* (2000).

BARTRIP, PETER, *Themselves Writ Large: The British Medical Association, 1832–1966* (1996).

BEALE, GEOFFREY [Pseudonym of C. P.], *Wise Wedlock: The Whole Truth* (1922; 1926).
—— *Wise Wedlock* (1922; 1940).

BECKER, GARY, 'An Economic Analysis of Fertility', in National Bureau of Economic research (ed.), *Demographic and Economic Change in Developed Countries* (Princeton, 1960).

BEDDOE, DEIRDRE, *Back to Home and Duty: Women between the Wars, 1918–1939* (1989).

BENN, CAROLINE, *Keir Hardie* (1992).

BENN, M., *Predicaments of Love* (1992).

—— and RICHARDSON, R., 'Uneasy Freedom: Women's Experiences of Contraception', *Women's Studies International Forum*, 7/4 (1984).

BERG, L. M. and STREET, ROBERT, *The Basis of Happy Marriage: The Art of Sexual Relationship* (1955; 1969).

BERGLER, E., 'Short Genetic Survey of Psychic Impotence', *Psychiatric Quarterly*, 1/19 (1945).

BERTRAND, C., *The British Press: An Historical Survey* (Paris, 1969).

BESANT, ANNIE, 'The Law of Population: Its Consequence and its Bearing upon Human Conduct and Morals' (1884), repr. in S. Chandrasekhar (ed.), *"A Dirty, Filthy Book": The Writings of Charles Knowlton and Annie Besant on Reproductive Physiology and Birth Control and an Account of the Bradlaugh–Besant Trial* (1981).

BEVAN, WILLIAM, *Prostitution in the Borough of Liverpool: A Lecture, etc.* (Liverpool, 1843).

BEYFUS, D., *The English Marriage: What it is Like to be Married Now* (1968).

BIBBY, CYRIL, *Sex Education* (1944).

BILLINGS, EVELYN, and WESTMORE, A., *The Billings Method: Controlling Fertility without Drugs or Devices* (Richmond, Australia, 1980).

BLAND, LUCY, 'Marriage Laid Bare: Middle-Class Women and Marital Sex c.1880–1914', in Jane Lewis (ed.), *Labour and Love: Women's Experience of Home and Family 1850–1940* (Oxford, 1986).

—— *Banishing the Beast: English Feminism and Sexual Morality, 1885–1914* (1995).

BLYTH, H. E., *Skittles: The Last Victorian Courtesan: The Life and Times of Catherine Walters* (1970).

BONAPARTE, MARIE, *Female Sexuality* (1953).

BONGAARTS, JOHN, 'A Framework for Analyzing the Proximate Determinants of Fertility', *Population and Development Review*, 4 (1978).

—— 'The Proximate Determinants of Natural Marital Fertility', in Rodolfo A. Bulatao and R. D. Lee (eds.), *Determinants of Fertility in Developing Countries* (Oxford, 1983).

—— and POTTER, R. G., *Fertility, Biology, and Behaviour: An Analysis of the Proximate Determinants* (New York, 1983).

BOOKER, H. S., and WALLIS, J. H., *Marriage Counselling: A Description and Analysis of the Remedial Work of the National Marriage Guidance Council* (1958).

BOSWELL, JAMES, *Boswell's London Journal, 1762–1763*, ed. Frederick A. Pottle (1950).

BOURKE, JOANNA, *Dismembering the Male: Men's Bodies, Britain and the Great War* (1996).

—— 'Housewifery in Working-Class England 1860–1914', in Pamela Sharpe (ed.), *Women's Work: The English Experience 1650–1914* (1998).

BOYLE, SHERON, *Working Girls and their Men* (1994).

BRANDON, RUTH, *The New Women and the Old Men* (1990).

BRECHER, EDWARD M., *The Sex Researchers* (1970).

—— and BRECHER, RUTH E., *An Analysis of 'Human Sexual Response'* (1967; 1969).

BRIANT, K. R., *Marie Stopes: A Biography* (1962).

BRIGGS, ASA, *The History of Broadcasting in the United Kingdom: Competition, 1955–1974* (Oxford, 1995).

BRISSETT, DENNIS, and LEWIS, LIONEL S., 'Guidelines for Marital Sex: An Analysis of Fifteen Popular Marriage Manuals', *Family Coordinator*, 1 (1970).

BRISTOW, EDWARD J., *Vice and Vigilance: Purity Movements in Britain since 1700* (Dublin, 1977).

BRITTAIN, VERA, *Testament of Youth* (1933).

—— *Testament of Experience* (1957).

—— *Chronicle of Youth: Vera Brittain's War Diary 1913–17*, ed. A. Bishop (1981).

BRITTON, DEREK, *Lady Chatterley: The Making of the Novel* (1988).

BRODIE, JANET F., *Contraception and Abortion in Nineteenth Century America* (New York, 1994).

BROOKE, STEPHEN, 'Gender and Working Class Identity in Britain during the 1950s', *Journal of Social History* (2001).

BROOKES, BARBARA, *Abortion in England* (1988).

BROWN, HELEN G., *Sex and the Single Girl* (New York, 1962).

BROWN, P. T., 'The Development of Sexual Function Therapies after Masters and Johnson', in W. H. Armytage, John Peel, and R. Chester (eds.), *Changing Patterns of Sexual Behaviour: Proceedings of the 15th Annual Symposium of the Eugenics Society 1978* (1980).

BRYDER, LINDA, *Below the Magic Mountain: A Social History of Tuberculosis in Twentieth-Century Britain* (Oxford, 1988).

BURKE, E. T., 'The Toll of Secret Disease', *Nineteenth Century* (1927).

BUSCHKE, A., and JACOBSOHN, F., *Sex Habits: A Vital Factor in Well-Being*, ed. Eden and Cedar Paul (1932).

BUSH, M. L., *What is Love? Richard Carlile's Philosophy of Sex* (1998).

BUTLER, JOSEPHINE, *The Constitution Violated* (Edinburgh, 1871).

—— *Recollections of George Butler* (Bristol, 1892).

CAINE, BARBARA, *Destined to be Wives: The Sisters of Beatrice Webb* (Oxford, 1985).

—— *English Feminism, 1780–1980* (Oxford, 1997).

CALDER, JENNI, *The Nine Lives of Naomi Mitchison* (1997).

CALDWELL, JOHN C., *Theory of Fertility Decline* (1983).

—— and CALDWELL, PAT, 'The Role of Marital Sexual Abstinence in determining Fertility: A Study of the Yoruba in Nigeria', *Population Studies*, 31/2 (1977).

—— McDONALD, PETER F., and RUZICKA, LADO T., 'Nuptiality and Fertility in Australia, 1921–1976', in Lado T. Ruzicka (ed.), *Nuptiality and Fertility: Proceedings of a Seminar Held in Bruges (Belgium), 8–11 January 1979* (Liège, 1979).

—— YOUNG, CHRISTABEL M., WARE, HELEN, LAVIS, DONALD R., and DAVIS, A-T., 'Australia: Knowledge, Attitudes and Practice of Family Planning in Melbourne, 1971', *Studies in Family Planning*, 4/3 (1973).

CAMPBELL, FLANN, 'Birth Control and the Christian Churches', *Population Studies*, 14 (1960).

CARPENTER, EDWARD, *Love's Coming-of-Age* (1896; 1923).

CARR-SAUNDERS, A. M., *The Population Problem* (Oxford, 1922).

CARSTAIRS, G. M., *This Island Now: The B.B.C. Reith Lectures 1962* (1963).

CARTER, ANGELA, 'Truly, It Felt like Year One', in S. Maitland (ed.), *Very Heaven: Looking Back at the 1960s* (1988).

CARTER, PAM, *Feminism, Breasts and Breastfeeding* (New York, 1995).

CARTWRIGHT, ANN, 'General Practitioners and Family Planning', *Medical Officer* (19 July 1968).

—— *Parents and Family Planning Services* (1970).

CAUTHERY, P. D., 'The Unwanted Pregnancy', *Forum* (1974).

CHALKER, REBECCA, *The Clitoral Truth: The World at your Fingertips* (New York, 2000).

CHARLES, E., *An Indian Patchwork* (1934).

—— *The Sexual Impulse: An Introduction to the Study of the Psychology, Physiology and Biochemistry of the Sexual Impulse among Adults in Mental and Bodily Health* (1935).

CHARLES, ENID, *The Practice of Birth Control: An Analysis of the Experience of Nine Hundred Women* (1932).

CHARTHAM, ROBERT S. R., *Mainly for Women: A Practical Guide to Love-Making in Marriage* (1964; 1966).

—— *Sex Manners for Women* (1964).

CHAUNCEY, GEORGE, DUBERMAN, MARTIN B., and VICINUS, MARTHA (eds.), 'Introduction', in *Hidden from History: Reclaiming the Gay and Lesbian Past* (1989; 1991).

CHEDZOY, ALAN, *A Scandalous Woman: The Story of Caroline Norton* (1992).

CHESNEY, KELLOW, *The Victorian Underworld* (1970; 1991).

CHESSER, EUSTACE, *Love without Fear (A Plain Guide to Sex Technique for Every Married Adult)* (1941).

—— *Sexual Behaviour: Normal and Abnormal* (1949).

—— *The Sexual, Marital and Family Relationships of the English Woman* (1956).

—— *Live and Let Live* (1958).

—— *Is Chastity Outmoded?* (1960; 1961).

—— *Sex and the Married Woman* (1968; 1970).

CHEW, ADA N., and CHEW, DORIS N., *Ada Neild Chew: The Life and Writings of a Working Woman*, ed. Anna Davin (1982).

CHINN, CARL, *They Worked All their Lives: Women of the Urban Poor in England, 1880–1939* (Manchester, 1988).

CHITTY, SUSAN, *The Beast and the Monk* (1974).

—— *That Singular Person Called Lear* (1988).

CLARK, ANNA, *Women's Silence, Men's Violence: Sexual Assault in England 1770–1845* (1987).

—— 'Whores and Gossips: Sexual Reputation in London 1770–1825', in Arina Angerman, Geerte Binnema, Annemieke Keunen, Vefie Poels, and Jacqueline Zirkzee (eds.), *Current Issues in Women's History* (1989).

—— *The Struggle for the Breeches: Gender and the Making of the British Working Class* (Berkeley, 1995).

CLARK, LEMON, 'Notes and Comments', *International Journal of Sexology*, 2 (1949).

CLARKE, MICHAEL, *Thackeray's Women* (De Kalb, Ill., 1995).

CLARKE, WILLIAM C., *The Secret Life of Wilkie Collins* (1988).

COHEN, D. A., 'Private Lives in Public Spaces: Marie Stopes, the Mother's Clinics and the Practice of Contraception', *History Workshop*, 35 (1993).

COLE, ESTELLE, *Education for Marriage* (1938).

COLE, MARGARET, *The Life of G. D. H. Cole* (1971).

COLEMAN, D., and SALT, J., *The British Population: Patterns, Trends, and Processes* (Oxford, 1992).

COLEMAN, S., *Family Planning in Japanese Society: Traditional Birth Control in a Modern Urban Culture* (Princeton, 1983).

COLLEY, L., *Britons: Forging the Nation 1707–1837* (1992).

COLLINS, JACKIE, *The World is Full of Married Men* (1968; 1969).

COLQUOUN, P., *A Treatise on the Police of the Metropolis* (1796).

COMFORT, ALEX, *Barbarism and Sexual Freedom* (1948).

—— *Sex in Society* (1963; 1964).

—— *The Anxiety Makers* (1967).

—— *The Joy of Sex* (1972).

COMINOS, PETER T., 'Late-Victorian Respectability and the Social System', *International Review of Social History*, 8/1–2 (1963).

COOK, HERA, 'Nudism: Sex, Gender and Social Change 1930–1955', unpublished manuscript (1994).

—— 'The Long Sexual Revolution: British Women, Sex and Contraception in the Twentieth Century' (D.Phil. thesis, University of Sussex, 1999).

—— ' "Unseemly and Unwomanly Behaviour": Comparing Women's Control of their Fertility in Australia and in England from 1890 to 1970', *Journal of Population Research (Australia)*, 17/2 (2000).

—— "Sex and the Experts: Medicalisation as a Two Way Process, Britain 1920–1950', in C. Usbourne and W. de Blecourt (eds.), *Mediating Medicine: Cultural Approaches to the History of Medicine* (2003).

COOTE, ANNA, and CAMPBELL, BEATRIX, *Sweet Freedom: The Struggle for Women's Liberation* (1982).

COSTELLO, J., *Love, Sex and War: Changing Values, 1939–45* (1986).

COSTLER, A. D. [pseud. A. Koestler], and WILLY, A., *The Encyclopaedia of Sexual Knowledge*, ed. Norman Haire (1934; 1941).

—— —— *The Encyclopaedia of Sex Practice*, ed. Norman Haire (1938; 1951).

COUSINS, SHEILA, *To Beg I am Ashamed: The Autobiography of a London Prostitute* (Paris, 1946; 1960).

COVENEY, LAL, KAY, LESLIE, and MAHONY, PAT, 'Theory into Practice: Sexual Liberation or Social Control (*Forum* magazine 1968–81)', in Lal Coveney, Sheila Jeffreys, Margaret Jackson, Leslie Kay, and Pat Mahony (eds.), *The Sexuality Papers: Male Sexuality and the Social Control of Women* (1984).

COX, GLADYS, *Youth, Sex and Life* (1935).

CRAFTS, N. F. R., 'A Time Series Study of Fertility in England and Wales, 1877–1938', *Journal of European Economic History (Italy)*, 13/3 (1984).

CRAIG, ALEC, *Sex and Revolution* (1934).

—— 'Report of Police Action and Proceedings Regarding "*An Introduction to the Study of the Psychology, Physiology and Bio-chemistry of the Sexual Impulse among Adults in Mental and Bodily Health*": A Study by Edward Charles, published on the 7th of February, 1935' (unpublished, British Library).

—— 'Censorship of Sexual Literature', in A. P. Abarbanel and Albert Ellis (eds.), *Encyclopaedia of Sexual Behaviour* (1961).

CROALL, J., *Neill of Summerhill: The Permanent Rebel* (1983).

CRYLE, PETER, *Geometry in the Boudoir: Configurations of French Erotic Narrative* (New York, 1994).

CUTHBERT, CROYDON, and WARNER, H. C., *Moral Problems* (1952).

DAUNTON, M. J., 'Housing', in F. M. Thompson (ed.), *The Cambridge Social History of Britain 1750–1950* (Cambridge, 1990).

DAVENPORT-HINES, RICHARD, *Sex, Death and Punishment* (1991).

DAVID, PAUL A., and SANDERSON, WARREN C., 'Rudimentary Contraceptive Methods and the American Transition to Marital Fertility Control, 1855–1915', in Stanley L. Engerman and Robert E. Gallman, (eds.), *Long Term Factors in America's Economic Growth* (Chicago, 1986).

DAVIDOFF, LEONORE, and HALL, CATHERINE, *Family Fortunes: Men and Women of the English Middle Class 1780–1850* (1987).

—— ' "The Hidden Investment": Women and the Enterprise', in Pamela Sharpe (ed.), *Women's Work: The English Experience 1650–1914* (1998).

DAVIDSON, JULIA O., 'Prostitution and the Contours of Control', in Jeffrey Weeks and Janet Holland (eds.), *Sexual Cultures, Communities, Values and Intimacy* (1996).

DAVIN, ANNA, 'Imperialism and Motherhood', *History Workshop*, 5 (1978).

DAVIS, KINGSLEY, and BLAKE, JUDITH, 'Social Structure and Fertility: An Analytic Framework', *Economic Development and Cultural Change*, 4 (1956).

DAVIS, MAXINE, *The Sexual Responsibility of Woman* (1957; 1964).

—— *Sexual Responsibility in Marriage* (1964; 1966).

DAVIS, PORTER P., *Handbook for Husbands (and Wives)* (New York, 1949).

DAVIS, T. C., *Actresses as Working Women: Their Social Identity in Victorian Culture* (1991).

DAYUS, KATHLEEN, *Where there's Life* (1985).

DEGLER, CARL N., 'What Ought to be and What Was: Women's Sexuality in the Nineteenth Century', *American Historical Review*, 79 (1974).

DE KOK, WINIFRED, 'Woman and Sex', in Lord Horder, Joan Malleson, and Gladys Cox (eds.), *The Modern Woman's Medical Guide* (1949; 1955).

DELANY, PAUL, *The Neo-pagans: Friendship and Love in the Rupert Brooke Circle* (1987).

DELL'OLIO, ANSELMA, 'The Sexual Revolution wasn't Our War', in *The First Ms. Reader* (New York, 1972).

DENNIS, NORMAN, SLAUGHTER, CLIFFORD, and HENRIQUES, FERNANDO D., *Coal is our Life* (1956; 1969).

DESMOND, HEATH, 'An Investigation into a Copious Vaginal Discharge during Intercourse: "Enough to Wet the Bed"—That "is not Urine" ', *Journal of Sex Research*, 20/2 (1984).

DIX, CAROL, *Say I'm Sorry to Mother: Growing up in the Sixties* (1978).

DIXON, JANET, 'Separatism: A Look Back at Anger', in Susan Hemmings and Bob Cant (eds.), *Radical Records: Thirty Years of Lesbian and Gay History, 1957–1987* (1988).

DOBSON, P., *Criminal Law* (5th edn., 1999).

DONOUGHUE, BERNARD and JONES, GEORGE W., *Herbert Morrison: Portrait of a Politician* (1973).

DOUGLAS, MARY, *Purity and Danger: An Analysis of the Concepts of Pollution and Taboo* (1966; 1994).

DRAPER, ELIZABETH, 'The Social Background', in M. D. Pollock (ed.), *Family Planning: A Handbook for the Doctor* (1966).

DRYSDALE, GEORGE, *Physical, Sexual and Natural Religion: By a Student of Medicine* (1855).

DUFFY, MAUREEN, *That's How it Was* (1962; 1983).

DUGDALE, A., 'Inserting Grafenberg's IUD into the Sex Reform Movement', in J. Wajcman and D. MacKenzie (eds.), *The Social Shaping of Technology* (Buckingham, 1999).

DYHOUSE, CAROL, 'Mothers and Daughter's in the Middle-Class Home c.1870–1914', in Jane Lewis, (ed.), *Labour and Love: Women's Experience of Home and Family 1850–1940* (Oxford, 1986).

EASTLAKE, LADY (née Elizabeth Rigby), 'Review *Vanity Fair, Jane Eyre,* and *The Governesses' Benevolent Institution—Report for 1847'*, *Quarterly Review*, 84 (1848).

EDWARDS, RUTH D., *Victor Gollancz: A Biography* (1987).

EHRENREICH, BARBARA, HESS, ELIZABETH, and JACOBS, GLORIA, *Re-making Love: The Feminisation of sex* (1987).

EICHENLAUB, JOHN E., *The Marriage Art* (1961; 1964).

EJLERSEN, METTE, *I Accuse!* (1969).

ELIAS, NORBERT, *The Civilising Process: State Formation and Civilization* (Oxford, 1939; 1976).

ELLIS, ALBERT, 'Is the Vaginal Orgasm a Myth?', in Manfred F. Demartino (ed.), *Sexual Behaviour and Personality Characteristics* (New York, 1963; 1966).

—— *The Sensuous Person* (1972).

ELLIS, HAVELOCK, *Psychology of Sex: A Manual for Students* (1933).

—— *Sex in Relation to Society* (1937; 1946).

EMBEY, PHILLIP, *Women's Change of Life* (1955).

ENGLAND, L., 'A British Sex Survey', *International Journal of Sexology*, 3/3 (1950).

—— 'Little Kinsey', in Liz Stanley (ed.), *Sex Surveyed 1949–1994: From Mass Observation's 'Little Kinsey' to the National Survey and the Hite Reports* (1995).

ERASMUS, CHARLES J., 'Changing Folk Beliefs and the Relativity of Empirical Knowledge', *Southwestern Journal of Anthropology*, 8 (1952).

EVANS, BARBARA, *Freedom to Choose: The Life and Work of Dr Helena Wright, Pioneer of Contraception* (1982).

EVANS, CHARLES B. S., *Man, Woman and Marriage*, preface N. Haire, (1932).

EVANS, RICHARD, *The Feminists: Women's Emancipation Movements in Europe, America and Australasia 1840–1920* (1977).

EXNER, M. J., *The Sexual Side of Marriage* (1932; 1951).

EYLES, LEONORA, *Commonsense about Sex* (1933).

FADERMAN, LILLIAN, *Surpassing the Love of Men: Romantic Friendship and Love between Women from the Renaissance to the Present* (1981; 1985).

FERRIS, PAUL, *The Nameless* (1967).

——— *Sex and the British: A Twentieth Century History* (1994).

FIELDING, MICHAEL, *Parenthood: Design or Accident? A Manual of Birth Control* (1928).

——— *Parenthood: Design or Accident? A Manual of Birth Control* (1928; 1934).

FILDES, VALERIE, *Breasts, Bottles and Babies: A History of Infant Feeding* (Edinburgh, 1986).

——— 'Infant Feeding Practices and Infant Mortality in England, 1900–1919', *Continuity and Change*, 13/2 (1998).

FINNEGAN, F., *Poverty and Prostitution: A Study of Prostitutes in Victorian York* (Cambridge, 1979).

FIRESTONE, SHULAMITH, *The Dialectic of Sex* (1970; 1971).

FISHER, KATE, 'An Oral History of Birth Control Practice c.1925–50: A Study of Oxford and Wales' (D.Phil. Thesis, University of Oxford, 1997).

——— ' "She was quite Satisfied with the Arrangements I Made": Gender and Birth Control in Britain 1920–1950', *Past and Present*, 169 (2001).

FISHER, SEYMOUR, *Understanding the Female Orgasm* [Paperback summary of *The Female Orgasm*', Allen Lane, 1973] (1973).

FLORENCE, LELLA S., *Birth Control on Trial* (1930).

——— *Progress Report on birth control* (1956).

——— *Lella Secor: A Diary in Letters, 1915–1922*, ed Moench B. Florence (New York, 1978).

FORSTER, MARGARET, *Georgy Girl* (1965; 1978).

FOUCAULT, MICHEL, *The History of Sexuality (La Volonté de savoir)* (1978; 1984).

FREMLIN, CELIA, *War Factory*, ed. D. Sheridan (1987).

FREUD, SIGMUND, *On Sexuality: Three Essays on the Theory of Sexuality and Other Works*, ed. James Strachey (1962; 1977).

FRIEDMAN, LEONARD J., *Virgin Wives: A Study of Unconsummated Marriages* (1962).

FROST, GINGER, *Promises Broken: Courtship, Class, and Gender in Victorian England* (Charlottesville, Va., 1995).

FRYER, PETER, *The Birth Controllers* (1965).

GAGNON, JOHN H., and SIMON, W., *Sexual Conduct: The Social Sources of Human Sexuality* (1974).

GARNHAM, ALISON and KNIGHTS, EMMA, *Putting the Treasury First: The Truth about Child Support*, Poverty Publication 88 (1994).

GARRET, EILIDH, 'The Trials of Labour: Motherhood versus Employment in a Nineteenth-Century Textile Centre', *Continuity and Change*, 5 (1990).

—— Szreter, Simon, Reid, Alice, and Schurer, Kevin, *Changing Family Size in England and Wales: Place, Class and Demography, 1891–1911* (Cambridge, 2001).

Gathorne-Hardy, Jonathon, *The Rise and Fall of the British Nanny* (1972).

Gavron, H., *The Captive Wife* (1966; 1968).

Gay, Peter, *Education of the Senses: The Bourgeois Experience, Victoria to Freud* (Oxford, 1984).

—— *The Tender Passion: The Bourgeois Experience, Victoria to Freud* (1986).

Gibson, Ian, *The English Vice: Beating Sex and Shame in Victorian England and After* (1978).

—— *The Erotomaniac: The Secret Life of Henry Spencer Ashbee* (2001).

Giles, Alison, 'Learning to Deal with Sexual Difficulties', *Family Planning*, 10/2 (1961).

—— Review of *The Art of Marriage*, by Mary Macaulay, *Family Planning*, 19/4 (1971).

Gillis, J. R., 'Servants, Sexual Relations and the Risks of Illegitimacy in London, 1801–1900', *Feminist Studies*, 5 (1979).

—— *For Better, for Worse: English Marriages, 1600 to the Present* (Oxford, 1985).

Gissing, George, *New Grub Street* (1891; 1968).

Gittins, Diana, *Fair Sex, Family Size and Structure, 1900– 39* (1982).

Gittins, D., 'Marital Status, Work and Kinship, 1850–1930', in J. Lewis (ed.), *Labour and Love: Women's Experience of Home and Family 1850–1940* (Oxford, 1986).

Glass, D. V., *Population Policies and Movements in Europe* (Oxford, 1940).

—— and Eversley, D. E. (eds.), *Population in History* (1965).

Gollancz, Victor, *Reminiscences of Affection* (1968).

Gordon, Linda, *Woman's Body, Woman's Right: A Social History of Birth Control in America* (New York, 1976).

—— and DuBois, Ellen, 'Seeking Ecstasy on the Battlefield: Danger and Pleasure in Nineteenth Century Feminist Sexual Thought', in Feminist Review (ed.), *Sexuality: A Reader* (1987).

Gordon, Michael, 'From an Unfortunate Necessity to a Cult of Mutual Orgasm: Sex in American Marital Education Literature, 1830–1940', in J. M. Henslin and E. Sagarin (eds.), *The Sociology of Sex* (New York, 1978).

—— and Bernstein, M. C., 'Mate Choice and Domestic Life in the Nineteenth-Century Marriage Manual', *Journal of Marriage and the Family*, 32 (1970).

—— and Shankweiler, Penelope J., 'Different Equals Less: Female Sexuality in Recent Marriage Manuals', *Journal of Marriage and the Family*, 3 (1971).

Gorer, Geoffrey, *Exploring English Character* (1955).

—— *Sex and Marriage in England Today: A Study of the Views and Experience of the under-45s* (1971).

Grafenberg, Ernest, 'The Role of the Urethra in Female Orgasm', *International Journal of Sexology*, 3/3 (1950).

GRANT, JOAN, *Time out of Mind* (1956).

GRANT, L., *Sexing the Millennium* (1993).

GRAY, A. H., *Men, Women and God: A Discussion of Sex Questions from the Christian Point of View* (1923; 17th edn. 1947).

GRAYLING, A. C., *The Quarrel of the Age: The Life and Times of William Hazlitt* (2001).

GREENWOOD, K., and KING, LUCY, 'Contraception and Abortion', in Cambridge Women's Studies Group (eds.), *Women in Society* (1981).

GREENWOOD, V., and YOUNG, J., *Abortion in Demand* (1976).

GREER, GERMAINE, *The Female Eunuch* (1970; 1971).

—— *Sex and Destiny: The Politics of Human Fertility* (1984).

GREG, W. R., 'Prostitution', *Westminster Review*, 53 (1850), repr. in K. Nield (ed.), *Prostitution in the Victorian Age* (1973).

—— 'Queen Bees or Working Bees?', *Saturday Review* (8 Oct. 1859).

—— 'Why are Women Redundant?', *National Review* (14 Apr. 1862).

GRIFFITH, EDWARD F., *Modern Marriage and Birth Control* (1935).

—— *Modern Marriage* (1935; 20th edn. 1947).

—— *Modern Marriage* (1935; 1963).

—— *Emotional Development* (1944).

—— *Modern Marriage* (1973).

—— *The Pioneer Spirit* (Upton Grey, 1981).

GRIFFITHS, TREVOR, *The Lancashire Working Classes: c.1880–1930* (Oxford, 2001).

GROVE, VALERIE, *Dear Dodie: The Life of Dodie Smith* (1996; 1997).

—— *The Complete Woman: Marriage, Motherhood, Career: Can she Have it All?* (1987; 1988).

GUTTMACHER, A. F., and MEARS, ELEANOR, *Babies by Choice or by Chance* (1960).

GUYON, RENÉ, *Sex Life and Sex Ethics*, ed. J. C. and I. Flugel (1934).

GUYOT, JULES, *A Ritual for Married Lovers*, trans. Gertrude M. Pinchot, (1859; 1933).

HACKER, R., 'Love Without Tears', *Sunday Pictorial* (25 Nov. 1956).

HAIRE, NORMAN, 'Contraceptive Technique', *Practitioner*, III/1 (1923).

—— *The Comparative Value of Current Contraceptive Methods, Reprinted from the Proceedings of the First International Congress for Sexual Research (Berlin October 10th to 16th, 1926)* (1928).

—— *Birth-Control Methods (Contraception, Abortion, Sterilisation)* (1936; 1937).

HAJNAL, J., 'European Marriage Patterns in Perspective', in David V. Glass and D. E. Eversley (eds.), *Population in History* (1965).

HALL, LESLEY A., *Hidden Anxieties: Male Sexuality, 1900–1950* (1991).

—— 'Forbidden by God, Despised by Men: Masturbation, Medical Warnings, Moral Panic, and Manhood in Great Britain, 1850–1950', *Journal of the History of Sexuality*, 2/3 (1992).

HALL, RUTH, *Marie Stopes: A Biography* (1977).

—— *Dear Dr Stopes: Sex in the 1920s* (1978).

Hall Carpenter Archives, *Walking after Midnight: Gay Men's Life Histories* (1989).

HAM, C. J., 'Power, Patients and Pluralism', in K. Barnard and K. Lee (eds.), *Conflicts in the National Health Service* (1977).

HAMBURGER, LOTTE, and HAMBURGER, JOSEPH, *Contemplating Adultery* (1992).

HAMER, E., *Britannia's Glory: A History of Twentieth Century Lesbians* (1996).

HAMILTON, CECILY, *Marriage is a Trade* (1909).

HAMMERTON, A. J., *Cruelty and Companionship* (1992).

HANNAM, JUNE, ' "I had not been to London": Women's Suffrage—A View from the Regions', in Sandra Holton and June Purvis (eds.), *Votes for Women* (2001).

HASTE, CATE, *Rules of Desire: Sex in Britain, World War I to the Present* (1992).

HASTRUP, KIRSTEN, 'A Question of Reason: Breastfeeding Patterns in Seventeenth and Eighteenth Century Iceland', in Vanessa Maher (ed.), *The Anthropology of Breastfeeding: Natural Law or Social Construct* (Oxford, 1992).

HAVIL, ANTHONY, *The Technique of Sex: Towards a Better Understanding of Sexual Relationship* (1939; 1959).

HEGELER, STEN, and HEGELER, INGE, *An ABZ of Love* (1963; 1969).

HEMYNG, BRACEBRIDGE, 'Prostitution', in Henry Mayhew (ed.), *London Labour and the London Poor* (1862).

HENDRICKSON, T., *Variations on a Sexual Theme* (1969).

HERON, A., *Towards a Quaker View of Sex: An Essay by a Group of Friends* (1964).

HIGGINS, NATALIE, 'Marriage in Mid 20th Century North England' (D.Phil. Thesis, University of Oxford, forthcoming, 2003).

HIGGINS, PATRICK, *Heterosexual Dictatorship: Male Homosexuality in Post-war Britain* (1996).

HIMES, NORMAN E., *The Medical History of Contraception* (New York, 1936; 1970).

—— and HIMES, VERA C., 'Birth Control for the British Working Classes: A Study of the First Thousand Cases to Visit an English Birth Control Clinic', *Hospital Social Service*, 19 (1929).

HIRSCH, PAM, *Barbara Leigh Smith Bodichon* (2001).

HITCHCOCK, TIM, *English Sexualities: 1700–1800* (1997).

—— 'Sociability and Misogyny in the Life of John Cannon, 1684–1743', in Tim Hitchcock and Michele Cohen (eds.), *English Masculinities, 1660–1800* (1999).

HITE, S., *The Hite Report* (1976).

HOGGART, LESLEY, 'The Campaign for Birth Control in Britain in the 1920s', in Anne Digby and John Stewart (eds.), *Gender, Health and Welfare* (1996).

HOGGART, RICHARD, *The Uses of Literacy* (1957).

—— *A Local Habitation* (*Life and Times*, I: *1918–1940*) (Oxford, 1989).

HOLMAN HUNT, DIANA, *My Grandfather, his Wives and Loves* (1969).

HOLROYD, MICHAEL, *Augustus John* (1974).

HOLTZMAN, ELLEN M., 'The Pursuit of Married Love: Women's Attitudes Toward Sexuality and Marriage in Great Britain, 1918–1939', *Journal of Social History*, 16/2 (1982).

HOPKINS, HARRY, *The New Look: A Social History of the Forties and Fifties in Britain* (1964).

HORRELL, S., and HUMPHRIES, J., 'Women's Labour Force Participation and the Transition to the Male-Breadwinner Family, 1790–1865', in P. Sharpe (ed.), *Women's Work: The English Experience 1650–1914* (1998).

HOWARD, JANE, *Please Touch* (New York, 1970; 1971).

HOWARTH, VYVYAN, *Secret Techniques of Erotic Delight* (New York, 1966).

HUDSON, DEREK, *Munby Man of Two Worlds: The Life and Diaries of Arthur J. Munby, 1828–1910* (1972).

HUDSON, L., and JACOT, B., *Intimate Relations: The Natural History of Desire* (1995).

HUMPHRIES, J., 'Female Headed Households in Early Industrial Britain: The Vanguard of the Proletariat', *Labour History Review*, 63 (1998).

HUMPHRIES, STEVE, *A Secret World of Sex* (1988).

HUNT, A., 'The Great Masturbation Panic and the Discourses of Moral Regulation in Nineteenth and Early Twentieth Century Britain', *Journal of the History of Sexuality* (1998).

HUNT, DAVID, *Parents and Children in History* (New York, 1970).

HUNT, E., *Diseases Affecting the Vulva* (1943).

HUTT, C. W., and THOMSON, H. H., *Principles and Practice of Preventive Medicine*, vol. ii (1935).

HUTTON, ISABEL E., *The Hygiene of Marriage*, (1923), ed. Margaret D. Smyth (1964).

—— *The Hygiene of Marriage* (1923).

—— *Memories of a Doctor in War and Peace* (1960).

HYDE, H. M., *The Other Love* (1970).

—— *The Hygiene of Life and Safer Motherhood* ([c. 1929]).

INGHAM, MARY, *Now We are Thirty: Women of the Breakthrough Generation* (1981).

IRVINE, JANICE M., *Disorders of desire: sex and gender in modern American sexology* (Philadelphia, 1990).

ISSACS, SUSAN, *Social Development in Young Children* (1933).

—— *The Nursery Years: The Mind of the Child from Birth to Six Years* (1929; 1932).

ITTMANN, K., *Work, Gender and Family in Victorian England* (New York, 1995).

—— 'Family Limitation and Family Economy in Bradford, West Yorkshire 1851–1881', *Journal of Social History*, 25/3 (1992).

JACKSON, MARGARET, *The Real Facts of Life: Feminism and the Politics of Sexuality, c.1850–1940* (1994).

——— ' "Something More than Blood": Conflicting Accounts of Pregnancy Loss in Eighteenth Century England', in R. Cecil (ed.), *The Anthropology of Pregnancy Loss: Comparative Studies in Miscarriage, Stillbirth and Neonatal Death* (Oxford, 1996).

JAMES, JOHN P., *The Facts of Sex* (1969).

JAMIESON, LYNN, 'Limited Resources and Limiting Conventions: Working Class Mothers and Daughters in Urban Scotland *c.*1890–1925', in Jane Lewis (ed.), *Labour and Love: Women's Experience of Home and Family 1850–1940* (Oxford, 1986).

JASPER, T., *The Top Twenty Book: The Official British Record Charts, 1955–1983* (Poole, 1983).

JEFFERIS, BENJAMIN G., and NICHOLS, JAMES L., *Search Lights on Health: Light on Dark Corners. A Complete Sexual Science and a Guide to Purity and Physical Manhood: Advice to Maiden, Wife and Mother, Love, Courtship and Marriage* (Toronto, 1894; 1905).

JEFFREYS, SHEILA, *The Spinster and her Enemies: Feminism and Sexuality, 1880–1930* (1985).

JEJEEBHOY, SHIREEN, *Women's Education, Autonomy, and Reproductive Behaviour: Experience from Developing Countries* (Oxford, 1995).

JOAD, C. E. M., *Guide to Modern Thought* (1933).

JORDAN, JANE, *Josephine Butler* (2001).

JORGENSEN-EARP, CHERYL, '*The Transfiguring Sword': The Just War of the Women's Social and Political Union* (Tuscaloosa, Ala., 1997).

JUKES, ADAM E., *Men who Batter Women* (1999).

KAUFMAN, JOSEPH J., and BORGESON, GRIFFITH, *Man and Sex* (1961; 1964).

KEATING, PETER, *The Haunted Study: A Social History of the English Novel, 1875–1914* (1989).

KEELER, CHRISTINE, and FAWKES, S., 'Nothing But ... Christine Keeler', in *Scandal* (1983).

KEGEL, A., 'Early Genital Relaxation: New Technique of Diagnosis and Nonsurgical Treatment', *Obstetrics and Gynaecology*, 8/5 (1956).

KELLY, GEORGE A., *The Catholic Marriage Manual* (New York, 1958).

KENT, SUSAN K., *Sex and Suffrage in Britain, 1860–1914* (1987; 1990).

KERR, M., *The People of Ship Street* (1958).

KEYNES, R., *Annie's Box: Charles Darwin, his Daughter and Human Evolution* (2001; 2002).

KINGSLEY, D., and BLAKE, J., 'Social Structure and Fertility: An Analytic Framework', *Economic Development and Cultural Change*, 4 (1956).

KINSEY, ALFRED C., POMEROY, WARDELL B., GEBHARD, PAUL H., and MARTIN, CLYDE E., *Sexual Behaviour in the Human Male* (Philadelphia, 1948).

——— ——— ——— ——— *Sexual Behaviour in the Human Female* (Philadelphia, 1953).

KIRK, D., 'Demographic Transition Theory', *Population Studies*, 50 (1996).

KIRK, M., MURPHY, MIKE, and HOBCRAFT, J., 'The Problem of Fertility, 1936–1986', in M. Murphy and J. Hobcraft (eds.), *Population Research in Britain: A Supplement to Population Studies*, 45 (1991).

KISCH, E. H., *The Sexual Life of Woman in its Physiological, Pathological and Hygienic Aspects* (1910; 1926).

KLEIN, JOSEPHINE, *Samples of English Culture*, vol. i (1965).

KLEIN, R., *The Politics of the NHS* (1989).

KNIGHT, P., 'Women and Abortion in Victorian and Edwardian England', *History Workshop* (1977).

KNODEL, JOHN, 'Two and a Half Centuries of Demographic History in a Bavarian Village', *Population Studies*, 24 (1967).

—— and VAN DE WALLE, ÉTIENNE, 'Lessons from the Past: Policy Implications of Historical Fertility Studies', in A. J. Coale and Susan C. Watkins (eds.), *The Decline of Fertility* (Princeton, 1986).

KNOWLTON, CHARLES, 'Fruits of Philosophy: An Essay on the Population Question' (1832), repr. in S. Chandrasekhar (ed.), *'A Dirty, Filthy Book': The Writings of Charles Knowlton and Annie Besant on Reproductive Physiology and Birth Control and an Account of the Bradlaugh–Besant Trial* (1981).

KOEDT, ANNE, 'The Myth of Vaginal Orgasm', repr. in Sneja Gunew (ed.), *A Reader in Feminist Knowledge* (1970; 1991).

KOHN, MAREK, *Dope Girls: The Birth of the British Drug Underground* (1992).

KRONHAUSEN, P. D., and KRONHAUSEN, E. D., *Sexual Response in Women* (1965).

LAING, R. D., *The Facts of Life* (1976).

LANE, W. ARBUTHNOT, (ed.), *The Modern Woman's Home Doctor* (1939).

LANGFORD, C. M., 'Birth Control Practice in Britain', *Family Planning*, 17/4 (1969).

—— 'Birth control Practice in Great Britain: A Review of the Evidence from Cross-sectional Surveys', in M. Murphy and J. Hobcraft (eds.), *Population Research in Britain: A Supplement to Population Studies*, 45 (1991).

—— *Birth Control Practice and Marital Fertility in Great Britain: A Report on a Survey Carried out in 1967–68* (1976).

LAQUEUR, THOMAS, *Making Sex: Body and Gender from the Greeks to Freud* (Cambridge, Mass., 1990).

—— 'Simply doing it', Review of *The Facts of Life: The Creation of Sexual Knowledge in Britain 1650–1950*, by R. Porter and L. Hall, *London Review of Books* (22 Feb. 1996).

LASSELL, MARGARET, *Wellington Road* (1966).

LATOUR, BRUNO, *Science in Action* (Cambridge, Mass. 1987).

LAUGHLIN, WILLIAM S., 'Primitive Theory of Medicine', in Iago Galdston (ed.), *Man's Image in Medicine and Anthropology* (New York, 1963).

LAWRENCE, DAVID H., *Lady Chatterley's Lover* (Florence, 1928; 1990).

——— *Sex, Literature and Censorship*, ed. Harry T. Moore (1955).

LAWRENCE, FRIEDA, 'Introduction' to David H. Lawrence, *The First Lady Chatterley* (1944; 1973).

LAZARSFELD, SOFIE, *Woman's Experience of the Male*, ed. Norman Haire (1935; 1955).

LEATHARD, AUDREY, *The Fight for Family Planning: The Development of Family Planning Services in Britain, 1921–74* (1980).

LECKIE, BARBARA, *Culture and Adultery: The Novel, the Newspaper, and the Law, 1857–1914* (Philadelphia, 1999).

LECKY, W. E. H., *European Morals from Augustus to Charlemagne* (1869).

LEECH, K., *Youthquake: The Growth of a Counter-Culture through Two Decades* (1973). Leeds

REVOLUTIONARY FEMINIST GROUP, 'Political Lesbianism: The Case against Hetero-sexuality' *Love your Enemy* (1979).

LEGMAN, GERSHON, *Rationale of the Dirty Joke: An Analysis of Sexual Humour* (1968).

LENEMAN, LEAH, *Alienated Affections: The Scottish Experience of Divorce and Separation, 1684–1830* (Edinburgh, 1998).

——— 'A Truly National Movement: The View from Outside London', in M. Joannou and June Purvis (eds.), *The Women's Suffrage Movement: New Feminist Perspectives* (2000).

LESSING, DORIS, *The Golden Notebook* (1962; 1973).

——— *Under my Skin: Volume One of my Autobiography, to 1949* (New York, 1995).

LESTHAEGHE, RON, *The Decline of Belgian Fertility* (Princeton, 1977).

——— and SURKYN, JOHAN, 'A Century of Demographic and Cultural Change in Western Europe: An Exploration of the Underlying Dimensions', *Population and Development Review* 9/3 (1983).

——— ——— 'Cultural Dynamics and Economic Theories of Fertility Change', *Population and Development Review*, 14/1 (1988).

LEVINE, D., *Reproducing Families: The Political Economy of English Population History* (Cambridge, 1987).

LEVINE, LENA (an exchange with J. Malleson), 'A Criterion for Orgasm in the Female', *Marriage Hygiene* (1948).

——— and LOTH, DAVID, *The Frigid Wife: Her Way to Sexual Fulfilment* (1962).

LEVINE-CLARK, M., 'Testing the Reproductive Hypothesis: Or What Made Working-Class Women Sick in Early Victorian London', *Women's History Review*, 11/2 (2001).

LEWIS, JANE, *Women in Britain since 1945* (Oxford, 1992).

——— CLARK, D., and MORGAN, D., *Whom God hath Joined: The Work of Marriage Guidance* (1992).

—— and KIERNAN, K. E., 'The Boundaries between Marriage, Nonmarriage, and Parenthood: Changes in Behaviour and Policy in Post-War Britain', *Journal of Family History*, 21/3 (1996).

—— LAND, H., and KIERNAN, K. E., *Lone Motherhood in Twentieth-Century Britain* (Oxford, 1998).

LEWIS, LIONEL S., and BRISSETT, DENNIS, 'Sex as Work', *Social Problems*, 15/8 (1967).

LIDDINGTON, JILL, and NORRIS, JILL, *One Hand Tied Behind Us: The Rise of the Women's Suffrage Movement* (1978; 1994).

LLEWELLYN DAVIES, MARGARET, *Maternity: Letters from Working Women Collected by the Women's Co-operative Guild* (1915; 1978).

—— *Life as we have Known it*, ed. Anna Davin (1931; 1977).

LONG, HARLAND W., *Sane Sex Life and Sane Sex Living* (Boston, 1919).

LONGFORD, Lord, *Pornography: The Longford Report* (1972).

LOUDON, IRVINE, *Death in Childbirth* (Oxford, 1992).

LOWE, RODNEY, and NICHOLSON, PAUL, 'The Formation of the Child Poverty Action Group (Witness Seminar)', *Contemporary Record*, 9/3 (1995).

LOWEN, ALEXANDER M., *Love and Orgasm: A Revolutionary Guide to Sexual Fulfillment* (New York, 1965; 1975).

LUNN, A., and LEAN, G., *The New Morality* (1964).

LUTYENS, MARY, *Edwin Lutyens* (1980).

—— *Millais and the Ruskins* (1967).

—— *The Ruskins and the Grays* (1972).

MACANDREW, RENNIE, [pseudonym of Andrew G. Eliot] *Friendship, Love Affairs and Marriage* (1939).

—— *Encyclopedia of Sex and Love Technique* (1941; 1951).

MACARTNEY, W. F. R., and MACKENZIE, COMPTON, *Walls have Mouths: A Record of Ten Years Penal Servitude* (1936).

MACAULAY, MARY, *The Art of Marriage* (1952; 1957).

—— *Marriage for the married* (1964).

McCALMAN, IAIN, 'Unrespectable Radicalism: Infidels and Pornography in Early Nineteenth-Century London', *Past and Present*, 104 (1984).

—— 'Females, Feminism and Free Love in an Early Nineteenth Century Radical Movement', *Labour History*, 38 (1980).

MacCARTHY, FIONA, *Eric Gill* (1989).

McDONALD, PETER, 'Gender Equity, Social Institutions and the Future of Fertility', *Journal of Population Research* (Australia), 17/1 (2000).

MacDougall's Party Book: A Complete and Detailed Explanation of How to Obtain Fullest Enjoyment in the Sexual Act without Fear of Unwanted Pregnancy (New York, 1934).

MacFarlane, Alan, review of *The Family, Sex and Marriage in England 1500–1800*, by Lawrence Stone, *History and Theory*, 18 (1979).
—— *The Culture of Capitalism* (Oxford, 1987).
McIntosh, Mary, 'Who Needs Prostitutes? The Ideology of Male Sexual Needs', in Carol Smart and Barry Smart (eds.), *Women, Sexuality and Social Control* (1978).
McIntosh, Tania, ' "An Abortionist City": Maternal Mortality, Abortion, and Birth Control in Sheffield, 1920–1940', *Medical History* (Great Britain), 44 (2000).
Mackenzie, Donald, and Wacjman, Judy (eds.), *The Social Shaping of Technology* (1999).
MacKinnon, Alison, 'Were Women Present at the Demographic Transition? Questions from a Feminist Historian to Historical Demographers', *Gender and History*, 7/2 (1995).
—— *Love and Freedom* (1997).
McLaren, Angus, 'Women's Work and Regulation of Family Size: The Question of Abortion in the Nineteenth Century', *History Workshop*, 4 (1977).
—— 'Abortion in France: Women and the Regulation of Family Size', *French Historical Studies*, 10 (1978).
—— *Birth Control in Nineteenth Century England* (New York, 1978).
—— *Sexuality and Social Order* (1983).
—— *Reproductive Rituals: The Perception of Fertility in England from the Sixteenth Century to the Nineteenth Century* (1984).
—— *A History of Contraception from Antiquity to the Present Day* (1990).
Macnicol, J., 'The Voluntary Sterilisation Campaign in Britain, 1918–1939', *Journal of the History of Sexuality*, 2/3 (1992).
Maher, Vanessa, 'Breastfeeding or Maternal Depletion', in Vanessa Maher (ed.), *The Anthropology of Breastfeeding: Natural Law or Social Construct* (Oxford, 1992).
Mahood, L., *The Magdalenes: Prostitution in the Nineteenth Century* (1990).
Maitland, S. E., *Very Heaven: Looking Back at the 1960s* (1988).
Makin, Peggy, *The Evelyn Home Story* (Glasgow, 1975).
Malleson, Joan, 'Vaginismus: Management and Psychogenesis', *BMJ* 2 (1942).
—— (an exchange with L. Levine), 'A Criterion for Orgasm in the Female', *Marriage Hygiene* (1948).
—— 'Vaginal Orgasm', *International Journal of Sexology*, 2 (1949).
—— *Any Wife or Any Husband* (1951; 1955).
—— 'Infertility due to Coital Difficulties: A Simple Treatment', *Practitioner*, 169 (1952).
—— 'Sex Problems in Marriage with Particular Reference to Coital Discomfort and the Unconsummated Marriage', *Practitioner*, 172 (1954).

MALLIER, A. T., and ROSSER, M. J., *Women and the Economy: A Comparative Study of Britain and the USA* (Basingstoke, 1987).

MALTHUS, T. R., *An Essay on the Principle of Population* (1872; 1914).

MANDERSON, LENORE, 'Women and the State: Maternal and Child Welfare in Colonial Malaya, 1900–1940', in Valerie Fildes, Lara V. Marks, and Hilary Marland (eds.), *Women and Children First: International and Maternal Welfare, 1870–1945* (1992).

MANNING, LEAH, *A Life for Education* (1970).

MARKS, LARA V., *Sexual Chemistry: A History of the Contraceptive Pill* (2001).

MARMOR, JUDD, 'Some Considerations Concerning Orgasm in the Female', *Psychosomatic Medicine*, 16 (1954).

MARWICK, M. D., 'Reminiscence in Retirement', *Family Planning* (Oct. 1965).

MASON, MICHAEL, *The Making of Victorian Sexual Attitudes* (Oxford, 1994).

—— *The Making of Victorian Sexuality* (Oxford, 1994).

MASSEY, D. E., *Sex Education Source Book: Current Issues and Debates* (1995).

MASS OBSERVATION, *Britain and her Birth Rate* (1945).

MASTERS, BRIAN, *The Life of E. F. Benson* (1991; 1993).

MASTERS, WILLIAM. H. and JOHNSON, VIRGINIA E., 'Orgasm, Anatomy of the Female', in A. P. Abarbanel and Albert Ellis (eds.), *The Encyclopaedia of Sexual Behaviour* (New York, 1961).

—— —— *Human Sexual Response* (1966).

MATTHEWS, J. J., 'They had Such a Lot of Fun: The Women's League of Health and Beauty between the Wars', *History Workshop*, 30 (1990).

MAYNARD, J., *Victorian Discourses on Sexuality and Religion* (Cambridge, 1993).

MEACHAM, S., *A Life Apart: The English Working Class 1890–1914* (1977).

MEADLEY, ROBERT, and KEELER, CHRISTINE, *Sex Scandals* (1985).

MEARS, ELEANOR, *Marriage: A Continuing Relationship* (1960).

MEDAWAR, PETER, 'Principle and Paradox in Eugenics', *Family Planning*, 10/4 (1962).

MERRILL, F., and MERRILL, M., *Among the Nudists* (1931).

MILES, DUDLEY, *Francis Place 1771–1854: The Life of a Remarkable Radical* (1988).

MILES, ROSALIND, *The Fiction of Sex* (1974).

MILLET, KATE, *Sexual Politics* (1969; 1971).

MITCHELL, JULIET, *Psychoanalysis and Feminism* (1974; 1990).

MITCHISON, NAOMI, *All Change Here: Girlhood and Marriage* (1975).

MORT, F., *Dangerous Sexualities: Medico-moral Politics in England since 1830* (1987).

MOSHER, CLELIA, *The Mosher Survey: Sexual Attitudes of 45 Victorian Women* (New York, 1980).

MURPHY, M., 'The Contraceptive Pill and Women's Employment as Factors in Fertility Change in Britain 1963–1980', *Population Studies*, 47 (1993).

MURPHY-LAWLESS, JO, *Reading Birth and Death: A History of Obstetric Thinking* (Cork, 1998).

NEAD, L., *Victorian Babylon: People, Streets and Images in Nineteenth-Century London* (2000).

'The Need for Prostitution', *Twentieth Century*, 172 (1964).

NEUHAUS, J., 'The Importance of being Orgasmic: Sexuality, Gender and Marital Sexual Difficulties in the United States, 1920–1963', *Journal of the History of Sexuality*, 9/4 (2000).

NEVILLE, RICHARD, *Play Power* (1971).

NEWMAN, LUCILE F. (ed.), *Women's Medicine: A Cross-Cultural Study of Indigenous Fertility Regulation* (New Brunswick, NJ, 1985).

NEWSON, JOHN, and NEWSON, ELIZABETH, *Patterns of Infant Care in an Urban Community* (1963; 1965).

——— *Four Years Old in an Urban Community* (1968).

NICHTER, MARK, 'Introduction', in Mark Nichter, (ed.), *Anthropological Approaches to the Study of Ethnomedicine* (Amsterdam, 1992).

NIELD, K. (ed.), *Prostitution in the Victorian Age: Debates on the Issue from Nineteenth-Century Critical Journals* (Farnborough, 1973).

NIVEN, DAVID, *The Moon's a Balloon* (1972).

NOONAN, J. T., *Contraception: A History of its Treatment by Catholic Theologians and Canonists* (Cambridge, Mass., 1965).

NORTON, CAROLINE, 'Letter to the Queen on Lord Chancellor Cranworth's Marriage and Divorce Bill, by Pearce Stevenson, Esq.' (1839), in James O. Hoge and Jane Marcus (eds.), *Selected Writings of Caroline Norton: Facsimile Reproductions* (Delmar, NY, 1978).

NOTESTEIN, FRANK W., 'Population: The Long View', in Theodore W. Schultz (ed.), *Food for the World* (Chicago, 1945).

OBELKEVICH, JAMES, 'Religion', in F. M. Thompson, (ed.), *The Cambridge Social History of Britain 1750–1950* (Cambridge, 1990).

OWEN, ROBERT D., *Moral Physiology* (1834).

PARKER, PETER, *Ackerley: A Life of J. R. Ackerley* (1989; 1994).

PARKIN, MOLLY, *Moll: The Making of Molly Parkin* (1993).

PAUL, L., *Coming to Terms with Sex* (1969).

PAYNE, SYLVIA, M., 'A Conception of Femininity', *British Journal of Medical Psychology*, 15 (1935).

PEARSALL, RONALD, *The Worm in the Bud: The World of Victorian Sexuality* (1969; 1993).

PEARSE, I. H., and CROCKER, L. H., *The Peckham Experiment: A Study in the Living Structure of Society* (1943).

PEEL, JOHN, 'The Manufacture and Retailing of Contraceptives in England', *Population Studies*, 17 (1963).

—— 'Contraception and the Medical Profession', *Population Studies*, 18 (1964).

PERETZ, ELIZABETH, 'The Costs of Modern Motherhood to Low Income Families in Inter-War Britain', in Valerie Fildes, Lara V., Marks, and Hilary Marland (eds.), *Women and Children First: International and Maternal Welfare, 1870–1945* (1992).

PETERSON, M. J., 'No Angels in the House: The Victorian Myth and the Paget Women', *American Historical Review*, 89 (1984).

—— *Family, Love, and Work in the Lives of Victorian Gentlewomen* (Bloomington, Ind., 1989).

—— 'The Victorian Governess: Status Incongruence in Family and Society', in M. Vicinus (ed.), *Suffer and be Still: Women in the Victorian Era* (Bloomington, Ind., 1972).

PETRE, DIANA, *The Secret Orchard of Roger Ackerley* (1975).

PFEFFER, NAOMI, *The Stork and the Syringe: A Political History of Reproductive Medicine* (Cambridge, 1993).

PHILLIPS, EILEEN, 'Introduction: Libertarianism, "Egotism", and Liberation', in Eileen Phillips (ed.), *The Left and the Erotic* (1983).

PIERPONT, R. (ed.), *Report of the Fifth International Neo-Malthusian and Birth Control Conference. Kingsway Hall, London, July 11th-14th, 1922* (1922).

PILLAY, A. P., *The Art of Love and Sane Sex Living, Based on Ancient Classics and Works of American and European Sexologists* (Bombay, 1964).

PLACE, FRANCIS, *Illustrations and Proof of the Principle of Population*, ed. Norman E. Himes (1930).

—— *The Autobiography of Francis Place (1771–1854)*, ed. Mary Thale (Cambridge, 1972).

POLLOCK, LINDA A., *Forgotten Children: Parent–Child Relations from 1500 to 1900* (Cambridge, 2001).

—— 'Embarking on a Rough Passage: The Experience of Pregnancy in Early-Modern Society', in V. Fildes (ed.), *Women as Mothers in Pre-industrial England* (1990).

PORTER, KEVIN, and WEEKS, JEFFREY (eds.), *Between the Acts: Lives of Homosexual Men, 1885–1967* (1991).

PORTER, R. and HALL, LESLEY A., *The Facts of Life: The Creation of Sexual Knowledge in Britain, 1650–1950* (New Haven, 1995).

PORTER, T., *Trust in Numbers: The Pursuit of Objectivity in Science and Public Life* (Princeton, 1995).

QUAIFE, G. R., *Wanton Wenches and Wayward Wives* (1979).

QUETEL, CLAUDE, *History of Syphilis* (1990).

RABY, P., *Samuel Butler: A Biography* (1991).

RADEMAKERS, JANY, and SANDFORT, THEO G. M. (eds.), *Childhood Sexuality: Normal Sexual Behaviour and Development* (2000).

RAINER, JULIA R. G., and RAINER, JEROME, *Sexual Pleasure in Marriage* (1959).

RAMA RAU, D., *An Inheritance: The Memoirs of Dhanvanthi Rama Rau* (1978).

RAPPAPORT, ERIKA D., *Shopping for Pleasure: Women in the Making of London's West End* (Princeton, 2000).

RATHBONE, ELEANOR, *The Disinherited Family* (1924), ed. Suzie Fleming (1986).

RATTRAY-TAYLOR, G., *Sex in History* (1953).

RAVERAT, GWEN, *Period piece: A Cambridge Childhood* (1952).

RAYNER, CLAIRE, *People in Love: A Modern Guide to Sex in Marriage* (1968).

REAY, BARRY, 'Sexuality in Nineteenth-Century England: The Social Context of Illegitimacy in Rural Kent', *Rural History*, 1/2 (1990).

—— 'Before the Transition: Fertility in English Villages, 1800–1880', *Continuity and Change*, 9 (1994).

REEVES, MARGARET, P., *Round about a Pound a Week* (1913; 1979).

REGER, J., and FLACK, SHIRLEY, *Janet Reger: Her Story* (1991).

REUBEN, DAVID, *Everything you Always Wanted to Know about Sex* but were Afraid to ask* (New York, 1970).

RIDDLE, JOHN M., *Contraception and Abortion from the Ancient World to the Renaissance* (Cambridge, Mass., 1992).

RILEY, DENISE, *War in the Nursery: Theories of the Child and Mother* (1983).

ROBERTS, ELIZABETH, *A Woman's Place: An Oral History of Working-Class Women, 1890–1940* (Oxford, 1984).

—— *Women and Families: An Oral History, 1940–1970* (Oxford, 1995).

—— 'The Working Class Extended Family: Functions and Attitudes 1890–1940', *Oral History* (1900).

ROBERTS, ELIZABETH J. (ed.), *Childhood Sexual Learning: The Unwritten Curriculum* (Cambridge, Mass., 1980).

ROBERTS, ROBERT, *The Classic Slum: Salford Life in the First Quarter of the Century* (1971; 1973).

ROBIE, W. F., *The Art of love* (Boston, 1921; 1963).

ROBINSON, JOHN A. T., *Honest to God* (1963).

ROBINSON, MARIE N., *The Power of Sexual Surrender* (1960).

ROBINSON, PAUL, *The Modernization of Sex* (New York, 1976).

ROLFE, C. N., 'Sexual Delinquency', in H. Llewellyn Smith (ed.), *The New Survey of London Life and Labour* (1935).

—— MALINOWSKI, B., VOGE, C. I., and CRICHTON-MILLER, H., *Preparation for Marriage: A Handbook Prepared by a Special Committee on Behalf of the British Social Hygiene Council*, ed. Kenneth M. Walker (1932).

ROLPH, C. H., *The Trial of Lady Chatterley: Regina v. Penguin Books Limited* (1961).

—— *Living Twice: An Autobiography* (1974).

ROPER, MICHAEL, and TOSH, JOHN, 'Historians and the Politics of Masculinity', in Michael Roper and John Tosh (eds.), *Manful Assertions: Masculinity in Britain since 1800* (1991).

ROQUES, F. W., BEATTIE, J., and WRIGLEY, J., *Diseases of Women* (1959).

ROSE, NIKOLAS, *Governing the Soul: The Shaping of the Private Self* (1990).

ROSE, PHYLLIS, *Parallel Lives* (1983; 1994).

ROSE, SONYA O., 'Girls and GIs: Race, Sex and Diplomacy in Second World War Britain', *International History Review*, 19/1 (1997).

ROSEN, ANDREW, *Rise up Women! The Militant Campaign of the Women's Social and Political Union 1903–1914* (1974).

ROSENFIELD, ALLAN, 'Maternal mortality and morbidity', in Benjamin P. Sachs, Richard Beard, Emile Papiernik, and Christine Russell (eds.), *Reproductive Health Care for Women and Babies* 1995).

ROSS, ELLEN, *Love and Toil: Motherhood in Outcast London, 1870–1918* (Oxford, 1993).

ROUTH, C. H. F., *The Moral and Physical Evils . . .* (1878; 1879).

ROUTH, GUY, *Occupation and Pay in Great Britain, 1906–79* (1980).

ROWBOTHAM, S., ' "Diary in the Life of Sheila Rowbotham", from *Red Rag* 1968', in *Dreams and Dilemmas: Collected Writings* (1983).

—— *Woman's Consciousness, Man's World* (Harmondsworth, 1973).

—— and MCCRINDLE, JEAN, *Dutiful Daughters: Women Talk about their Lives* (1977).

ROWNTREE, GRISELDA, and PIERCE, RACHEL, M., 'Birth Control in Britain: Part One', *Population Studies*, 15/1 (1961).

—— 'Birth Control in Britain: Part Two', *Population Studies*, 15/2 (1961).

RUSHBRIDGER, ALAN, *A Concise History of the Sex Manual* (1986).

RUSSELL, BERTRAND, *Marriage and Morals* (1929; 1968).

—— and RUSSELL, PATRICIA (eds.), *The Amberley Papers: The Letters and Diaries of Lord and Lady Amberley*, vols. i and ii (1937; 1966).

RUZICKA, LADO, T., and CALDWELL, JOHN, C., *The End of the Demographic Transition in Australia* (Canberra, 1977).

RYAN, MICHAEL, *Prostitution in London* (1839).

RYDER, N. B., and WESTOFF, C. F., *Reproduction in the United States, 1965* (Princeton, 1971).

SADLER, R., ACLAND, R. S., and BENTLEY, G. B., *Sexual Morality: Three Views*, ed. C. L. Gough (1965).

SAGAR, KEITH, *D.H. Lawrence: Life into Art* (1985).

SANDERS, DEIDRE, *The Woman Book of Love and Sex* (1985).

SANGER, MARGARET, *Happiness in Marriage* (1927).

—— and STONE, HANNAH, *The Practice of Contraception: An International Symposium and Survey. From the Proceedings of the Seventh International Birth Control Congress, Zurich, Switzerland, September 1930* (Baltimore, 1931).

SANTOW, GIGI, 'Coitus Interruptus in the Twentieth Century', *Population and Development Review*, 19/4 (1993).

—— 'Coitus Interruptus and the Control of Natural Fertility', *Population Studies*, 49 (1995).

—— and BRACHER, M., 'Premature Discontinuation of Contraception in Australia', *Family Planning Perspectives*, 24 (1992).

SAVAGE, GAIL, ' "The Wilful Communication of a Loathesome Disease": Marital Conflict and Venereal Disease in Victorian England', *Victorian Studies*, 34 (1990).

—— 'Erotic Stories and Public Decency: Newspaper Reporting of Divorce Proceedings in England', *Historical Journal*, 41/2 (1998).

SCARRY, ELAINE, *The Body in Pain* (Oxford, 1995).

SCHNEIDER, JANE, and SCHNEIDER, PETER, *Festival of the Poor: Fertility Decline and the Ideology of Class in Sicily, 1860–1980* (Tucson, Ariz., 1996).

SCHOFIELD, MICHAEL, *The Sexual Behaviour of Young People* (1965; rev. edn. 1968).

—— *The Sexual Behaviour of Young Adults* (1973).

SCHWARZ, OSWALD, *The Psychology of Sex* (1949).

SCHWARZKOPF, JUTTA, *Women in the Chartist Movement* (1991).

SCOTT, GEORGE R., *Sex and its Mysteries* (1929; 2nd edn. 1948).

—— *Modern Birth Control Methods* (1933; 2nd edn. 1947).

—— *The New Art of Love* (1934).

—— *The New Art of Love* (1934; 1955).

—— *The History of Prostitution: From Antiquity to the Present Day* (1936; 1996).

—— *Sex in Married Life* (1938).

SCOTT, GILLIAN, *Feminism and the Politics of Working Women: The Women's Co-operative Guild, 1880s to the Second World War* (1998).

SEAMAN, BARBARA, *Free and Female* (1972).

—— *The Doctors' Case against the Pill* (1970).

SECCOMBE, WALLY, 'Starting to Stop: Working-Class Fertility Decline in Britain', *Past and Present*, 126 (1990).

—— 'Men's "Marital Rights" and Women's "Wifely Duties": Changing Conjugal Relations in the Fertility Decline', in John R. Gillis, Louise A. Tilly, and David Levine (eds.), *The European Experience of Declining Fertility: A Quiet Revolution 1850–1970* (Oxford, 1992).

—— *Weathering the Storm: Working-Class Families from the Industrial Revolution to the Fertility Decline*, (1993).

—— *A Millenium of Family Change: Feudalism to Capitalism in Northwestern Europe* (1995).

SEDGWICK, E. KOSOFSKY, *Epistemology of the Closet* (1990).

SEGAL, LYNNE, *Slow Motion: Changing Masculinities, Changing Men* (1990).

—— *Straight Sex: The Politics of Pleasure* (1994).

SEIDLECKY, STEFANIA, and WYNDHAM, DIANA, *Populate and Perish: Australian Women's Fight for Birth Control* (Sydney, 1990).

SEVELY, JOSEPHINE L., *Eve's Secrets: A New Perspective on Human Sexuality* (1987).

'Sex Manuals: How Not To', *Newsweek* (18 Oct. 1965).

SHANLEY, MARY L., *Feminism, Marriage and the Law in Victorian England, 1850–1895* (1989).

SHAPIRO, PAULINE, 'The Unplanned Children', *New Society* (1962).

SHEARD, S., 'Profit is a Dirty Word: The Development of Public Baths and Wash-houses in Britain, 1847–1915', *Social History of Medicine*, 13/1 (2000).

SHERFEY, MARY J., *The Nature and Evolution of Female Sexuality* (New York, 1966; 1973).

SHORTER, E., *The Making of the Modern Family* (1975).

—— KNODEL, JOHN, and VAN DE WALLE, ÉTIENNE, 'The Decline of Non-Marital Fertility in Europe', *Population Studies*, 25 (1971).

SHOWALTER, E., *Sexual Anarchy: Gender and Culture at the Fin de Siecle* (1991).

SIKES, H. M. (ed.), *The Letters of William Hazlitt* (1905; New York, 1978).

SINGER, IRVING, *The Goals of Human Sexuality* (1973; 1974).

SLATER, ELIOT, and WOODSIDE, MOYA, *Patterns of Marriage: A Study of the Marriage Relationships of the Urban Working Classes* (1951).

SLOAN, DOUGLAS G., 'The Extent of Contraceptive Use and the Social Paradigm of Modern Demography', *Sociology*, 17/3 (1983).

SMITH, F. B., 'Sexuality in Britain, 1800–1900: Some Suggested Revisions', in Martha Vicinus (ed.), *A Widening Sphere: Changing Roles of Victorian Women* (1977).

—— *Radical Artisan: William James Linton 1812–97* (Manchester, 1973).

SMITH, RICHARD, 'Elements of Demographic Change in Britain since 1945', in James Obelkevich and P. Catterall (eds.), *Understanding Post-war British Society* (1994).

SNELL, K. D. M., *Annals of the Labouring Poor: Social Change and Agrarian England, 1660–1900* (Cambridge, 1985).

—— and ELL, PAUL, S., *Rival Jerusalems: The Geography of Victorian Religion* (Cambridge, 2000).

SOGNER, SOLVI, 'Historical Features of Women's Position in Society', in N. Frederici, Karen O. Mason, and Solvi Sogner (eds.), *Women's Position and Demographic Change* (Oxford, 1993).

SOLOWAY, RICHARD A., *Birth Control and the Population Question in England, 1877–1930* (1982).

—— *Demography and Degeneration: Eugenics and the Declining Birth Rate in Twentieth-Century Britain* (Chapel Hill, NC, 1990).

—— ' "The Perfect Contraceptive": Eugenics and Birth Control Research in Britain and America in the Inter-War years', *Journal of Contemporary History*, 30 (1996).

SPENCER, ROBERT F., 'Primitive obstetrics', *Ciba Symposia*, 11 (1949).

SPITZER, ALLEN B., 'The Historical Idea of Generation', *American Historical Review*, 78 (1973).

SPRING RICE, MARGERY, *Working-Class Wives: Their Health and Conditions* (1939; 1981).

STANLEY, LIZ, *Sex Surveyed 1949–1994: From Mass Observation's 'Little Kinsey' to the National Survey and the Hite Reports* (1995).

STEAD, W. T., 'The Maiden Tribute of Modern Babylon', *Pall Mall Gazette*, 42/6336–8 (1885).

STEARNS, PETER N., 'Working-Class Women', in Martha Vicinus (ed.), *Suffer and be Still* (1972).

STEDMAN JONES, G., *Languages of Class: Studies in English Working Class History, 1832–1982* (Cambridge, 1983).

STEPHENS, MARGARET, *Women and Marriage: A Handbook* (1910; 1918).

STEWART, W. A. C., *Progressives and Radicals in English Education, 1750–1970* (1972).

STOCKHAM, ALICE B., *Tokology: A Book for Every Woman* (Chicago, 1883; 1897).

STOCKS, M. 'Climate of Opinion', *Family Planning*, 8/3 (1959).

STONE, ABRAHAM, and STONE, HANNAH, *A Marriage Manual: A Practical Guide Book to Sex and Marriage* (Australia, 1936; 1954).

STONE, LAWRENCE, *The Family, Sex and Marriage in England 1500–1800* (1977).

—— *Road to Divorce: England 1530–1987* (Oxford, 1990; 1995).

STOPES, MARIE, *Married Love: A New Contribution to the Solution of Sex Difficulties* (1918).

—— *Married Love* (1918; 1937).

—— *Wise Parenthood* (1918; 3rd edn. 1919).

—— *Wise Parenthood* (1918).

—— *Contraception: Theory, History and Practice* (1923; 1925).

—— *Contraception: Theory, History and Practice* (1923; 1928).

—— *The First Five Thousand: The First Report of the First Birth Control Clinic in the British Empire* (1923).

—— *Enduring Passion* (1928; 1931).

—— *Enduring Passion* (1928; 1937).

STOTT, M., *Forgetting's No Excuse* (1975).

SUMMERFIELD, PENNY, and FINCH, JANET, 'Social Reconstruction and the Emergence of Companionate Marriage, 1945–59', in D. Clark, (ed.), *Marriage, Domestic Life, and Social Change: Writings for Jacqueline Burgoyne* (1991).

SWYER, G. I., PATON, W. D. M., PIRIE, N. W., MORRIS, N. R. and EDWARDS, R. G., 'The Scientific Basis of Contraception', supplement 'Towards a Population Policy for the United Kingdom', *Population Studies* (1970).

SZRETER, SIMON, 'The Idea of the Demographic Transition and the Study of Fertility Change: A Critical Intellectual History', *Population and Development Review*, 19/4 (1993).

—— *Fertility, Class and Gender in Britain, 1860–1940* (Cambridge, 1996).

—— 'Victorian Britain, 1837–1963: Towards a Social History of Sexuality', *Journal of Victorian Culture*, 1 (1996).

—— and GARRET, EILIDH, 'Reproduction, Compositional Demography and Economic Growth: Family Planning in England Long Before the Fertility Decline', *Population and Development Review*, 26/1 (2000).

TAIT, LAWSON, *Diseases of Women and Abdominal Surgery*, vol. i (Leicester, 1889).

TAIT, WILLIAM, *Magdalenism: An Inquiry into the Extent, Causes and Consequences of Prostitution in Edinburgh* (1840).

TAJ, A. M., and MASON, KAREN O., 'Differences between Women's and Men's Reproductive Goals in Developing Countries', *Population and Development Review*, 13 (1987).

TALBOT, JAMES, *The Miseries of Prostitution* (1844).

TAYLOR, BARBARA, *Eve and the New Jerusalem* (1983).

TAYLOR, DAVID, *Crime, policing and punishment in England, 1750–1914* (1998).

TAYLOR, G. R., *Sex in History* (1953).

TAYLOR, LAURIE, 'The Unfinished Sexual Revolution: The First Marie Stopes Memorial Lecture', *Journal of Biosocial Science*, 3 (1972).

TEBBUTT, MELANIE, *Women's Talk? A Social History of Gossip in Working-Class Neighbour-hoods, 1880–1960* (1995).

TEIFER, LEONORE, 'Medicine, Morality and the Public Management of Sexual Matters', in Lynne Segal (ed.), *New Sexual Agendas* (1997).

TENENBAUM, JOSEPH, *The Riddle of Sex: The Medical and Social Aspects of Sex, Love and Marriage*, Introd. Vera Brittain (1930).

THANE, PAT M., 'The Debate on the Declining Birth Rate in Britain: The "Menace" of an Ageing Population, 1920s–1950s', *Continuity and Change*, 5/2 (1990).

THOMPSON, DOROTHY, *The Chartists: Popular Politics in the Industrial Revolution* (Aldershot, 1986).

THOMPSON, E. P., *The Making of the English Working-Class* (1980).

—— and YEO, EILEEN (eds.), *The Unknown Mayhew: Selections from the Morning Chronicle 1849–50* (1971).

THOMPSON, PAUL, *The Edwardians: The Remaking of British Society* (1975; 1977).

THOMPSON, T., *Dear Girl: The Diaries and Letters of Two Working Women 1897–1917* (1987).

THOROGOOD, M., and VESSEY, M. P., 'Trends in Use of Oral Contraceptives in Britain', *British Journal of Family Planning*, 16 (1990).

THWAITE, ANN, *Emily Tennyson: The Poet's Wife*, (1996).

TIETZE, CHRISTOPHER, *The Condom as a Contraceptive* (New York, 1960).

—— 'The Use-Effectiveness of Contraceptive Methods', in V. Clyde Kiser (ed.), *Research in Family Planning* (Princeton, 1962).

TILLY, L., and SCOTT, J. W., *Women, Work and Family* (1989).

—— and COHEN, M., 'Women's Work and European Fertility Patterns', *Journal of Interdisciplinary History*, 6/3 (1976).

TOFT, MOGENS, *Sexual Techniques: An Illustrated Guide* (1969).

TOMALIN, CLAIRE, *The Life and Death of Mary Wollstonecraft* (1974).

—— *Katherine Mansfield: A Secret Life* (1988).

—— *The Invisible Woman* (1990).

—— *Several Strangers: Writing from Three Decades* (1999).

TOMES, NANCY, ' "A Torrent of Abuse": Crimes of Violence between Working Class Men and Women in London, 1840–1875', *Journal of Social History*, 11 (1978).

TOMKINSON, MARTIN, *The Pornbrokers: The Rise of the Soho Sex Barons* (1982).

TOSH, JOHN, *A Man's Place: Masculinity and the Middle Class Home in Victorian England* (1999).

TOWNSEND, P., *The Family Life of Old People: An Inquiry in East London* (1957).

TRALL, RUSSELL T., *Sexual Physiology: A Scientific and Popular Exposition of the Fundamental Problems in Sociology* (1866; 1919).

—— *Sexual Physiology and Hygiene: An Exposition Practical, Scientific, Moral and Popular, of Some of the Fundamental Problems of Sociology* (1891; 1914).

TRAVIS, A., *Bound and Gagged: A Secret History of Obscenity in Britain* (2000).

TRISTAN, FLORA, *Flora Tristan's London Journal, 1840* (1980).

TRUDGILL, ERIC, *Madonnas and Magdalens: The Origins and Development of Victorian Sexual Attitudes* (1976).

TRUSSELL, J., and KOST, K., 'Contraceptive Failure in the United States: A Critical Review of the Literature', *Studies in Family Planning*, 18 (1987).

UDRY, J. R., 'Coitus as Demographic Behaviour', in Ronald Gray, Henri Leridon, and Alfred Spira (eds.), *Biomedical and Demographic Determinants of Reproduction* (Oxford, 1993).

VAN DE VELDE, TH. H., *Ideal marriage: Its Physiology and Technique*, trans. Stella Brown, ed. J. J. Abraham (1928; 1952).

—— *Ferility and Sterility in Marriage: Their Voluntary Promotion and Limitation* (1931).

—— *Sex Hostility in Marriage: Its Origin, Prevention and Treatment* (1931).

—— *Sex Efficiency through Exercises: Special Physical Culture for Women* (1933).

VAUGHAN, PAUL, *The Pill on Trial* (1972).

VICINUS, MARTHA, *A Widening Sphere: Changing Roles of Victorian Women* (Bloomington, Ind., 1977).

—— 'Distance and Desire: English Boarding School Friendships, 1870–1920', in Martha Vicinus, Martin B. Duberman, and George Chauncey, (eds.), *Hidden from History: Reclaiming the Gay and Lesbian Past* (1989; 1991).

—— *Independent Women: Work and Community for Single Women, 1850–1920* (Chicago, 1985).

VICKERY, AMANDA, 'Golden Age to Separate Spheres? A Review of the Categories and Chronology of English Women's History', *Historical Journal*, 36/2 (1993).

VINCENT, DAVID, 'Love and Death and the Nineteenth-Century Working-Class', *Social History*, 5/2 (1980).

—— *The Rise of Mass Literacy: Reading and Writing in Modern Europe* (2000).

VOGE, C. I., *The Chemistry and Physics of Contraceptives* (1933).

VON URBAN, RUDOLF D., *Sex Perfection* (1952; 1969).

WAGNER, PETER, *Eros Revived: Erotica of the Enlightenment in England and America* (1988; 1990).

WALKER, KENNETH M., *The Physiology of Sex* (1940).

—— *I Talk of Dreams* (1946).

—— *Love, Marriage and the Family* (1957).

—— *Sexual Behaviour: Creative and Destructive* (1966).

—— and FLETCHER, P., *Sex and Society* (1955).

—— and STRAUSS, E. B., *Sexual Disorders in the Male* (1939; 4th edn. 1954).

WALKOWITZ, JUDITH R., *Prostitution and Victorian Society: Women, Class and the State* (1980).

—— 'Male Vice and Female Virtue', in Ann Snitow, Christine Stansell, and Sharon Thompson, (eds.), *Powers of Desire: The Politics of Sexuality* (New York, 1983).

WALT, GILLIAN, 'Policy Making in Britain: A Comparative Study of Fluoridation and Family Planning, 1960–1974' (D.Phil. thesis, London School of Economics, 1976).

[WALTER], *My Secret Life* (Amsterdam, 1880; 1995).

WARDLAW, RALPH, *Lectures on Female Prostitution: Its Nature, Extent, Effects, Guilt, Causes, and Remedy, etc.* (Glasgow, 1842).

WARNER, MARINA, 'Our Lady of the Boarding School', in Margaret Laing (ed.), *Woman on Woman* (1971).

WATKINS, ELIZABETH ROSE, *On the Pill: A Social History of Oral Contraceptives in America, 1950–1970*, (Baltimore, 1998).

WATKINS, SUSAN C., *From Provinces into Nations: Demographic Integration in Western Europe, 1870–1960* (Princeton, 1991).

WEAR, A., 'The History of Personal Hygiene', in R. Porter and W. F. Bynum (eds.), *Companion Encyclopaedia of the History of Medicine* (1993).

WEATHERHEAD, LESLIE D., *The Mastery of Sex through Psychology and Religion* (1931).

—— *The Mastery of Sex through Psychology and Religion* (1931; 1942).

WEEKS, JEFFREY, *Sex, Politics and Society: The Regulation of Sexuality since 1800* (1981; 1989).

—— *Sexuality and its Discontents* (1985).

—— 'Sexual Values Revisited', in Lynne Segal (ed.), *New Sexual Agendas* (1997; Basingstoke, 1998).

WEINBERG, MARTIN S., SWENSSON, ROCHELLE G., and HAMMERSMITH, SUE K., 'Sexual Autonomy and the Status of Women: Models of Female Sexuality in U.S. Sex Manuals from 1950 to 1980', *Social Problems* (1983).

WEINER, J. H., *Radicalism and Freethought in Nineteenth-Century Britain: The Life of Richard Carlile* (Westport, Conn., 1983).

WELDON, FAY, *The Fat Woman's Joke* (1967; 1982).

WELLINGS, KAYE, FIELD, J., JOHNSON, A. M., WADSWORTH, J., and BRADSHAW, SALLY, *Sexual Attitudes and Lifestyles* (1994).

WHELPTON, PASCAL K., CAMPBELL, ARTHUR C., and FREEDON, RONALD, *Family Planning, Sterility and Population Growth* (New York, 1959).

WHITE, C., *Women's Magazines 1693–1968* (1970).

WHITEHEAD, CLAYTON S., and HOFF, CHARLES A., *Sex Revelations and the New Eugenics: A Safe Guide for Young Men—Young Women* (Chicago, 1936).

WHITEHORN, K., 'Catholics and Birth Control', *Family Planning*, 13/1 (1964).

WHITING, P., 'Female Sexuality: Its Political Implications', in Michelene Wandor (ed.), *The Body Politic: Women's Liberation in Britain 1969–1972* (1972).

WHORTON, J. C., 'Inner Hygiene: The Philosophy and Practice of Intestinal Purity in Western Civilization', in Y. Kawakita S. Sakai, and Y. Otsuka (eds.), *History of Hygiene: Proceedings of the 12th International Symposium on the Comparative History of Medicine—East and West* (Tokyo, 1991).

WILLIAMS, COLIN C., *Examining the Nature of Domestic Labour* (Aldershot, 1988).

WILMOTT, PETER, *Adolescent Boys of East London* (1966).

—— and Young, Michael, *Family and Kinship in East London* (1957: 1962).

—— and YOUNG, MICHAEL, *The Symmetrical Family* (1973).

WILSON, COLIN, *Sex and the Intelligent Teenager* (1966).

WILSON, ELIZABETH, *Only Halfway to Paradise: Women in Postwar Britain, 1945–1968* (1980).

—— *The Sphinx in the City* (1991).

—— *Women and the Welfare State* (1977).

WILSON, HARRIETTE, *Harriette Wilson's Memoirs*, (1825), ed. L. Blanch, (1957).

WIMPERIS, VIRGINIA, *The Unmarried Mother and her Child* (1960).

WOLLSTONECRAFT, MARY, *A Vindication of the Rights of Women* (1792).

Women's Group on Public Welfare, *Our Towns: A Close up* (London, 1943; New York, 1985).

WOODS, R. I., WATTERSON, P. A. and WOODWARD, J. H., 'The Causes of the Rapid Infant Mortality Decline in England and Wales, 1861–1921 part II', *Population Studies*, 43 (1989).

WOODSIDE, MOYA, 'Orgasm Capacity among 200 English Working-Class Wives', in Albert Ellis and A. P. Pillay (eds.), *Sex, Society and the Individual* (Bombay, 1953).

WOOLER, T. J., *Black Dwarf*, 11 (1823).

WOOLF, MYRA, *Family Intentions* (1971).

WOYCKE, JAMES, *Birth Control in Germany, 1871–1933* (1988).

WRIGHT, HELENA, *The Sex Factor in Marriage* (1930; 1940).

—— *Sex Fulfilment in Married Women* (1947).

—— Review of *The condom as a Contraceptive* by C Tietze, *Family Planning*, 9/3 (1960).

WRIGLEY, E. A., 'Family Limitation in Pre-Industrial England', in Orest A. Ranum and Patricia Ranum (eds.), *Popular Attitudes towards Birth Control in Pre-industrial France and England* (New York, 1972).

—— 'Explaining the Rise in Marital Fertility in England in the "Long" Eighteenth Century', *Economic History Review*, 51/3 (1998).

—— 'Marriage, Fertility and Population Growth in Eighteenth century England', in R. B. Outhwaite (ed.), *Marriage and Society: Studies in the Social History of Marriage* (1981).

—— OEPPEN, J. E., SCHOFIELD, R. S., and DAVIES, R. S., *English Population History from Family Reconstitution, 1580–1837* (Cambridge, 1997).

—— and SCHOFIELD, R. S., *The Population History of England, 1541–1871* (1981).

WYATT, GAIL E., NEWCOMB, MICHAEL D., and RIEDERLE, MONIKA H., *Sexual Abuse and Consensual Sex: Women's Developmental Patterns and Outcomes* (1993).

WYNDHAM, JOAN, *Love is Blue* (1986).

—— *Love Lessons* (1986).

ZWEIG, FERDYNAND, *Women's Life and Labour* (1952).

—— *The Worker in an Affluent Society: Family Life and Industry* (1961).

Index

abortion 2, 5, 7, 20, 22, 40, 42, 121, 122,
    185
  abortifacients 43–4
  concealment of, in 1970s 108
  law reform and 289, 290–1, 304, 331,
    343
  mortality 288
  new technique 116–17
  proximate determinant 20, 22–3
  class and 43, 331
  women's awareness of risks in
    20th c 142
absorption, of semen by vagina 201–2,
    246
abstinence 107–10, 144, 155–62
  breastfeeding and 35
  definition of 107–9
  female preference for 117, 121, 157
  genitals and 155
  rejection, in sex manuals 110, 155 n.
    48
  role of late marriage 110
  separate beds and 158
  in USA 59–60
  see also coital frequency
adoption (1950s) 185
adultery 339
  and absence of contraception,
    pre-1800 45
  middle-class men and 185
  mistresses 210, 238, 239–40
  1940s 184
AIDs 340
Aimeè Ben 55

Age Concern 313
anal intercourse 128–30
Anderson, Michael 321
animals 293
Andrews, A. 344
Arran, Lord 338
The Art of Marriage 228
Austin, John 70, 76, 82–3, 100
Austin, Sarah (née Taylor) 70,
    82–3, 97
Australia 5, 49, 51–2, 266–8
autonomy, female 18, 62, 69, 278
  active female sexuality, rejection
    of 213–19
  breastfeeding and 31–6
  female sexual activity, and 71–3,
    331
  definition 3–4
  Freud and 215, 233
  growth of in 20th c 176, 296, 317
  rejection of 19th c. 71, 85, 111
  Stopes, and female sexuality 192
  van de Velde, absence of 202
agency, female 23, 26–7
  conjugal rights and 111–12
  see also autonomy, female

Bailey, Derrick Sherwin 229–30
Baker, J. R. 136
Banks, Joseph 76–7, 88, 99
Barnes, F. and K.C. 343
Baruch, D. 344
BBC (British Broadcasting
    Corporation) 285, 286

Beale, G. Courtenay
    (pseudonym) 194, 198, 200–1,
    204, 345
Bentley, G. B. Canon 286–7
Berg, Louis 237, 344
Besant Annie 60–1
bestiality 220
bidets, moral aspect 128, 136
Birmingham 96, 126, 138, 289–90, 307
biological processes 6
    conception 107, 130–1
    and fertility 20–32
    lubrication and first sexual
        intercourse 199
    fortnightly cycle female
        desire 200–1
    menstruation 44
    women's awareness of 31, 32 n. 40
    see also breastfeeding; pregnancy;
        proximate determinants
birth control (i.e. all methods
    including abortion):
    development of 40–1, 47–9, 52–3,
        55–9
    free services 307–8, 335
    government action 280, 302
    and population control, 1950s 297,
        301
    rational choices and 303, 311
    unnatural 75
    see also abortion; abstinence;
        communal control of fertility;
        contraception
Birth Control Association 274
Birth Control Campaign 301
birth control clinics:
    numbers of 272–3
    for unmarried women 288–90
    see also Family Planning Association
Birth Control Investigation
    Committee 123

birth control manuals:
    authors of 124–6
Birth Control Methods 125
Birth Control on Trial 126
birth control tracts 19th c 41, 53–61
Blake, Judith 19–20
Black Dwarf 71, 73
Blacker, C. P. 195
Blooman, Mrs and Charlie 315
bodies, physical:
    damage to, from breastfeeding 32
    impact of high fertility, on 11–12,
        30–1, 38
    GPs and 273–4
    interwar changes in dress, exercise,
        etc. 138
    mind/body dualism 24
    pain, impact on body and mind 28
    as unchanging substratum 12,
        250–1, 260
bohemians and socialists 101, 144, 165
Bone, Margaret 52, 268
Bongaarts, John 20
Borgeson, Griffith 236, 344
Boswell, John 46
Boulton, W. 343
Bovet, T. 343
bowel control 144, 147, 150–1
Bowman, Elaine Kellet 303
Bracher, Marie 52
Bradlaugh, Charles 60
Bradshaw, Sally 319
Braine, Bernard 306
breastfeeding 6, 11, 29, 192
    as contraceptive method 130
    female autonomy and 31–6
    as reproductive labour 31–2, 36
    pleasure and 32
    rates of 33–4
    post-partum infecundability 21–2
Briant, Keith 277

Briggs, Asa 285
Brisset, Dennis 188
British Eugenics Society 300
British Medical Association
    (BMA) 280–1, 283, 290–1, 304–5
British Medical Journal 272–3
*British Society for the Study of Sex
    Psychology* 194
Brittain, Vera 145
Brodie, Janet Farrell 59
Brook, Helen 288–9, 293
    Brook clinic 288–9
Brooke, Rupert 122
Bross, B. 343
Buschke, Abraham 204, 344
Butler, Josephine 92
Butt, Ronald 310
Butterfield, O. 343
Byron, Lord 78

Canada 5
Calderone, M. S. 343–4
Caldwell, Jenni 172
Caldwell, John 29–30
Cambridge birth control clinic 126,
    138
Cannon, John 45–6, 84
Caprio, F. S. 344
Carlile, Richard 70
    birth control 53–61, 70–1
    sexuality 74–5
    unnatural 75
Carlile, Jane 74
Carlyle, Thomas 99
Carter, Angela 271
Carter, Pam 29, 128 n. 27
Carstairs, G. M. 285
Catholics:
    contraception and 278, 304
    GPs 274, 304–5
    press censorship and 305

response to sex research 253
    see also religion
censorship 183, 216, 227, 342
    diminishing 292–3
    masturbation and 211–12
    theatre censorship 290
cervical caps 112, 114, 132–5
    and damage in childbirth 134–5
    description 132
    effectiveness interwar 142
    see also vaginal contraception
cervical mucus 281
Charles, Edward 212–5, 219 n. 41, 220,
    342–4
Charles, Enid 126
    contraception, use of 128, 132
    condom use 138–9
    effectiveness 139–42
    sample, class of 140
Chartham, R. 343
chastity 213, 303–4, 306
Chesser, Eustace 184, 221, 342–6
    anal sex 129
    duration sexual intercourse 203
    influence of Freud upon 210–11,
        221
    petting 230–1, 321
    premarital sexual intercourse
        283–4, 321
Child Poverty Action Group 309
children 16, 23, 312–3
    financial responsibility for 64
    masturbation, 122–4, 147, 210, 215
    labour and fertility decline 72
    nannies 147
    parental authority 119
    pleasure and 28, 38
    sexual development 166, 169–7
childbirth 29, 192
    morbidity resulting from 11, 30–1,
        87, 134–5

childbearing 20, 29–31
    family size, impact on mother's
        health 11–12, 38, 134–5
    decision-making process 25
    see also family size; reproductive
        labour
Chitty, Susan 83
Church of England 81–2, 197
    approval birth control 304
    Bishop of Woolwich 285
    family size and 285
    premarital sex, 1960s and 285–7
    subordination of women 229
    women's decision making and 27
    see also religion
Circular 5/66 302
Clark, Anna 66, 71
Clark, LeMon 250, 343
clitoris:
    emotion and 239
    inhibitions fading 259
    and masturbation, interwar
        period 207–10
    new brides and 230–1
    orgasm 214–17, 253–60
    see also genitals; vaginal orgasm
Coal is Our Life 179, 181
Cochran, Joan 343
coital frequency 7, 20, 22, 131
    conception and 107
    contraceptive effectiveness and 50,
        265–6
    fertility rates and 63, 265
    high frequencies 242
    low rates of 266–7
    in sex manuals 155–6
    see also abstinence
coital interlocking 245–7, 249
Cole, Estelle 223–4, 343
Cole, G. D. H. 174–5
Cole, Margaret 129, 174

Cole, Martin 289–90, 303
Colley, Linda 69
Colquhoun, Patrick 79
Comfort, Alex 188, 286–7, 289–50, 341,
    344–6
commercialization sexuality 12,
    339–40
community control of fertility 16, 40,
    64, 184, 322–3
community control of sexuality 179,
    184, 273–4, 279–80, 286
condoms 46, 58, 77, 102, 202
    effectiveness 141–2, 267
    male dislike of 138–9
    rate of use, 20th c. 112, 330
    re-usable 138
    rubber, improved technology
        137–8, 276–7
    supply of 274
conjugal rights 1, 26, 94, 117, 130, 228,
    235–8
    legal basis 2 n. 3, 94
    male insistence on 1, 35, 200–1,
        237–8
    wife's refusal of 46, 111–12, 144, 157
    sex manuals interwar and 199–201
    theological justification 229–30
    working-class women and 111–12
Conservatives, *see* Tory
Contagious Diseases Acts 79, 94–5
    Anti-Contagious Diseases Acts
        campaign 81, 94–5
    see also Butler, Josephine
contraception (i.e. methods not
        including abortion) 5, 20, 122–41,
        185
    anatomical contraception 51
    developing knowledge of 115–16,
        122–4, 132–3, 141
    female-controlled 57, 60, 114–16,
        132, 267 n. 14

grafenberg rings 131, 141
herbal recipes 44
'holding back' 127–8
intra-cervical pessaries 131
interuterine pessaries 131
IUDs 131
knowledge and research 19th c. 55
male control of 115, 119, 134, 138,
    144, 291, 295
male rejection of 138, 144, 277, 291
modification sexual response
    and 55–6, 123, 143–4, 166
'natural' method 281
rates of use 7, 112–16, 268–70, 327,
    329–38
quality control 123–4, 267
rubber and 41–2, 137–8
safe period 130–1, 141
sponges 55, 57–60, 75–6, 87, 126–7,
    141
see also abortion; anal sex; birth
    control; breastfeeding; caps;
    condoms; diaphragms; pill (oral
    contraception); spermicides;
    withdrawal
contraceptive effectiveness 22, 40–1,
    44, 56, 108–9, 122–3
and class 127, 153–4
and combined methods 141–2, 154
housing, sanitation and 51–2, 127
ineffective methods 40, 51, 56,
    127–8, 130–2
interwar 139–42
measuring effectiveness 50, 139–40
the pill and 270
constipation 135, 151
see also bowel control
Costler, A. [pseud. Koestler, A.] 344
Cox, G. 343
Cox, Katherine 122
Craig, Alec 211–12

cultural generations 166–7
cunnilingus, *see* oral sex

Daily Express 283
Daily Telegraph 301
Dante, Alighieri 312
Darwin, Charles 88
Darwin, Emma 88
Davidson, Leonore 85
Davis, Maxine 343
Davis, Paul 109
Davis, Porter [pseud.] 345
deference, 118, 253
    erosion of 312–17
    patient's rights groups and 313–14
    'rational' decisions and 303, 311, 316
Diachylon 116–17
diaphragms 112, 114, 131
    and constipation 135
    description 132
    effectiveness interwar 141–2
    FPA and 275–6, 290
    fitting 133, 134–5, 247 n. 8
    rates of use 114–16, 272
    see also vaginal contraception
Dickinson, Robert Latou 258
Diseases Affecting the Vulva 152
Divine Comedy 312
divorce 210, 223, 285, 321
    law reform 94, 290
domestic service 66
    sexual exploitation and 78, 85
domestic violence 119 n. 88
Don Juan 78
double standard
    19th c. 92–3, 100–1, 104
    20th c. 180–1, 184, 232, 240, 338
douching 135–7
    C. Knowlton and 58
    claim widely used, 19th c. 58
    effectiveness 122, 141

douching (*cont.*)
  home-made solutions 135
  rates of use 114–5, 136
  see also spermicides; vaginal
    contraception
Drabble, Margaret 271
Drysdale, George 60–1
Dubois, Ellen 110
Dunnell, Karen 108, 327, 331

Easterlin, Richard 24–5
Eastern Europe 291
economic position:
  fertility, marriage and 322–5
  men: changing labour market
    19th c. 64; paid employment 118
  women: childbearing and 336–7;
    economic autonomy 118; and
    sexual caution 66; middle-class
    women, 19th c. 67; neo-liberal
    economics and 340; paid
    employment 5, 17, 23, 38, 96;
    20th c. 324, 335–7; relative to
    men of own class 62; risk, of
    sexuality 7, 12–13; working–class
    women 19th c. 65–6, 104
education 5, 12, 19
  free schools movement 183
  remote determinant 23
  women and lower infant
    mortality 35–6
  women's fertility and 95–6
  see also sex education
effectiveness, *see* contraceptive
  effectiveness
Eichenlaub, John 237, 343–4
Elias, Norbert 7–8
Ellis, A. 343
Ellis, Havelock 191, 194
Ehrenreich, Barbara 189
emotion 95, 111, 159, 171, 219

association with women 24
body and 125, 257, 194–6
control of 98–9, 144, 241, 253
romantic love 13, 29, 65, 68, 75
men and 236, 238–40
psychoanalysis and 191, 234–5
in sex manuals 220–1
spousal closeness and
  education 95
sexual intercourse and 228–9, 232,
  see also vaginal orgasm
*The Encyclopedia of Sexual
  Knowledge* 342
Enduring Passion 155–6, 203
England, Leonard 168
Equal Pay Act 290
Erasmus, Charles 47
Essay on the Principle of Population 54
eugenics 4, 126, 196, 296, 299–300,
  309–10
Eugenics Review 125
*Everything You Always Wanted to Know About
  Sex* But Were Afraid to Ask* 344
Every Woman's Book 71, 74
extramarital sex, *see* adultery
Eyles, Leonora 165, 222, 343–5

Family Doctor 283
Family Formation 327
Family Planning Association 159
  achievements 296
  class and 316–17, 27
  clinics 272
  diaphragms 275–6, 290
  female autonomy 278
  female dominated 274–5
  husbands' involvement 277
  pill and 277, 278–9, 290
  Report on Family Planning 275–7,
    303
  sex manual authors and 227, 228

  19th c. 88–9, 99, 107
  20th c. 265
  female health and 11–12, 38–9, 105
  religious adherence and 285–6
  sexual indulgence and 156–7
  sexual mores and 264
fatherhood:
  avoidance of 26, 99
  desire for children 38
  and fertility decline 118–21
  financial responsibility 73, 323–4
  lack of support for wife 100
  loving fathers 118, 120
fathers, unmarried 17, 64, 84 n. 66, 282, 322–3
  see also illegitimacy
fellatio, *see* oral sex
feminism 2, 23, 184, 204, 253
  awareness of, 1950s 229–30, 277
  influence on sex manuals 237
  rejection of passionlessness 201, 241–3
  first wave 96, 152–3, 182; provincial roots 210; rejection of birth control 115; conjugal rights and 199–201; USA 199–200, 226
  second wave 185, 313, 315–16; Women's Liberation and pill 301
Ferris, Paul 195, 294
fertility decline 15–16, 76–7, 99
  decline post 1930s 25–6, 263–70
  gender and 38–9, 105–6, 119–21
  future time planning and 88
fertility rates:
  1750–1975 14–15
  gross fertility rate 15
  marital fertility rate 264–6
  sexuality and 12–14, 63, 97
  total fertility rate 14

women's reproductive labour and 11
Fielding, Michael 133–4, 136
Fildes, Mary 71, 73–4
Fildes, Valerie 32–3
Fisher, Kate 115, 119
first sexual intercourse 291, 335
  age at and sexual revolution 319–20
  ignorance and 100, 171–2, 197–9
  husbands and 228, 277
  meanings of 319, 321–2
  within marriage 326–7
First World War, illegitimacy rates 102
Florence, Lella Secor 126, 127, 133, 275 n. 17
  Birmingham birth control use 139
  breastfeeding 34, 130
  Cambridge Birth Control Clinic 139,
  condom use 139
Food and Drug Administration, USA 267
Forum 130
Foucault, Michael, 90–1
France 33, 48–9, 55, 69, 76, 137
freethinkers and republicans 70–1, 73–5, 77
Freud, Sigmund H.:
  absence physical sexual feelings and 160, 168, 222–4
  female sexuality 173, 214–15, 246, 231, 234–6
  impact on social change 175–6, 221–4, 255, 303
  infant masturbation 147, 210, 215, 222–4
  libido 167–8, 222
  masturbation 147, 210
  rejection of 234–5, 236, 238
frigidity 223–4
  absence vaginal orgasms 231

frigidity (*cont.*)
  as resistance to male
    domination 234–5, 236, 238

Gardiner, Gerald Q.C. 284
Garret, Eilidh 54
Garrity, Terry, *see* J. [pseud.]
Gathorne-Hardy, Jonathon 147–8, 150
Gavron, Hannah 154–5
Gay, Peter 83, 171
Geldenhuys, J. n. 343
gender 6
  education and gender
    stratification 96
  gendered response to birth
    control 115
  separate sexual cultures 19th c. 85
  separate sexual cultures 20th c. 19,
    166, 179–82
  sexual liberalisation and 130, 232,
    241
  diminishing gender gulf 186
  see also double standard
genitals, female 97, 99, 161
  hygiene, customary
    standards 145–7
  touching, rejection of 111, 149,
    151–4
  rejection of 99
  see also clitoris; masturbation; vagina;
    vaginal orgasm
Germany 129 n. 29, 216, 342
Getting Married 283–4
Gill, Eric 144 n. 3
Godwin, William 54
The Golden Notebook 232, 240
Gollancz, Victor 144
Gollancz, Ruth 144
Gordon, Linda 110, 299
Gordon, Michael 188–9
Gorer, Geoffrey:

absence of sexual feelings 173
male control of contraception 134,
  119
male sexual ignorance 172
toilet training 150
Grafenberg, Ernst, 250
Grant, Joan 198
Gray, Arthur Herbert 197, 343
Gray, Euphemia 97–9
Greene, Hugh 285
Greer, Germaine 256, 281
Griffith, Edward Fyfe 125, 343, 345
  anxiety and masturbation 212
  conjugal rights 201
  male dislike of condom use
    138
The Guardian 271, 314–16
Gurley Brown, Helen 240 n. 52
Guttmacher, Alan 125
Guyon, Rene 212

Hacker, Rose 242
Haire, Norman 342–3
  rejection Stopes 195
  use of contraception 125, 126, 133,
    135, 136, 137–8, 140–2
Hajnal, John 16, 322–3
Hall, Catherine 85
Hall, Lesley 159, 189
Hall, Ruth 195
Ham, C. J. 313
Hammerton, James 94
Hardie, Keir 159
Hastings, D. 343
Hastrup, Kirsten 33
Havil, A. [pseud. Phillip, E. E.] 344
Hazlitt, William 103–4
Hedley, Dennis 159
Hendrickson, T. 344
Hess, Elizabeth 189
Himes, Norman 54, 77, 343

Hoggart, Richard 128, 129, 180
homosexuality 13, 175, 178, 179, 186,
    188, 282, 338–9
  dominant role and
    heterosexuality 218–19
  impact of the Second World
    War 184
  sex manual authors and 344
  Sexual Offences Act 290
  see also lesbian
Honest to God 285
household formation 17, 321, 323–4
housing, and use of contraception:
  absence running water 127, 145,
    154–5
  effectiveness and 127, 142, 153–4
  heating 136–7
  privacy 127, 135, 142, 148–9
  sanitation 127, 135
Howarth, Vyvyan 129 n. 29, 345
Hughes, Agnes 159
Human Sexual Response 251, 255
Humanae Vitae 304
Humphries, Jane 72
Hunt, E. 152
Hutton, Isabel 195, 196–7, 198, 343
hygiene, personal:
  class and 145, 153–5
  contraception and 52, 127
  'dirt' and 95, 145, 148,
  genital 95, 144–7, 192
  health improvements and 145
  history of 145–6
Home, Evelyn, *see* Makin, Peggy
Iceland 33
Ideal Marriage 221, 246
  Goethe, Rousseau, Stendhal in 196

ignorance, sexual 7, 166, 167, 198–9, 220
  absence, physical sexual
    awareness 169, 171–7

creation of 167–77
  diminishing 168–9, 173–4, 176–7,
    221, 230
  lack of recognition, physical sexual
    desire 174
  menstruation and 151
  unmarried women and 97–8
  see also reticence
illegitimacy 123, 185, 322
  rates of (1840s–1980) 101–2, 105
    (1960s) 282, 289, 293
  see also fathers unmarried; mothers
    unmarried
Illustrations and Proofs of Population 54
industrialisation 16, 19, 23, 38, 64
infanticide 40, 161
infertility 4, 20–1
  male 21
  venereal disease and 21 n. 18
infidelity, *see* adultery
Ingham, Mary 287–8
Ireland and media censorship 303
Irvine, Janice 189
Is Chastity Outmoded? 283–4
Issacs, Susan 147, 150
'Itsy Bitsy Teeny Weeny Yellow Polka
    Dot Bikini' 293
Ittman, Karl 72

J. [pseud. Garrity, Terry] 240, 344
Jackson, Margaret 189
Jacobs, Gloria 189
Jacobsohn, Freidrich 204, 344
James, John [pseud.] 345
Japan 291
Jeffreys, Sheila 189
Jejeebhoy, Shireen 35, 95–6
John, Augustus n. 3 144 n. 3
John, Ida 144 n. 3
Johnson, E. W. 343
Johnson, Virginia, *see* Masters, William

Joseph, Keith 307–12, 316
Journal of Royal College of Practitioners
    314
Joy of Sex 188, 244, 342

Karezza 128
Kaufman, Joseph 236, 344
Keeler, Christine 286
Kelly, G. A. 343
Kelly, G. L. 343
Kenyan Asians 307
Kind, R. W. 292
Kingsley, Charles 83, 88
Kingsley Fanny 83, 97
Kinsey, Alfred 205–6, 226, 249
Knight, Jill 301
Knodel, John 33
Knowlton, Charles 58–61, 77
Koedt, Anna 256–8
Krafft-Ebings, R. 191

Labour Party 278, 290, 302, 308
Lady Chatterley's Daughter 284
Lady Chatterley's Lover 216–17, 235, 284
Lafitte, François 275
Lambert, Joan 294
Lancet 280
The Law of Population 61
Laquer, Thomas 167 n. 6
Lawrence, David Herbert 220, 235
    and female sexuality 215–17
    love 284, 287
    sexual morality 284
Lawrence, Frieda 216
Leathard, Audrey 296, 316–17
Leck, Bryan 306
Leigh-Smith, Barbara (later
    Bodichon) 92, 94
legislative change 7, 118
    abortion (1967) 290–1
    divorce (1857) 94

local authority initiatives
    and 302–3, 307
Married Women's Property Acts 96
NHS Amendment (Family
    Planning) Bill (1967) 302–7
NHS Reorganisation Bill 307–9
social legislation (1960s) 290–1
see also censorship
Lesthaeghe, Ron 25–6.
lesbian 201
    genital sexuality 175–7, 198, 201
    Second World War 184, 201
Lessing, Doris 232, 239–40, 257–9
Levine, Lena 248–50
Lewis, Jane 271, 296, 319
Lewis, Lionel 188
Lewis-Faning, E. 115
libertine male sexuality 20th c. 189,
    219–21, 225, 259, 343–4
    double standard and 240
    support for prostitution 242
Linton, William James, use of
    contraception 75–6
Local Authorities and birth
    control 272, 280, 302–4, 306–7
Long, W. H. 343
Longden, Anne 82
Loth, D. 345
Love Without Fear 211, 221, 226, 342
Lowen, Alexander 235–6, 344
Lutyens, Edwin 100, 173
Lutyens, Emily 100, 173
Lutyens, Mary 99
Lysol 147

Macandrew, Rennie [pseud. Eliot,
    A. G.] 230, 231, 343
Macaulay, Mary 228, 233, 275 n. 17, 343
Mackinnon, Alison 26
McLaren, Angus 42
Makin, Peggy 225–6

Malaya 34
male domination 7, 69–70, 94, 184–5,
    218–9, 232, 237, 277
  Biblical justification of (1950s) 229
  physical sexual practice 218–19, 232,
    237
  psychoanalysis and 214–16, 234–6
male sexual response, physical:
  condoms 138–9
  duration of sexual
    intercourse 202–4
  female orgasm and 204, 214–17
  impotence 161
  in *Married Love* 198, 201
  need for sexual relief 35, 95, 200–1
  spontaneity and 204, 216–18
  withdrawal and 52, 56–7
male sexuality 16, 21
  contraceptive methods and 127
  emotional involvement in 83, 232,
    239–40
  female sexual response and 134,
    180–1, 234, 239–40
  high fertility and 88–9
  insistence on conjugal rights 35
  jokes and gossip 161, 179–80
  lack of sexual experience 82, 84,
    100
  low sexual interest 174, 189, 202
  in *Married Love* 194
  predatory male sexuality 2–3,
    180–1, 189, 202
  professional male life cycle, 19th c.
    77
  reputation and 71–2
  selfishness 100, 235–7
  sexual liberalization and 241
  varied sexual cultures 82–3, 99
  venereal disease and 95, 238–9
  see also libertine male sexuality; male
    domination; male sexual

response; penis; prostitution and
    male sexuality; semen
Mallard, Dr C. Killick 138
Malleson, Joan 159, 233, 234, 248–50,
    275 n. 17, 343–4
Malthus, T. H. 54, 68, 75, 297
Manderson, Leonore 34
marriage:
  (1950s) 321
  age at 16, 53–4, 68, 84–5, 264–5,
    266–7, 323–4
  changes in 63–7, 68, 336, 339
  as fertility control 16–18
  men and 324
  non-consummation of 97, 158–9
  proportion never married 107, 322
  proximate determinant 20–1
  rates of 263–4, 323–4
  wages and 323–4
marriage guidance:
  and sex manual authors 227–9,
    342–3
Married Love 124, 155, 172, 188, 226, 192,
    342
  positive view of sexuality 192–7, 221
  sales 194, post-Second World
    War 226
Married Women's Property Acts 96
Mason, Michael 58, 93
Mass-Observation 156–7, 168–9, 184,
    285, 321
masturbation 13, 78, 144
  class and 148–50
  enduring prohibitions against 147
  infants, children and 147
  prevalence 149, 226
  medical attitudes 152–3, 160, 207–11
  touching partner's genitals 207–11,
    224, 230, 238
  women and experience of 149, 232,
    258–9

Masters, William and Johnson,
    Virginia 35, 191, 251–7, 344
Matrimonial Causes Act (1875) 94
Mayhew, Henry 65–7
Maynard, John 82
Mead, Margaret 151
Mears, Eleanor 125, 343
medical model 257, 319
medics:
    contraception and 132–3, 272–4, 280
    GPs and the pill 272–4, 279–81
    to masturbation 152–3, 160
    patient's sexual problems 97, 158–9,
        241
    as sex and birth control manual
        authors 122–4, 345
    tampons and 152–3
menopause 20–1, 22
Miles, Dudley 55
Mill, John Stuart 99
Miller, H. 344
Millet, Kate 256
menstruation 11, 22, 44, 75 n. 40, 133,
    151–3, 192
· Miles, H. J. 343
Miles, Rosalind 257–8
MIND 313
Minertzhagen, Daniel 100
Ministry of Health 280–1, 292, 312
miscarriage 20, 22, 44, 87, 122–3
Mitchison, Dick 172
Mitchison, Naomi (née Haldane)
    172–3
modesty 71, 127, 128, 150, 338
Monty Python's Flying Circus 306
Moral Physiology 75, 77
Morrison, Herbert 157
mortality
    infant 36
    maternal 6, 30, 144 n. 3
Mosher, Clelia 109 n. 58

mothers 4, 30, 38
    health of 134–5
    sex education and 98, 149–50, 151
    in working-class family 121
mothers, unmarried 2, 13
    abortion 288, 293, 331
    adoption 288
    economic position 64–7, 72
    financial cost to government
        308–11
    impact on women 65–7, 84 n. 66,
        122–3, 282–3
    Joseph, Keith and 308–11
    new poor law and 64
    promiscuity 287–8, 289–90
    working class 309–11
    see also illegitimacy
Murphy, Michael 268–70
My Secret Life 58–9
The Myth of the Vaginal Orgasm 256

*National Association for the Welfare of
    Children in Hospital* 312–13
National Health Service:
    contraception and 279–81, 296–301,
        308
    NHS Amendment Act (Family
        Planning) 1967 302–7
    NHS Reorganization Bill 307–9
    Platt Committee 312
    prescription charges 279–80
    women and 134
National Marriage Guidance
    Council 228
national service 313
National Society for Women's
    Suffrage 96
National Survey of Health and
    Development 268
Neuhaus, Jessamyn 189
The New Art of Love 219

new Poor Law 64
New Statesman 283
New Zealand 5, 342
Newfield, Maurice, *see* Fielding,
    Michael
News of the World 280
Newson, Elizabeth and John 149–50
Newsweek 191
non-penetrative sex 256–7
Noonan, John 46
North, Lydia 98
north-west European marriage
    system 16–18, 318, 322–3, 331
nudism 183, 212

Oakley, E.G. 345
Observer 273, 300, 305
O'Connell Davidson, Julia 83
Oh Calcutta! 293
Old Poor Law 17
Olsen, H. 343
Oral contraception, *see* the pill
oral sex 128, 130, 230–1, 237
orgasm, female 218, 248–51, 254–60
    clitoral stimulation and 208–9
    ejaculation 250–1
    estimates, interwar-1950s 233
    'holding back' 127, 141
    male response and 203–5
    male domination and 214–17
    new interpretations 251
Owen, Robert 53, 55
Owen, Robert Dale 53–61, 57, 75

paid employment, *see* economic
    position
Paget, James 98
Parkin, Molly 149
Parkinson-Smith, F. [psued.] 345
Patient's Association 313
patient's rights 312–14

Paul, Leslie 253
The Peckham Experiment 158
pederasty 220
Peel, John 305
Pember Reeves, Amber 122–3
Penguin Books 284
penis 146–7, 151, 245
Pepys, Samuel 45
Peterson, M. J. 98
petting (physical sexual activity not
        including sexual intercourse) 84,
        98, 102–4, 230–1, 260, 321–2
    definition of 321
    middle class and 97–8, 100–1
    rates of, 20th c. 321
Physical, sexual and natural religion 60
Pierce, Rachel 115
Pillay, A. P. 343
Pilkington, Roger 283
the pill (oral contraception) 7, 256,
        268–74, 277–82, 290–2, 332–5
    cost 279–80
    effectiveness 272
    fertility rates and 268–70, 281–2
    female pressure to prescribe 278–9,
        280
    GPs and 273, 281, 290
    health warnings and major side
        effects 292, 308
    rates of use 268–70, 281, 292
    promiscuity and 289–90, 294
    religious response to 304–5
    saying no 1–3
    young women and 287–8, 291–2,
        296, 298, 317
Place Elizabeth 42 n. 4, 43
Place, Francis 39, 70
    birth control 42, 53, 56, 71
    fatalism and family size 42–3, 54
    female-controlled birth control 57
Platt Committee 312

Pope Pius IX 304
Popenoe, Paul 343
population control 4, 61, 297–302
   coercive measures 298, 300, 302
   FPA and 300
   feminism and 298–9
   and Joseph, Keith 311–12
   racism and 301–2, 307
   supporters of 301–2, 307, 311–12
population growth 11, 40, 54, 81
   international 297–9
   Malthus and 54
   as rhetorical strategy 306–7
   shift to towns, mid-19th c. 81
Potter, Georgiana 100
Potter, Robert 20
Powell, Enoch 280
The Power of Sexual Surrender 234–5
The Practice of Birth Control 126
pregnancy 11, 12–13, 17, 28, 87, 192
   fear of unwanted 116, 130, 142
   not to be seen in public 156
   sexual activity during 35
premarital pregnancy 17, 64, 101–2,
      322,
   class and 328–31
   concealment of (1970s) 108
   impact on women 84 n. 66, 122–3
premarital sexual intercourse 17, 64
   class and 101, 319, 329–30
   definition of 321, 332
   paradigm shift 294, 332, 334–5
   petting and 321
   public anxiety concerning 282–90
   public acceptance of 212, 231, 293–5
   rising incidence of 271–2, 283–4,
      321–5, 328–9, 332–3, 334–5
   Second World War and 184
   see also north-west European
      marriage system; petting;
      premarital pregnancy

Princeton European Fertility
      Project 16
Profumo, John 286
Progress on Birth Control 126
promiscuity 284, 287–8, 294–5, 328, 339
   and birth control 288–90, 294
   definition of 293–4
   sexual immorality 308
prostitution 13, 61, 178, 220, 237
   associated with birth control 73–4
   associated with sexual pleasure
      73–4, 104, 217
   class and 80, 104
   definition of, 19th c. 73, 79
   blurred boundaries mid-20th c.
      238–9
   genital hygiene and 58
prostitution and men:
   class of male users 80
   male manual authors 219, 238, 242
   prositution and, 19th c. 7, 72, 78–94,
      100, 157, 161
   middle class and 19th c. 78–87
proximate determinants 20–2
prudery 97, 99, 100, 106, 148
   class and 111, 128 n. 27, 150, 185
psychoanalysis, *see* Freud, S. H.
puberty 21
Pulse 314

Quaife, G. R. 44
Quakers 286, 343

racism 301–2, 307
Race Relations Acts 290
Rainer, J. and J. 344
rape 220, 228, 241
rational choices, and fertility
      control 303, 311
Rayner, Claire 255, 343
Reay, Barry 64, 322

Rendall's pessaries 136
The Republican 71
religion:
   class 20th c. 185–6
   middle class 19th c. 78, 81–2, 106
   new sexual morality 285–7
   Quakers 286
   remote determinants 20, 23–4, 26
   sex manuals and 197, 343
   working class and 66
Report of the Wolfenden Committee on
   Homosexual Offences and
   Prostitution 282–3, 338
reproductive labour 11
   body and 28–31, 32
   breastfeeding as 31–2, 36
   child labour and 72
   class and 31
   finished family size, 19th c. 38–9, 88
   women's attitudes to 26, 38–9
reticence and sexuality 100, 166, 170–1,
   181–2, 184
   as desirable 253
   diminishing 182–3, 185–6, 292,
   304–6
   Foucault and 90–1
   growing 98–9
   gendered variation in 179–82
   historical cultures of 48
   spousal finances and 179
Reuben, David 344
The Riddle of Sex 196
Roberts, Elizabeth 119
Roberts, Robert 111, 132, 148–9, 180
Robins, Patricia 284
Robinson, Jean 314
Robinson, J.A.T., Bishop of
   Woolwich 285
Robinson, Kenneth 302, 308
Robinson, Marie 234–5
Rolling Stones 293

Rolph, C. H. 284
Rowntree, Griselda 115
Royal College of Obstetricians and
   Gynaecologists 152, 290–1
Royal Commission on
   Population 303
Royal Commission on Venereal
   Disease 80
Ruskin, John 97, 99
Russell, John Lord Amberley
   76

Salford 111
Sanderson, Warren 109
Sanger, Margaret 343
Santow, Gina 42, 49, 52
Scarry, Elaine 28
Schneider, Jane and Peter 117
Schofield, R. S. 17
Schwarz, Oswald 239
Scotland 268
Scott, George Ryley 125, 219–20,
   344
Seaman, Barbara 255
Seccombe, Wally 25, 26, 109, 112,
   119
Second World War:
   condoms 102
   deference and 313
   housing 154
   illegitimacy rates 102
   premarital sexuality 184
   sexual change and 183
Sedgewick, Eve Kosofsky 6
Sellwood, Emily 68
semen 51, 56, 58–9, 138–9, 198, 201–2,
   246–7, 252
The Sensuous Woman 240, 344
Sex and its Mysteries 219
Sex in Society 286
Sex in the Human Female 226

Sex in the Human Male 205, 226
sexual abuse of women 241–3
Sexual Attitudes and Lifestyles 130, 147,
    319–20, 326
Sexual Disorders in the Male 158
The Sexual Impulse 212, 342
sex education 157, 168
    and mothers 98, 149–50
    see also sexual learning
sex manuals 187–244
    abstinence 110
    definition of 187
    content of 192–3, 220–1, 243–4
    FPA and 343
    historiography 187–8
    marriage guidance and 342–3
    pornography and 220–1
    separation sex and reproduction
        in 192–3
    sexual pleasure 202
    readership 193–4, 227
    sales 194, 227, 237
    venereal disease in 196–7
    USA manuals 225–6, 237–8
sex manual authors 341–6
    (1950s) 191–2, 225, 237–8
    eugenics and 343
    female authors 344
    interwar 192, 203–4
    nationality of 342
    occupations 345
    religious commitment 343
    sexual mores and 190, 192
sexology 189, 190–2
sexual activity, non-marital:
    cohabitation 21, 63–6, 104, 333
    fluid sexual mores, early 19th
        c. 68–9, 79–80
    rejection of 284
    single women and 332–5
    see also promiscuity

Sexual Attitudes and Lifestyles 319–20,
    326–7
sexual desire, women 2, 12, 60, 97–9,
    133, 197–8, 292
    uncontrolled fertility and 89, 119
    working-class women, 19th
        c. 104–5
sexual intercourse 5, 12, 111, 188–9
    descriptions in manuals 198
    duration of 133, 202–5
    gendered conduct of 133, 218–19,
        228–232, 237
    modernization of 205–6, 215
    'real thing' 211
    spontaneity and control 204, 206,
        216–18
    Stopes and 198, 199, 201–2, 216
    woman active during 119, 133–4,
        216–7, 218, 220
    under age 16 294–5
    see also first sexual intercourse;
        vaginal orgasm
sexual learning 166, 168, 185
    absence of 173–5, 198
    definition of 170–1
    and lesbian and gay sexuality 176–7
    middle class women 19th c. 83, 97–8
    petting and 82–4, 98–9
    physical and social progression
        of 84, 169, 170–1
    prevention of 169–70
    sexual pleasure and 171
sexual mores:
    change and birth control 41,
        281–2
    class and, 19th c. 66, 68, 84–5
    class and, 20th c. 148, 149–50,
        185–6
    early-mid 20th c. 179
    English compared to French 48–9
    public debate 282–95

regional and social variation early
19th c. 63
sexual rebellion 166
sexual pleasure, mutual:
absence of 100, 111, 117, 172–3
as defined by males 213, 217–8, 201,
236–7
domination by one partner and 218
sex manuals and 197, 201
vaginal orgasm and 232, 239–40
sexual pleasure, women 12, 83, 84,
103–4, 134
association with birth control and
prostitution 19th c. 73–4, 104
ignorance and 172
lack of female satisfaction,
responsibility for 234–5, 244
low levels of desire 175, 177
rejection of, by men 134, 180–2
rejection of, by women 105,
111–12,
USA evidence of, 60, 109 n. 58
use of contraception and 142
withdrawal, diminished 112,
114–15, 157
sexual revolution 7, 271–2, 292–4,
325
birth control and 171, 281–2
claim unrelated to pill 319, 336–7
family forms and 338–9
millenarian hopes 317, 340
pill and 318
The Times 310, 316
young women and 336–7
sexuality:
absence of sexual pleasure 165, 169,
180–1
dirt and 95, 145, 148
Freudian model of sexuality 173
highly sexually active 178–9
hypocrisy, sexual 93

individual right to define 6, 160,
222–3, 258–9
link with fertility control 41
separation sexuality and birth
control 61, 124,
separation sexuality and
reproduction 192–4, 256–7, 259,
336–7
sexual change over 20th c. 182–6
social order and 16
theoretical approaches to 12, 319
see also ignorance, sexual
sexuality, women:
fertility, impact upon 12, 105,
119–20
Foucault, and 90
relative lack of interest in varied acts
and positions 130, 232
reputation and 71
Shankweiler, Penelope 188–9
Sharples, Eliza 74–5
Sherfey, Mary Jane 254–6
Sicily 117
Slater, Eliot 118, 126
Sloan, Douglas 108
Smith, Ben 82
Smyth, Margaret 196, 343
social construction 6, 12, 210, 338
physical sexual events and 12,
189–90
see also sexual learning
social purity movement 5, 95
Sogner, Solvi 26–7
Soloway, Richard 300, 309
Spencer, Robert F. 47
sperm, *see* semen
spermicidal pessaries 135–7
as combined method 135, 141–2
expense 136
irritation caused by 135–6
of lard 132

spermicidal pessaries (*cont.*)
    male controlled method 115
    method failure 141, 144
    see also douching
statistics, use of 14, 18–19
Stedman Jones, Gareth 66
Stephens, Margaret 197, 342
sterilization 298, 299
Stevenson, T. H. C. 77, 80
stillbirths, rate of 11
Stoddard, Sara 69
Stone, A. and H. 343
Stott, Mary 314–5
Stopes, Marie 51, 109, 124–5, 207, 209,
    211, 226–7, 234, 343–5
    active vagina 246–8
    anatomical contraception 51
    coital frequency 155–6
    and emotion 194–5
    female sexuality 171, 199, 187–92
    feminism and 200
    Lawrence, D. H. and 216
    lesbianism 176–7, 201
    male approach of 277
    male duration of sexual
        intercourse 203–4
    male rejection of 195, 213–14, 216,
        277
    rejection of 195, 213–5
    separation of reproduction and
        sexuality 192–3
    wooing and physiological
        desire 172–3, 199
Street, Robert 237, 344
Strauss, E. B. 158
Stuttaford, Tom 311, 316
Sunday Pictorial 284
Sunday Telegraph 292
Sunday Times 294
Surkyn, Johan 25–6
Swyer, G. I. 49, 51

syphilis 110, 196–7, 220
    middle-class men and 19th
        c. 80–2
    mortality late 19th c. 80–1
    mortality early 20th c. 94, 196–7
    see also venereal disease
syringing, see douching
Szreter, Simon 18, 107, 109–10, 117,
    323

Taylor, Sarah, *see* Sarah Austin
Teifer, Leonore 257
Tenenbaum, Joseph 196–7, 343–4
Tennyson, Alfred Lord 68
Thompson, E. P. 304
thrombosis 292
Thynne, Christopher 148
The Times 293, 310, 316
Times Educational Supplement 294
Tizard, Leslie J. 353
Toft, M. 344
Top Twenty 293
Tories 302, 307–9
Tosh, John 85
Trall, Russell Thatcher 199–200, 342
Tufill, S. G. 344
Tynan, Kenneth 293
Tyrer, A. H. 343

United States of America 5, 49, 51–2
    demography and sexual change 205
        n. 60, 266–8
    female assertiveness in 69, 226
    female contraception, use of 59–60,
        267, 272
    feminism 199, 226
    Kinsey's findings 185 n. 61, 205–6,
    sex manuals from 225–6, 237–8,
        341–2
    sexology 189, 190–2
    sexual pleasure resistance 110–11

use of contraception and fertility
  rates, 19th c. 59–60
urbanization 16, 23–4, 105, 81

vagina 21, 117
  capacity for sensation 232–4,
    245–61
  damage in childbirth 134–5
  during arousal 254
  hymen and first intercourse 199
  lubrication and desire 199
  muscles of 247–8
  insertion of objects into 133, 152–3
  passive 245–6, 254, 256
  vaginismus 160
  see also vaginal orgasm
vaginal contraception 114–16, 133, 136
  modesty and 127
  gendered conduct of sexual
    intercourse and 133
  medical ignorance and 133, 152–3
  muscles vagina, and 246–7
  women's dislike of 114–16, 133, 136
  see also caps, cervical; diaphragms
vaginal orgasm 225
  definitions of 248–50
  emotion and 232, 239–40, 257–9
  psychoanalysis and 215, 231, 235–6,
    246
  uterine suction 246
Velde van de T.H. 125, 221, 246
  conjugal rights 201
  contraception use of 51, 128, 135,
    137–8, 144
  female sexual sensation 246–7
  sexuality and 196, 209, 221, 236,
    246–8
venereal disease 11, 21 n. 18, 47, 87, 99,
    308, 345
  anti-Contagious Diseases Acts
    campaign 94

gonorrhoea 46
  in sex manuals 196–7
  women's exposure and conjugal
    rights 110
  see also syphilis
Vickers, Joan 303
A Vindication of the Rights of Women 55
Voge, C. I. 136

Wade, Emily 75–6
Wallis, J. H. 343
Walker, Kenneth 173, 193, 343–6
  abstinence 158–9
  masturbation 212
  ribaldry and male sexuality 161
  tolerance and 211
Walker, Sarah 97, 103–4
Walkowitz, Judith 80
Walt, Gillian 296, 307, 316–17
'Walter' 58–9
Weatherhead, Leslie 177, 194, 343
Weeks, Jeffrey 188, 194, 271, 296, 311,
    317, 319, 340
Wellings, Kaye 319
Wells, H. G. 122, 144,
West, Rebecca 122–3
Weymouth, Alexander 148
What is Love? 71
Whitehorn, Katherine 305
Whitehouse, Mary 285
Williams, Rosie 100
Wilson, Elizabeth 296, 311, 317
Wilson, Harold 278
widowhood 38
Wise Parenthood 124, 131, 193
Wise, P. 131
withdrawal 42–53, 55, 56–7, 117, 300
  in 19th-c. birth control tracts 56
  claim obvious technique 42, 52
  development of 47
  definition 42

withdrawal (*cont.*)
  diminished female sexual
    pleasure 114–17, 295
  effectiveness 49–53
  evidence pre-1800 42, 44
  partial withdrawal 51, 56
  rates of use 20th c. 112–14, 330
  required practice 47, 52–3, 55–7
  Stopes' rejection of 202
  see also duration of sexual
    intercourse
Withers, Mary 84 n. 66
Wise Parenthood 124
Witt, E. 343 n.
Wolfenden Report, see *Report of
    Wolfenden Committee on Homosexual
    Offences and Prostitution*
Woman 130
women:
  absence of control over fertility 19th
    c. 59, 88
  altruism and 26
  changing life course 326
  desire for children 31
  fertility, impact upon female
    sexuality 12, 105, 119–20
  Foucault, and 90
  growth in equality 19th c. 118–19
  health 134, 154; and infant
    mortality 36; and
    reproduction 11–12, 30–2, 38, 87,
    134–5
  labour discounted 29
  mothers and wives 23, 37–8
  rejection sexual pleasure 105–7
  relative lack of interest in varied
    sexual acts and positions 130, 232
  reputation and sexuality 71

  rising expectations, 1950s 25–6
  response to contraception 70–1,
    73–5, 115–17, 121, 157
women, single:
  absence sexual experience, middle
    class 82–3
  access to birth control 2–3, 273,
    286–9, 335
  bearing costs relaxed sexual
    mores 2–3, 65–7, 185
  birth control, impact of 332–335
  control of 2–3, 308–9, 296
  emotion 240
  fear of pregnancy 73
  genital sexual desire and 198
  ignorance, sexual 97–9, 169–70
  life course 330
  and pill 287–8, 290–2, 330–1
  sexual activity of 63–6, 68–9,
    324–35
  sexual desire of, in manuals 197–8
  see also first sexual intercourse;
    mothers, unmarried; petting;
    premarital intercourse;
    promiscuity
Women's Liberation 298–9, 301, 315
Woodside, Moya 114, 118, 126
Wooler, Thomas 71, 73
Woolf, Myra 265
Working Class Wives 134, 154
Wright, Helena 219, 223, 234, 343–5
  clitoral stimulation and
    masturbation 209–10, 213
  female sexual satisfaction 233
  gender roles 209
Wrigley, E. A. 17

Zweig, Ferdynand 118, 324